*Against Principalities and Powers* is a fascinating and engaging work on communal identity and moral discourse in Paul's letter to the Ephesians. This text creates a dialogical forum between theologians and scholars of African religions. Darko's focus on Africa provides an in-depth understanding of African people's spiritual cosmology, worldview, culture and society as it relates to the broad themes in the book. Using a comparative lens, Darko exegetically explores and articulates a deep knowledge of Pauline writings, making this a significant text for African theology, African religions and World Christianity scholars.

**Jacob K. Olupona, PhD**
Professor, African Religious Traditions,
and African and African American Studies,
Harvard Divinity School, Cambridge, Massachusetts, USA

AF259057

In clearly academic yet jargon-free writing, Darko draws the reader into the background world of early Jewish and Gentile converts to Christianity offering fresh insights into the spirit cosmology that informs their hearing and living the Scriptures. Under his analysis the parallels between the wisdom sayings of their sages and philosophers, and the injunctions in the Epistles, with Ephesians being the prime example, situates the often misunderstood and contested injunctions in household living within their context in a way that invites attention to re-read these texts with generosity, regardless of one's theological inclinations.

The over-spiritualization of all problems, demonization, and divination which pervades post-missionary African Christianity in its ecclesiology are juxtaposed with first-century Christianity with a much-needed corrective that encourages these Christians to understand and hold human responsibility and divine action in tandem.

A must read for academic and lay alike who care for the future of biblical interpretation in context and communion.

**Rev Esther E. Acolatse, PhD**
Associate Professor of Pastoral Theology and Intercultural Studies,
Knox College, University of Toronto, Canada

There is perhaps no topic where the gulf separating the West from the non-Western world is as deep and broad as the issue of the demonic. The question of whether evil spirits exist and are involved in our daily lives has been firmly decided in the Western educational tradition. The answer is unequivocally "no"! Such a belief system is relegated to an outmoded and primitive worldview that has no place in the modern world. But in this important and well-researched volume, Daniel Darko has effectively challenged this assumption by demonstrating the convergence of the African worldview with the biblical worldview, especially as reflected in the New Testament letter to the Ephesians. Evil spirits do exist and pose an ongoing threat. Ephesians, however, gives us a theological framework for understanding this realm and how we should live in light of this reality. Every Christian should read this book and allow it to shatter their deeply embedded assumptions. The present role of the resurrected and exalted Christ will take on far greater significance in your life.

**Clinton E. Arnold, PhD**
Dean and Professor of New Testament,
Talbot School of Theology, Pasadena, California, USA

Dan Darko's *Against Principalities and Powers* offers an insightful and careful study that reflects on the intersection between the worlds of spirits in Ephesians and African cosmology. It is impossible to encounter African expressions of Christianity in any shape or form without finding in it an engagement with the Holy Spirit, spirits, and principalities and powers. This is an important study that will serve as a major resource in the field of biblical and African Christian spirituality for years to come.

**J. Kwabena Asamoah-Gyadu, PhD**
Baeta-Grau Professor of Contemporary African Christianity
and Pentecostal Theology,
Trinity Theological Seminary, Legon, Ghana

In this very important study, Daniel Darko fills a gaping hole in the investigation of the role of spiritual beings in Ephesians, a topic that has suffered an abysmal neglect. Professor Darko clearly establishes that rather than being tangential, spiritual beings play a significant role in the identity formation and moral discourse of the letter. He demonstrates his clear grasp of the subject from his engagement with primary and secondary literature that deal with the issue both in Greco-Roman antiquity and Jewish literature. Drawing parallels without equating the practices and norms of the Jewish, Greco-Roman and New Testament worlds, he shows the benefits of a new way of looking at Scripture from one's social location, and with non-Western eyes in particular. With this study and his well-reasoned, compelling arguments, Darko has provided an alternative and complementary reading of Ephesians that merits the engagement of students and scholars going forward.

**J. Ayodeji Adewuya, PhD**
Professor of New Testament,
Pentecostal Theological Seminary, Cleveland, Tennessee, USA

This careful interdisciplinary work provides insights on Ephesians, its message of unity, Greco-Roman and ancient Jewish cosmology and demonology, and traditional African cosmology, theology and spirits. As such, it also models a self-aware, respectful intercultural reading too often lacking among Western interpreters.

**Craig S. Keener, PhD**
F. M. and Ada Thompson Professor of Biblical Studies,
Asbury Theological Seminary, Wilmore, Kentucky, USA

# Against Principalities and Powers

# Against Principalities and Powers

## Spiritual Beings in Relation to Communal Identity and the Moral Discourse of Ephesians

### Daniel K. Darko

HIPPOBOOKS

Published 2020 by HippoBooks, an imprint of ACTS and Langham Publishing.

Africa Christian Textbooks (ACTS), TCNN, PMB 2020, Bukuru 930008, Plateau State, Nigeria.
**www.actsnigeria.org**

Langham Publishing, PO Box 296, Carlisle, Cumbria, CA3 9WZ, UK
**www.langhampublishing.org**

ISBNs:
978-1-78368-767-1 Print
978-1-78368-835-7 ePub
978-1-78368-836-4 Mobi
978-1-78368-837-1 PDF



**British Library Cataloguing-in-Publication Data**
A catalogue record for this book is available from the British Library

ISBN: 978-1-78368-767-1

Cover & Book Design: projectluz.com

I dedicate this book to my daughters
– Esther and Deborah Darko –
that they may be ever mindful of the fullness and power of God's salvation,
and endeavor to live fearlessly to the glory of God.

# Contents


Acknowledgements . . . . . . . . . . . . . . . . . . . . . . . . . . . . . . . . . . . . . . . . . . xiii

Abbreviations . . . . . . . . . . . . . . . . . . . . . . . . . . . . . . . . . . . . . . . . . . . . . . xv

1  Introduction . . . . . . . . . . . . . . . . . . . . . . . . . . . . . . . . . . . . . . . . . . 1

2  Towards Greco-Roman Spirit Cosmology . . . . . . . . . . . . . . . . . . . . 19

3  Spiritual Beings in Judaism and Early Christianity . . . . . . . . . . . . . . 53

4  Spirit Cosmology of Ephesians 1–3 . . . . . . . . . . . . . . . . . . . . . . . . . 81

5  Spiritual Beings in the Moral Discourse of Ephesians 4–6 . . . . . . . . 115

6  Parallels and Particulars with African Spirit Cosmology . . . . . . . . . 163

7  Conclusions . . . . . . . . . . . . . . . . . . . . . . . . . . . . . . . . . . . . . . . . . . 213

Appendix 1 . . . . . . . . . . . . . . . . . . . . . . . . . . . . . . . . . . . . . . . . . . . . . 219

Appendix 2 . . . . . . . . . . . . . . . . . . . . . . . . . . . . . . . . . . . . . . . . . . . . . 223

Bibliography . . . . . . . . . . . . . . . . . . . . . . . . . . . . . . . . . . . . . . . . . . . . 237

Index of Names . . . . . . . . . . . . . . . . . . . . . . . . . . . . . . . . . . . . . . . . . . 269

Index of Subjects . . . . . . . . . . . . . . . . . . . . . . . . . . . . . . . . . . . . . . . . . 273

# Acknowledgements

Many are the people and experiences that have shaped my interest and research on this subject matter. Growing up as a Christian in a village populated by adherents to African Traditional Religion, Islam and a small dedicated number of Christians gave me invaluable exposure and has enabled me to pose crucial questions in the inquiry. Moreover, my extensive tertiary education in Europe (Croatia and England) brought me into contact with friends, churches and intellectual traditions that challenged me to reconcile my default posture towards intellectual curiosity and my upbringing with African worldview against the backdrop of post-enlightenment worldview. For this, Clinton E. Arnold and Judith Gundry were very helpful when they supervised my Master of Theology thesis on a related topic; they shared insights and challenged me to provide an adequate rationale for certain assumptions in my quest to decipher the import of Ephesians. Arnold has subsequently been a mentor who has persistently impressed upon me to bring the West in dialogue with Africans in the study of the cosmology of Ephesians. His personal support and works have aided my scholarship in no small way.

This book could not have been completed around this time without the help of student volunteers and colleagues in Africa, Europe and the United States. Of particular note are some men and women at Central University (Ghana) and the Legon Pentecostal Union in the University of Ghana who assisted in conducting the field research. Matthew Durnphy, my Teaching Assistant at Gordon College, and Esther Darko computed the field research data and provided useful insights in the analysis. My younger daughter, Deborah Darko, was a great companion and support in the process of writing.

The team at Langham Publishing were very helpful in many ways. Pieter Kwant and Luke Lewis took special interest in the work while Vivian Doub worked closely with me in the acquisition and editorial processes. I feel honored to be able to contribute to the incredible work of Langham Publishing. Any error or problem in this book is my own, and perhaps should serve as reminder of my fallibility. I hope it helps the West and rest to hear Ephesians in a manner that would resonate with the early Christian readers in Asia Minor.

# **Abbreviations**

| | |
|---|---|
| AB | Anchor Bible |
| Ang | Angelos |
| ANRW | Aufstieg und Niedergang der romischen Welt |
| BASP | Bulletin of American Society of Papyrologists |
| *Bib* | *Biblica* |
| *BibInt* | *Biblical Interpretation* |
| *BR* | *Biblical Research* |
| *BTB* | *Biblical Theology Bulletin* |
| *BSac* | *Bibliotheca Sacra* |
| BZNW | Beihefte zur Zeitschrift für die neutestamentliche |
| *CBQ* | *Catholic Biblical Quarterly* |
| *CBR* | *Currents in Biblical Research* |
| *ConJ* | *Concordia Journal* |
| *CQ* | *Classical Quarterly* |
| CRAI | Comptes rendus de A'Académie des inscriptions et belles-letters |
| *CSR* | *Christian Scholar's Review* |
| *CT* | *Christianity Today* |
| *CTR* | *Criswell Theological Review* |
| DLNT | Dictionary of the Later New Testament and Its Developments |
| DNTB | Dictionary of New Testament Background |
| DPL | Dictionary of Paul and the Letters |
| *DSD* | *Dead Sea Discoveries* |
| DSS | Dead Sea Scrolls |
| *ECC* | *Early Christianity in Context* |
| *ERT* | *Evangelical Review of Theology* |
| *ExpTim* | *Expository Times* |
| Evangel | Evangel |
| *EvQ* | *Evangelical Quarterly* |

| GNTC | Greek New Testament Commentaries |
| *GTJ* | *Grace Theological Journal* |
| HNT | Handbuch zum Neuen Testament |
| HR | History of Religion |
| HTKNT | Herders theologischer Kommentar zum Neuen Testament |
| *HTR* | *Harvard Theological Review* |
| *IBMR* | *International Bulletin of Missionary Research* |
| ICC | International Critical Commentary |
| Int | Interpretation |
| *IRM* | *International Review of Mission* |
| *JAC* | *Jahrbuch für Antike und Christentum* |
| *JBE* | *Journal of Biblical Equality* |
| *JBL* | *Journal of Biblical Literature* |
| *JECS* | *Journal of Early Christian Studies* |
| *JETS* | *Journal of the Evangelical Theological Society* |
| *JJS* | *Journal of Jewish Studies* |
| *JPT* | *Journal of Pentecostal Theology* |
| *JQR* | *Jewish Quarterly Review* |
| *JRS* | *Journal of Roman Studies* |
| *JRT* | *Journal of Reformed Theology* |
| *JS* | *Journal of Semantics* |
| *JSNT* | *Journal for the Study of the New Testament* |
| JSNTSup | Journal for the Study of the New Testament: Supplement Series |
| *JSP* | *Journal for the Study of Pseudepigrapha* |
| *JR* | *Journal of Religion* |
| *JRT* | *Journal of Religious Thought* |
| *JTS* | *Journal of Theological Studies* |
| *JTSA* | *Journal of Theology of South Africa* |
| LCL | Loeb Classical Library |
| LNTS | Library of New Testament Studies |
| *LQ* | *Lutheran Quarterly* |
| LXX | Septuagint |
| MS | Mission Studies |
| *MSJ* | *Master's Seminary Journal* |

| | |
|---|---|
| Neot | Neotestamentica |
| NIBNTT | New International Dictionary of New Testament Theology |
| *NovT* | *Novum Testamentum* |
| NTAbh | Neutestamentliche Abhandlungen |
| NTG | New Testament Guides |
| *NTS* | *New Testament Studies* |
| NTT | New Testament Theology |
| PNTC | The Pillar New Testament Commentary |
| *PGM* | *Papyri Graecae Magicae* [The Greek Magical Papyri] |
| *PSB* | *Princeton Seminary Bulletin* |
| *ResQ* | *Restoration Quarterly* |
| *RevExp* | *Review and Expositor* |
| *RivB* | *Rivista Biblica* |
| *RSBul* | *Religious Studies Bulletin* |
| *RSR* | *Religious Studies Review* |
| SBLMS | Society of Biblical Literature Monograph Series |
| SBLSP | Society of Biblical Literature Seminar Papers |
| *Semeia* | *Semeia* |
| *SJT* | *Scottish Journal of Theology* |
| SNTSMS | Society for New Testament Studies Monograph Series |
| SNTW | Studies of the New Testament and Its World |
| SP | Sacra Pagina |
| *ST* | *Studia Theologica* |
| SVTP | Studia in Veteris Testamenti Pseudepigrapha |
| *SwJT* | *Southwestern Journal of Theology* |
| TDNT | Theological Dictionary of the New Testament |
| *TJ* | *Trinity Journal* |
| *TJCT* | *Trinity Journal of Church and Theology* |
| *TLNT* | *Theological Lexicon of the New Testament* |
| TTP | Testaments of the Twelve Patriarchs |
| TSAJ | Texts and Studies in Ancient Judaism |
| *TynBul* | *Tyndale Bulletin* |
| *TZ* | *Theologische Zeitschrift* |
| *VC* | *Vigiliar Christiianae* |

| | |
|---|---|
| *VE* | *Vox Evangelica* |
| WBC | Word Biblical Commentary |
| *WD* | *Wort und Dienst* |
| WUNT | Wissenschaftliche Untersuchungen zum Neuen Testament |
| YCS | Yale Classical Studies |
| *ZNW* | *Zeitschrift für die Neutestamentliche Wissenschraft und Kunde der Alteren Kirche* |

# Introduction

Ephesians is distinct in its reference to spiritual beings, portrait of spiritual activity and size devoted to prayers proportionately in the Pauline corpus. However, research interest has focused primarily on its theological themes, social identity construct or function of the household code. It is not a secret that the bulk of scholars inadvertently come to the text with the prism of post-European enlightenment, cynical about the notion of transcendent realities and ambivalent to the idea of personal evil spirits. Consequently, much of the contributions have sought to answer questions about or have addressed existential issues and pivoted away from the most pervasive feature in the letter, namely the role of spiritual beings. Methodologically, priorities to linguistic analysis (*verba*) in the historical-grammatical approach above social history of author-reader framework misconstrues the interface of language, worldview and culture in the quest for authorial aims (*voluntas*).[1] Words are symbols that find meaning in the context of their usage. For example, religion and culture were inseparable in the Greco-Roman world; the distance between modern biblical scholarship and custodians of the Bible (the church) has not been wider partly due to how the NT has been approached. A post-enlightenment esoteric approach to biblical studies has not only dominated academic inquiry but it has also diminished the value of its findings to Christian communities. The world concept of the early Christians was assumed in NT writings; the

---

1. G. Samuel, *A Short Introduction to Judging and to Legal Reasoning* (Cheltenham: Edward Elgar Publishing, 2016), 5–103. The history of hermeneutics show clear shifts in the mode of reasoning in philosophy, legal and biblical interpretation after the enlightenment. The emphasis on *verba* – words – to adequately convey intent (*voluntas*) or shape interpretation in deciphering meaning became more pronounced from the eighteenth century. Biblical scholars may be cautious about claims to objectivity since the concurrent mode of reasoning in legal and biblical hermeneutics over the centuries shows obvious influence by philosophical, scientific and social trends on interpretation. Some biblical scholars have erred on the basis of genre criticism – interpreting sacred/religious texts as though they are legal or philosophical texts.

understanding of religious texts presupposes or assumes religious prism of sort to make sense of religious concepts and prescriptions.

The naming and framing of spiritual beings in Ephesians made sense to the early readers whose worldview differed from our modern Western one, especially in regard to the role of transcendent forces in human affairs. The worldview of Asia Minor predates the Enlightenment and modern civilization. To decipher the message of Ephesians, one does not need to agree with its cosmology. It is, however, imperative to grasp the world concept in which its message is framed. The letter would espouse no cogent message, and its readers would find it incomprehensible if its spirit cosmology was fashioned in the framework of post-enlightenment artisans. In other words, understanding the worldview of the ancient text is crucial to deciphering the conditions, socio-religious features and ultimate aims of religious communities.

The quest to understand the identity of Christ followers features prominently in recent studies on Ephesians.[2] Significant amount of research has been conducted particularly on the social identity (sect or otherwise) being espoused in the letter. In a previous work, I highlighted a tension in prevailing scholarship arguing for "sectarian" features in the rhetoric of differentiation on the one hand, and apologetic aims of the household code, on the other.[3] I showed the misleading character of those social reconstructions and brought to bear the consistent strategy of the letter's moral discourse. Moreover, social scientific theories have been applied to Ephesians either to test the efficacy of methodologies or to reconstruct social history to shed light on group identity or group dynamics of the early Christian communities. Social scientific studies have made contributions to our understanding of Ephesians. However, the traditional Western worldview and biases have left a comprehensive study of spiritual beings in Ephesians largely unattended – despite their dominant feature in the letter. The idea of a personal God, Holy Spirit and Jesus Christ as spiritual agents on behalf of the church has not been problematic. Conversely, the nature of principalities and powers (referring to the language of the powers) named in the letter and the idea of evil spirits rather seem to evoke some

---

2. See Tet-Lim N. Yee, *Jews, Gentiles and Ethnic Reconciliation: Paul's Jewish Identity and Ephesians* (SNTSMS 130; Cambridge: CUP, 2005); M. Shkul, Reading Ephesians: Exploring Social Entrepreneurship in the Text (LNTS 408; London: T&T Clark, 2009); R. Roitta, *Behaving as a Christ-Believer: A Cognitive Perspective on Identity and Behavior Norms in Ephesians* (Linköping: Linköping University, 2009).

3. D. K. Darko, *No Longer Living as the Gentiles: Differentiation and Shared Ethical Values in Ephesians 4:17–6:9* (LNTS 375; London: T&T Clark, 2008).

consternation. Arguably, attention to the role of spiritual beings in regard to the communal identity and moral framework of Ephesians would have enhanced some of the findings from social-scientific studies.

The premise with which we establish what to study, mode of analysis and justify our findings is mostly shaped by the concept of reality we assume and informed by the logic (thought pattern) of the investigator. The claim to new or novel insights is commonplace in our discipline – whether or not there is an end that such findings lead to or if an idea itself and/or peer appraisal is the end in itself. Biblical studies have honed the art of exegetical analysis with particular attention to philology and grammatical analyses in deciphering authorial intent. Culture, social anthropology or in the case of religious texts, religious beliefs is too often relegated to the background. Perhaps, an inadvertent blind spot is the lack of appreciation for ancient thought patterns, "primitive" cultural mores and religious experiences that are not necessarily shared by the mainstream in Western traditions. Historically, the shift in worldview during and after the European enlightenment, preceded by medieval quest for faith-reason integration, has affected our orientation, interest and even how we determine the value of our subject of inquiry.

Students of my biblical hermeneutics class in non-western countries are often struck by the assumptions underlying historical-grammatical method, especially the notion that one may be able to decipher the import of religious texts simply by knowing original languages and applying the rules of grammar. Working in multiple languages, they point to the significance of culture, worldview and religious traditions in good interpretation. As one African student posed, "Do you read English books and make sense of them only by the study of English morphology and syntax?" My answer is, "Of course not!" It is important to examine texts like Ephesians against the cultural background, worldview and pre-conversion belief systems of its earliest readers – this will enable us to probe and identify prescriptions on how new believers may navigate their new identity as Christ followers in their socio-religious context. When a religious text becomes an object of academic inquiry, it often stands to lose some of its religious fervor and become an object of "speculation" devoid of religious import.

This work aims to examine Ephesians as a religious correspondence to Christ followers in western Asia Minor, intended to effect real and concrete outcomes in their beliefs and lived experiences. I do not claim exactitude in the historical reconstructions but aim for proximate knowledge.

## 1.1 Recalling Changing Trends in Philosophical Thought on Spirit Cosmology

How did we arrive at the worldview that informs our academic discourse in Europe and North America? Why is the notion of transcendent realities such a contentious or uncomfortable subject in the study of religious texts? The belief in the transcendent powers in established religious traditions – mysticism or superstitious practices – was commonplace in the ancient world. The dominant world concept was one that perceived spiritual beings as active both in the celestial and terrestrial realms. This worldview enhanced the place of religious institutions and religious leaders in sociopolitical affairs. For example, the Christianized Europe accorded religious leaders important places in civic affairs. Education institutions and scientific advancement would be borne and developed in Europe with religious impetus. We need not rehearse the fact that Rome, Portugal, Spain and later Great Britain wielded significant influence with explorations and conquests that were sanctioned, if not funded, by Christian institutions. Hitherto, the epoch of scholasticism in the Middle Ages had challenged the status quo in regard to prevailing cosmology: Religious worldview and superstitious beliefs had to be explained rationally. Faith ought to make sense. Figures like Thomas Aquinas left their mark in the efforts to integrate faith and reason – to articulate in essence what constitutes a reasoned faith. Emphasis on the life of the mind, spiritual discernment and social engagement garnered popular appreciation and served as the segue to philosophical enlightenment.[4]

Martin Luther's ninety-five theses emerged in a European context with strong appetite to unmask the mystical and unearth the rationale for religious practices. Thus, the Reformation coincided with European enlightenment in the seventeenth and eighteenth centuries to introduce approaches to theological inquiry and biblical interpretation that would eventually concede to the tenets of "rational faith," owing to the changing worldviews in Europe and later in the United States. Faith in God ultimately gave way to faith in reason and science. As one scholar notes, "the Reformation saw reawakening of human interest in the awe of the supernatural order. The Enlightenment era saw theorists looking to nature to find clues on how life should be lived."[5] The place of humanity in

---

4. The scope of this work does not allow for a sketch on how philosophies of education began to shift from this period through the enlightenment to modern intellectual traditions in Western society.

5. G. L. Gutek, *Historical and Philosophical Foundations of Education: A Biographical Introduction* (Upper Saddle River: Merrill Prentice-Hall, 2001), 110.

determining how the world works and how humans ought to live became more attractive than the idea of a God who is in charge of creation. "Man was put at the center of the universe and allowed to be the supreme artisan of its destiny."[6] The debate between Catholics and reformers during the reformation garnered popular interest in the need to subject Christian doctrines to critical scrutiny. Inter-church tensions further served as a gift to non-ecclesial philosophers of enlightenment to challenge foundations to Christian beliefs.

> The enlightenment philosophes were highly critical of the established church. By proposing that knowledge came from the senses, experience, reason and feelings rather than history, tradition, or a universal authority, the Enlightenment thinkers tended to undermine the theological and philosophical presuppositions of seventeenth and eighteenth-century Christians.[7]

Perhaps, the academy is blindsided today to normalize post-enlightenment sensibilities in our approach to sacred text, which too often engenders false confidence in our ability to challenge the reasoning of biblical authors. Postmodern philosophy has dented claims to objective truth and methodologies derived from modernist philosophical enterprise. Though hardly admitted, NT scholars have been susceptible to the influence of the modern social, cultural and philosophical currents. The prism with which we read is the prism of our world/worldview. We do not need to accept the world concept of the Greco-Roman author and readers, but intellectual honesty demands that we venture to understand and appreciate their worldview if we want to understand the message of ancient texts written for Christians in Asia Minor. This study aims to augment prevailing scholarship by arguing that we should acknowledge post-enlightenment anachronism and endeavor to bring spirit cosmology to where it belongs in the study of Ephesians.

## 1.2 Review of Scholarship on Principalities and Powers

Ephesians stands out proportionately in its reference to "rulers and authorities" or principalities and powers in the Pauline corpus. Generally, the portrait of God, Jesus Christ and the Holy Spirit in the epistle are not debated, except on rare occasions where semantic ambiguities require further inquiry to determine

---

6. M. J. Anthony and W. S. Benson, *Exploring the History and Philosophy of Christian Education: Principles for the 21st Century* (Eugene: Wipf & Stock, 2003), 231.

7. Anthony and Benson, *History and Philosophy of Christian Education*, 233.

if "spirit" refers to human spirit or a spiritual agent. However, the identity of principalities and powers is a subject of debate. Some appeal to etymology, philology or general use of lexemes in the Pauline corpus to establish the meaning and/or reference to these powers. Still others have narrowed the scope to the social location of Ephesians (Asia Minor) as the backdrop to shed light on how the language of the letter may be understood. As far back as 1888, Otto Everling argued that "principalities and powers" in the NT and Ephesians in particular be read against the background of Hellenistic Jewish and Greco-Roman religious conventions to grasp their fullest import[8] – that is as personal spiritual forces whose overlord is Satan. Martin Dibelius[9] later locates the discussion in theological themes to assert that Paul's theology of the spirit is better understood in his eschatological and christological framework. Dibelius finds the spirit world in Paul to be one that includes the activity of evil spiritual powers both in the undisputed and disputed letters. Grundmann reiterated that these "powers" are personal spiritual beings that may be conceived of in light of popular understanding of the spirit-world in its milieu, as evident in Greek magical texts.[10]

Conversely, a shift in German scholarship during and in the aftermath of World War II saw new attempts to personify evil and employ social/existential readings to the language of principalities and powers in Paul. Hitherto, the impact of the Enlightenment in social thought and the tendency to characterize transcendent notions as superstitions and myths were gradually paving way for existential reading. For example, Heinrich Schlier had identified a wide variety of references to the "powers" and argued that they connote personal agents and hostile forces.[11] Apparently, Christ disarmed these forces (*entmächtigt*) on the cross but they still remain operative until their ultimate demise (*entmächtigung*) in the second advent of Christ. For Schlier, these powers take the form of

---

8. O. Everling, *Die Paulinische Angelologie und Dämonologie: Ein biblisch-theologischer Versuch* (Göttingen: Vandenhoek & Ruprecht, 1888), 119.

9. M. Dibelius, *Die Geisterwelt im Glauben des Paulus* (Göttingen: Vandenhoek & Ruprecht, 1909), 169–175.

10. W. Grundmann, *Der Begriff der Kraft in der Neutestamentlichen Gedankenwelt* (BWANT 8; Stuttgart: Kohlhammer, 1932), 39–55. See review in C. E. Arnold, *Power and Magic: The Concept of Power in Ephesians* (Grand Rapids: Baker Books, 1989), 43–44.

11. H. Schlier, *Principalities and Powers in the New Testament* (London: Burns & Oates, 1961). The original work was published in German in the 1930s. Once a disciple of Rudolf Bultmann, Schlier became a Catholic. This work is not primarily on Ephesians but deals with the subject in Galatians and the work of Christ in the NT in general. His interpretation of "stoicheia" in Galatians 4 in light of astral forces prompted major responses at the time. Clearly, events in World War II and existentialist philosophy influenced how scholars like Schlier, Bultmann and Berkhoff read the terms for "principalities and powers" in the NT.

"anxiety, death or care in the present age"; they exercise control in the world and persistently seek to undermine godly living. Bultmann[12] concurred and followed to demythologize the "powers."[13]

Hendrik Berkhof became a prominent figure in this field of study following his publication of *Christ and the Powers*.[14] Berkhof argues that understanding Paul's language for principalities, powers, and thrones in their first century usage is crucial to formulating cogent theological rationale for civic engagement. "These terms were not new to the religious vocabulary of Paul's readers,"[15] he argues. Paul, however, redefines their mythical import with Jewish apocalyptic framework in order to address prevailing social issues; "the apocalypse think primarily of the principalities and powers as heavenly angels: Paul sees them as social structures of earthly existence."[16] Demythologization becomes the means to appropriate Paul's language of the powers to Christian ethics or social engagement. However, Berkhof concedes that Paul does not demythologize the powers entirely in Ephesians. Ephesians is one text in which the language of the powers is unambiguous in its reference to satanic/evil spiritual forces.[17]

In his monograph entitled *Angels and Principalities: The Background, Meaning and Development of the Pauline Phrase Hai Archai Kai Hai Exousiai*,[18] Wesley Carr builds on the notion of the powers as social evil and social structures to contend that there are no such things as evil spiritual powers in Paul's writings. He insists that the language rather points to holy or pure angelic beings. Carr prioritizes philological analysis in his method of inquiry. However, Carr's inability to make sense of Ephesians 6:12 leads him to suggest that we consider the verse as a second century interpolation into original text.

---

12. R. Bultmann, *Jesus Christ and Mythology* (New York: Charles Schribner's, 1958).

13. O. Cullmann, *Christ and Time: The Primitive Christian Conception of Time and History*, 3rd volume (trans. F. V. Filson; London: SCM, 1962). Though not directly related to the study of Ephesians, Cullmann argued around the same time that the language of "authorities" in Romans 13 may be read to have dual meaning in conveying the sense of human authorities and angelic forces. Cullmann was not aiming to define the powers per se but examined how Christians lived at the time within this framework. It is accurate that some use of the terms elsewhere in Paul convey the import of human authorities.

14. H. Berkhof, *Christ and the Powers* (trans. H. H. Yoder; Scottdale: Herald Press, 1962).

15. Berkhof, *Christ and the Powers*, 17.

16. Berkhof, 23.

17. Berkhof, 30–31.

18. W. Carr, *Angels and Principalities: The Background, Meaning and Development of the Pauline Phrase Hai Archai Kai Hai Exousiai* (SNTS 42; Cambridge: CUP, 1981).

This conjecture has been challenged for its lack of material evidence.[19] Arnold presents the strongest and most comprehensive critique to Carr, exposing the pitfalls of Carr's view as well as its speculative nature.[20] Berkhof and Carr acknowledge explicitly that Ephesians 6.12 is an outlier in their observations since it refers to evil spiritual forces. Walter Wink follows the broader thesis of Bultmann and Berkhof in their demythologizing endeavor to argue that we read the powers as existential or social structures.[21] According to Wink, "Paul substitutes the terminologies for Satan, Beliar, Azazzel, demons or evil spirits within Jewish apocalyptic thought with 'quasi-hypostatised' words as sin, flesh and death."[22] In other words, Paul departs from spirit cosmology of his Greek and Jewish context to construct or redefine new ways to understand the powers.

Subsequently, academic treatment of the term "spirit" in modern societies that perceive reality as that which is concrete, tangible, and accessible to the five senses, would pivot to esoteric abstractions or find ways to minimize the import of spirit cosmology in the Roman world. Apparently, etymological analyses and social reading of Pauline lexemes of principalities and powers leave more questions than answers. Benoit[23] found it difficult to trace Pauline terminology for the powers to any particular tradition. He posits that they probably mediated through Second Temple Judaism into early Christian thought. Benoit underscores Jewish belief in good and evil spirits; these spirits also "hover between humanity and God."[24] If Paul borrowed from this tradition, argues Benoit, then he meant to convey that personal evil spiritual powers do exist. Lee[25] suggests that the origin of these concepts may be traced specifically to Jewish apocalyptic and astrological beliefs. He contends that we read the powers against the background of Rabbinic literature in particular, and perhaps the broader Greco-Roman background.

---

19. See P. T. O'Brien, "Principalities and Powers: Opponents of the Church," in *Biblical Interpretation and the Church: Text and Context* (ed. D. A. Carson; Exeter: Paternoster, 1984), 110–150, 125–128; and R. A. Wild, "The Warrior and the Prisoner: Some Reflections on Ephesians 6:10–20," *CBQ* 46, no. 2 (1984): 284–285.

20. C. E. Arnold, "The 'Exorcism' of Ephesians 6:12 in Recent Research: A Critique of Wesley Carr's View of the Role of Evil Powers in First Century AD Belief," *JSNT* 30 (1987): 71–87.

21. Wink uses the exact or common phrases in Berkhof's work to "unmask the powers."

22. Walter Wink, *Naming the Powers: Language of Power in the New Testament* (Philadelphia: Fortress, 1984), 100.

23. P. Benoit, "Pauline Angelology and Demonology: Reflexions on the Designations of the Heavenly Powers and On the Origin of Angelic Evil According to Paul," *RSBul* 3 (1983): 1–18.

24. Benoit, "Pauline Angelology and Demonology," 16.

25. J. Y. Lee, "Interpreting the Demonic Powers in Pauline Thought," *NovT* 12 (1970): 54–69.

Forbes later refutes the notion that Paul's language of the powers is grounded in Jewish apocalyptic thought and characterizes it as grossly misleading. Conversely, his study of δυναμεις/ἄρχων, ἐξουσίας and κυρίοτητες leads to the conclusion that Paul draws from middle Platonism[26] and other Greek conventions instead. Apparently, Pauline usage denotes the complex idea of personal spirits and "personified abstractions" in Greek traditions.[27] According to Forbes, while Paul's belief in personal evil spirits is self-evident, he renders these terms and characterizes the "spiritual world" in terms of personal abstractions. "He (Paul) is willing to virtually hypostatize Law, Sin and Death, and treat them as 'spiritual powers,' quasi-personal realities."[28] Thus, "the Law, Sin and Death are for Paul the primary powers confronting humanity, and also the primary forces defeated by Jesus."[29] He asserts, "it was thoroughly acceptable to take abstract features of the nature of God, or of the cosmos, and to understand them as personified beings: gods, demigods or souls."[30] Paul then uses lexemes of principalities and powers not as referents to personal spiritual beings but abstract concepts in Christian ideological framework. Forbes finds this usage applicable in the undisputed letters of Paul. His reader would have benefited from the treatment of clear points of departure from undisputed Pauline and disputed letters such as Ephesians and Colossians. As others noted above, Forbes realizes that his interpretation could not apply to how we read the powers in Ephesians and indicates that the use of διάβολος, ἄρχων, ἐξουσίας in Ephesians and other correspondence to Ephesus (i.e. 1 & 2 Timothy) do refer to spiritual beings.[31] Previous attempts to demythologize the powers in

---

26. C. Forbes, "Pauline Demonology and/or Cosmology? Principalities, Powers and the Elements of the World in their Hellenistic Context," *JSNT* 85 (2002): 51–73. It is important that one does not read Philo and Plutarch as if they did not believe in the existence of spiritual beings in the cosmos. Far from it. Philo writes as a Jew with a Jewish framework and sympathy to Plato whom he suggests learned much of his wisdom from Moses. Plutarch is perhaps the most religious philosopher from the first century. The argument pertains to specific use of words and spirit cosmology of Philo and Plutarch. Forbes's lack of clarity in stating the scope of his inquiry leaves this part of his account somewhat ambiguous if not misleading.

27. C. Forbes, "Paul's Principalities and Powers: Demythologizing Apocalyptic?" *JSNT* 82 (2001): 61–62.

28. Forbes, "Paul's Principalities and Powers," 83.

29. Forbes, 63.

30. Forbes, "Pauline Demonology and/or Cosmology?" 71.

31. Forbes, "Paul's Principalities and Powers," 65–69.

Paul and others who employed sociopolitical readings realize that Ephesians does not fit their interpretation well.[32]

Gombis offers two interrelated readings of the powers in Ephesians that are noteworthy; one that finds Ancient Near East (ANE) and Hebrew conventions as the backdrop for deciphering a pattern and rationale for the feature of the powers in Ephesians. First, he identities a pattern in divine warfare discourses in ANE and in Hebrew literature – "conflict, victory, kingship, house-building and celebration"[33] – as a lens to interpret "the Drama of Ephesians." He indicates that Israel's neighbors "utilized the divine warfare as a rhetorical tool to proclaim the supremacy of their deity."[34] He further argues that the device features in Hebrew scriptures to characterize Yahweh's supreme status over the gods of the nations. Ephesians purportedly utilizes the device for similar aims or appropriates it to convey its message.[35]

Second, Gombis locates Paul's concept of the powers in his Jewish worldview where Satan/Beliar, angelic beings, gods and other suprahuman agents were either perceived or believed to exist in the cosmic realm. The present age in Pauline thought is thus "dominated by supra human cosmic powers that are in rebellion against God and his purposes for creation."[36] These powers are responsible for disrupting God's order in his creation. Gombis reads Ephesians 6:10–13, not in terms of warfare against spiritual beings, but a battle against social injustice, as he explains here. "This is not a purely negative task but involves the people of God imagining new and renewed patterns of life that

---

32. A common pattern in the review is how scholars tried to explain Paul to accommodate their world-concepts. Paul is made to conform to the interpreter's worldview instead of attempting to understand Paul in his worldview.

33. T. G. Gombis, "Ephesians 2 as a Narrative of Divine Warfare," *JSNT* 26, no. 4 (2004): 403–418, (404 in particular). Also T. Longman III and D. G. Reid, *God as a Warrior* (Carlisle: Paternoster, 1995). This builds on a pattern or similar features previously proposed by Longman and Reid in their treatment of OT texts. Gombis applies it here to his reading of Ephesians.

34. T. G. Gombis, *The Drama of Ephesians: Participating in the Triumph of God* (Downers Grove: IVP Academic, 2010), 28. Gombis does not clarify if the readers actually believed that the events actually occurred in the cosmic realm or are left to imagine such events.

35. T. G. Gombis, "Cosmic Lordship and the Divine Gift-Giving: Psalm 68 in Ephesians 4:8," *NovT* 47, no. 4 (2005): 367–380; "Ephesians 3:2–13: Pointless Digression, or Epitome of the Triumph of God in Christ," *WTJ* (2004): 313–323. The author indicates that the device helps to decipher how Paul explains his weak standing as a prisoner in this pericope (3:2–13) to Christ followers that did not know him. He indicates, "Ephesians is most likely written to churches that were unfamiliar with him (Paul), and he needs to make explicit the paradox of his situation so that his imprisonment might rightly be understood" (p. 316).

36. Gombis, *Drama of Ephesians*, 44–57. Gombis reads "the rulers of this age" in 1 Cor 2 as suprahuman agents as well. Paul's use of rulers and authorities does not always convey the sense of personal spiritual agents, and this reading of 1 Corinthians is problematic at the very least.

are redemptive and life-giving. We resist participating in broader systems of injustice and exploitations and pray for wisdom to forge creative pathways of renewal that are redemptive and life-giving and represent a return to shalom."[37]

Thus, "the drama of Ephesians involves the powers and authorities who are cosmic rulers responsible for large-scale patterns of injustice, oppression, exploitation and idolatry."[38] The pre-Christian past in Ephesians 2:1–3 is one that is perverted by Satan and marked by enslavement to sin and moral decadence. Accordingly, Christ followers are no longer subject to these forces of evil but stand victorious in Christ. In this vein, "the church must be faithful to its call because it stands as the monument to the triumph of God over Satan and the powers of evil."[39] Gombis's reading does not only propose a Jewish background to Ephesians, but also presents the powers as spiritual agents whose activities occur in the sociopolitical and moral arena of human existence.

As shown above, previous scholarship posits that understanding the origin of Pauline terminology of "rulers and authorities" or "principalities and powers" would richly enhance our understanding of their import in his letters. A major contribution to the discussion, and one that has received widespread support, is the work of Clinton Arnold. Arnold's 1989 monograph entitled *Power and Magic: The Concept of Power in Ephesians in Light of Its Historical Context*[40] makes a compelling case to read the powers in Ephesians as personal evil spiritual forces. The stated aim is "to acquire a more complete understanding of the nature and motivation for the inclusion of the power-motif in the epistle by studying the author's development of the theme against the backdrop of the spiritual environment of Western Asia Minor in the first century."[41] Arnold provides material evidence from the broader religious context of Asia Minor and the empire to shed light on the subject.[42] A careful study of religions, magic, and astrological practices indicates a widespread belief in spiritual powers and

---

37. Gombis, *Drama of Ephesians*, 57.

38. Gombis, 58.

39. Gombis, 106.

40. C. E. Arnold, *Power and Magic: The Concept of Power in Ephesians in Light of Its Historical Context* (Cambridge: CUP, 1989).

41. Arnold, *Power and Magic*, 2.

42. Arnold points to the anachronistic nature of reading Ephesians against the background of Gnosticism or Gnosis in the first century, thereby suggesting the need to eliminate Gnosticism in the study. He situates the context in the vicinity of western Asia Minor, arguing that the circular nature of the letter warrants such regional scope.

familiar usage of the terminology for the powers outside Christianity.[43] His study of selected passages[44] from Ephesians leads to the conclusion that the terminologies for the "powers" refer to personal evil spiritual forces, and it is the way that the early readers would have understood them.[45] Arnold asserts that, "a knowledge of Hellenistic magic may very well be the most important background of understanding why the author highlights the power of God and the 'powers' of evil in Ephesians."[46] Arnold posits that, "the whole of the epistle is moving in this direction. It focuses on the unseen dimension of Christian existence, envisioning a host of evil spiritual forces under the leadership of the devil continuing to assail believers and causing them to fall."[47] He suggests that evidence from magic, astrology and cultic practices of the ancient world be adduced in the quest to understand the nature of these powers, the dreadful conditions of the readers of Ephesians and authorial aims to mitigate that.

Arnold's work, especially his *Power and Magic* and subsequent work on Colossians,[48] have made a lasting contribution in the way we read the powers in Ephesians. His apt critique of demythologization and sociopolitical readings has left us with a widely accepted reading of the powers as personal evil spiritual forces in Ephesians;[49] this reading is consistent with the conventions of the time and sheds better light of a consistent reading of Ephesians.[50] Methodologically,

---

43. The core of Arnold's work resides in the section devoted to the historical-religious background of Asia Minor where he employs primary sources such as the PGM, T. Solomon, *Prayer of Jacob*, fragments from magic and astrology to show that both Jews and Gentiles in Asia employed magic, astrology and engaged rituals associated with deities like the patron goddess, Artemis Ephesia.

44. Ephesians 1:10, 15–23; 2:2; 3:10, 14; 4:8–10; 6:10–20.

45. Two chapters (4 and 5) are devoted to showing the disposition of believers and the power of God available to meet their dreadful and diabolic spiritual climate. Drawing from the prayers in 1:15–23; 3:14–19; and 3:20–21, he stresses divine enabling by the Holy Spirit, and the power of Christ for the church that need to be appropriated in the struggle against evil spiritual powers. According to Arnold, Ephesians addresses the fears of the believers "directly and instructs the new and older believers alike on how to resist the powerful influence of these evil forces." Arnold, *Power and Magic*, 122.

46. Arnold, *Power and Magic*, 39.

47. Arnold, 142.

48. C. E. Arnold, *The Colossians Syncretism: The Interface between Christianity and Folk Belief at Colossae* (Grand Rapids: Baker, 1996).

49. Elsewhere in Paul the language of "rulers and authorities" does not always refer to evil spiritual forces. However, they are used consistently in Ephesians in support of Arnold's argument.

50. Arnold's high dependence on the PGM evinces mixed reactions. On one hand, it helps to explain how magic was used and understood. On the other hand, the PGM is composed of many fragments from Egypt but Arnold makes the connection primarily with the Asia Minor setting in the study. The frequency of communication and commerce between Rome, Alexandria and Ephesus by the first century, even franchise of gods like Isis known in the first

his scope in the reconstruction of the socio-religious background and conceptualization of their import would be significant in this particular study.

## 1.3 Central Issues of Inquiry

Building on the reading of the "powers" as personal spiritual forces in Ephesians and a broader scope of background study, comprising Greco-Roman and Jewish conventions, this work examines the role of spiritual beings in the cosmological framework of Ephesians, underlining how it informs the epistle's construction of communal identity and ethical imperatives in advancing group solidarity. First, I move the issue from lexicography, philology and etymological analyses to frame the discussion in the cosmological framework or worldview within which the portrait of spiritual beings would make sense. Thus, I re-examine the evidence from Jewish, Greek and folk religious practices (like Arnold) in an attempt to reconstruct the proximate spirit cosmology of the author and his readers. Second, previous studies focused primarily on the *nature* of the powers in Ephesians, but this study aims to investigate the *role* or *function* of spiritual beings as a whole, including the role of God, Jesus Christ and the Holy Spirit. It becomes apparent that the message of Ephesians could be misconstrued by one-sided study of spiritual beings – be they personal evil spiritual powers or the portraits of God, Christ and the Holy Spirit. The interface of material and spiritual dimensions of the world, and the notion of divine activity in human affairs become integral features to understand the message of the letter. Third, the role of spiritual beings relative to the identity construction of Christ followers and their moral aspirations is examined to establish the spiritual being's influence, impact, and role in the framing of communal disposition, in-group identity and praxis. Previous studies of social identity of the letter emphasized Jew-Gentile relations, in-group (Christ followers) and out-group (unbelievers) relations and intrapersonal relations. This study augments those relations by exploring the prominence and significance of spirit cosmology in identity construction, spiritual formation, and mutual obligation to maintain solidarity in the household of God.

---

three centuries, is the reason those who disagree with Arnold may not want to overstretch their position. On a different note, Arnold assumes that the religious context would naturally lead to fear of malevolent forces. It is not always the case that people who engage in magic, astrology or cultic practices do so for security; a range of possibilities could be added: (a) living in a social structure that expresses great interest in spiritual beings and prides in its religious affiliation, (b) striving for success through spiritual assistance could be a factor, (c) consulting and depending on spiritual aid to enhance individual prowess or blessings for major undertakings (marriage, work, etc.).

This study also builds on earlier literary, historical-grammatical and social-scientific approaches to explore the cosmos as a habitat for spiritual and physical realities. It reconstructs spirit cosmology with source material from the religious culture, ancient texts, numismatics, epitaphs and Second Temple Judaism, among others, in the NT era. It will become apparent that early Christianity, as a fledging Jewish movement, shared a world concept similar to other Greco-Roman traditions. The entire letter of Ephesians – not selected verses – will be examined not only to study the demonology, but also christological, pneumatology or *theo*-logical impetus for group identity and moral aspirations. Worldview informs truth-claims hence its significance in the study of a religious text such as Ephesians.

## 1.4 Spiritual Beings in the Literary Structure and Rhetorical Framework

Apart from the actual naming of spiritual beings and the permeating framework in every chapter of Ephesians, its literary structure and rhetorical framework further underscore the significance of our subject of inquiry in the argument and communication strategy.[51] The opening paragraph accentuates "every spiritual blessings in the heavenly realms"[52] accorded in Christ as the basis for an elaborate eulogy – invocation of God's blessings to evoke gratitude and a cause for praise (1:3–14). Moreover, the closing of the body of the letter makes a passionate plea to frame Christian living as spiritual warfare, requiring vigilance, discipline and virtue in utmost readiness to withstand the stratagems of evil spiritual forces (6:10–20). The opening and ending in the literary structure bookends the rest of the discourse with spiritual overtones and highlights activities of spiritual beings. Hubing makes an important observation, in this regard, in a recent monograph[53] in which he examines the literary forms of Galatians against the background of Greco-Roman letter writing conventions.

---

51. J. A. D. Weima, *Paul the Ancient Letter Writer: An Introduction to Epistolary Analysis* (Grand Rapids: Baker Academic, 2016), 11–12. Weima makes a case to observe the important role of epistolary features in our understanding of Paul's letters in the entire NT. His chapters on letter opening (pp. 11–50) and letter closing (pp. 165–204) demonstrate with concrete examples how these features serve to enhance persuasion. While Ephesians does not feature prominently in his examples, the import of the epistolary opening and closing further draws a reader's attention to how the author of Ephesians characterized the role of spiritual beings to be central to his entire discourse.

52. Unless otherwise stated, all Scripture translations in this work are the author's own.

53. J. Hubing, *Crucifixion and New Creation: The Strategic Purpose of Galatians 6:11–17*, LNTS 508 (London: T&T Clark, 2015).

His study of papyri letters vis-à-vis the literary structure of Paul's letters aptly provides valuable insights into the way we read Galatians 6:11–17 as the end of the body of the letter. He argues with substantive evidence to ascertain that "the body closing" in ancient common letter traditions functions as recapitulation and/or accentuation of the motive, summation of main issues and grounds for further exploration to key issues of inquiry. That Ephesians 6:10–20 serves as the conclusion of the body of the letter warrants attention in the way it buttresses the author's main points in this regard. The opening and concluding paragraphs in the structure of Ephesians suggests that the idea of "spiritual blessings" (1:3) and/or the struggle "against the rulers, against the authorities, against cosmic powers over this present darkness, against spiritual forces of evil in the heavenly places" (6:12) are of significant import in the literary structure and communicative strategy.

Andrew Lincoln's use of rhetorical criticism leads him to identify features of *peroratio* in Ephesians 6:10–20.[54] His observations from literary forms in Aristotle, Cicero and Quintilian seem to support the notion that the pericope is framed to evoke the kind of response expected of an epilogue that serves the function of *peroratio*. Aristotle's fourfold features of peroratio is well known: It makes "(1) the audience well-disposed towards yourself and ill-disposed towards your opponents, (2) magnify or minimize the leading facts, (3) excite the required state of emotion in your hearts, and (4) refresh their memories."[55] For Quintilian, these features may be compressed into two as (1) the recapitulation of the key points and (2) strategic harnessing of strong emotional response.[56] Cicero[57] indicates that an effective *peroratio* must include some metaphor in the composition.[58] In Ephesians 6:10–20, the battle imagery and analogy with military armory seems to serve such aims while evoking a strong sense of urgency. Moreover, corresponding terms and concepts in the opening (1:3–14) and closing paragraph (6:10–20) suggests that they function as *peroratio*, clearly accentuating spiritual activity in the framework of the letter. For example, the reference to heavenly realms (1:3; 1:20; 2:6; 3:10) is revisited in 6:10–20. The powers as personal evil spiritual powers (1:20–21; 2:2; 3:10; 4:27) feature prominently in this pericope as well. As Lincoln further explains,

---

54. A. T. Lincoln, "'Stand, therefore . . .': Ephesians 6:10–20 as Peroratio," *Biblical Interpretation*, 105–106.

55. Aristotle, *Rhetoric* 3.19 (trans. W. Rhys Roberts).

56. Quintilian, *Inst.* 6.1.1–15.

57. Cicero, *Part. Or.* 15.53.

58. Quintilian, *Inst.* 6.1.2.

"The virtues required in the first four pieces of the armor reinforce the appeal of the immediately preceding paranetical part of the letter, with its concerns that the readers live a righteous life in the world, while the two items reflect the whole thrust of the first part of the letter, that the readers appropriate all that has been achieved for them in their salvation and the gospel that has made it known."[59]

If we accept Lincoln's observation, then it would not be far-fetched to surmise that the *peroratio* encapsulates what the author seeks to convey in the preceding discourse regarding the nature and posture towards Christian living, necessitating readiness and vigilance in the spiritual battle. That would also echo the crucial role of this framework in what the letter seeks to convey.

## 1.5 The Structure of the Book

This book is structured to explore spirit cosmology of the world behind Ephesians (Greek, Roman and Jewish) prior to a careful study of the role of spiritual beings in Ephesians. The study of the text is followed by reconstruction of parallel spirit cosmology in Africa in an attempt to strip the findings off esoteric imaginations to concretize how Christ followers in Asia Minor would have received the message being conveyed. Chapter 2 focuses on spirit cosmology of Asia Minor and beyond with additional insights from elsewhere in the Roman empire, the social location and religious worldview of the readers' pre-conversion past. Chapter 3 provides a survey of the role of spiritual beings in Jewish world concept – the worldview of the Jewish author (Paul of Ephesians) – and an early Christian portrait of spirit cosmology. Chapter 4 investigates the status and role of spiritual beings in Ephesians 1–3 against the backdrop aforementioned. These first three chapters of Ephesians have been read traditionally as a theological discourse and it will become evident that the section makes no overt demand from the readership but explicates and underscores the unfolding plan of God with the agency of Jesus Christ and the Holy Spirit in regard to their salvific status. Chapter 5 examines Ephesians 4–6 to make sense the portrayal of divine activity and human responsibility in the paranetic discourse. Chapter 6 is devoted to the reconstruction of spirit cosmology in Africa to demonstrate and help the reader to imagine the radical differences between the worlds/worldviews behind the text, shared in many ways by Africans, and the framework with which an

---

59. A. T. Lincoln, "'Stand, therefore . . .': Ephesians 6:10–20 as Peroratio," *Biblical Interpretation*, 105–106.

interpreter from the Euro-American context looks at the text. It is anticipated that this would increase awareness of exegetical blind spots and generate a new interest/desire for western and non-western scholars to appreciate what each worldview brings to the complex task of exegesis in our discipline. As a native of Ghana in West Africa, I will examine African scholars closely to bring to light some useful elements that may aid cross-cultural hermeneutical endeavors. Chapter 7 summarizes key findings and makes some proposals for consideration, cooperation and constructive engagement in reading Ephesians and perhaps other books of the New Testament.

# 2

## Towards Greco-Roman Spirit Cosmology

The early Christians perceived reality and the world differently from how post-European enlightenment Christians in the western hemisphere may do. Reality as that which is accessible by the five senses seem incompatible with the notion that spiritual beings are active in every aspect of human affairs. At the basic level, the worldview of the early Christians accommodated the belief that spiritual beings are partly responsible for certain conditions and moral failings. Christian origins held that a teenage virgin could be impregnated by a spirit supernaturally to give birth to fully human and fully divine baby (Jesus). Moreover, central to Christian faith is the idea that human separation from God or the fall of humanity (caused by deception by the devil manifesting in the form of a serpent – Gen 3) could be mitigated by faith in the Son of God who died for the sins of the world; that his death offers opportunity to those who believe to be saved from the consequences of sin and alienation from God.

These early Christians were products of a social location and worldview that made matters of faith and life intelligible. Their view of the cosmos was one that found an interplay of matter and spirit, the physical and metaphysical and the natural and supernatural. Greeks, Romans and Jews perceived the world as a place where human life and deeds could be influenced by spiritual agents. Today's dichotomy between science and religion, physics and metaphysics, even critical thinking and spirituality would be foreign to the first-century followers of Christ, as we shall see below. Similarly, the subject of "behavioral science" as a discipline that focuses on neural decision-making processes and communication patterns in behavioral formation, to the exclusion of belief systems, would be inconceivable to them. Rooted in post-enlightenment epistemology, behavioral science examines the cognitive prowess of the *individual* and how it shapes moral judgment and social interaction *apart from spiritual powers*. Even outside religious studies, it is not uncommon to find critical distancing of "all things spiritual" from "all things scientific" in the quest to understand issues of group identity and moral framework. Undoubtedly, post-Darwinian scholars of the NT have been exposed to rich scientific advancement and findings about human origins and our solar system at levels unknown to their forebears. However, Christianity is rooted in ancient traditions, thoughts and texts that continue to shape its dogma and praxis. It is imperative then that we understand and appreciate how these early Christians perceived the inhabited world and their fate in it relative to transcendent powers such as the God in whom they believed.

Global Christianity has brought about one more challenge to otherwise uncontested trends in scholarship. The decline of Christianity in the western hemisphere where members possess, produce and control most of its resources and the growth of Christianity in the non-western world, where most of the worldviews of its adherents seem rather closer to those of the early Christians, begs answers to the legitimacy of post-enlightenment assumptions in biblical interpretation. Biblical texts are impregnated with cultural-specific norms and thought patterns; the writers communicated from socio-cultural contexts using the acceptable modes of reasoning in language, logic and referents of their time. This chapter endeavors to reconstruct an aspect of the worldview of early Gentile followers of Christ, especially those in western Asia Minor, to recall the religious culture and worldview from which they converted to Christianity and shed some light suggestively on how they comprehended the issues of identity, community and moral aspirations in Ephesians – relative to the role of spiritual beings.

The chapter examines how spiritual beings and belief systems in the Greco-Roman world informed moral discourse and behavioral patterns. It does not intend to be exhaustive in differentiating minute details of traditions, religions and worldviews. The aim is to show that while some differences existed, there was a widely held belief that spiritual beings were active and instrumental in human affairs. This reconstruction is representative but not selective; it does not cover every belief, tradition or deity in the region. I will show how philosophers and rhetoricians depicted transcendent forces in the affairs of humankind. It is not my intention to dismiss the views of sophists and philosophers who challenged extreme elements in the religious culture. There were indeed a few outliers with marginal impact hence the focus on the general worldview of first-century communities. In fact, it is common knowledge in ancient philosophy that those who expressed atheist viewpoints overtly faced expulsion from their cities owing to intolerance by the citizenry.[1] I make no claim that Greco-Roman philosophers were monolithic in their spirit cosmology either. Instead, I contend that they shared broader perspectives that would aid our understanding of Ephesians. Moving the discussion from "word study," etymological analysis and source critical approaches, I contend that a good grasp of the worldview and religious culture will offer better insights into how we approach and interpret Ephesians as a letter – beyond selected words or verses – in regard to the role of spiritual beings. I will also examine folk religions, astrology and magical practices and how they imparted social dynamics. Here, the attention will be narrowly focused on Ephesus, other cities in Asia Minor and relevant widespread traditions. I hope this inquiry into spirit cosmology will shed light on how we read the portrait of group identity and moral discourse in Ephesians.

## 2.1 Spiritual Beings in Greco-Roman Thought

Ancient philosophical pursuits and religious piety were inseparable in many cases. As Epictetus notes, "true philosophy and piety are one and the same thing."[2] Intellectual traditions were fused in the cosmology in which spiritual beings were intricate parts of human existence. This was the norm and permeated every fabric of society, urban or rural. Moral philosophers and rhetoricians exerted more influence in the urban sectors whereas rural folks participated in traditions and practices grounded in multifaceted beliefs of transcendent powers. This does not suggest that religious activities in urban sectors were comparatively less than the rural areas. On the contrary, the connectedness of culture and religion persisted in major cities, with elaborate festivities associated with gods and goddesses. The Greek and Roman gods presided over the success and failure of individuals and communities. Philosophers from Miletus to Anatolia to Rome wrote about their beliefs and spirit cosmology. The gods were significant to the identity of the people and an important part of the culture and functioning of a good society. "One of the chief glories of Greek philosophy is that it fostered the light of reason and rolled back the darkness of superstition and fear. But the rational approach did not always lead to agnosticism – far from it. As the subject developed, the

---

1. See Cicero, *Nature of the Gods* 1.63 and Critias, *DK* 88. B. 25. Cicero writes about some who rejected divination but held belief in the existence of the gods (Cicero, *Div.* 1.5).

2. Epictetus, *Ench.* 31.1.

main current of speculation set ever more strongly in the direction of a theistic, or pantheistic, interpretation of the world."[3]

It is impossible to measure the degree by which religion influenced morality, culture and politics, but it is certain that intelligence, prudence and devotion to the gods were not either/or categories. The intelligentsia were also devotees of magic and/or astrology.

Zeus was at the center of cosmological speculations in early Greek philosophy.[4] For example, classical Ionians appointed priests into significant roles in their monarchy in order to give prominent voices to the gods in deliberations.[5] Socially, public figures that resisted or disparaged religious events could be subjected to severe punishment. Even Socrates was not spared but charged with "misconduct" when he criticized the validity of certain rituals to the gods.[6] For Plato, the divine Creator is the center of the universe. "The heavens, in his view, declare the rational purposes of the Maker, whose handiwork constitutes a 'cosmos', a single, ordered, and beautiful whole, infused with life and intelligence."[7]

Popular philosophical traditions held deep religious convictions – be it Platonists, Stoics, Cynics and Epicureans. "Socrates offers a cock to Asclepius . . . Xenophon builds a temple. . . Socrates models himself upon God . . . and is divinely commissioned."[8] Cynic philosophy held that Julian sought spiritual guidance and indulged in rituals like the other citizens.[9] Pseudo-Diogenes claims that Diogenes "calls himself heaven's dog who lives freely under Zeus, and attributes what is good to Zeus and not his neighbors. It is in his living according to nature (*kata physin*) and not according to popular opinion (*kata doxan*) that is equivalent to his being free under God."[10] Epictetus indicates that the pursuit of philosophy itself must be guided by the gods.[11] He thus argues for a prominent role of the gods in the affairs of the cosmos. "Be assured that the essential property of piety towards the gods is to form right opinions concerning them, as existing and as governing the universe with goodness

3. J. V. Luce, *Introduction to Greek Philosophy* (London: Thames & Hudson, 1992), 161.

4. Luce, *Greek Philosophy*, 20–22, 59–72.

5. Luce, 29.

6. Luce, 87, 92–93.

7. Luce, 107.

8. A. J. Malherbe, *Paul and the Popular Philosophers* (Minneapolis: Fortress, 1989), 23.

9. Malherbe, *Paul and Popular Philosophers*, 23.

10. Malherbe, 110–111. See Pseudo-Diogenes *Epistle* 7 and Pseudo-Heraclitus, *Ep.* 4.

11. Epictetus, *Dis.* 3.22.95–98.

and justice. And fix yourself in this resolution, to obey them, and yield to them, and willingly follow them in all events, as produced by the most perfect understanding. For thus you will never find fault with the gods, nor accuse them as neglecting you."[12]

As ambiguous as Plato's cosmology appears in *Timaeus,* it is evident that he ascribes origin of the cosmos to a deity and/or Demiurge, whom Socrates had previously described as "the maker and father of the universe."[13] Plato indicates that there are intermediary gods and demons serving as agents of God in the world. These powers "serve as channels through which divine power might reach the world."[14] He ascribes moral failings to lack of spiritual discipline since commitment to the gods does impact civil obedience. It is on this note that the ideal city state ought to reserve prominent places in its landscape to the gods, who would also serve as models of human conduct. Plato is insistent that citizens embraced religious obligations as civic duty. Thus, "If a good man sacrifices to the gods and keeps them constant company in his prayers and offerings and every kind of worship he can give them, this will be the best and noblest policy he can follow; it is the conduct that fits his character as nothing else can, and it is his most effective way of achieving a happy life."[15]

Plato and other philosophers stressed the role of the gods as guardians of moral decency in human interactions. The idea that the gods protected the vulnerable and avenge the cause of the defenseless served as a check in society; they rewarded good deeds and punished injustice. Plato asserts in the *Laws (V)* that unfair acts against foreigners tend to attract expedient reaction from the gods. He states:

> As to foreigners, one should regard agreements made with them as particularly sacrosanct. Practically all offenses committed as between or against foreigners are quicker to attract the vengeance of God than offenses as between fellow citizens. The foreigner is not surrounded by friends and companions, and stirs the compassion of gods and men that much more, so that anyone who has the power to avenge come to his aid more readily; and that power is possessed pre-eminently by the guardian spirit or

---

12. Epictetus, *Ench.* 31.

13. R. H. Nash, *The Gospel and the Greeks: Did the New Testament Borrow Pagan Thoughts?* (Philipsburg: P&R Publishing, 2003), 27.

14. Nash, *Gospel and the Greeks,* 31.

15. Plato, *Laws* 4.716e (trans. T. J. Saunders).

god, companion of Zeus the God of Strangers, who is concerned in each case.[16]

Xenocrates (396–315 BCE), a follower of Plato, similarly attributes the creation of the cosmos to a god whose power extends to the oversight on how life is lived in it.[17] To some degree, Aristotle was less of a religious man than other Athenian philosophers. However, he also shared their belief in God and argues that the inability of humans to explain mysteries and complexities in the material world is suggestive of the fact that these are acts of God.[18] "Aristotle too in his ideal state prescribes the institution of priesthoods of the gods, though in a slightly grudging manner: he lists them fifth of the various institutions of the state 'though they are first in importance.'"[19] His proposal for an ideal polis also allows for the erection of sculptures, paintings and shrines that are pleasant in sight in prominent places.

Middle Platonism similarly encouraged religious practices and devotion to the gods.[20] It understood spirit and matter as inseparable dimensions of one cosmos. To that extent, "neo-Pythagoreanism might mean nothing more than astrology, occultism, twaddle about mysterious properties of numbers."[21] Unlike in our post-enlightenment prisms, critical thinking and spirituality belonged together. To believe in the reality of supernatural powers to influence human thoughts and praxis was not akin to ignorance in Greek philosophy, which would ultimately form the foundations of western intellectual tradition. This cosmology among ancient philosophers developed and permeated traditions and cultures from which some Gentiles would become Christ followers.

Plutarch, a contemporary of Paul, was perhaps the most religious of all known middle Platonists. He forthrightly condemns atheism and excessive superstition simultaneously.[22] Plutarch argues that superstition is engineered by fear and leads to undesirable consequences. He emphasizes that while gods exist in every country, there is no legitimate cause for unwarranted superstitions. He defines superstition as "an emotional idea and assumption productive of a fear which utterly humbles and crushes a man, for he thinks that there are gods, but

---

16. Plato, 729e–730b.

17. Nash, *Gospel and the Greeks*, 26.

18. Aristotle, *Metaphysics* 12.7 (1072B). Here he elaborates on his understanding of God and his role in the world.

19. Price, *Religions of the Ancient Greeks,* 134.

20. Nash, *Gospel and the Greeks*, 45.

21. A. H. Armstrong, *An Introduction to Ancient Philosophy* (Boston: Beacon, 1963), 148.

22. Plutarch, *Mor.* 165–171.

that they are the cause of pain and injury."[23] Plutarch labels the Jewish Sabbath as a superstitious endeavor[24] perhaps due to the consequences associated with a breach thereof. He cites the case of Midas and Aristodemus as example of individuals who suffered as a result of superstitious beliefs.

Greek and Roman traditions adhered to the belief that blessings and protection of the gods are important for conjugal relations to flourish. The gods are entreated to bless couples during matrimonial ceremonies. In his address to Pollianus and Eurydice, Plutarch indicates that the wife desists friendship with anyone outside the husband's circle of friends. Plutarch provides the rationale for which she must embrace his friends and adopt his religion. "The gods are first and most important friends. Wherefore it is becoming for a wife to worship and to know only the gods that her husband believes, and shut the front door tight upon all queer rituals and outlandish superstitions. For with no god do stealthy and secret rights performed by a woman find any favor."[25]

The philosopher indicates that these gods contribute to successful marriage, and thereby discourages Eurydice from any attempt to bribe them for favor with her husband. The wife should abstain from the common practice of women to seek spiritual aid to enhance their marriage, he argues. Plutarch points to a loathsome outcome of one such pursuit:

> King Philip was enamoured of a Thessalian woman who was accused of using magic charms upon him. Olympias accordingly made haste to get the woman into her power. But when the latter had come into the queen's presence and was seen to be beautiful in appearance, and her conversation with the queen was not lacking in good-breeding or cleverness, Olympias exclaimed, "Away with these slanders! You have your magic charm in yourself." And so a wedded and lawful wife becomes an irresistible thing if she makes everything, dowry, birth, magic charms and even the magic girdle itself, to be inherent in herself, and by character and virtue succeeds in winning her husband's love.[26]

---

23. Plutarch, 165B.
24. Plutarch, 169.
25. Plutarch, *Mor.* 140D.
26. Plutarch, *Mor.* 141B.

Plutarch further points to the nature of spirit cosmology of the time in which some spirits are regarded as good spirits and others were regarded evil or demons.[27]

> The great majority and wisest men hold this opinion: they believe that there are two gods, rivals as it were, the one the Artificer of good and the other of evil. There are also those who called the better one a god (θεός) and the other a daemon (δαίμονια), as, for example, Zoroaster the sage, who they record, lived five thousand years before the time of the Trojan War. He called the one Oromazes and the other Areimanius; and he further declared that among all other things perceptible to the senses, Oromazes may be best compared to light, and Araimanius, conversely, to darkness and ignorance . . . Oromazes, born from the purest light, and Areimanius, born from darkness, are constantly at war with each other.[28]

Thus, even from the perspective of a philosopher, spiritual beings were known to influence human lives be it marriage or other aspects of life. Moreover, the contemporary of Paul (Plutarch) held that there were such things as good and evil spirits portrayed in the light–darkness antithesis in the pre-Christian world.

Students of religion may observe that each religion seems to have adherents who take their belief and traditions to the extreme; the permeating religious movements in the Greco-Roman world and extreme expressions thereof similarly attracted criticisms against extremes. Epicurean philosophers were outspoken and condemned religious superstitions in sharp terms. However, this in no way made them atheists since they professed belief in the gods and their activities in the cosmos.[29] Epicureans believed in the gods but argued that they do not seek vengeance, retribution nor interfere in human conduct in their pursuit of happiness. They held that superstition is engineered by fear and ignorance. They argued that gods and spirits exist and remained active in the cosmos but they do not concern themselves in human affairs in the way others make them to be. This tenet should not be misconstrued as indictment on theism.

---

27. Plutarch, 369B.

28. Plutarch, 369C–F.

29. Luce, *Greek Philosophy*, 142–145.

The Stoics were by far the most influential philosophical school in the NT era and known for their religious convictions.[30] Unlike Epicureans, they believed that the Supreme Being (God) is active not only in the cosmos but also concretely in the affairs of humankind. "They thought that God and the world were related like soul and body. God is the soul of the world, and the world is the body of God."[31] The principle that governs the orderly cosmos is the law of nature. Apparently, this governing principle "may take the form of *fire* or *logos* – theologically identified as *Zeus*."[32] The duty of humankind is thus to live "according to nature," which is tantamount to subscribing to the will of the impersonal God.[33] By designating *fire* as the "molding principle," they argued that the cosmos has a spiritual dimension.[34] "The metaphorical use of the word *fire* allowed some Stoics to tie the physical universe to the Greek high God Zeus in a somewhat pantheistic manner . . . living 'according to nature' means allowing our human reason – as a connecting point with divine reason that permeates the universe – to govern our lives."[35]

Epictetus entreated his followers to model their lives after Zeus.[36] The attributes of the impersonal God may thus be emulated in stoic moral discipline (see Eph 4:24; 5:1–2).

Dio Chrysostom claims that his own vocation as an orator came by divine appointment – as a calling. He attributes his success to the enabling of the gods.[37] According to Chrysostom, it is inherently human to yearn for the gods as a child craves her parents. "Human beings are right to love the gods for the benefits they have received and because they are related to them, and they wish in every way to be with the gods and enjoy their company. This is why many foreign peoples, who are poor and lack artistic skill, attribute the name of the gods to mountains, unpruned trees and shapeless stones, although such things bear no resemblance to the gods than does the human form."[38]

---

30. Price, *Religions of the Ancient Greeks*, 138.

31. Nash, *Gospel and the Greeks*, 58–59.

32. See L. H. Martin, *Studies in Hellenistic Religions* (Eugene: Cascade, 2018), 35–62 and 143–170.

33. Nash, *Gospel and the Greeks*, 61.

34. S. J. Grenz, *The Moral Quest: Foundations of Christian Ethics* (Downers Grove: InterVarsity, 1997), 83.

35. Grenz, *Moral Quest*, 83.

36. Epictetus, *Illiad* 1.526.

37. Dio Chrysostom, *Discourse* 32.11–12.

38. Dio Chrysostom, *Or.* 12.60ff.

Seneca asserts that wise and perfect men are "full of virtues and divine."[39] The Roman stoic argues that a "holy spirit" indwells and empowers humans for good cause.

> We do not need to uplift our hands towards heaven, or to beg the keeper of a temple to let us approach his idol's ear, as if in this way our prayers were more likely to be heard. God is near you, he is with you, he is within you. This is what I mean, Lucilius: a holy spirit indwells within us, one who marks our good and bad deeds, and is our guardian. As we treat this spirit, so are we treated by it. Indeed, no man can be good without the help of God.[40]

Seneca describes a common practice in which mountains, caves and rivers are turned into places of worship in the Roman world. "We worship the sources of mighty rivers; we erect altars at places where great streams burst suddenly from hidden sources; we adore springs of hot water as divine, and consecrate certain pools because of their dark waters or their immeasurable depth."[41]

Building upon the idea of divine activity in the cosmos, Cicero indicates that divination is a legitimate means to inquire into future events, as is common among Assyrians, Chaldeans, Greeks and Egyptians. Cicero notes that it is the way by which "men may approach very near to the power of the gods."[42] It was commonplace to employ rituals or magic to predict future events in the Roman world.[43] Cicero reckons that prominent philosophers shared this view about divination as well.

> For example, Socrates and all of the Socratic School, and Zeno and his followers, continued in the faith of the ancient philosophers and in agreement with the Old Academy and with the Peripatetics. Their predecessor, Pythagoras, who even wished to be considered an augur himself, gave the weight of his great name to the same practice; and that eminent author, Democritus, in many passages, strongly affirmed his belief in a presentiment of things to come. Moreover, Dicaearchus, the Peripatetic, though he accepted divination by dreams and frenzy, cast away all other kinds; and

---

39. Seneca, *Const. Sap.* 6.8.

40. Seneca, *Ep.* 41.273.

41. Seneca, 41.275.

42. Cicero, *Div.* I. 1.1.

43. The idea of prophesy as a spiritual gift and openness to receive "spiritual gifts" was therefore nothing out of the ordinary in the world-concept or logic of the era.

my intimate friend, Cratippus, whom I consider the peer of the greatest of the Peripatetics, also gave credence to the same kinds of divination but rejected the rest.[44]

However, Cicero does not want divination to weigh above rational inquiry in decision-making processes or in exercising good judgment. Moreover, Musonius Rufus would like children to prefer divinely inspired instruction from Zeus over that of biological fathers. Apparently, sound moral laws come from Zeus who is able to instruct and enable children to acquire praiseworthy virtues. "His (Zeus) command and law is that man be just and honest, beneficent, temperate, high minded, superior to pain, superior to pleasure, free of all envy and malice; to put it briefly, the law of Zeus bids man to be good. If you obey your father, you will follow the will of man; if you choose the philosopher's life, the will of God."[45]

He contends that the fact that humankind embodies the image of God is the reason humans ought to imitate good moral qualities of God (see Eph 5:1–2).

> In general, of all creatures on earth man alone resembles God and has the same virtues that He has, since we can imagine nothing even the gods better than prudence, justice, courage, and temperance. Therefore, as God, through the possession of these virtues, is unconquered by pleasure or greed, is superior to desire, envy and jealousy; is high-minded, beneficent, and kindly (for such is our conception of God), so also man in the image of Him, when living in accord with nature, should be thought of as being like Him, and being enviable, he would forthwith be happy, for envy none but the happy.[46]

Musonius Rufus "exemplified this imitation of God, since not only did he frequently speak of it but also he was publicly taunted for it: 'Zeus the Saviour whom you imitate and emulate . . .' someone once said to him on the street."[47]

A survey of the general concept of spiritual beings in ancient Greek literary works and social thought shows the belief in a spiritual being as the author or maker of the cosmos. The maker of the cosmos also presides over and guides its affairs. Human failings (sin) had spiritual consequence. Yet, human

---

44. Cicero, *Div.* 1.3.5.

45. Musonius Rufus, *Discourse* XVI.

46. Musonius Rufus, *Discourse* XVII.

47. J. T. Dillion, *Musonius Rufus and Education in the Good Life: A Model of Teaching and Living Virtue* (Dallas: University Press of America, 2004), 88.

conduct could also be divinely enabled to yield positive outcomes, to the extent that the vocation of Dio Chrysostom could be explained in terms of divine calling. Spirits indwell and empower human agents to exhibit good behavior. Deities possess virtues worthy of human imitation in this worldview. However, not all spirits are good spirits – a holy spirit helps to achieve positive results whereas demons work to effect negative outcomes. This world concept was commonplace, transcending geographical boundaries in Greek and Roman antiquity. Our subsequent discussion will further shed more light on how concurrent folk religions accentuate the worldview.

## 2.2 Religious Practices in the Wider Society

Greco-Roman cultures did not separate religion from culture or politics. The prism of social anthropology allowed for a world in which spirits inhabited animate and inanimate objects and spiritual activity permeated every aspect of human life. Religious culture was not isolated from social life, to the extent that public events were held at temple precincts. As the welfare of the *oikos* was connected to the prosperity of the *polis* so were the gods who presided over cities instrumental in ensuring concord and prosperity in households. In Anatolia, pagan temples ornamented the landscape of cities and attracted participants in festivities at the precincts.[48] Hellenization paved way for large-scale commercial and religious interchange between Egypt, Asia Minor and other parts of the Roman empire. This exchange came along with religio-cultural influences. The link between the seaports of Alexandria and Asia Minor via the Cayster river and the harbour at Ephesus helped to harness that. Ephesus was the largest city in Asia Minor and center of commerce and communication in the region.[49]

Transport and communication between prominent cities of the time (Rome, Ephesus and Alexandria) came along with mass migrations and exchange of culture, deities and other religious practices. First-century Alexandria was a major intellectual and cultural hub modelled after Greek tradition – this did not diminish its religious culture. Egyptian gods were imported to Asia Minor and

---

48. M. C. Tenney, *New Testament Times* (London: IVP, 1965), 112.

49. While scholars continue to debate the provenance of Ephesians, we should not lose sight of the fact there was no better hub for distribution than Ephesus in the entire region, whether the letter was first delivered to believers there or not. If anyone wanted to circulate a religious text to early Christians in the region, why is it so difficult to entertain the thought that the center for religion, commerce and communication would have been one of the natural starting points?

worshipped across the Roman world. For example, Isis became a very popular deity in the empire. Greeks and Romans worshipped and held her in high esteem. Isis was "the protector of women and marriage, goddess of maternity and the new born, guarantor of the fertility of fields and the abundance of harvest, and protector of people both by land and sea."[50] Archaeological remains shows an altar in Ephesus that was dedicated to Egyptian gods bearing the inscription to "Σαράπιδι, Ισιδι, Ἀνούβιδι, Θεος συννᾶοι (Sarapis, Isis, Anubis, temple sharing gods)."[51] Polytheism was the norm. In fact, monotheism was rare in most of the Roman empire, thereby making Judaism and Christianity unique. A first-century statue bearing the image of Isis was dedicated to the Artemis of Ephesus. This same statue was dedicated to tax collectors (τελώνιον) in the city's fishing industry.[52] Numismatic evidence points to inhabitants of Colossae and elsewhere that worshipped the Ephesian Artemis, Laodicean Zeus, Asclepius, Hygeia, Leto, Demeter, Helios, Selene, Dionysius, Athena, Men, Isis, Serapis etc.[53] Devotees outsourced, franchised or imported gods they found useful in meeting their needs. Shrines for Artemis and Asclepius were erected in many places across Asia Minor. Various gods and goddesses attracted devotees in different parts of the world – regardless of the powers of a patron deity of a city. For example, "a dedication from Pergamum dating to the first century CE show that two 'bearers of holy vessels' (ἱεραφόροι) offered statues or reliefs of Sarapis, Isis, Anubis, Harpokrates, Osiris, Apis, Helios, Ares and the Dioskouroi, by order of Isis."[54]

## 2.2.1 Religion, Politics and Civic Duties

The Greek polis, even in Roman times, had religion as an intricate component. As noted previously, Plato and Aristotle were keen to spell out the role of religion in their ideal polis. Religion was intertwined with public life – politics and piety could not be separated.[55] Those who followed the "customs of their

---

50. V. M. Warrior, *Roman Religion* (New York, NY: Cambridge, 2006), 107.

51. J. C. Walters, "Egyptian Religions in Ephesos," in *Ephesos: Metropolis of Asia* (Valley Forge: Trinity, 1995), 284.

52. Walters, "Egyptian Religions in Ephesos," 291.

53. Arnold, *Colossian Syncretism*, 107–108.

54. Walters, "Egyptian Religions in Ephesos," 300.

55. Festus, 284. Cf. V. M. Warrior, *Greek Religion: A Sourcebook* (Cambridge: Focus, 2009), 55–74. The sources presented in this section covering "prayer and sacrifice" echo this dynamic in Greek culture. Religion was part of normal life in or outside the home.

city" attracted the favor of the gods.[56] It was taken for granted that the gods could use human agents as mediums to communicate to devotees both at the state and personal levels by means of dreams, prophecy and in other ways.[57] Greek cities usually had their own patron deities. It is noteworthy that real estate of patron deities was usually situated at notable places in the landscape of the city. The operating budget of patron shrines eventually became public responsibility with the rationale that they do serve the common good. This is the backdrop of the arguments of philosophers who advocated for cities to devote substantial amounts of their budget to religious practices. Aristotle, for instance, suggested that a quarter of a city's revenue be directed to the gods but Hippodamus preferred a third.[58]

Finances for religious activities came in more than one form. The Greeks gave tithes to gods or goddesses such as Zeus/Apollo and the Artemis of Ephesus. We are told that Xenophon built a small replica of the shrine of Artemis a few kilometers outside Olympia and offered tithes annually to the goddess. An inscription from the site reads, "This place is sacred to Artemis. He who owns it and enjoys its produce must offer in sacrifice a tenth each year, and from the remainder must keep the temple in good condition. If someone fails to do these things, the goddess will take care of it."[59] There was no such thing as "separation of church and state" in the period under consideration. "There is no religious sphere separate from that of politics and warfare or private life; instead, religion is embedded in all aspects of life, public or private."[60] Temple precincts were sacred and safe places for banking transactions. The storage of wealth also made temple sites susceptible to robbery. The penalty for temple robbery could be death without burial.

The Romans similarly placed religion at the center of public and private life. Political leaders dabbled in religious activities openly. Similar to the Greeks, some Romans argued that the state would be better served by appointing religious leaders to run all matters of religion and politics. Cicero, among others, discussed this as a matter of great importance.

> Many things, O priests, have been devised and established with
> divine wisdom by our ancestors; but no action of theirs was ever

---

56. Xenophon, *Memorabilia* 4.3.16.

57. Warrior, *Roman Religion*, 9. See Suetonius, *Life of Tiberius* 2, Cicero, *Div.* 1.48 and Cicero, *Nature of the Gods* 2:10–12.

58. Aristotle, *Pol.* 1330a8–16, 1267b33–7.

59. S. Price, *Religions of the Ancient Greeks* (Cambridge: CUP, 1999), 3.

60. Price, 3.

more wise than their determination that the same men should superintend both what relates to the religious worship due to the immortal gods, and also what concerns the highest interests of the state, so that they might preserve the republic as the most honorable and eminent of the citizens, by governing it well, and as priests by wisely interpreting the requirements of religion.[61]

Political success was attributed to divine favor as also kings and high-ranking officials made regular sacrifices to the gods for the welfare of the state.[62]

The western Asia Minor provenance of Ephesians is undisputed – the debate is rather on what specific city may have first received the letter. As a city, Ephesus had about fifty temples by the time of the NT. The shrine of Artemis Ephesia was one of the seven wonders of the ancient world. The temple was about four hundred and twenty-five by two hundred and twenty-five feet wide, secured by one hundred and twenty-seven columns and standing at sixty feet tall.[63] The influence of Artemis permeated culture, sports[64] and commerce in Ephesus and the surrounding region. "The Artemis cults, embraced by Greeks and non-Greeks alike, had spread throughout much of the known world by the first century CE. There is evidence to that effect in Greece, Italy, France, Spain, Phoenicia, and Palestine."[65] Festivities associated with the goddess were citywide events, thereby attracting observers and participants from various parts of the world.[66]

Artemis performed miracles, cured diseases, regulated commerce and aided decision-making processes.[67] She possessed maternal instincts of sympathy and attentiveness,[68] and availed herself to those in difficult conditions. "The ancient

---

61. Cicero, *Or.* 1.1 (trans. C. D. Yonge).

62. Cf. Livy, 2.2.1–2.

63. Pliny, *Nat.* 36.95–97.

64. E. C. Blake and A. G. Edmonds, *Biblical Sites in Turkey* (Istanbul: Redhouse, 1977), 62. The authors show that much of the popularity of the goddess came through sports and Eastern orgiastic rituals.

65. C. L. Brinks, "'Great Is the Artemis of the Ephesians': Acts 19:23–41 in Light of Goddess Worship in Ephesus," CBQ 71, no. 4 (2009): 780.

66. I will proceed hereon to elaborate on the influence of Artemis since the vicinity that was impacted the most by her rituals and services is also the region in which Ephesians was first circulated.

67. W. H. Stephens, *The New Testament World Pictures* (Nashville: Broadman, 1987), 239.

68. Cf. R. S. Kraemer, *Women's Religions in the Greco-Roman World: A Sourcebook* (Oxford: OUP, 2004). This compilation is a good source for the study of female deities in the Greco-Roman world. It becomes apparent that being a female goddess, like Artemis, does not mean she advanced a particular feminist agenda.

cult of Artemis was central to the city's sense of communal identity. Pride was taken both in the local cult and in the fact that the deity was worshipped all over the Greek world."[69] As such, she commanded unsurpassed loyalty and attracted goodwill from all walks of life. "It was because of her supra-natural powers that she could intercede between her followers and the cruel fate which plagued them. To those who called upon Artemis, she was saviour (Σώτειρα), lord (Κυρία) and queen of the cosmos (Βασιλης Κόσμου) whose being and character could be described in superlatives: μεγίστη, ἁγιωτάτη, and ἐπιφανεστάτη."[70] The power of Artemis, portrayed in the imagery of a lion, was engraved on the arms of her statue. Other objects engraved include bulbous ornaments on her chest, bee eggs, ostrich eggs, steer testicles, grapes, nuts, and different kinds of animals on her skirt. It is uncertain as to what each of these symbols represented. The lion and other wildlife motif may have denoted superior power over evil powers associated with those animals.[71] An earlier conjecture aligned her with orgiastic activities[72] but that view has subsequently been debunked with evidence rather pointing to ascetic practices among her devotees.

Perhaps one of the pronounced displays and intersections of socio-cultural, political and religious activities in Ephesus was the annual procession in honor of Artemis. "All of the local girls in marriageable age (παρθένους) and all the local boys entering the military training (ἐφήβους) were required to take part of the ritual."[73] In order words, religious activity was deemed civic responsibility. Xenophon of Ephesus (second century CE) comments on the influence of Artemis during the annual procession.

> The local festival of Artemis was in progress with its procession from the city to the temple nearly a mile away. All local girls had to march in procession richly dressed as well as the young men of Habrocomas' age. He is around sixteen, already a member of the ephebes, and took first place in the procession. There was a great crowd of Ephesians and visitors alike to see the festival, for it was the custom at this festival to find husbands for the girls and wives for the young men. So as the procession filed past, first the sacred

---

69. Price, *Religions of the Ancient Greeks*, 22.

70. R. Oster, "The Ephesian Artemis as an Opponent of Early Christianity," *JAC* 19 (1974): 40.

71. Arnold, *Power and Magic*, 26.

72. Arnold, 27. Also J. G. Griffiths, "Xenophon of Ephesus on Isis and Alexandria," in *Hommages a, Maarten J. Vermaseren Vol. 1* (EPRO 68; Leiden: Brill, 1978): 419.

73. Thomas, "At Home in the City of Artemis," 85.

> objects, the torches, the baskets and the incense; and horses, gods, hunting equipment, some for war, most for peace . . . Each of the girls was dressed as if to receive a lover.[74]

The procession followed an orderly protocol with horses and dogs in their special places.[75] Participation was an act of patriotism. Morally, Artemis was a champion of chastity – one who enabled devotees to remain chaste. As a virgin, she helped young women to preserve their virginity until marriage.[76] It was customary for priests in the Artemision to take girls of marriageable age through rituals to authenticate their virginity prior to presenting them as suitable to marry heroic figures or men of nobility.

> The chastity ordeal takes place in the Artemision of Ephesus, where the priest of Artemis tells of a cave in a grove at the back of the temple, on the wall of which is hung a magical syrinx. The cave is forbidden except to women who are pure virgins. When a girl enters, the doors of the cave are closed behind her; if she is a virgin, the syrinx plays beautiful music, the doors of the cave open automatically, and the girl appears crowned with sprigs of pine. If not, a scream is heard, the crowd is bid to leave until three days later, when a virgin priestess opens the cave to find the syrinx cast to the ground, and no trace of the young woman.[77]

Hymns accompanied the rituals and festivities as was the custom. "The standard structure (of such hymns) was invocation of the god, honoring the god through recounting of one or more divine deeds, and finally a prayer for divine favor."[78] These hymns and rituals were meant to honor, appease and win her favor. It is noteworthy that similar processions were conducted annually in Athens in honor of Zeus. It was a fact of the matter that gods, goddesses and other spiritual beings existed and had crucial roles in the well-being and flourishing of societies – be it a polis, small community or household.

---

74. Xenophon of Ephesos 1.2, trans. of the whole in B. P. Reardon, *Collected Ancient Greek Novels* (Berkeley: University of California Press, 1989) citing from Price, *Religions of the Ancient Greeks,* 30.

75. Xenophon, *Ephesiaka* 1.2.6–7.

76. S. L. Glahn, "The Identity of Artemis in First Century Ephesus," *BSac* 172 (2015): 316–334. The article makes a persuasive case, showing the potential mistaken identity with the Greek Artemis.

77. Thomas, "At Home in the City of Artemis," 96–97.

78. Price, *Religions of the Ancient Greeks,* 37.

## 2.2.2 Asia Minor as a Locale of Deep Religious Conviction

The reputation of ancient Ephesus for its magical arts is well attested. The city's identity and pride were linked to her reputation as the home of magic and Artemis. Apparently, the inhabitants established a connection between the powers of Artemis and the Ephesia Grammata. Evidently, Artemis features in magical formulae in the *Papyri Graecae Magicae* (PGM).[79] But we do not have evidence in support of activities of official magicians at the shrine of Artemis; it is only a conjecture that magic was practiced at her precincts.[80] The pantheistic beliefs of the time allowed for a hybrid of religious beliefs and practices. People sought aid and paid homage to multiple spiritual entities either to ward off evil or seek favor.

There is evidence of an imperial cult in Ephesus, but nothing to suggest that it supplanted the widespread loyalty to the mother goddess and other cults in any significant way. The relationship between the imperial cult and local deities rather suggests a public support for a broader religious culture in Asia Minor. Any suggestion that citizens turned to imperial cults at the expense of traditional religions would be misunderstanding the nature of polytheistic culture and the sociopolitical function of imperial cults. Devotees did not leave one god for the other. Numismatic evidence bearing the image of four temples, statue of Artemis and three emperors has been discovered showing adherence to multiple deities as a common practice.[81]

The shrine of Artemis was a sanctuary and a place of refuge for those charged with criminal offences and stood susceptible to public retaliation.[82] Tatius writes about a murderer and adulterer who were admitted in the precincts for such reasons; he laments the wisdom of making such provision to put an adulterer in close proximity to virgins in the sacred space. He bemoans, "a murderer and adulterer, living in the house of the goddess of purity! Oh, an adulterer dwelling with the virgin! . . . You have made . . . the home of Artemis a bedroom for adulterers and whores."[83] Citizens and

---

79. C. C. McCown, "The Ephesia Grammata in Popular Belief," in *Transactions of the American Philological Association* 54 (1923): 129–130; Clinton, *Power and Magic*, 22–24, and H. D. Betz, *The Greek Magical Papyri in Translation Including the Demonic Spells* (Chicago: University of Chicago Press, 1986), IV. 2523, 2720–21, 2816ff.; LXXVIII. 11–12.

80. Arnold, *Principalities and Powers*, 21. Arnold reckons that the ornamentations on the famous image of Artemis were sometimes interpreted magically.

81. W. M. Ramsay, *The Letters to the Seven Churches – Updated Edition* (Peabody: Hendrickson, 1994), 169.

82. History shows that there were Roman, Greek and Egyptian political leaders that fled to the temple to seek refuge. Cf. Josephus, *Ant.* 15.89; *Porphery Chronnica* 3.3; 6.1.

83. Achilles, *Tatius* 8.8.10–11.

aliens in Ephesus extended devotion to other deities as well including Isis, Agathe Tyche, Aphrodite, Apollo, Asclepius, Boulaia, Cabiri, Concord, Cybele, Dionysus,[84] Enedera, Hecate, Hephaestus, Heracles, Hestia, Nemesis, Pan, Pion (a mountain god), Pluto, Poseidon, Theos Hypsistos, Tyche Soteira, Zeus and several river deities.[85] The popularity of Artemis saw a decline by the second century CE. It is suggested that a trend of new skepticism in Asia Minor and Europe, as Christianity attracted more following in Ephesus, accounted for her decline in fame and interest in other gods like Sarapis and Mithras who were popular outside Asia Minor as well.[86] The demise of Artemis paved the way for the rise of "Demeter, the bringer of daily bread, and her daughter Kore; Sosipolis, the Saviour of the city; the μαντεῖος ('oracular sanctuary') of Clarion Apollo; and others."[87] This period is, however, beyond the first-century timeframe of Ephesians.

Unlike Ephesus, cities like Pergamum did not have a popular patron deity (Epidaurus), but the city was known as the home of Asclepius. Many Greek gods claimed healing powers but only three were regularly attested to have wrought healing, namely Hercules, Isis and Asclepius. Public inscriptions attested to Asclepius's ability to heal all kinds of diseases,[88] including blindness, epilepsy, dropsy, paralysis and to raise the dead.[89] His healing prowess ranged from dream cure at its sanctuary and cures that were administered by trained physicians.[90] In other words, orthodox medicine and spiritual healing were both administered at the precincts. Unlike quack doctors, healing services at the shrine acquired notoriety and credence. Apparently, the dream healing of Asclepius became popular.

---

84. Plutarch, *Lives, Antony* 24.3. Plutarch records some women and boys having some celebrations at the Dionysian cult in Ephesus when Anthony entered the city. This occurred in the first century. He indicates that there was a significant number of devotees to the cult in Ephesus.

85. C. E. Arnold, "Ephesus," in *DPL*, eds. G. H. Hawthorne, R. P. Martin and D. G. Reid (Leicester: IVP, 1993), 250.

86. D. Knibbe, "Via Sacra Ephesiaca – New Aspects of the Cult of Artemis Ephesia," in *Ephesos: Metropolis of Asia* (Valley Forge: Trinity, 1995), 146–147.

87. Knibbe, "Via Sacra Ephesiaca," 146.

88. Aelius Aristides, *Heracles* 40.12.

89. W. Cotter, *Miracles in Greco-Roman Antiquity: A Sourcebook for the Study of New Testament Miracles Series* (New York: Routledge, 1999), 14–26. Cotter provides a long list of inscriptions from antiquity and from several witnesses recounting healings that were done by Asclepius. The witness confirms a worldview in which several miraculous healings were ascribed to the work of spiritual agents.

90. D. C. Duling and N. Perin, *The New Testament: Proclamation and Paranesis, Myth and History* (Fort Worth: Harcourt Brace, 1994), 70.

Many reportedly received divine healing intervention of Asclepius during the rite of "incubation," (dream healing) sleeping in the precincts of the temple in order to receive a visionary epiphany from the god. When Asclepius appeared to the sick person, his healing powers were imparted and the person was healed. This appearance and apparent healing constituted the essence of initiation into the divine mystery of Asclepius.[91]

The Asclepeium in Pergamum, among others in Asia Minor, organized extensive clinical and health services. The temple had a section that people could receive medical treatments.[92] Thus, devotees and the wider populace who had health problems visited the precincts for cure, in the way that people would visit hospitals today. One of the protocols at the site was that a priest would typically take the ailing through a ritual with a pledge to live a life of moral purity if cured. Sometimes, effective healing was contingent upon the moral standing of the candidate. Sin or a history of wrongdoing could hinder divine healing. Consequently, these practices reinforced moral sensibilities and common decency among citizens. An inscription at the entrance of the shrine of Asclepius in Epidaurus read, "pure must be he who enters the fragrant temple; purity means to be wise in holy things."[93] The god was known for being the most humane of all Greek gods. He was ascribed titles such as the savior, benefactor, and friend of human beings. The attributes of the god of medicine and medical arts (Asclepius) included being caring, compassionate and sympathetic to human suffering.[94] The point being that divine healing was a viable medical practice, not opposed to what we call orthodox medicine, but practiced alongside primitive health care. These realities defined the pre-Christian past of those who became Christ followers. Even health care was connected to pagan worship of sorts.

Dionysius (Bachhus), the god of wine, grapes, theater, and fertility, had a large following in Asia Minor. He was the patron of Pergamum during the reign of King Attalid in 3 BCE. Dionysius's rituals attracted people of all classes. As the god of the vine, the rituals included public gatherings for common meals and drinks. It was not uncommon for festivities to result in drunkenness *en masse*, orgies and various forms of debauchery.[95] "To talk about wine and

---

91. Arnold, *Principalities and Powers*, 41.

92. Blake and Edmonds, *Biblical Sites in Turkey*, 65.

93. Fergusson, *Background of Early Christianity*, 208.

94. H. Koester, *History, Culture and Religion of the Hellenistic Age: Introduction to the New Testament Vol. 1* (New York: Walter De Gruyter, 1982), 176.

95. See Arnold, *Principalities and Powers*, 45.

drinking immediately brought Dionysian expressions in the conversation, and to live a riotous, wanton, debauched, drunken life was characterized as a 'Dionysian mode of life.'"[96] Dionysus was believed to have once appeared in the form of an animal; he also lived in wine. The rituals included eating raw meat from live animals and consuming lots of wine simultaneously as a way to embody the god and his power within the individual.[97] Inebriations were associated with Dionysian empowerment.[98] To be filled with wine then was associated with being filled with the power of Bacchus (see Eph 5:18).

Livy, the Roman historian (*ca.* 59 BCE – 17 CE), recounts the spread and influence of Bacchic rituals in Rome and elsewhere in the empire that prompted the senate to enact regulations against extreme practices thereof, and also in attempt to curtail its rapid spread. Livy suggests that Bacchic rituals were partly to blame for excessive drinking accompanied by uncontrollable levels of vices and crime in Rome.[99]

> At first these were divulged to only a few; then they began to spread amongst both men and women, and the attractions of wine and feasting increased the number of his followers. When they were heated with wine and the nightly commingling of men and women, those of tender age with their seniors, had extinguished all sense of modesty, debaucheries of every kind commenced; each had pleasures at hand to satisfy the lust he was most prone to. Nor was the mischief confined to the promiscuous intercourse of men and women; false witness, the forging of seals and testaments, and false information, all proceeded from the same source, as also poisonings and murders of families where the bodies could not even be found for burial. Many crimes were committed by treachery; most by violence, which was kept secret, because the

---

96. C. L. Rogers, "The Dionysian Background of Ephesians 5:18," in *Bibliotheca Sacra* 136, no. 543 (July–Sept 1979): 253. Rogers shows in his article that the cult was worshipped in many parts of the then world, including Palestine. The celebrations of the god varied from place to place but two things were always present, namely emphasis on fertility and sexual practices. They would always drink, dance, play flutes, cymbals, drums or tambourines in the festivities.

97. E. Fergusson, *Background of Early Christianity* (Grand Rapids: Eerdmans, 1993), 243.

98. R. S. Kraemer, "Ecstasy and Possession: The Attraction of Women to the Cult of Dionysus," *HTR* 72, no. 1/2 (1979): 57. Temporary drunkenness and sexual intercourse with others, even for those who were married, were not considered as sin or vice to the devotees during worship ceremonies. One could not say drunkenness is bad to such people when they understood it as a manifestation of power (compare Eph 5:18).

99. Livy, 39.8.

cries of those who were being violated or murdered could not be heard owing to the noise of drums and cymbals.[100]

Livy reminds the reader of the spread of certain cults at the time and the social effect of religion in cities. He bemoans the shamelessness and indecency associated with these rituals. Later, Clement of Alexandria reiterates that orgies and nefarious activities occurred at the celebrations of Dionysus and Aphrodite. "The bacchanals hold their orgies in honor of the frenzied Dionysus, celebrating their sacred frenzy by eating of raw flesh, and go through the distribution of butchered victims crowned with snakes, shrieking out the name of Eva by whom error came in the world."[101] Rogers indicates that,

> The purpose of the intoxication by wine and also the chewing of ivy, as well as eating raw animal flesh, was to have Dionysus enter the body of the worshipper and fill him with "enthusiasm" or the spirit of the god. Dionysus was to possess and control such ones so that they were united with him and partook of his strength, wisdom, and abilities. This resulted in the person doing the will of the deity (either willingly or unwillingly) and having the ability to speak inspired prophecy, and was often thought to be the source of artistic or poetical ability.[102]

A myth had it that the god died and came back to life and, as a result, his devotees trusted him for their own immortality. Imagine the conditions of Christ followers who hitherto participated in these rituals and now dwelled in environs where they regularly occurred.

There were several other gods and temples in Pergamum, as was the norm in cities of the time. For example, the Altar of Zeus was erected on the conical hill in front of the Temple of Athene in 240 BCE, one of the most visible and prominent real estates. Zeus also impacted the city's culture and religious life in significant ways.[103] "Forty feet high, it stood on a projecting ledge of rock and looked exactly like a great throne on the hillside. All day long it smoked with

---

100. Livy, 39.8.

101. Clement of Alexandria, "Exhortation the Heathen," in *The Ante-Nicene Fathers* (Edinburgh: T&T Clark, 1989): 175. Clement further exposed the immorality inherent in the worship of Dionysus and Aphrodite and characterizes their orgies as imposture and quackery. This is an example of how immorality was linked with the cultic celebrations that were common in Asia Minor. Clement indicates that Christianity faced challenges in defining and observing what was morally acceptable in his Alexandrian context.

102. Rogers, "The Dionysian Background to Ephesians 5:18," 255.

103. G. B. Caird, *The Revelation of Saint John* (Peabody: Hendrickson, 1966), 37.

the smoke of sacrifices offered to Zeus. Around its base was carved one of the greatest achievements in the world of sculpture, the frieze which showed the Battle of Giants, in which the gods of Greece were victorious over the giants of the barbarians."[104] Zeus was called *Zeus Soter* (Zeus the savior) and was second only to the patron deity. He gave victory over enemies and protected members against external aggression. Some have gone as far as to suggest that the structure of Zeus perhaps forms the backdrop of John's reference to "Satan's throne" in Pergamum (Rev 2:13)[105] – a place "where Satan dwells" and from which he reigns.[106] The main issue in this study, however, is to ascertain that the cities in the vicinity of Ephesus shared the spirit cosmology and religious practices that may inform our understanding of spirit cosmology of Ephesians.

Religion, magic and astrology were widespread in Asia Minor.[107] There was no distinction between social ethics and religious piety. This spirit cosmology permeated the culture, ethics, entertainment and even health care provision. The framework aforementioned is consistent with what we find elsewhere in other Asia Minor cities such as Colossae, Hierapolis and Smyrna. At Smyrna (40 miles from Ephesus), the patron goddess was Cybele. The city was known for being the first to have a temple for the imperial cult (in the region), a privilege awarded when it was preferred over Ephesus in 26 CE to host the temple of Tiberius[108] owing to its savvy political maneuvering. Smyrna was known for its beautiful temples and magnificent architecture. It hosted, among others, the temples of Cybele, Zeus, Apollo, Nemeseis, Aphrodite[109] and Asclepius. The most famous of all streets in Smyrna was "the street of gold,"

---

104. W. Barclay, *The Revelation of John, Vol. 1* (Philadelphia: Westminster, 1976), 89.

105. Swete, *Apocalypse*, 34–35.

106. J. F. Walvoord. *The Revelation of Jesus Christ* (Chicago: Moody, 1966) 67. See also G. R. Beasley-Murray, *Revelation* (Grand Rapids: Eerdmans, 1983) 84, 92, and G. E. Ladd, *Revelation of John* (Grand Rapids: Eerdmans, 1972), 46. Ladd adds that the city was also the center of the imperial cult that served as a great threat to the early church. For Ladd, "Satan's throne" may refer to the altar of Zeus or worship of Asclepius or the emperor worship, which could be depicted as the throne of the emperor (Satan).

107. See L. J. Kreitzer, *Hierapolis in the Heavens: Studies in the Letter to the Ephesians* (London: T&T Clark, 2007). In the attempt to argue for Hierapolis as the destination of Ephesians, Kreitzer provides a very good account of the religious landscape of Hierapolis and its immediate context. While I find his primary thesis unconvincing, his reconstruction of the religious context is aptly supported by the evidence. It becomes apparent to a student that Ephesus, Pergamum, Colossae, Hierapolis and Smyrna in western Asia Minor shared the worldview being provided here in great detail.

108. W. Barclay, *The Revelation of John, Vol. 1* (Philadelphia: Westminster, 1976), 75.

109. Aphrodite is a goddess of love, beauty and fertility and her worship includes sacred prostitution that occurs at her sanctuary.

which ran from the temple of Zeus to the temple of Cybele.[110] Paganism did not only contribute to the beautification of Smyrna, "the fairest of the cities of Ionia" or the "queenly city crowned with towers," but it also shaped its culture, architecture and social ethics. Major entertainments occurred in the form of religious festivities.

Generally, sports were linked to religion in some way. The Greeks held sporting events in honor of gods or sought spiritual support to guarantee victory over opponents. Athletes employed charms or wore talismans to help them to succeed. Sporting events were performed as tributes to gods or goddesses. The four main Greek games (Olympic, Pythian, Isthmian and Nemean) were primarily held in honor of the gods: "The games at Olympia were celebrated in honor of Apollo, the Isthmian at the Isthmus near Corinth were in honor of Poseidon, and the Nemean at Nemea between Corinth and Argos were also in honor of Zeus."[111] Athletes, their parents, brothers and trainers had to take oaths before Zeus Horkios to establish their commitment to honesty and fairness in their preparation; that they had not violated any of the rules in preparing for the games.[112] This tradition was known among Romans as well. The Roman games (Ludi) were held on days that were set aside to honor the gods. The chief magistrate would customarily organize grand processions where statutes of the gods would be paraded. In such occasions, boys attaining manhood were given prominent places, also as a rite of passage. The procession often preceded the commencement of games.[113] "Thus both gods and humans participated in the festival."[114] Sports and religion were inseparable aspects of culture.

A significant part of spirit cosmology in the NT world, as it relates to our subject of inquiry, is the personal affinity devotees developed with deities. These gods were perceived to be real and intimately involved in human affairs. Greek and Romans believed in the ability of the deities to appear in human form and interact with them. A shared identity among the devotees was often couched around relationships with prominent gods or goddesses. The use of fictive kinship language to describe fraternal relationships among devotees

---

110. Barclay, *Revelation*, 74.

111. Warrior, *Greek Religion*, 135.

112. Warrior, 139, and Pausanias 5.24.9–11. This is the equivalent of a modern-day doping text and medical examination to make sure that all athletes are clean and ready for fare competition.

113. Dionysius of Halicarnassus, 7.72.1–13.

114. Warrior, *Roman Religion*, 115.

or in reference to deities was commonplace in Greek, Roman[115] and Egyptian settings of antiquity.[116] For example, citizens of Ephesus referred to Artemis as the mother goddess. Kinship language was employed mainly to harness group identity and promote cohesion among devotees.

Evidently, cultural norms were enshrined in values attributed to spiritual agents in the social context of Ephesians. There were occasions when what Christ followers would consider to be vices would be validated as a legitimate part of cultic rituals (e.g. drunkenness, orgies, temple prostitution). These religious beliefs enhanced moral judgment and regulated social conduct to some degree. Philosophers and orators argued that people consider their obligation to the gods in matters of ethics in general and with sexual conduct in particular – even in sex trade. Dio Chrysostom indicates that,

> In dealing with brothel-keepers and their trade . . . Such men bring individuals together in union without love and intercourse without affection, and all for the sake of filthy lucre . . . Yes, and they respect no man nor god – not Zeus, the god of family life, not Hera, the goddess of marriage, not the Fates, who bring fulfillment, not Artemis, protectress of the child-bed, not mother Rhea, not the Eileithyiae who preside over human birth, not Aphrodite, whose name stands for the normal intercourse and union of male and female. No, we must proclaim that neither magistrate nor lawgiver shall allow such merchandising or legalize it.[117]

Plato argues that "holy marriage with the blessings of the gods" ought to be preserved by appropriate sexual boundaries.[118] The fear of the gods or desire to appease them served as motivation to abstain from indecency. In the case of Artemis, she helped young women to preserve their virginity until marriage. Basic necessities such as security and health care were imbedded and offered at sacred precincts. The general public was immersed in cultic activities through economic systems (banking), entertainment and civic events. The people of the NT world operated in a cosmological framework in which spiritual beings inspired, provided and rewarded human endeavors. The sacred and secular were intertwined. "One belonged to the πολις which in turn belonged to the gods who

---

115. See S. C. Barton and G. H. R. Horsley, "A Hellenistic Cult Group and the New Testament Churches," *JAC* 24 (1981): 7–41.

116. R. W. Daniel, "Notes on the Guilds and Army in Roman Egypt," *BASP* 16 (1979): 37–46.

117. Dio Chrysostom, *Or.* 7.133–137.

118. Plato, *Laws, VIII,* 841 (trans. Trevor J. Saunders).

were present in and for the πόλις. There was, then, the solid conviction that 'the city, with its population, divine and human, was the one essential fact in the life of civilized men.'"[119] Religion permeated culture to the extent that prominent figures claimed divine origin (birth with a deity) and were sometimes deified.[120]

### 2.2.3 Household Gods, Rituals and Ancestors

The Greek *oikos* and the Roman *familia* comprised all members of the household, including slaves and children of slaves. It was customary for households to have their own gods for protection, productivity and family welfare. The *pater familias* (literally "father of the household") was responsible for rituals in the *oikos*. Hierocles affirms the common belief that the gods preside over homes, weddings and births.[121] Plato reckons that "if a man honors and respects his relatives, who share the worship of the family gods and have the same blood in their veins, he can reasonably expect to have the gods of birth look with benevolence on the procreation of his own children/household (*oikos*) . . ."[122] These gods were accorded sacred space in the house – a designated space to themselves. It is the mark of good citizenship to erect shrines for the great gods in the *oikos*.[123] Proliferation of household gods and shrines in first century CE prompted philosophers to call for state censorship; to foster proportionate devotion to household gods, state religious activities, politics and entertainment. For Cicero, "No one shall have gods for himself, either new gods or aliens, unless they have been recognized by the state. Privately they shall worship those gods they have duly received from their ancestors. In cities they shall have shrines; in the country they shall have groves and places for the Lares. They shall preserve the rites of the family and their ancestors."[124]

Another area of religious practice was rituals to deceased parents or ancestors. A list of things that children could do to honor their parents included decent burial and to venerate them after death.[125] Romans considered reverence for the deceased family obligation since the ancestors continued to have stakes

---

119. R. Strelan, *Paul, Artemis and the Jews in Ephesus* (Berlin: Walter De Gruyter, 1996), 27.

120. Plutarch, *Life of Alexander* 28.1–6; Suetonius, *Life of Julius* 88; Pliny, *Natural History* 2.93–94.

121. Hierocles, *Duties, On Marriage* 4.22.21–24 (4.502, 1–507).

122. Plato, *Laws* 5.729c.

123. Aristotle, *Ath. Cons.* 55.3.

124. Cicero, *Laws* 2:19.

125. P. Balla, *The Child-Parent Relationship in the New Testament and Its Environment* (Peabody: Hendrickson, 2005), 17. To honor one's parent is a duty that could not be taken for

in the welfare of the household. These rituals included food or drink offerings to the dead at their burial site.[126] In one Roman epitaph, a woman expresses her love and hope for reunion with her deceased husband.[127] It was held that offerings and prayers (libations) to the ancestors kept them connected to their loved ones. "Ovid describes two festivals in honor of the dead, the Parentalia and Feralia, that were celebrated from 18–21 February. He reports the reputed origins of these practices, while also recounting several rituals that involve sympathetic magic."[128] People offered prayers to ancestors and sometimes dressed family members in the likeness of the deceased as part of these rituals.[129]

At thirty, Greek men were deemed mature and fit to marry, and to participate in civic duties. Girls became adults by fifteen, at which stage they could legally be given out for marriage. It was however not uncommon for a girl to be given out for marriage at thirteen. The "rite of passage" had religious components in which the gods were invoked and assumed lordship over households. It was a usual practice to seek some spiritual support to ward off perceived evil against family members.

## 2.3 Magic and Astrology

The ancient world took for granted that humanity was under the constant influence of transcendent forces for good or evil. Magic,[130] astrology and sorcery[131] were employed throughout the then world as a means to deal with

---

granted at this time. Balla provides elaborate accounts of how this ensued during the era of the New Testament.

126. Varro, *On the Latin Language*, 6.1, and Ovid, *Fasti* 5.421–6.

127. Warrior, *Roman Religion*, 33–34.

128. Warrior, 31. Cf. Ovid, *Fasti* 2.533–570.

129. The Romans were deeply involved in ancestral worship. This observation is significant for an inquiry on how the widespread tradition influenced early Christian belief in "saints" and formation of doctrines around key figures like Mary of Nazareth (the mother of Jesus) during the Roman Empire.

130. I do not find the case to distinguish magic from religion convincing. Magic was not a mere art in antiquity but served a people who believed in the manipulation of transcendent powers to do their bidding. For those interested in this discussion on religion and magic, see R. Conner, *Magic in the New Testament: A Survey and Appraisal of the Evidence* (Oxford: Mandrake, 2010), 3–10, and P. Schäfer, "Magic and Religion in Ancient Judaism," in *Encountering Magic: A Princeton Seminar and Symposium*, eds. Peter Schäfer and Hans G. Kippenberg (Leiden: Brill, 1997), 32–33.

131. Plutarch, *Mor.* 706D. Sorcery and magic were used together in some occasions to deliver people from demonic possession or protect those oppressed by evil spirits, as Plutarch explains in the *Table Talk.*

evil powers, gain favors or manipulate people to do one's bidding.[132] Their use was so rampant[133] that leading voices such as Plato argued that some forms of magic be regulated by statutes.[134] Magic served *ex opere operato* (to meet a desired effect by utterance) in the quest for protection, good fortune, or love. Even prostitutes employed magic to attract clients. Sportsmen used magic to gain a competitive edge over their opponents. A magical tablet found describing the scene of a horse race gives a glimpse of how athletes employed spells in this regard. It reads:

> I conjure you up, holy beings and holy names; join in aiding this spell, and bind, enchant, thwart, strike, overturn, conspire against, destroy, kill, break Eucherius the charioteer, and all his horses tomorrow in the circus in Rome. May he not leave the barriers well; may he not be quick in the contest; may he not outstrip anyone; may he not make turns well; may he not win any prizes . . . may he be broken; may he be dragged along by your power, in the morning and afternoon races. Now! Now! Quickly! Quickly![135]

It was the belief that spirit-induced sicknesses could be cured, and sexual prowess could be enhanced by magic.[136] Magic was ubiquitous. Professional magicians and sorcerers travelled across the empire to trade their services. In his treatise *On Those Hired for Pay*, Lucian recounts some incidents with foreign magicians and astrologers in Rome. Romans typically hired Greek migrants known to combine philosophy, magic and astrology as private consultants. By the first century, the influx of foreign magicians coupled with how much they exploited people for huge sums had become a nuisance. Cicero recounts consternation in Rome due to the overwhelming influence of augurs and astrologers.[137] Consequently, Tiberius instituted strong measures and expelled some from the city. However, Dio Cassius, Tacitus and Suetonius sought to

---

132. M. W. Dickie, *Magic and Magicians in the Greco-Roman World* (London: Routledge, 2001). See Pliny the Elder, *Natural History*, 28. Pliny recounts the ubiquitous nature of magic, superstitions or witchcraft in the Greco-Roman world. He goes to the extent of explaining the magical formulae in some occasions.

133. D. E. Aune, "Magic in Early Christianity," in *Aufstieg und Niedergang der römischen Welt* II.23.2 (Berlin/New York: Walter de Gruyter, 1980), 1521. Aune shows evidence of magic at all levels of social class in the Greco-Roman world.

134. Plato, *Laws* 10.909.

135. A. F. Segal, "Hellenistic Magic: Some Questions of Definition," in *Studies in Gnosticism and Hellenistic Religions* (Leiden: Brill, 1981), 358.

136. Arnold, *Power and Magic*, 18.

137. Cicero, *Div.* 1.12–25.

embarrass the emperor by revealing his hypocritical act; for the emperor had retained Thrasyllus (a Greek) as his private astrologer and sorcerer during the time he sought to expel others.[138]

Divination was not set apart from magic per se. "It should be no occasion for surprise that for many Romans there was no sharp distinction between magic-working and divination in general. The distinction, in particular, between magic and astrology was blurred."[139] For our purposes, divination and magic were all part of the world concept in which transcendent spiritual forces played a major role in human affairs. Divination was a common practice of spirituality. As one ancient writer puts it, "the gods know all things. By means of sacrifices, birds, voices and dreams they send signs to whomever they wish."[140] Pliny reckons that, "there is no one who does not fear to be spellbound by curse tablets."[141] Tacitus writes about the effect of magical spells and incantations.[142] Moreover, the mingling of Egyptian, Greek and Roman divination and incantations was common. Magical arts in the Roman world included (a) complicated rituals, (b) magical spells and recipes, (c) recitation of names or syllables, (d) reliance on professional technicians, (e) syncretism, and (f) coercion and manipulation of spiritual powers.[143]

It appears that the elite could indulge more in magic since its expensive resources were not affordable to the poor. Apollonius of Tyana, a mid-first- and early second-century CE magician from Asia Minor, was known for his magical arts, especially for his prediction about a plague that later came on the city of Ephesus. Metzger ranks Ephesus the third in the Greco-Roman world for magical practices, sorcerers and various forms of charlatans.[144] "Perhaps even more than Pisidian Antioch, Corinth, and Antioch-on-the-Orontes, this city of traders and sailors, of courtesans and rakes, swarmed

---

138. Dickie, *Magic and Magicians*, 195–196.

139. Dickie, 193.

140. Xenophon, *The Cavalry Commander*, 9.9. Also *Memorabilia* 1.1.3; Cicero, *On Divination* 1.5.

141. Pliny, *Natural History* 24.4.19.

142. Tacitus, *Ann.* 2.69.

143. B. Witherington III, *The Acts of the Apostles: A Socio-Rhetorical Commentary* (Grand Rapids: Eerdmans, 1998), 578. Also Arnold, *Principalities and Powers,* 22. Some describe the aspects of ancient magic under two rubrics, namely (a) ritual and (b) performance. The *ritual* takes the form of repetitive and formal routines whereas *performance* includes utterances that are made to effect the anticipated bidding.

144. B. M. Metzger, "St. Paul and the Magicians," *PSB* 38 (1944): 27.

with soothsayers and purveyors of charms."[145] The social location of the early readers of Ephesians necessitates that we approach a sacred text to a religious community in the region with this framework. For they held these beliefs and indulged these practices.

Ephesus was particularly famous for what was known as the *Ephesia Grammata* – a magical formulae that includes six names – *askion, kataskion, lix, tetrax, damnameneus, aisia.*[146] These words were believed to have contained extraordinary powers to ward off demons, provide access to supernatural powers and aid those who appropriated them effectively in conjuration or in the form of talisman. Clement of Alexandria refers to the *Ephesia Grammata,* as told to him by Androcydes, and describes its appropriation as demonic in nature.[147] In sports, a wrestler from Ephesus wearing the *Ephesia grammata* on his ankle is alleged to have been defeating his Milesian opponent until the "letters" were discovered and removed later – after which he suffered three successive defeats.[148] Magical spells were inscribed on animal skin and worn as necklaces for protection.[149] One may apply magic to ward off diabolic forces.[150] In some cases, the conjurer would have to fulfill certain obligations to yield the desired effect. For example, a person desiring protection from demonic forces may be required to abstain from pork at a specified time frame.[151] Magic was also utilized to solicit love, as this spell shows:

> To make [a woman] mad after man: You should bring a live shrew-mouse, remove its gall and put it in one place; and remove its heart and put it in another place. You should take its whole body. You should pound it very much while it is dry; you should take a little of what is pounded with the blood of your second finger and the

---

145. O. Meinardus, *St. Paul in Ephesus and the Cities of Galatia and Cyprus* (Athens: Lycabettus, 1979), 91.

146. See Arnold, *Power and Magic,* 15. Arnold explains that these terms were first mentioned in a fourth-century BCE Cretan tablet and well attested to in literature, including the works of Clement of Alexandria and Hesychus.

147. Clement of Alexandria, "The Stromata," in *Ante-Nicene Fathers,* eds. A. Roberts and J. Donaldson (Grand Rapids: Eerdmans, 1989), 454–455. The appearance of these letters in Clement's writings also suggests that magical arts in Asia Minor and Egypt had a lot in common.

148. Arnold, *Power and Magic,* 15.

149. PGM IV. 2695–2700.

150. PGM IV. 3007–86.

151. PGM IV. 3080–3085. The use of the charm for protection also needs to be according to standard, which also suggests that it is a Jewish magical formula.

> little finger of your left hand; you should put it in a cup of wine; and you should make the woman drink it. She is mad after you.[152]

Thus, a woman could be induced to love a partner under the influence of magical powers.

Furthermore, magic was employed to restrain a hot-tempered person from causing harm and to regulate their conduct. Apparently, an embittered manifesting in rage could subside if the subject was prepared to undergo certain rituals to regain control over his bad temper (see Eph 4:31–32).[153] Magic could ward off the "spirit of anger." One such recipe requires the candidate to hold his thumb and repeat this spell seven times: "ERMALLOTH ARCHIMALLOTH stop the mouths that speak against me, because I glorify your sacred and honored names which are in heaven."[154] The effectiveness of magic was contingent upon the ability to follow the recipe closely, including being able to pronounce the names and stand at the prescribed location in the right posture.

The polytheistic religious outlook allowed for engaging multiple spiritual instruments to meet one's needs. Some powerful gods were invoked in magic for immediacy; the common ones included Hekate, Artemis, Selene, Kore, Kronos, Serapis, and Aphrodite.[155] Hekate is the goddess of protection. She features in Greek magic and is often associated with Artemis Ephesia. The spiritual climate placed no limitations on the spiritual sources that could be adduced to meet one's needs. Whatever powers worked at a given time for a particular cause could be solicited or employed. The thought of someone being able to highjack a person's wishes was a legitimate cause for anxiety.

The cosmos is God's design and this God ensures social order. Human beings are not the center of the world, but inhabitants of a world created and governed by a deity. Social ethics was not always based on human ability to do good; spiritual powers were able to subject people to the bidding of another by manipulation. Even in public speaking, one could be restrained from conveying their honest thoughts by means of magic.[156] A gambler may employ magic to defeat a fellow contestant;[157] an opponent in sports could be charmed to

---

152. PGM XIV. 1206–14. Also PGM VII. 300a–310. The PGM contains many love charms and recipes, which implies that the use of spells was a common practice in the Hellenistic world. Ethical concepts were not only grounded in philosophy but perhaps more influenced by religious superstitions in the then world.

153. PGM VII. 940–68; XXXVI. 35–60.

154. PGM XXXVI. 161–77.

155. PGM IV. 1715; V. 4–5; IV. 2523, 2720–2721; V. 1–53.

156. PGM VII. 396–404.

157. PGM VII. 423–28.

perform poorly;[158] and magic could be utilized for favor, friendship and fame.[159] The PGM shows that magic was even used as a form of contraception. A woman would wear a certain talisman in the waning of the moon to prevent unwanted pregnancy.[160]

Astrology was also practiced alongside magic, sorcery and divination; the stars, sun, and moon were means to unlock mysteries. The fate of cities, nations and individuals could be known through astrology. The origin of astrology is often traced to Mesopotamia, but the practice later spread throughout Asia and other parts of the world[161] through migrations.[162] The sun (Helios), moon (Selene) and planets were all believed to have close connection with angelic beings. "The Greco-Roman world believed that their daily lives were tightly connected by the sun, moon, planets, and stars, which explain their deep involvement with astrology and the zodiac."[163] It must be noted that astrological arts and magic were not isolated from cultic worship, as noted above.

Astrology was prevalent in Asia Minor. An inscription in Miletus showing evidence of astrology read: "Holy one, protect the city of the Milesians and all those inhabiting it." Another inscription stood below these six sectors that read, "ἀράγγελοι protect the city of the Milesians and all those inhabiting it."[164] Astrology was utilized to determine the right place for important banquets or make salient political decisions, according to the handbook of astrology.[165] Koester indicates that many resorted to astrology and magic when they realized that philosophy alone could not grant them the freedom they craved.[166] The philosophers themselves did not dismiss or distant themselves from these practices. Thus, the equation of intellectual pursuit to anti-religious devotion in modern thought is radically different from how the great founders of our Greek and Roman intellectual heritage understood their place in the world. Astrology

---

158. PGM VII. 390–93.

159. PGM XII. 270–350.

160. XXXVI. 320–32.

161. Koester, *History, Culture and Religion*, 156. Also E. McNall Burns and P. L. Ralph, *World Civilization Vol. 1*, 5th ed. (New York: Norton & Co., 1974), 233–234.

162. W. A. Meeks, *The First Urban Christians: The Social World of the Apostle Paul* (New Haven: YUP, 1983), 18–19. Meeks discusses the way religious practices spread in the entire Hellenistic world and Mesopotamia as people moved to settle from one place to the other.

163. G. M. Burge et. al. *The New Testament in Antiquity: A Survey of the New Testament within Its Cultural Contexts* (Grand Rapids: Zondervan, 2009), 339.

164. Arnold, *Power and Magic*, 29.

165. Koester, *History, Culture and Religion*, 159.

166. Koester, 159. This assertion leans on the assumption that philosophy was not that active in magic, astrology and other religious practices but that was not the case.

was regarded "as the highest of all sciences, and together with manticism it was defended by the stoics, especially as both corresponded with stoic determinism and gave unsurpassed expression to a basic notion of the time, the 'sympathy' of the macrocosm and the microcosm, the world and man."[167] It was even possible to pursue astrology, viewed as a combination of science and religion, as vocation. Professional astrologers were called *mathematici* or *Chaldaei*: The former denotes mathematical calculation whereas the latter alludes to its Mesopotamian origin. The practice was widespread, even among Jews (see 1 Enoch 72:13, 19; 75:3; 2 Enoch 30:6).

Another religious phenomenon known across cultural and geographical borders in the ancient world is the concept of the "evil eye." The evil eye is a difficult and complex phenomenon to define yet it is powerfully engrained in human consciousness and social interactions, especially in the Middle East where its influence continues even today. It is the belief that a look of envy or getting looks from an observer can emit or deploy an evil omen to the object of beholding.[168] The effects of this belief – threat and dread thereof – was present in every human interaction, professional or otherwise. John H. Elliott has conducted the most extensive and exhaustive study of this phenomenon spanning from 3000 BCE to 600 CE from Mesopotamia, Egypt, Greece, Rome, Israel and in the context of early Christianity.[169] His second volume covering Greece and Rome (our context), in particular, aptly shows the connection between envy and the evil eye phenomenon in society. While some find his methodological appropriation with etymological analysis problematic, what is not in dispute is the fact that the phenomenon prevailed prior to and within the time frame of Ephesians. The notion that spiritual powers could be deployed to cause harm and/or alter fate by a second party's look of envy made sense within the prevailing worldview. The need to protect oneself from such malevolent acts was not tantamount to naivete.

---

167. M. Hengel, *Judaism and Hellenism* (Philadelphia: Fortress, 1974), 238–239. This is to say that religious superstition was not only common among the uneducated. The educated Jews and ordinary people in the Gentile communities were influenced in one way or the other by religious superstition.

168. Today travelers to the Middle East would find stones or special objects in the markets intended, even as souvenirs, to ward off the effects of "the evil eye."

169. J. H. Elliott, *Beware the Evil Eye: The Evil Eye in the Bible and the Ancient World – Introduction, Mesopotamia, and Egypt Vol. 1* (Eugene: Cascade, 2015); *Beware the Evil Eye: The Evil Eye in the Bible and the Ancient World – Greece and Rome Vol. 2* (Eugene, Cascade, 2016); *Beware the Evil Eye: The Evil Eye in the Bible and the Ancient World – The Bible and Related Sources Vol. 3* (Eugene: Cascade, 2016); *Beware the Evil Eye: The Evil Eye in the Bible and the Ancient World – Post-Biblical Israel and Early Christianity through Late Antiquity Vol. 4* (Eugene: Cascade, 2017).

The discussion so far has shown the nature of spirit cosmology in the Greco-Roman world, with particular attention to Asia Minor. The worldview and belief systems were not region-specific but widespread, spanning centuries. Cultic celebrations were public events and entertainment (e.g. Artemis in Ephesus). Luke's portrait of magic and the popularity of Artemis in Ephesus (Acts 19) corresponds well with what we know from extra-biblical accounts of the region at the time. Religion was part of social events.[170] Sportsmen sought spiritual help (e.g. magic), pagan temples served as hospitals (e.g. the temple of Asclepius), and young virgins found husbands with divine assistance. Furthermore, pagan temples were prominent features in city landscapes and marked some of the most beautiful architecture in the cities of Asia Minor. Moreover, monetary units bore images of patron deities to underscore their presence in economics. Some coins even featured emperors and astrological symbols side by side, implying subservience of political leaders to the law of the sky (stars in particular).[171]

The popular view was that humanity stood under continued influence of invisible powers, either by mainstream deities, astrology or magic.

> Fate, demons, and gods of every description haunted the atmosphere; spells, incantations, and magic were the means by which the individual could fend off the dangers that encircled him. Security was obtained by bribing the deities, or by ascertaining from horoscopes what course of action to pursue, or by discovering some potent charm to keep the threatening powers of darkness at bay. The uncertainty of the future held the masses of mankind in mental and spiritual bondage.[172]

This world concept defined reality and informed the logic of Gentile Christians in their pre-conversion past. Ephesians was written to a people within this context, informed by its beliefs and influenced by its worldview.

---

170. Thomas, "At Home in the City of Artemis," 84.

171. Koester, *History, Culture and Religion*, 159.

172. Tenney, *New Testament Times*, 124.

# 3

# Spiritual Beings in Judaism and Early Christianity

The origins of Christianity are rooted in Judaism. The Jesus movement was a Jewish sect that saw its mission in light of the fulfillment of messianic prophecies about Yahweh's covenant community. Jesus and his disciples were Jews; they thought as Jews, worshipped as Jews and perceived the world in the prism of Jewish conventions. They worshipped in synagogues, participated in Torah reading and celebrated Jewish festivals. Christians must guard against supersessionist viewpoints or replacement theologies[1] that see Christianity as an anti-Jewish movement in its inception. There was no separation of Judaism and Christianity until about late first or second century.[2] Failure to grasp this symbiotic relationship between Judaism and Christianity misconstrues how we imagine the social context, worldview and appreciate why Gentile membership of the church was such a constant cause for contention. While overlaps did exist in the broader framework of spirit cosmology of Jews and non-Jews, it is

---

1. M. R. Wilson, *Exploring Our Hebraic Heritage: A Christian Theology of Roots and Renewal* (Grand Rapids: Eerdmans, 2014), 245–257. This important study, especially the pages listed here, provides insight into the origins of the church and point to the danger of the view that the church came to supersede or replace Judaism.

2. See M. Zetterholm, *The Formation of Christianity in Antioch: A Social Scientific Approach to the Separation between Judaism and Christianity* (London: Routledge, 2003), 202–240. It is quite difficult to establish a dating for "the parting of the Way" between Judaism and Christianity. Zetterholm, among others, has suggested that the dispute between Peter and Paul in Galatians 2 may have marked its inception. We however find evidence in later writings, the Gospel of Matthew and others in Pauline corpus, showing that Jews and Gentiles in Christian communities were still wrestling with issues of continuity and discontinuity. The parting of the way may have happened from region to region by the end of the first century into the early parts of the second century CE. Traces may be found in writings of the church fathers and Rabbis of the time as well. While Christians sought to make differentiations, some rabbis also expressed the need for a break since Christianity was becoming a movement of Gentile majority. Revisions in Jewish morning prayers suggests that both sides may have contributed to the break simultaneously.

rather within the monotheistic framework, religious rituals and sacred writings of Israel/Jews that the foundation of Christianity rests. In a nutshell, it is in the story of Israel that we find the mission, message and meaning of Christianity.

## 3.1 Towards Spirit Cosmology in Judaism – A Survey

The journey of Abraham from his Chaldean home and social location to becoming the founding father of Israel is thoroughly *theo*centric. His departure from home was in obedience to divine call; he entered into a divine-human covenant accompanied by a promise of offspring, a nation and land (Gen 12, 15 and 17). Abraham's experiences occurred after his (human) encounter with the divine and elaborate divine orchestration and interventions to develop the Hebrews, as God's chosen people, into a nation. Communal identity and belief in divine intervention prior to and in the post-exilic era underlie the people's anticipation for the restoration of the kingdom of Israel. It is noteworthy that all founding leaders of Christianity were Jewish and operated in this continuum. It is only in Jewish cosmology that the message of God's salvific work in Christ makes sense. Unlike Greeks, Romans and other surrounding nations, Second Temple Judaism was anchored in the belief that God is one.[3] The *Shema* was thus a pivotal statement of confession: "Hear, O Israel: The LORD our God, the LORD is one" (Deut 6:4 ESV). Monotheism remained central to the social identity of Jewish communities wherever they settled. Their identity and sense of belonging were harnessed through the stories about their origin, history with God and religious traditions. Israel's social and moral boundaries were divinely given and sanctioned codes. For example, circumcision had deep spiritual significance as the mark of a covenant between God and his people. The governing principles and rituals of their community are necessitated by and enforced within the framework of Yahweh's covenant with his people – Yahweh blesses compliance and punishes disobedience; leaders were appointed by God as also prophets were chosen as covenant enforcing agents among the people of God. Yahweh's chastisement may come in the form of defeat at

---

3. Jews had migrated to many parts of the empire by the first century. Significant numbers settled in Syria, Egypt, and Asia Minor. There were smaller Jewish communities in Phoenicia, Cyrene, Greece and Rome. Judaism was not monolithic but had many sects at the time. For example, the Pharisees and Sadducees could not agree on the question of the immortality of the soul. The Essene preferred an ascetic way of life. However, the tenets of Judaism that were held by all Jews and linked to their national identity included the belief in one God – the God of Abraham, Isaac and Jacob. Other core beliefs included the conviction that they are a chosen people and a community in covenant relationship with God. They subscribed to the Torah and considered the Temple in Jerusalem as the center of Jewish community and piety.

war, national disaster and even captivity by foreign nations. The rise and fall of Israel was contingent upon her standing with God. Ancient Israel did not exist for itself, but as a people of God living up to and enjoying the privileges of covenant relationship with God.[4]

The origins of Israel and her relationship with God begins with the call of Abram and the promise to make him a great nation (Gen 12). This must not be confused with how the Christian story develops. Yahweh's covenant with Abram and how it unfolded in posterity defines the people of Israel and their place in the world. The Christian story (theological anthropology and soteriology), however, begins with creation and fall of humankind – a state from which salvation in Christ ensues. Abraham becomes an important figure in God's plan of redemption after several failed attempts to restore relationship with humans (Gen 3–11). Israel would become the chosen matrix and means by which Yahweh's plan for *the nations* would be actualized. The Abrahamic narratives recount how a pagan husband heard the voice of God and took decisive action to follow God's lead with his wife. To ponder a person's ability to hear from a deity with certainty and commit to follow his guidance was not unthinkable in Abram's spirit cosmology. In other words, migration and property ownership could be orchestrated by divine agency – the Maker of the world could take away lands from sinful pagans and give them to the descendants of Abraham (Gen 12). Abraham believed that the God he encountered is the Supreme God within his Chaldean belief system.

Creation is the act of this one Supreme God in the cosmology of Israel. It is he who brought order out of chaos and spoke things into being, except for humankind. Yahweh created humankind in his image and likeness and gave them the mandate to manage his creation (Gen 1 and 2; Ps 8). Humans owe their origin to a spirit being to whom they are accountable in how they live and steward his creation. It was Yahweh or Yahweh Elohim who commissioned the first persons to be cosmic managers – not human initiative. Later, human relationship with God and fate would be altered in consequence of a breach in dietary restrictions (Gen 2–3). The failings of one person after the other to meet God's expectations is what would ultimately lead God to call and make a covenant with their Chaldean ancestor, Abram. For the Hebrew people, God is the architect and initiator of a covenant that would result in their very existence.

---

4. It would make no sense to many people in today's western world to conceive of an entire nation claiming its origins to a pagan ancestor who heard and heeded the voice of God to leave his homeland to a place where the spiritual being would locate them.

Hebrew identity has always been linked to divine initiative and covenant relationship with Yahweh. The God of Abraham, Isaac and Jacob was with Joseph prior to and during his time in Egypt (Gen 37–50). Yahweh delivered Israel from their Egyptian oppressors and resettled them in the land of promise. According to the Pentateuch, the subsequent religious duties and moral obligations were all given by God during the exodus, and as the Hebrews developed into a nation. Yahweh's appointed leaders ensured that his people did not transgress covenant obligations such as the Sabbath, Torah observance, dietary laws etc. However, the belief in the transcendent was not limited to Yahweh. Israel acknowledged the religions and deities of other nations to be real but demonized them. God's covenant community was barred from indulging in pagan religions, customs and other activities.

Israel's neighbors and the ancestral people of Abram (Chaldeans) shared the notion that the universe is created and ordered by spiritual beings. Arguably, traces if not parallels of OT cosmology are found in the *Enuma Elish* and texts like *The Epic of Atrahasis*. There was no distinction between the sacred and secular in those ancient cosmologies. "The gods provided, or they did not. Misfortune was seen as judgment of the gods. The way in which one lived life had religious significance; nothing was beyond the realm of the religious."[5] It is in this vein that the "speaking serpent," later associated with the devil, would instigate rebellion against God (Gen 3). Moses's triumph with plagues upon Egypt (Exod 5–12) were all taken for granted that what was at stake was not a mere release of enslaved migrants but a spiritual battle against the gods of the land.

Spirit cosmology permeates the Hebrew scriptures. For example, Yahweh allowed and dared Satan (an adversary) to test the loyalty of Job (Job 1). Job's family and his entire livelihood suffered in an spiritual battle unbeknown to Job that was ensuing behind the scenes. Elsewhere in the Bible, we have references to incidents such as a "lying spirit" persuading a king to follow false prophets (1 Sam 22:21–23). Israel's first king, Saul, was particularly amiable to spiritual forces. His first encounter with Prophet Samuel occurred in the cause of his pursuit for spiritual direction (1 Sam 10) and later, King Saul consulted a witch at Endor after the death of Samuel (1 Sam 28). "Faced with the imminent prospect of a perilous battle with the Philistines, he can no longer bear God's silence, and he rides out to Endor, to a woman who

---

5. P. T. Vogt, *Interpreting the Pentateuch: An Exegetical Handbook* (Grand Rapids: Kregel, 2009), 102.

conjures the dead."[6] David's music could deliver Saul from the oppression of evil spirits (1 Sam 16:14–23). Furthermore, King Manasseh was notorious for indulging in soothsaying, augury, witchcraft and dealing with mediums (2 Kgs 21:6). The biblical account shows fewer incidents or mentions of evil spirits effecting people who disobeyed God prior to the exile compared to the higher number of mention of evil spirits, the devil or Beliar, in the exilic and post-exilic narratives. One exilic narrative (Daniel) shows the challenges and successes of Jewish migrants working alongside magicians and astrologers, and even on an occasion when an evil spirit attempted to intercept Yahweh's answer to Daniel's prayer (Dan 1:20). A DSS parallel to Daniel 4 recounts an incident with Nabonidus (Babylonian king) who when punished by God had to undergo exorcism.

> [I, Nabonidus,] was smitten [with severe inflammation] lasting seven years. Beca[use] I was thus changed, [becoming like a beast, I prayed to the Most High,] and He forgave my sins. An exorcist – a Jew, in fact, a mem[ber of the community of exiles – came to me and said,] Declare and write this story, and so ascribe glory and gre[at]ness to the name of G[od Most High. Accordingly, I have myself written it down].[7]

An observer may notice that the formula for exorcism aforementioned is either sparse or not found in pre-exilic texts. Direct reference to Satan, Beliar or the devil features prominently more so in post-exilic Jewish texts. For example, the *Martyrdom and Ascension of Isaiah* attributes the failings of Manasseh to satanic influence. Consequently, Beliar (ruler of the world) rejoiced for being able to lead the king to indulge in iniquity, sorcery, magic, augury and divination.[8] There are traces of activities of evil spirits (not only pagan deities) in the Second Temple period.[9] Two Jewish texts from the period are relevant to our inquiry, namely *Testament of the Twelve Patriarchs* (TTP) and *Testament of Solomon*. These representative texts underscore prevailing thoughts on the role of evil spirits and their influence on human affairs.

---

6. J. Ratzinger, *Jesus of Nazareth: From the Baptism in the Jordan to the Transfiguration* (San Francisco: Ignatius Press, 2007), 2.

7. 4Q242 (trans. M. Wise).

8. "The Martyrdom and Ascension of Isaiah" 2:2–5, in *The Old Testament Pseudepigrapha Vol. 1: Apocalyptic Literature & Testaments*, ed. J. H. Charlesworth (Garden City: Doubleday, 1983), 143–176.

9. It is possible that living with Gentiles in exile or the Hellenization project of Alexander the Great and its subsequent impact on the empire are responsible for how spiritual opposition was characterized by the time of the New Testament.

Jewish communities in the diaspora maintained their monotheistic faith and commensurate norms. This does not, however, mean that there were no transgressors from traditional beliefs, even in the homeland.[10] In Egypt, Anatolia and elsewhere, some Jews succumbed to the influence of the dominant culture and imbedded religious customs. There is evidence of magic and astrology among Jews, even when there was no political pressure from Rome to compromise their faith.[11] Until Hadrian, Jews had the backing of Rome to practice their religion yet syncretism prevailed.[12] Josephus recounts exemptions from military service and freedom to practice religion in Asia Minor.

> Hyrcanus sent also one of these ambassadors to Dolabella, who was the prefect of Asia, and desired him to dismiss the Jews from military services, and to preserve to them the custom of their forefathers, and to permit them to live according to them. And when Dolabella had received Hyrcanus' letter, without any farther deliberation, he sent an epistle to all the Asiatics, and particularly to the city of Ephesus, the metropolis of Asia, about the Jews.[13]

This freedom does not imply that Jews isolated or dissociated themselves from society; they lived and maintained social interactions with their neighbors.[14]

Diaspora Jews dreaded the influence of evil powers like the rest of society. As such, some yielded to the mediums employed by their Gentile neighbors to mitigate those fears. It was not uncommon for Jews to indulge in magic –

---

10. F. Josephus, *The Works of Josephus,* trans. W. Whiston (Lynn: Hendrickson, 1980), 251. *Ant.* 12.3.2. Josephus shows that there was a good size number of Jews in Asia Minor (Ionia) that wanted to be joint partakers of the rights of citizens, but they retreated when they were asked to worship the pagan gods as one of the conditions for gaining that right. See P. R. Trebilco, *Jewish Communities in Asia Minor* (Cambridge: CUP, 1991), and R. C. Kroeger and C. C. Kroeger, *I Suffer not a Woman: Rethinking 1 Timothy 2:11–15 in Light of Ancient Evidence* (Grand Rapids: Baker, 1997), 54–56. The Kroegers indicate that the Jewish population in Ephesus as at the first century was about seventy-five thousand people.

11. Philo, *Spec. Laws* I: 315–316, trans. C. D. Yonge (Peabody: Hendrickson, 1993), 564. Philo implies that some itinerant Jews claimed to be prophets filled with the Holy Spirit, but their claims were inaccurate. He warns Jews against those whose aim was to exhort them to be cheerful among pagan multitudes, worship in their temples with them and offer pagan sacrifices. He calls them imposters. He clearly implies that some Jews tried to lead others to worship pagan gods.

12. E. P. Sanders, *Judaism: Practice and Belief 63BCE–66CE* (London: SCM, 1992), 20.

13. Josephus, *Ant.* 14.233–224.

14. J. M. G. Barclay, *Jews in the Mediterranean Diaspora: From Alexander to Trajan 323 BCE–117 CE* (Berkeley: University of California Press, 1996), 82–102, 259–281. Barclay provides a nuanced account of how we may imagine levels of assimilation or acculturation of Jews in the diaspora.

contrary biblical injunctions (see Deut 18:10–12, 20; Mic 5:12)[15] and rabbinic teachings.[16] Evidence abounds in the PGM and elsewhere of Jewish names in magical spells. One popular name was *Iao Sabaoth*. It is uncertain whether the Jewish names in magic formulae always originated from Gentiles or Jews in the PGM. What is certain though is that some Jews practiced magic. A reader of diaspora Judaism should always bear in mind that Second Temple Judaism did not have monolithic theology. Various sects and movements held different theological viewpoints (Pharisees, Sadducees etc.). However, all Jews subscribed to four main pillars – the Shema, circumcision, the Torah observance and temple worship. None of the sects embraced Gentile religious practices and/or intermarriage with Gentiles, but transgressions did occur (Acts 16:2; 2 Tim 1:1–7 [intermarriage] and Acts 19 [magic]).

Texts from Jewish mysticism attest to pagan rituals in diaspora Judaism. The *Sepher Ha-Razim* contains magical formulae and invocations to Aphrodite, Helios and Hermes. It features three kinds of magic, namely magic for healing, magic for revelation/divination and magic to control enemies.[17] Similarly, The *Sefer Yesira* contains evidence of Jewish magic. God is portrayed as the Great Artist and Magician in the *Sefer Yesira*. God's name and the twenty-two Hebrew letters are utilized as magical formula.[18] The Chaldean heritage of Abraham resurfaces in this text as Abraham is portrayed as a magician (*SY 61*).[19] Though these two texts, *Sepher Ha-Razim* and *Sefer Yesira*, appeared later than the first century CE, they do provide valuable insight into Jewish engagement with magic. The discovery of eighty Jewish incantation bowls in Nippur, Khuzestan, Hamadan and Nehavan, dating approximately 226–635 CE, further echo the

---

15. M. J. Geller and D. Levene, "Magical Texts from the Genizah (with a New Duplicate)," in *JJS* 44, no. 2 (1998): 334–335. It is important to note that Jewish magic was not employed as prayer in their synagogues. Despite some similarities between prayer and magic, they are not the same or used for the same purpose. Both magic and prayer invoked divine favor or appeal to God, seek protection and quote sacred texts, such text in the liturgy would have been some scriptural verses. On the other hand, "(1) prayer is obligatory upon men, while magic is used only as necessary. (2) Magic is specifically designed to counter the activities of demons and other evil agents (e.g. the evil eye, witchcraft etc.). (3) Magic uses various "powers" against supernatural agents . . . , which is not normal in liturgy. (4) Magic is unconcerned with piety of the client . . . (5) Magic often depends upon the client's belief in the authority of the magician to influence demons, while prayers are either biblical psalms or usually anonymous compositions."

16. H. Dandy, *The Mishnah: Translated from the Hebrew with Introduction and Brief Explanatory Notes* (Oxford: Oxford University Press, 1991), 305. Sotah 9.13.

17. D. E. Aune, "Magic," in *The International Standard Bible Encyclopedia Vol. 3*, ed. G. W. Bromiley (Grand Rapids: Eerdmans, 1990), 217.

18. P. Hayman, "Was God a Magician? Sefer Yesira and Jewish Magic," *JJS* 40, no. 2 (1989): 225–237. The article shows portions of the text depicting God in magic formulae.

19. Hayman, "Was God a Magician?," 234.

fact that these practices were present in Judaism. The bowls contain magical texts that include a quote from Zechariah 3:2.[20] This does not, however, suggest that all Jews dabbled in magic, but it points to shared spirit cosmology and fear of evil spiritual forces in the milieu. Moreover, some Jews intermarried with Gentiles, participated in synagogue worship and yielded to wider cultural influences (cf. Acts 16; 2 Tim 1:1–7).

Many Jews in the Roman world employed magic and astrology to the extent that the only way to distinguish Jewish from Greek or Roman magical practices was the ability to recognize the names in a recipe. Figures like Abraham, Moses and Solomon were associated with magic and/or astrology. "Moses' role as a wonder-worker and recipient of divine wisdom and Jews' legendary knowledge of the divine name made Jewish lore attractive also to non-Jews interested in magic."[21] Arnold outlines three features of Jewish magic at the time: "(1) a great respect for Hebrew phrases which seemed to have magical power; (2) a sense of efficacious power in the [divine] name; and (3) an overwhelming regard for angels and demons."[22] Ancient Jewish traditions made association with the wisdom of Solomon and magic as well. Apparently, Solomon had the ability to exorcise.[23] According to Josephus, God enabled him with the wisdom to "expel demons" and "compose incantations." "And he (Solomon) left behind him the manner of using exorcisms, by which they drive away demons, so that they never return, and this method of cure is of great force unto this day."[24] Josephus claims to have witnessed an occasion in the presence of Vespasian when Eleazer exorcised with Solomonic recipe.[25]

The *Testament of Solomon* provides important details on these practices among some Jews in Asia Minor. The text is a haggadic-type folktale about

---

20. Aune, "Magic," 217.

21. S. R. Garrett, *The Demise of the Devil: Magic and the Demonic in Luke's Writings* (Minneapolis: Fortress, 1989), 13.

22. Arnold, *Power and Magic*, 31.

23. D. C. Duling, "Solomon, Exorcism, and the Son of David," *HTR* 68, no. 3/4 (1975): 235–252. Duling demonstrates that the notion that Solomon had wisdom that enabled him to thwart evil forces was not only common in the Gentile land but also in Palestine (cf. Josephus, *Antiquities* 8.2.5). The main thesis of his article was to examine the relationship between Solomon, the Son of David who has power to exorcise, and reference to Jesus as the Son of David in the Gospels. His thorough examination of ancient literature and the Gospels leads him to a conclusion that, it would appear that Solomon-as-exorcist, who may be called the "Son of David" in a more or less casual way, could have had an effect on early Christian tradition in as far as Mark modified the conception for its own purposes. If so, the concept should no longer be omitted from the discussions of Son of David Christology (p. 252).

24. Josephus, *Ant.* 8.45–46 (trans. W. Whiston).

25. Josephus, 46–49.

Solomon's task of building the temple and the lore of magic, astrology, angelology, demonology, and primitive medicine.[26] The author is unknown, but his Jewish origin is undisputed. The text probably originated from Asia Minor, as many scholars think, but Babylon, Egypt or Galilee have also been suggested for possible provenance as well.[27] As Arnold explains:

> (1) The Solomonic magical tradition is epigraphically attested for Asia Minor. (2) One of the only two geographical terms in the document is Lydia (southern Asia Minor; see 8:4). The other is Olympus (northeastern Greece; see 8:4). While it is explainable why the writer of the document would have mentioned Olympus, famous as the reputed home of the gods in Greek mythology and religion, it is difficult to see why the writer would have mentioned the territory of Lydia unless the writer lived there or near there and was familiar with some local traditions. (3) The document explicitly names "Lix Tetrax" (7:5), two of the six Ephesia Grammata purportedly written on the cultic statue of the Ephesian Artemis. (4) T. Sol. also reports a demon telling Solomon, "I shall harm you when I order (you to be bound) with the bonds of Artemis" (8:11), which is best understood as the Ephesian Artemis, a patroness of magic.[28]

The large amount of magical apparatus found in Pergamum and what we know of magic in Anatolia further explain why a Jewish text mentioning Artemis and two of the six words of *Ephesia Grammata* would originate in Asia Minor.[29]

The *Testament of Solomon* (T. Sol.) bears three main features that are relevant to this inquiry: (a) it shows that astral powers are able to influence morality and life in general, (b) it provides a glimpse of how magic was utilized by Jews, and (c) shares terminology for spiritual forces with Ephesians. It shows that, apparently, Solomon possessed wisdom and authority to deal with spirits of the air, earth, and the underworld (18:2–3). The testament indicates that

---

26. D. C. Duling, "Testament of Solomon: A Translation and Introduction," in *The Old Testament Pseudepigrapha: Apocalyptic Literature & Testaments Vol. 1*, ed. J. H. Charlesworth (Garden City: Doubleday, 1983), 935.

27. The factors that led to this suggestion include the widespread Jewish communities and their involvement in magical practices in the Greco-Roman world. I will contend below that Asia Minor is the most likely place of its origin.

28. Arnold, *Colossian Syncretism*, 51.

29. D. C. Duling, "Testament of Solomon," 943–944. There are no concrete facts presented in favor of other locations that have been suggested. Duling leaves us with more uncertainty but I think the internal evidence raised by Arnold should be accepted in favor of Asia Minor.

these powers were embodied in a ring handed to Solomon by the archangel Michael to thwart evil forces (T. Sol. 1:6–7). Solomon could subsequently order demons to make full self-disclosure in order to deal with them accordingly. For example, the demon Onoskelis identified himself as a strangler and perverter of the character of men (T. Sol. 4:5). At Solomon's behest, Asmodeus could not mislead but explained, "I cause the wickedness of men to spread throughout the world. I am always hatching plots against newlyweds; I mar the beauty of virgins and cause their hearts to grow cold . . . I spread madness about women through the stars and I have often committed a rash of murders" (T. Sol. 5:7–8). Asmodeus claims to be responsible for sexual promiscuity, defilement and sexual assaults.

Lix Tetrax, a demon named after two of the six *Ephesia Grammata*, had primary functions to cause divisions, make whirlwinds and render households non-functional (7:5).[30] The testament features a group of seven spirits that introduced themselves as "heavenly bodies" and "rulers of this world of darkness;"[31] they claim to be agents of deception, strife, war, distress, tyranny and harm to rulers (8:1–4). They indicate that the city of Lydia in Asia Minor, Olympus and some mountains were their operational constituencies. Solomon confronted these powers in regard to their identity and roles.

> Then I Solomon, continued questioning them, beginning from the first. "Tell me what you do." He responded, "I am Deception. I plot deception and I devise the most evil heresies . . ." The second said, "I am strife, I cause strife by making available clubs, pellets, and swords, my implements of war . . ." Likewise, the third said, "I am called Fate. I cause every man to fight in battle rather than make peace honorably with those who are winning . . ." The fourth (Distress) said, "I cause men to lack moderation; I divide them into factions; I keep them separated. Since strife follows my footsteps, I set men against each other and do many similar things to them . . ." The fifth said, "I am error, King Solomon, and I am leading you into error, and I led you into error when I made you kill your brothers. I lead people into error by hunting for graves and I teach them (how) to dig them up. I lead (men's) mind to stray away from religion and I do many bad things . . ." Likewise, the sixth said, "I

---

30. Unity in the churches and peace in Christian homes would then be a demonstration of victory over *Lix Tetrax*, names very familiar to the readers of Ephesians.

31. See Ephesians 1:20; 6:12 for the same terminology for evil powers. Reference to Heavenlies in Ephesians also assumes a sphere where the heavenly bodies dwell.

am Power. I raise up tyrants, I dispose kings, and I grant power to
all those who are enemies . . . ." Similarly, the seventh said, "I am
The Worst, and you, King, I shall harm when I order (you to be
bound) with the bonds of Artemis . . ." (T. Sol. 8:5–11)

Obyzouth strangled newborn babes at night while Lecherous, who was a
demon residing in cemeteries, plagued societies with epilepsy. According to
Lecherous, the only one who could defeat him is the Saviour, the one who is to
come (17:2–5). The Testament of Solomon echoes Jewish beliefs that diseases
are caused by sin or demonic powers.

Another text that sheds more light on demonology in the Second
Temple period is the *Testament of the Twelve Patriarchs* (TTP). Authored by
a Hellenistic Jew, it purports to be an account of the last words of each of the
sons of Jacob meant for their children or posterity (Gen 34–50). An earlier date
puts its composition at 250 CE but some scholars date it at 137–107 BCE.[32] It
is noteworthy that the TTP has been subjected to intense scrutiny due to some
parallels it has with Johannine epistles, and alleged Christian interpolations.[33]
For our purposes, the link of NT books with Asia Minor provenance further
reiterates the nature of spirit cosmology among Jews and Christ followers in
the region. A Jewish scholar explains that "it [TTP] asserts the traditional
values of Torah ethics and ideals of Israel as found in most ancient Hebrew
literature."[34] It probes the conscience and portray haunting experiences of the
sons of Jacob with regard to how they treated their brother Joseph with the
goal that posterity must know in order for them to choose a better way of life.
The TTP is here examined with a narrow focus on its spirit cosmology, without
necessarily addressing the issue of whether it is distinctly Jewish or Christian
or both. As indicated above, early Christianity was a movement within Judaism
with a distinct theology of messianic hopes and God's salvific work beyond
Jewish cultural and geographical boundaries. The TTP delineates how these
pseudonymous sons of Jacob explained the role of spiritual beings in their lives.

In the TTP, Reuben recalls that God exposed his secret affair at the age of
thirty, shortly after he had defiled the marriage bed of his father with Bilhah,

---

32. C. Leviant, *Masterpiece of Hebrew Literature* (Philadelphia: Jewish Publication Society,
2008), 41–42.

33. J. H. Charlesworth, *The Old Testament Pseudepigrapha: Apocalyptic Literature &*
*Testaments* (Garden City: Doubleday, 1983), 775–780, and M. De Jonge, *Jewish Eschatology, Early*
*Christian Christology and the Testaments of the Twelve Patriarchs: Collected Essays of Marinus*
*De Jonge* (Leiden: Brill, 1991), 154–237. The debate is whether it is an authentic Jewish text or
a Jewish text that was slightly edited by a Christian sometime in the first or second century CE.

34. Leviant, *Masterpiece of Hebrew Literature*, 41.

a woman he raped while she was asleep. A severe spiritual consequence was averted when he repented of his wrongdoing and fasted from wine and choice food. He perceived his conduct to be subject to divine law and order.[35] Reuben warns that his offspring desists from such sins in order to avoid the influence of Beliar. They must be vigilant of the activities of Beliar and resist his efforts to promote sexual deviance among them.[36]

Simeon indicates that it was the "spirit of error" and "jealousy" that prompted him to rise against Joseph. Simeon was able to comport himself only by the power of God.[37] He reckons that evil spirits cannot harm those who take refuge in God (3.5). Levi offered his children to make a choice between light and darkness in regard to how they chose to live their lives; it was also a choice between "the Law of the Lord or the works of Beliar." He admonished that the prudent path is to be clothed in and by God: "Arise, put on the vestments of the priesthood, the crown of righteousness, the oracle of understanding, the robe of truth, the breastplate of faith, the miter for the head, and the apron for prophetic power," he entreats.[38] His use of a clothing metaphor to characterize moral standing against diabolic influence, as we see in Ephesians, is not uncommon. There is no middle ground in this cosmology as success or failure depended on affiliation with God or Beliar.

The Testament of Judah alludes to Genesis 38 to admonish Judah's children about the spiritual consequences of poor moral judgment. Judah's wife is called Anan in this account, not Shua as in the Bible (Gen 38:2). He reckons that God has blessed him, but it is his inanity to indulge in wine that led to rebellion against God. "The spirit of envy and promiscuity" exploited his moral failings and urged him to commit an affair with the Canaanite woman.[39] Anan's dislike of the Mesopotamian wife of Er (Tamar), and the sexual deviance associated with her (from Onan to himself), are all regarded as a chain of punishment from God.[40] In other words, moral failure could be engineered by forces of evil and attract divine chastisement. Judah further warns against drunkenness and underscores the unbearable spiritual consequence thereof (see Eph 5:18).

> And now, my children, I tell you, do not be drunk with wine, because wine perverts the mind from the truth, arouses impulses

---

35. *T. Reuben* 1:6–10.

36. *T. Reuben* 2:2, 8–9.

37. *T. Simeon* 2:11–13.

38. *T. Levi* 8:2.

39. *T. Judah* 13:2–3.

40. *T. Judah* 10–13.

of desire, and leads the eyes into the path of error. For the spirit of promiscuity has wine as its servant for the indulgence of the mind. If any one of you drinks wine to the point of drunkenness, your mind is confused by sordid thoughts, and your body is kindled by pleasure to commit adultery.[41]

An angel of God revealed to Judah that women could gain mastery over great and small men when indiscretion gives room to drunkenness and debauchery.[42] Judah identifies four spirits that operate through wine and insists that his children be vigilant against "desire, heated passion, debauchery and sordid greed" (16:1). The right cause of action is to live in the fear of God, Judah explains. "So understand, my children, that two spirits await an opportunity with humanity: the spirit of truth and the spirit of error. In between is the conscience of the mind which inclines at its will."[43]

Issachar emulated his father's dedication to God and encourages his progeny to do "only the will of God."[44] They would be able to ward off the spirit of error[45] in so doing. He is insistent that their being distant from the Lord is to "ally themselves with Beliar."[46] There is no middle ground – one is either with God or with Beliar (2 Cor 6:15). However, love for the Lord and fellow human being is able to put "every spirit of Beliar" to flight.[47] Thus, moral uprightness is a means to fight Beliar and defeat his aim to promote immorality and evil of various forms. Zebulun attests to God's faithfulness for sparing his household from diseases[48] and urges his children to show mercy to others so that God may preserve them in time of tribulation (9:8). Unlike Zebulun, Dan became susceptible to the spirit of jealousy and anger from Beliar that ensnared him and urged him with the thought to kill Joseph.[49] The *Testament of Dan* (TTP) portrays the spirit of anger as a destructive force; it "always moves with falsehood at the right of Satan, in order that such deeds may be done through savagery and deception."[50] When anger and falsehood perturbs the soul, "the

---

41. *T. Judah* 14:1–3.

42. *T. Judah* 15:5–6.

43. *T. Judah* 20:1–2.

44. *T. Issachar* 4:3.

45. *T. Issachar* 4:4.

46. *T. Issachar* 6:1.

47. *T. Issachar* 7:6.

48. *T. Zebulun* 5:2–5.

49. *T. Dan* 1:7–9.

50. *T. Dan* 3:5.

Lord withdraws from it and Beliar rules it."[51] Spiritual forces belie nefarious deeds but God is able to deliver people from diabolic influence.[52] It is prudent, therefore, to guard against "Satan and his spirits" (see Jas 4).

While the other brothers recount their bad deeds towards Joseph in the TTP, Naphtali is unique in expressing his love and admiration for his brother, recounting how Rachel developed deep affection for him as she noticed similar features with him and her son, Joseph. Naphtali makes an observation that the law of God is opposed to the law of Beliar as light is to darkness.[53] He admonishes his children to shun the ways of Beliar and follow the will of God.[54] For Naphtali, good conduct draws a person to God and puts the devil to flight.[55] Conversely, "the one who does not do good to men and angels will curse . . . the devil will inhabit him as his own instrument."[56] Gad held grudges against Joseph and that made him subject to severe diabolic influence. "For among all men the spirit of hatred works by Satan through human frailty for the death of mankind; the spirit of love works by the law of God through forbearance for the salvation of mankind."[57] It is noteworthy that Gad is an exception for his lack of reference to "Beliar" in the TTP.

Asher posits that "evil" is associated with evil spirit and "good" with God who judges wrongdoing. "Evil is overmastered by Beliar, who, even when is undertaken, presses the struggle so as to make the aim of his action into evil, since the devil's storehouse is filled with the venom of evil spirit."[58] Asher admonishes his progeny to turn to God as a defeat of the devil; those who turn away from God live to please Beliar. "Flee from the evil tendency, destroying the devil by your good works," he exclaims.[59] He reckons that evil spirits do torment evil souls and manifest their works by evil deeds.[60] As we see in Ephesians, the cosmic framework is dualistic – evil spirits on one hand and God on the other. Moreover, human conduct is influenced by spiritual forces inasmuch as

---

51. *T. Dan* 4:7. Here, Dan makes a direct link between anger and diabolic influence as we find in Ephesians 4:26–27.

52. *T. Dan* 5:9–11.

53. *T. Naphtali* 2:6–7.

54. *T. Naphtali* 3:2.

55. *T. Naphtali* 8:4.

56. *T. Naphtali* 8:6.

57. *T. Gad* 4:7; 5:6–11.

58. *T. Asher* 1:8–9.

59. *T. Asher* 3:2.

60. *T. Asher* 6:4–5.

human activity has spiritual consequences. Good is enabled by God whereas evil spirits tend to influence those who indulge in bad behavior.

The Testament of Joseph highlights God's faithfulness at the onset and proceeds to recount his ordeal with the seductive wife of an Egyptian official (Gen 39). Joseph's fate lay with God who ultimately rewarded his faithfulness and loyalty. Apparently, the unnamed wife had devised elaborate seductive ploys to lure Joseph prior to the recorded events in Genesis.[61] On occasion, she proposed to poison her husband if Joseph would marry her thereafter. To which Joseph remarked, "she was wholly beautiful and splendidly decked out to entice me, but the Lord protected me from her manipulations."[62] Her enchantment proved futile as Joseph devoted himself to prayer and fasting during the ordeal. He was thus unaffected when Beliar led her to offer him a meal mixed with enchantment.[63] For Joseph, the ordeal was a spiritual battle, but God preserved him against Beliar – the spirit at work in the woman. Joseph exhorts his progeny to trust God for his deliverance, if Beliar incites Egyptians to oppress them later.[64]

According to Benjamin, there is protection in God for those who fear him and love their neighbors. "Even if the spirits of Beliar seek to derange you with all sorts of oppression, they will not dominate you, any more than they dominated Joseph, my brother."[65] It is imperative that one flees from Beliar because he comes along with moral corruption, destruction, oppression, greed, turmoil and desolation.[66] Conversely, children should avail and align themselves to the Spirit of God in purity of heart, and good deeds will ultimately dispel the spirit of Beliar.[67]

The cosmology in the Second Temple period, as observed in the Testament of Solomon and Testaments of the Twelve Patriarchs, show a continued quest for covenant faithfulness. Their standing with God in the Abrahamic covenant and its accompanying statutes enshrined in the Torah places the patriarchs and their progeny alongside God, as long as they remained faithful in a world plagued by malevolent powers. Unlike pre-exilic emphasis or warnings against the gods of the nations, here we see sin or wrongdoing being attributed to

---

61. It is unknown why the name of this woman is not mentioned here or in the Hebrew Bible.

62. *T. Joseph* 9:5.

63. *T. Joseph* 7:5.

64. *T. Joseph* 20:1–3.

65. *T. Benjamin* 3:3.

66. *T. Benjamin* 7:1–2.

67. *T. Benjamin* 6:1.

the work of Beliar or evil spirits. Moral boundaries are not couched only in terms of wrong versus good deeds, but also as activities of Beliar versus the will of God. These notions of the spirit world and social pressures on diaspora Jews help to explain their conditions and parallel concepts with the dominant culture on matters of religious, social and moral boundaries.

Moreover, some Jews indulged in astrology and magic. Israel had been warned to abstain from the gods and religious practices of their neighbors, yet some transgressed. Yahweh prohibited idol worship, worship of stars, moon and heavenly hosts (Exod 20:4; Deut 5:8) but not all Jews would comply. The ubiquity of astrology and its apparent efficacy drew many Jews into it – to the extent that some began to link Abraham to astrology. As Solomon was associated with magic so was Abraham associated with some rationale for astrology. Philo indicates that the Chaldean heritage of Abraham is good enough grounds to surmise that he did practice astrology prior to his encounter with Yahweh.[68] Philo did not condone astrology, but he was not immune to its influence either. We find at least one incident where he explains the breastplate of a high priest in astrological parlance.[69] Even a conservative sect like the Essenes could not resist astrology entirely. Members of the community found it useful to employ astrology in the selection of candidates to join their community (4Q186).[70] Moreover, these beliefs and background may be borne in mind when we read of a magi from Abraham's homeland or Persian origin (μάγοι[71] ἀπὸ ἀνατολῶν Matt 2:1, 7, 12, 16) that "saw the star" of Jesus and came to worship him (εἴδομεν γὰρ αὐτου τὸν ἀστέρα ἐν τῇ ἀνατολῇ – Matt 2:2).[72] The NT does not endorse magic and/or astrology, but this observation shows

---

68. Philo, *Spec.* 1:87.

69. Philo, *J. W.* 5.217–218, and E. M. Yamauchi and M. R. Wilson, *Dictionary of Daily Life in Biblical & Post Biblical Antiquity Vol. 1* (Peabody: Hendrickson, 2014), 104. The reader may find Yamauchi and Wilson's chapter on astrology helpful in the way it discusses the origin of astrology and traces its use in the wider social context as well as reference in Old and New Testament texts.

70. Yamauchi and Wilson, *Dictionary of Daily Life*, 104. It is suggested here that perhaps the interest in Enoch and Jubilees in the Qumran sect explains their willingness to embrace astrology to some degree.

71. This word translates as "magicians" or "wise men." The resonance with what the readers knew of magic and astrology is obvious yet our English translations obscure this word to the one who does not read Greek. Matthew refers to the visitors as magi four times in his infancy narrative (Matt 2:1, 7, 12, 16).

72. To translate μάγοι as "wise men" is quite misleading because it denotes not those who possess wisdom per se but "experts in astrology, interpretation of dreams and various other secret arts." The birth of the Saviour of the world is (1) announced to Gentiles and (2) initiates another call of persons to obedient response, from the home of Abraham, to witness and worship him.

(1) its prevalence and (2) astrology as the mode with which God revealed the birth of the Savior of the world to Gentiles.

Philo's spirit cosmology, though influenced by Platonism, is thoroughly Jewish. Its Jewish framework is consistent with the ones aforementioned. The early part of Philo's *Giants* addresses two opposing forces of good and evil, noting that the descendants of Noah were influenced by demons to engage in wicked acts (Gen 6:1–2).[73] He shares the cosmic dualism in which good spirits and demons are active in the world as opposing forces.[74] Apparently, Prince Mastema (evil spirit) initiated and instigated the test of Abraham to sacrifice his son, Isaac.[75] Prince Mastema was shamed when Abraham triumphed in obedience to God (18:12–13). Philo also believed in the indwelling of the Holy Spirit in humans,[76] and the Spirit's role in inspiring prophetic speech.[77] "Philo speaks of the prophet as being completely overborne by the Spirit."[78] The general world concept, relative to the role of spiritual beings, did not differ significantly from non-Jewish cultures in the Greco-Roman world. Beyond cosmology, writers like Philo and Aristobulus sought to harmonize Jewish thoughts and moral philosophy with that of their Greek counterparts. Philo describes Plato "as the sweetest of all writers" or the "most holy Plato."[79] His admiration of Greek culture is quite obvious.

> Zeno is appreciated for having "lived under the direction of virtue to an unsurpassed degree" (Lib 53). Homer is identified as "the greatest and most reputed of poets." The words of Sophocles are in Philo's eyes "as true as the Delphi oracles" (Lib 19), while Euripides is frequently quoted as the quintessential tragedian whose pieces provoked overwhelming applause among the audience in the theatre (Lib 14). The poets in general are spoken of as "educators through all our days" who teach wisdom to the public in the same

---

73. Philo, *Gig.* II (6).

74. Philo, *Gig.* IV (16).

75. Philo, *Jubilee* 17:15–16.

76. Philo, *Al. Int.* 1.31–44.

77. Philo, *Giants* 27.

78. Anthony C. Thiselton, *The Holy Spirit: In Biblical Teaching through the Centuries and Today* (Grand Rapids: Eerdmans, 2013), 29.

79. Philo, *Every Good Man Is Free*, 13.

way as parents do to their children (Lib 143). Philo hardly treats these writers as representative of a foreign or even other culture.[80]

Jews were by no means immune to the religious and social influence of their surrounding cultures and neither were they resilient enough to withstand them. Some Jews were loyal to Jewish conventions, but a significant number proactively dabbled in the practices of non-Jews, even divinations, magic and astrology.[81]

It is noteworthy that these transgressions were not true of all Jews. Members of Jewish sects such as Pharisees and Essenes took strong conservative stances in the homeland. Conversely, Sadducees, who were religious elites with significant influence on temple worship and in the Sanhedrin, were more or less clients to Roman patrons.[82] Thus, the reason we find Jesus in contention with Pharisees so often is partly because of the similarity (not difference) of their teachings; they also emphasized good interpretation of Torah,[83] believed in resurrection of the dead whereas Sadducees neither stressed strict Torah observance nor Jewish customs.[84] For Jesus, the Pharisees' main problem was misunderstanding the spirit of the Law and their misplaced application (see Matt 5–7). There were miracle workers and people with ability to predict the future during the Second Temple period. For example, Josephus predicted the rise of Vespasian to the imperial throne; which came to pass and partly contributed to his lasting relationship with the Flavian dynasty.[85] According to

---

80. M. R. Niehoff, *Philo on Jewish Identity and Culture* (TSAJ 86; Tübingen: Mohr Siebeck, 2001), 138–139.

81. *Contra* P. R. Trebilco, *Jewish Communities in Asia Minor,* 142. Trebilco argues that Judaism in Asia Minor was not affected by the surrounding pagan practices. He sees inscriptions or amulets bearing Jewish and pagan names as the work of Gentiles, but the discussion above suggests the contrary is rather the case.

82. F. J. Murphy, *Early Judaism: The Exile to the Time of Jesus* (Peabody: Hendrickson, 2002), 213–244. This chapter provides a further account of prevailing Jewish movements in Palestine by the time of Jesus. It gives a cursory review of biblical and extra-biblical material relating to the subject matter. The reader gains understanding of the Scribes, Pharisees, Sadducees, Essenes and the Sanhedrin.

83. Josephus, *J. W.* 2.

84. Josephus, *Ant.* 18.12.

85. Josephus, *War* 3.401–403. See W. den Hollander, *Josephus, the Emperors and the City of Rome: From Hostage to Historian* (AJEC 86; Leiden: Brill, 2014), 68–93. Den Hollander provides a very good reconstruction of how the relationship of Josephus and Vespasian developed. These pages aptly place in proper context the impact of his prophetic utterance to the relationship with Vespasian and Titus.

Josephus, the true prophet has the divine spirit whereas the false one does not.[86] The entire ministry of Jesus is framed in the prophetic and messianic hope in Second Temple Judaism. Thus, healing miracles and prophetic utterances were not unique to early Christianity. The main issue is discerning the power in which one performed miraculous acts – *By what spirit do you perform miracles?* In a nutshell, Jewish identity is linked to divine initiative and the call of the great ancestor Abraham. Their sense of belonging, conduct and social boundaries make sense only in the ensuing spirit cosmology under investigation.

## 3.2 Spiritual Beings in Early Christianity

The spiritual dimension of the cosmos in Jewish cosmology was wrapped in their identity as a people of covenant relationship with God. Early Christianity was not a separate movement but one within Judaism. The worldview of early Christians was, therefore, one in which the physical and spiritual dimensions of the cosmos were inseparable, where cosmology and anthropology were fused together. The ministry and message of Jesus were comprehended in light of the fulfillment of Jewish messianic prophesies. I proceed to survey the pivotal role of God or the 'Holy Spirit' in the account of Christian origins, based on the Lukan corpus, the closest we have to a history of the early church, without much attention to the self-evident recurrence and encounters with evil spirits in the other gospels.[87] For Luke Timothy Johnson, "the most important character of all in Luke–Acts may be God, who never directly appears but who in various ways directs the action, and with reference to whom the entire narrative unfolds."[88] Luke's infancy narrative (Luke 1–2) shows that the coming of the Davidic messiah (anointed one) was preceded by an Elijah figure's (John) prophetic ministry also in fulfillment of prophecy. The witness of Simeon and Anna in the temple and their utterances reflect a people who found their messianic hopes being fulfilled in God's timing in their lifetime. In other words, John and Jesus did not come by mere coincidence but by divine

---

86. Josephus, *Ant.* 8.408. Also Thiselton, *The Holy Spirit*, 22–32. Thiselton devotes ten pages to the discussion on the "Spirit in Judaism," and here the reader finds how pervasive the notion of Holy Spirit or Divine Spirit was in the Second Temple Jewish thought.

87. Cf. R. Stronstad, *The Charismatic Theology of St. Luke* (Peabody: Hendrickson, 1984). Stronstad's findings and conclusions suggests that the birth, witness and expansion of the church are all attributed to the work of the Spirit. In other words, the Holy Spirit is pivotal in what God is doing in the new era.

88. L. T. Johnson, *The Gospel of Luke* (Collegeville: Liturgical, 1991), 5.

design and orchestration; they were part of a larger story in the unfolding plan of God. The Spirit was actively involved with John, Elizabeth, Zechariah and Simeon, all within the Jewish eschatological framework.[89] Jesus was named, circumcised and dedicated according to the Jewish custom. His coming into our world was supernatural at its inception. The angel Gabriel (spirit being) announced to a virgin (Mary) that she would conceive a child by the Holy Spirit in contradiction of natural science or human biology. Later, Joseph's suspicion and desire to separate from Mary would be curbed by divine revelation by means of dreams. It is a foundational Christian tenet that the conception and birth of Christ came by divine activity – "the Savior of the world" came through the work of spiritual beings. Both Matthew and Luke devote the first two chapters of their gospels to recount how Jesus's birth came by divine activity, and the Son of God was spared an assassination attempt by divine intervention. For Luke, the Holy Spirit was pivotal at every stage in bringing the plan of God into effect. Even the family's migration to and from Egypt was undertaken by divine guidance. To question this cosmological framework is to cast doubt on Christian origins.

Jesus was publicly acclaimed and affirmed as the Son of God at his baptism, "You are my Son" (Luke 3:22). The Holy Spirit descended on him and he was led by the "Spirit" to be tempted by the devil (Luke 4:1–3). His victory over Satan during temptation commences a Spirit-empowered ministry. Even the weapon used to defeat Satan during his temptation was the "written" word of God (Luke 4). Jesus's triumph in the spiritual contest sets the stage for a ministry marked by remarkable demonstration of power over evil spiritual forces. Central to the teachings and work of Jesus is the idea of the kingdom of God. It triumphs over the ruler of the world and accords freedom to those enslaved by the forces of darkness. As Jesus explains in his hometown synagogue, his ministry is accredited by the Spirit in fulfillment of prophesy.

> And he came to Nazareth, where he had been brought up. And as was his custom, he went to the synagogue on the Sabbath day, and he stood up to read. And the scroll of the prophet Isaiah was given to him. He unrolled the scroll and found the place where it was written, "The Spirit of the Lord is upon me, because he has anointed me to proclaim good news to the poor. He has sent me to proclaim liberty to the captives and recovering of sight to the blind, to set at liberty those who are oppressed, to proclaim the

---

89. D. L. Block, *A Theology of Luke and Acts* (Grand Rapids: Zondervan, 2012), 212–213.

year of the Lord's favor." And he rolled up the scroll and gave it back to the attendant and sat down. And the eyes of all in the synagogue were fixed on him. And he began to say to them, "Today this Scripture has been fulfilled in your hearing." (Luke 4:16–21 ESV)

Luke does not hesitate to place the Holy Spirit at the center of the ministry of Jesus. "The work of the Spirit is probably the most comprehensive aspect of Luke's theology because it spans the period from before the birth of John and Jesus to the later moments of Paul's ministry."[90] Exorcism, miracles and spiritual encounters were regular features in the ministry of Jesus. Moreover, "in the narrative world of Luke's Gospel, Satan genuinely does possess the authority and glory of the kingdom of the world, for many are indeed under his sway."[91] Miracles were pointed to us evidence that Jesus is the son of God who reigns over all (Luke 7:18–23). The manifestation of God's power in this regard, as reported by the disciples, was evidence of God's supreme reign (Matt 10:5–15).

The Gospel of Mark gives prominence to spiritual encounters in Jesus's ministry. We read of a fierce exchange when Jesus was accused of using an evil spirit to cast out devils (see Mark 3:22; Matt 12:24; Luke 11:15; John 7:20; 8:48–52; 10:20). John records miraculous signs, including turning water into wine (John 2), feeding the masses and raising the dead (John 11). John thoroughly reflects the cosmology of his day, even with the divine logos doctrine. The idea of incarnation makes sense only in the spirit cosmology being recounted in this book. Furthermore, the resurrection of Jesus is crucial in how we conceive spirit cosmology in the early church. Paul argues that Christianity stands or falls on belief in the resurrection (1 Cor 15). To believe that Jesus was crucified, died, buried and rose again is to believe in God's ability to infuse life into a dead person to come alive and never die thereafter – in the case of Jesus. The mystery of ascension notwithstanding.

Christian salvation is premised on human transgression in divine plan, the consequence of which includes alienation from God, God's punitive acts, and subservience to the control of evil spiritual forces. The celestial and terrestrial are intertwined in this worldview. Evil spirits lie behind diseases as Satan could also influence people to conduct immoral deeds (e.g. Judas, Ananias and Sapphira [Luke 22:3; Acts 5]). Malevolent forces are constantly engaged in human affairs seeking to rob sinful people of a better life and

______

90. D. Morphew, *The Mission of the Kingdom: The Theology of Luke–Acts* (Cape Town: Vineyard International, 2011), 48.

91. Garrett, *Demise of the Devil*, 41.

plague them with undesirable conditions. Sin is a theological term denoting a breach of relationship with a spiritual being or beings – a violation of the wishes of God that leads to spiritual and social consequences. All humanity stands condemned in this regard, according to the Christian story (Rom 3:23). Rituals of atonement are usually required to pacify transgressors for forgiveness and restoration so that God may continue to be with, bless and protect his people. Premised on Jewish sacrificial systems, the death of Jesus atones for sins and restores humanity's broken relationship with God, according to the Christian gospel. The idea of death by crucifixion serving as a sacrifice for sins, and emphasis on the shedding of Jesus's blood, would, in this context, be understood in the prism of divine-human relationship. Consequently, God requires a response of obedience to his gracious reach to restore humanity's broken relationship with him and in accordance with his moral order. Christian soteriology and eschatology all point towards this end – a time when God's people will live and spend eternity with him. The gospel makes no sense in any epistemology that cannot accept this cosmology. Otherwise, from what are Christians saved and to what end?

The birth of the church is marked by a spiritual experience – in the outpouring of the Holy Spirit on the day of Pentecost in Jerusalem. In the same way that Jesus was conceived by the Spirit so was the church birthed in/by the Holy Spirit. The Pentecost experience fulfills Jewish prophesy of divine visitation in "the last days" (Joel 2:28–29; Acts 2:17–18). The disciples who had ran away or denied knowing Jesus during his trial proceedings would garner courage by the enabling of the Spirit to proclaim the message of the kingdom of God (Acts 2:1–39). Major epochs in the expansion of the church were marked by dramatic spiritual encounters such as the healing of a cripple at the gate of the temple (Acts 3), divine judgement on falsehood (Acts 5), the extraordinary "conversion" experience of Saul[92] (Acts 9), Peter in the home of a Roman centurion (Cornelius) by divine arrangement (Acts 10), and in the launching of the outreach to Gentiles in Antioch (Acts 13). Salvation through Jesus was understood as deliverance from sin, evil forces and moral decadence. The subsequent virtues that are enabled by the Spirit in the convert become

---

92. J. B. Green, *Conversion in Luke-Acts: Divine Action, Human Cognition, and the People of God* (Grand Rapids: Baker, 2015), 4–16. This important and short study delves into the nature of conversion and observes some salient issues in the Lukan narratives. Green challenges the view that "repentance" and "conversion" explain two different experiences, especially as it relates to Paul on the road to Damascus. He argues that the two words may be used interchangeable. I do not use the word "conversion" here as any particular *terminus technicus* but simply as descriptor for non-Christ followers who became members of the church.

the "fruit of the Spirit" (Gal 5:22–23) and talents empowered by the Holy Spirit are "gifts of the Holy Spirit" (Rom 12:6–8; 1 Cor 12:4–11; Eph 4:9–12) in Christian theology. The ministry of Christ's apostles and followers included proclamation and miraculous deeds in various forms including to magicians and exorcists who encountered the power of the Holy Spirit, were converted and became Christ followers in Asia Minor (Acts 19:1–20). The early Christians had a worldview in which spirits were active in human affairs, consistent with Greek, Roman and Jewish world concepts.

The Anatolian discourse in Acts also provides insight into early Christian perceptions of spiritual beings in the region (see Acts 18:24–28 and 19:1–7). A fear of evil spirits and the routine spiritual activity partly accounted for why some converts struggled to break from their past.[93] Elsewhere, Nicolaitans are said to engineer participation in pagan rituals in the region (Rev 2:6, 15).[94] Tradition says that the most bewildering thing that John the apostle witnessed on his visit to Ephesus was Christian participation in pagan rituals.[95] Evidently, the interlink of pagan rituals, entertainment and social life would have presented real problems for Gentile Christ followers in how they negotiated their new identity and social network.[96] Genuine converts openly denounced magic and previously held religious allegiance. "According to the magic theory, the potency of a spell is bound up to its secrecy; if it be divulged, it becomes ineffective. So these converted magicians renounced their imagined power by rendering their spell inoperative."[97] It should come as no surprise

---

93. J. D. G. Dunn, *The Acts of the Apostles* (Valley Forge: Trinity Press International, 1996), 260–261, and I. H. Marshall, *Acts: Introduction and Commentary* (Leicester: Inter-Varsity Press, 1980), 312. While some may interpret the account in Acts 19 to mean that those who brought the magical books did so after their decision to be part of the church, Dunn and Marshall indicate that the narrative rather implies that they had been in the church for some time before bringing those books. Marshall further explains that some of the pagan converts did not change instantly: "The history of the church in Corinth shows that Christians took some time to be persuaded that sexual immorality and idol-worship were ultimately incompatible with Christian faith (1 Cor 6:9–10)."

94. H. B. Swete, *The Apocalypse of St. John* (New York: Macmillan, 1907), lxxv. See also Ladd, *A Commentary on the Revelation of John,* 44 and 52. Ladd explains that the heresy of the Nicolaitans was the same as that of the woman named Jezebel in Thyatira (Rev 2:20) and indicates the influence of pagan practices on some of the churches in Asia Minor.

95. F. Cimok, *A Guide to the Seven Churches* (Istanbul: A Turizm Yayinlari, 1998), 28.

96. P. Borgen, *Early Christianity and Hellenistic Judaism* (Edinburgh: T&T Clark, 1996), 22.

97. F. F. Bruce, *The Book of the Acts* (Grand Rapids: Eerdmans, 1976), 391.

that unbelievers saw evidence of God's ability to protect them from evil forces as good reason to become Christ followers.[98]

Early Christian beliefs were counter to the religions of the social context, though not necessarily indifferent to traditional virtues and some social norms. These Christians saw paganism, magic and astrology as the work of the devil; that magic was commonplace in the era did not evade NT writers.[99] Both Jesus (Mark 5:1–20) and the early church (Acts 19) took for granted that Satan is an active spiritual agent working against God's plan in human affairs. Conner goes as far as to argue that the miracles of Jesus mirror the magic of his day; he clarifies that the difference lay in the fact that Jesus attributed the source of his miracles to God's power.[100] Jesus was even accused of utilizing a demonic spirit (John 7:20; 8:48–52) and employing the spirit of Beelzebul in exorcism (Mark 3:22). Jesus, however, objected to the charge and defended his ministry, saying his miracles derived from the power of God. The apostolic fathers similarly defended Christianity against such accusations and admonished fellow Christians to desist from pagan practices.[101] The *Didache* is emphatic on this issue, "you shall not practice magic, you shall not practice witchcraft or sorcery."[102]

Luke's account of the origin of the church records three encounters with magicians who were all Jews – Simon Magus (Acts 8:4–25), Bar-Jesus (Acts 13:4–12) and the sons of Sceva, the Jewish high priest (19:8–20). Simon had perceived Christian workers as magicians. Bar-Jesus conceived business as usual in wanting to obstruct God's work with magic. At Ephesus, the sons

---

98. Those of us who have been Christian workers in pagan contexts have had to explain what the gospel is and what it means to become a Christian. I have personally burnt charms, talismans and concoctions from people that had been in a church for several months. They did not see the need to do so until they were told they were demonic and needed to be destroyed.

99. See D. E. Aune, "The Apocalypse of John and Greco-Roman Revelatory Magic," *NTS* 33 (1987): 481–501; and S. R. Garrett, "Light on a Dark Subject and Vice Versa: Magic and Magicians in the New Testament," in *Religion, Science, and Magic: In Conflict and in Concert*, ed. J. Neusner et. al. (New York: Oxford University Press, 1989), 142–165. These scholars argue that NT writings show awareness and engage magical practices apologetically in the writings.

100. R. Conner, *Magic in the New Testament: A Survey and Appraisal of the Evidence* (Oxford: Mandrake, 2010). The book makes observations from NT texts and shows parallels between Greco-Roman magic and the miracles of Jesus. While I consider some of his assertions and conclusions to be problematic, he does well to highlight similarities that cannot be taken for granted in the attempt to remove the Lord Jesus (divine) from his immediate socio-religious context. A similar argument had been made previously by M. Smith, *Jesus the Magician: Charlatan or Son of God?* (San Francisco: Harper & Row, 1978).

101. Ignatius, *Ephesians* 19.3; Origen, *Contra Celsus* 1.60; Justin Martyr, *1 Apology* 14; and Tertullian, *On Idolatry* 9.

102. *Didache* 2.2. Cf. *Didache* 5.1.

of Sceva thought they could employ the "name" of Jesus as a typical magic formula to cast out evil spirits.[103] The triumph of Christ over spiritual forces in Asia Minor is echoed by John in his admonition to believers in the region (Rev 9:4; 12:12; 13:8). At the same time, exorcism[104] was a regular feature in the missionary enterprise of the church. The Christ followers were exposed to various forms of religious pressures; they could not participate in rituals associated with pagan deities, even rites of passage for young people were no longer attractive to believers. Imagine the challenge they faced with health care as they could not participate in healing rituals of Asclepius.[105]

Paul met Jewish opposition in Asia Minor.[106] Believers saw satanic work behind human opponents (see Rev 2:9). In Anatolia, Jews who participated in pagan activities were labeled "the synagogue of Satan."[107] In later years, Christ followers renovated and turned pagan temples into places of worship when mass conversions served as a visible manifestation of victory over the forces of evil. An inscription in a northern Arabian church at Ezraa, "The Church of St George" (circa 515 CE), attests to the practice that had been in existence for centuries prior; it reads, "What was once a lodging place of demons has become a house of God; where once idols were sacrificed, there are now choirs of angels; where God was provoked to wrath, now he is propitiated."[108] The belief in personal evil spirits working against Christ followers was commonplace in Christian thought for ages.[109] Church leaders like Justin Martyr argued

---

103. E. Haenchen, *Acts of the Apostles* (Oxford: Basil Blackwell, 1971), 564. Haenchen explains that there were magical papyri found with the inscription, "I adjure you by Jesus, the God of the Hebrews." The sons of Sceva probably thought Paul was invoking such a magical formula in his exorcism and thereby sought to imitate him.

104. The view that Jesus used magic in some healing performances would need to be discussed when addressing exorcism in the gospels, which the limited space and scope of this work does not allow. It is noteworthy that those who pose the question of Jesus's use of magic do accept that the people in Jesus's day believed that demonic influence on people is real.

105. See Letters to the Seven churches in Asia Minor in Revelation 2–3. They enumerate some of the temptations the believers faced and exhort them to stand firm in the strength of the Lord.

106. P. H. Towner, "Mission Practice and Theology under Construction," in *Witness and Gospel: The Theology of Acts*, eds. I. H. Marshall and D. Peterson (Grand Rapids: Eerdmans, 1998), 432–433.

107. The synagogue of Satan is certainly an enemy to the church of God. It is a place where Satan dwells and influences the lives of people. It could even imply that the people were Jews who indulged magic or astrology and still claimed to be devout Jews.

108. R. Burns, *The Monuments of Syria: A Guide* (London: Tauris, 1994), 121.

109. See W. Tabbernee, *Early Christianity in Contexts: An Exploration across Cultures and Continents* (Grand Rapids: Baker, 2014). This is an excellent compilation of essays on early Christianity in a cross section of the empire. A careful reader may observe how the notion of the

that Satan had persistently sought to duplicate and discredit the work of God through mystery cults but to no avail.[110] The prevalence of these beliefs contributed to the flourishing of Christian movements like Nicolaitism and Montanism in Asia Minor towards the end of the first century. Later, beliefs associated with the spirit of those who died for their faith would serve as impetus for theology on Christian martyrdom. "From the second century, if not earlier, relics of martyrs were collected, and, especially in the post-Constantinian era, the cults of individual martyrs or of groups such as the Forty Martyrs of Sabaste were established throughout Asia Minor and Cyprus."[111]

The NT contains several letters attributed to Asia Minor readership apart from Ephesians; these include the Gospel of John, Galatians, Colossians, Philemon, 1 Timothy, 2 Timothy, Titus, 1 Peter, the epistles of John and Revelation. Paul himself spent a significant amount of time in the region. The author of Ephesians would have been familiar with the spiritually intense climate of the region. The spirit cosmology sketched so far, and its implications was not a regional phenomenon but widespread in the empire. It is important that Ephesians, as a letter to Asia Minor with several mentions of activities of spiritual beings, be examined closely in light of the worldview of its provenance. It is anticipated that an analysis of the text against this backdrop would help in placing its communal identity and moral discourse in proper perspective. It will become apparent that the supremacy of God, among other things, would provide security and divine enabling to believers to live as members of the household of God and the believers would be secure as long as they kept good standing with God (see Eph 1:19–23; 4:8–10; Col 1:15–20; 2:15, 20).

The early Christians believed in God who comes to redeem humanity from sin, Satan and death. God reconciles humans to himself through the death of Jesus on the cross. Christ is the Savior, mediator as well as a model for good conduct to the community of faith (Col 2:6). As is well articulated in the writings of Paul, the Holy Spirit fills, edifies and empowers Christ followers to live up to expectation (Rom 12:6–13; 1 Cor 12 and14). Christ followers are *who they are* and *live the way they do* because of the salvific work of God through Jesus Christ and the empowering agency of the Holy Spirit.

---

real presence of spiritual beings in human affairs echoes the beliefs and practices of Christians and non-Christians alike.

110. A. A. Bell, *A Guide to the New Testament World* (Waterloo: Herald Press, 1994), 153.

111. Tabbernee, *Early Christianity in Contexts*, 317.

## Conclusion

The early Christian worldview did not deny the role of spiritual beings in human affairs and neither did Christians play down the existence of evil spirits or the power of God. As a Jew, Paul and his contemporaries held that Satanic powers are real and capable of misleading and negatively influencing the people of God.[112] The cosmology of the former Pharisee went beyond a belief in the immortality of the soul and God's power to effect resurrection of the dead (Phil 3); he embodied the broader worldview of the Jewish community that had its identity rooted in the God of Abraham, Isaac and Jacob. Ephesians does not depart from this framework and/or spirit cosmology of the early Christians. To reject this world concept or minimize its import is to remove a central feature that explains the logic of Christian beliefs. Jesus's ministry included visible demonstration of power over demonic powers and diseases (Mark 2:1–11; 5:1–20). The NT takes for granted that Satan and his cohort exist as personal evil spiritual forces and it also shows how God's power transcends all powers of evil (Jas 2:19; Rev 9:20). We are informed about the nature of evil powers (Luke 4:33; 6:18), their activity (1 Tim 4:1; Rev 16:14), their *modus operandi* (Eph 6:10–20) and their eternal doom (Matt 25:41) in the NT.[113] It is in this framework that we proceed to examine the manner in which this worldview informs group identity and moral aspirations for Christ followers in Ephesians.

---

112. See Baruch 4:7; Pss 95:5; 106:36–37; Gen 3:1–15; 4:1–6; 6:1–10; Lev 17:7; Deut 32:17; 2 Chr 11:15; Isa 13:21; 34:14, etc.

113. Cf. M. F. Unger, *Demons in the World Today* (Wheaton: Tyndale House, 1971), 9.

# 4

# Spirit Cosmology of Ephesians 1–3

The world concept of Greek, Roman and Jewish antiquity in relation to spiritual beings, as seen in previous chapters, was not different from what we find in early Christian thought and literature. Converts to Christianity came from these cultures, lived in these social locations and maintained ties with relatives in these cultures. This chapter examines how this worldview informs the framing and portrait of group identity in this part of Ephesians. We shall observe the role of spiritual beings in the cosmic plan of God and in the unfolding mystery. It will become evident that Ephesians shares the prevailing spirit cosmology of the time and portrays the Christian community as one that was borne out of divine initiative and shaped according to God's pre-planned agenda.

Previously, scholars have noted the prominence of cosmic language in Ephesians,[1] partly accounting for an earlier conjecture that the letter was influenced by gnostic thought.[2] The import of spirit cosmology in the communal identity construction, purpose of existence and ultimate end in the epistle has, however, received little to no significant attention in scholarship. Studies of social identity have utilized social theories, models and concepts to examine Christian communities, often focusing primarily on social-

---

1. A. T. Lincoln and A. J. M. Wedderburn, *The Theology of the Later Pauline Letters* (NTT, Cambridge: CUP, 1933), 89.

2. H. Schlier, *Der Brief an die Epheser* (Dusseldorf: Patmos, 1957); E. Kasemann, *Leib und Leib Christi* (Tubingen: Mohr, 1933).

anthropological issues.[3] Apart from my previous work,[4] studies on the role of spiritual beings in the identity construction of Christ followers in Ephesians has rather been sparse. However, a surface reading of Ephesians 1–3 would show that perhaps the most dominant theme in the first three chapters is divine acts and interventions pertaining to the place of humanity in God's ultimate plan for the cosmos. In this chapter, I examine the role of spiritual beings in Ephesians 1–3, and how it relates to its framing of group identity. For example, is God the main architect in the formation of the community or is it a human endeavor with divine assistance or both? In light of the spirit cosmology, what is the status of humanity in the reordering of the cosmos? I employ traditional exegetical methods against the backdrop of prevailing spirit cosmology to examine the place and role of spiritual beings in the discourse. The three foci in cosmological studies comprise the physical, social[5] and spatial[6] dimensions of the world. The chapter focuses on the spatial/spiritual dimension and investigates the nature of the cosmic framework as it pertains to the role of God, Jesus Christ and Holy Spirit on one hand, and that of the "principalities and powers," on the other.

## 4.1 Invocation for Divine Initiatives and God's Cosmic Plan 1:3–14

The prescript of Ephesians is instructive in the way the standard Pauline greeting establishes shared author-reader identity in Christ and parentage[7]

---

3. Cf. R. Roitto, *Behaving as a Christ-Believer*, 167–172. Roitto makes good observations about the relationship between spiritual beings and issues of identity in Ephesians. The subject, however, gains no significant attention, partly due to the scope of his study, despite the observation that "God is the original cause and fundamental rationale of their identity in Christ" (p. 167).

4. D. K. Darko, "Spirit-Cosmology in the Identity and Community of Ephesians," *Pleroma* 15, no. 1 (2013): 59–71.

5. C. H. Kahn, *Anaximander and the Origins of Greek Cosmology* (New York: Columbia University, 1964), 219–230. The term κόσμος was used to refer to a variety of things such as adornment, order etc. but the emphasis here is the understanding of the world, worldview and concepts of spiritual entities in the universe.

6. Sasse, "κοσμέω etc." *TDNT* 3.871–878. Sasse shows that the idea of spiritual dimension of the cosmos is commonplace in Plato. Spatial/spirit cosmology and the cosmos as creation of θεός is also known in Plato as also in Aristotle, Sasse observes.

7. D. K. Darko, "Adopted Siblings in the Household of God: Kinship Lexemes in the Social Identity Construction of Ephesians," in *The Handbook to Social Identity and the New Testament* (London: T&T Clark, 2014), 333–346. Here, I discuss the kinship framework of the letter and how Paul employs fictive kinship to argue for shared identity of the members of the community otherwise referred to as the household of God. The designation of a spiritual being as the "father" or "mother" of a group or city was commonplace in Greek antiquity, as shown in previous chapters.

to God (inclusive; 1:1–2). Paul is called, commissioned and validated by the will of God – "an apostle of Christ Jesus by the will of God" (1:1). He does not transact his own business but serves as a steward tasked to put God's wishes into effect. "Of Christ Jesus" and "in Christ Jesus" point to the centrality of Christ in the framing of shared identity of the author and readers. They have become children of God with common identity in Christ. The greeting (1:2) also has a collective note in the use of the first person plural – referring to God as the father of Christ followers, and Jesus Christ as their Lord – thereby assuming Paul's affinity for the children of God. Thus, the opening aligns the author and readers with Christ in shared identity with God.

The eulogy (1:3–14) further employs inclusive pronouns (we and you [plural]) to enumerate praiseworthy acts of God: God has blessed "us in the heavenly realms with every spiritual blessing." *Every spiritual blessing* has been interpreted to denote blessings from "the Spirit of God," as gifts of the Spirit[8] or noncorporeal benefits "mediated by the Holy Spirit."[9] The adjective πνευματικός refers to that which pertains to the spirit, qualifying the nature of blessings or the manner in which they were administered. In Pauline usage, we find no precedence in its usage to refer to the "human spirit" or "spiritual life."[10] Its appearance in 1:3 seems to explain the nature of the blessings and not the source. Πνευματικός is not *terminus technicus* for the Holy Spirit and neither is the Holy Spirit named as the benefactor in this context. Further elaboration on the components of these blessings bear no resemblance to what is elsewhere named as the gifts of the Holy Spirit in the Pauline corpus (Rom 12; Eph 4; 1 Cor 12–14). Spiritual blessings do not imply that which is unearthly, immaterial or mystical in substance. The language is better understood against the backdrop of Greco-Roman spirit cosmology. Spiritual beings bless people to succeed materially in the readers' world, as noted in previous chapters. The invocation invites beneficiaries to bless the divine benefactor who provided them with "every spiritual blessing." The blessings in question are all encompassing and supersede anything that could be given by or desired from other deities. The

---

8. F. Thielman, *Ephesians* (Grand Rapids: Baker Academic, 2010), 46–47. Cf. Best, *Ephesians*, 114. For Best, spiritual blessings "belongs to the sphere of the Spirt . . . in the sense in which the gifts of Gal 5:22 are ultimately from the Spirit." Conversely, nothing in this passage suggests that the Spirit is the subject providing blessings. It is noteworthy that the virtue list in Gal 5:22–23 is characterized as the fruit of the Spirit and not as gifts, if one should find Best's explanation useful.

9. R. Schnackenburg, *The Epistle to the Ephesians* (London: T&T Clark, 1991), 50.

10. G. D. Fee, *God's Empowering Presence: The Holy Spirit in the Letters of Paul* (Peabody: Hendrickson, 1994), 32.

subject is God who could mediate these blessings by the agency of the Holy Spirit, Jesus Christ or provide "every spiritual" need in other ways. Blessings from a spirit being do not have to be mediated or administered by a spirit being per se. Moreover, the manner in which beneficiaries access these blessings do not require ethereal state removed from corporeal existence. God is active in human affairs in the mundane and magnanimous. The import is to invoke a deep sense of gratitude among believers in acknowledgement and expression of praise for what God has done to accord them with their new standing with him in the world.

The reference to "heavenly realms . . . in Christ" (1:3) does not suggest that which is heavenly vis-à-vis the earthly.[11] The five appearances of ἐπουράνιος in Ephesians (1:3, 20; 2:6; 3:10; 6:12) are all in plural to denote a spatial dimension of the cosmos[12] and perhaps echoing the concept of multilayer heavens in Jewish cosmological thought (2 Cor 12:2–4 and T. Levi 3:1–8). The heavenlies is the sphere that Christ ascended to and from which he exercises dominion over principalities and powers. It is the celestial realm or unseen dimension of the cosmos inhibited by humans.[13] This is (a) the locus of spiritual blessings (1:3);[14] (b) a place where the ascended Christ exercises dominion (1:20); (c) and where Christ followers are now seated with him (2:6). It is also (d) the realm from which God demonstrates his "manifold wisdom" through the church to the powers (3:10) and the theatre of spiritual warfare between human beings and spiritual powers (6:12). It is "a spiritual dimension of existence, one in which the forces of good and evil conduct [a] campaign for the hearts and mind of people."[15] Yet, this dimension of the cosmos is inseparable from the

---

11. Fee, *God's Empowering Presence*, 667. See the parallel usage in 2:6.

12. *Contra* Lincoln, *Ephesians*, 481.

13. R. M. Pope, "Of the Heavenly Places," *ET* 33 (1911–1912): 366. C. J. A. Lash, "Where Do Devils Live? A Problem in the Textual Criticism of Ephesians 6.12," *VC* 30 (1976): 161–174. A. T. Lincoln, "A Re-Examination of 'the Heavenlies,' in Ephesians," *NTS* 19 (1972/73): 468–483, and H. Odeberg, *The View of the Universe in the Epistle to the Ephesians* (Lund: C. W. K. Gleerup, 1934). Lincoln and Odeberg provide an extensive account of the meaning of the word and its import in Ephesians.

14. Lincoln, "A Re-Examination of 'the Heavenlies,'" 471. For Lincoln, God in Christ has blessed them and sealed them with the Spirit (cf. v. 13). These benefits are to be found in ἐν τοῖς ἐπουρανίοις and ἐν Χριστῷ, the latter phrase signifying that believers partake of the benefits because they are incorporated into the status of ascended Christ as their representative who is himself in the heavenlies.

15. L. J. Kreitzer, *The Epistle to the Ephesians* (Peterborough: Epworth, 1989), 55–56.

current sphere of human existence.[16] Celestial and terrestrial dichotomy does not exist in this cosmic imagination. This framework permeates the letter and the post-enlightenment reader must keep that in mind.[17] The world was conceived differently from the milieu of post-eighteenth-century philosophical mode of reasoning and scientific advancement.

The cosmology allowed for blessings or curses from spiritual beings to impact human lives in tangible ways. In Ephesians, God is the one who initiates the creation of the community of Christ followers; it did not originate as a reaction to an emergency or as an afterthought. God planned it beforehand and chose members before the foundation of the world (1:4). It is purposeful undertaking being executed with good pleasure. That is to say that the community originates with the initiative of God (spiritual agent) to reconstitute certain persons to participate in his grand plan for the cosmos. Human beings are secondary actors. Roberts captures this in the assertion that, "the story of Ephesians is truly the story *of God*, a drama in which God is the primary *actor* and the entire cosmos his *stage* . . . In Ephesians, God is gathering a people for himself and for his purpose."[18] The prepositional phrase ἐν τοῖς ἐπουρανίοις ἐν Χριστῷ is locative, suggesting the realm/sphere of Christ.

Jesus is also instrumental in mediating and executing God's plan. The phrase "in Christ" and its antecedents, "in him" or "in the Lord," appear thirty-four times in Ephesians alone compared to 164 in all of the Pauline corpus[19] to buttress the significant role of Christ in the epistle. Matera's observation in 1:3–13 and concise summation is noteworthy.

> The role of Christ is absolutely integral to the mystery of God's will. Repeatedly employing the preposition "in" (*en*), Paul notes that God has blessed the Ephesians *in* Christ (1:3), and elected them *in* him (1:4). *In* his Beloved he bestowed grace upon them (1:6), and *in* him they received redemption (1:7). *In* Christ, God has set

16. Lincoln, "A Re-Examination of 'the Heavenlies' in Ephesians," 475, 482–483. Cf. R. L. Foster, "Reoriented to the Cosmos: Cosmology & Theology in Ephesians Through Philemon," in *Cosmology and New Testament Theology*, eds. J. T. Pennington and S. M. McDonough (London: T&T Clark, 2008), 108–111. Foster makes a distinction between "the universe" (κόσμος) in the general sense and the heavenly realms.

17. Also M. MacDonald, "Citizens of Heaven and Earth: Asceticism in Colossians and Ephesians," in *Asceticism in the New Testament*, eds. L. E. Vaage and V. L. Wimbush (London: Routledge, 1999), 287.

18. M. D. Roberts, *Ephesians: The Story of God Bible Commentary* (Grand Rapids: Zondervan, 2016), 24. Roberts does not develop this idea but the words capture the essence of what is going on in the eulogy.

19. J. A. Allan, "The 'In Christ' Formula in Ephesians," *NTS* 5 (1958): 54.

forth his favor (1:9), for he had determined to sum up everything *in* Christ, whether in heaven or on earth (1:10). Therefore *in* Christ the Ephesians were chosen (1:11), for they first hoped *in* him (1:12), and *in* him they heard the whole truth (1:13).[20]

The eulogy also ascribes the origin of the church to God's initiative, and it is he who also chose its members (1:4).[21] God chose them before the foundation of the cosmos and held it as a mystery to be unveiled in the present age. He did this out of his own volition and pleasure. Members did not exist when the plan was put in place and neither could they have done anything to bring it into effect. It is noteworthy that divine election and predestination language here apply to the plan and timing of God's act.[22] In other words, he chose them before the foundation of the world to be "holy and blameless" a term that has a cultic, not moral, connotation to denote a people worthy before God. Love was the motivation with which God predestined them to be his adopted children. The imagery is that of a loving God adopting and embracing a select group of people into his household with all rights and privileges appertaining. "Paul is saying that the goal of the adoptive sonship of believers is a relationship with God similar to that of Jesus's own filial relationship with God."[23] Ephesians 1:3–14 is premised on God's benevolence in the form of spiritual blessings: he chose, loved, adopted and sealed them to be a part of his beloved household.[24]

God's blessings are mediated through Christ to the praise of his glory or honor (1:6).[25] Redemption was a common parlance in ancient slave transactions denoting the paying of a price to secure what is otherwise held captive or a manumission and restoration to the original status. The idea of "redemption through his blood" (1:7) points to the shedding of the blood of Jesus for the salvific status of those God selected. God deemed it prudent to choose this

---

20. F. J. Matera, *New Testament Christology* (Louisville: Westminster John Knox, 1999), 148. Cf. C. F. D. Moule, *The Origins of Christology* (Cambridge: CUP, 1977), 54–69.

21. Ephesians addresses the community as a whole. It is important to read it as a product of collectivist culture addressing members in collectivist cultural framework vis-à-vis a twenty-first century individualistic outlook in western countries.

22. This verse does not address the question nor answer the doctrine of predestination.

23. Thielman, *Ephesians*, 52.

24. Thielman, *Ephesians*, 53, and Schnackenburg, *Ephesians*, 54. These two scholars read the phrase "in the beloved" as synonymous with "in Christ." For Thielman (p. 54), it could be taken as the embodiment of the community of Christ. I would argue that the phrase may be taken to refer to beloved members of the community. Christ has mastery over them all (collectively) and members may describe their experience as being "in Christ." The believers are beloved because God reached out to them in love and are loved by God.

25. Note the purpose phrase "to the praise of glory/honor" in the pericope.

way to redeem them from transgressions in "all wisdom and understanding" (1:8). The pre-conversion past was a life of bondage and transgressions (2:1–3), yet the injured deity who has legitimate cause and power for vengeance, chose forgiveness in order to restore relationship with humankind (1:7–8). God's motivation is love and his posture was undergirded by grace. Ultimately, he aims to ultimately sum up the entire cosmos in Christ in the fullness of time (1:9–10), the climax "in which God's mystery in Christ is revealed, realized and developed."[26]

The spiritual blessings aforementioned are not limited to election, adoption, forgiveness and redemption but they also include spiritual marking (sealing) of members as God's own. God has sealed them with the Holy Spirit to mark his ownership, thereby guaranteeing future inheritance for the saints (1:13, 14). The seal identifies them as authentic people of God. Conversely, cosmic powers of evil can no longer claim custody or assume legitimate control over the lives and affairs of the saints. By informing believers that they are sealed Paul is assuring them of their security with God in what is also an invincible mark and a sign to opposing spiritual forces. This should not be taken as a mere metaphor with no theological significance. The custody issue in the cosmic realms resumes in 2:1–3 when pre-conversion life and the current status of unbelievers is portrayed as living under the "ruler of the power of the air." The idea is that members may be identified by the seal of the Spirit in the unseen realms (identity marker) as the Spirit also guarantees their place in the inheritance of the saints. "The presence of the Spirit is the believer's assurance that God will bring his plan to fulfillment, the result of which is the praise of God's glory."[27] Thus, we find God, Jesus Christ and the Holy Spirit working in concert for the benefit of the church. It is important to note that in 1:3–14, the work of these three was pre-planned: It was predestined (1:5, 11), according to his pleasure (1:5, 9), his will (1:5, 9) and plan (1:9, 11). Gentile inclusion did not come by happenstance. Paul (of Ephesians) seeks to "encourage and reassure his Gentile readers that they have been included in God's story by way of Christ and the Spirit."[28] He therefore provides assurance in these salient details about their identity and ultimate destiny in God's plan.

---

26. Schnackenburg, *Ephesians*, 59.

27. W. F. Taylor Jr. and J. H. P. Reumann, *Ephesians and Colossians* (Minneapolis: Augsburg, 1985), 38.

28. G. D. Fee, *Pauline Christology: An Exegetical-Theological Study* (Peabody: Hendrickson, 2007), 343.

## 4.2 A Plea for Divine Aid for Wisdom and Revelation 1:15–23

Paul makes inference to the preceding theocentric eulogy as the basis to express gratitude to God also for two qualities he had heard to be present in the Ephesian believers, namely (a) their faith in the Lord Jesus and (b) love for all God's people. He prays that God may grant them spiritual insight – "spirit/ Spirit," characterized by "wisdom and revelation" – to understand him. The anarthrous use of πνεῦμα could be taken as a reference to the human spirit or inner attitude. Some argue that it refers to the Holy Spirit[29] or specifically the outpouring of the Holy Spirit.[30] Wisdom denotes insight or knowledge whereas revelation conveys disclosure or unveiling what hitherto was concealed. The prayer is offered so that God may provide this need. The sentence structure appears to favor the rendering of πνεῦμα as referring to the Holy Spirit – that he may grant them through Holy Spirit "the wisdom to understand what he also reveals to them about God and his ways."[31]

Prayer is recorded in a letter usually to show the desire of the author for divine assistance on a subject matter. Paul prays that members may have full grasp of their status with God, which others describe as "experiential awareness,"[32] "transformed imagination,"[33] or "interior understanding,"[34] (1) *to know* the hope of God's calling, (2) *to know* his inheritance in the saints, and (3) *to know* the magnitude of God's power (1:18–19). The *knowing* and *revealing* of their status with God are important cognitively in regard to group identity and standing with the Supreme God. Prayer for the community, if granted, would provide impetus for confidence in who they are as a group in relation to God. The petition to "know the magnitude of God's power" follows to reinforce the idea of supremacy of Christ and their security in Christ amidst the pervading influence of dreadful spirits. The power of God in question is the same that resurrected Jesus from death. Knowledge about the exalted position of Christ above principalities and powers is indicative of God's surpassing power at work

---

29. Hoehner, *Ephesians*, 257, and Lincoln, *Ephesians*, 57.

30. *Contra* P. S. Williamson, *Ephesians* (Grand Rapids: Baker Academic, 2009), 47. Williamson claims that Paul is praying that the Holy Spirit be poured out to enable members to "know God more deeply." The problems with Williamson's reading is that he does not understand the term "spirit" to refer to the Holy Spirit.

31. Fee, *God's Empowering Presence*, 676.

32. Talbert, *Ephesians and Colossians*, 56.

33. Gombis, *Drama of Ephesians*, 60–61.

34. Williamson, *Ephesians*, 48.

for the church (1:20–22). This power is immeasurable and effective through the working of his might in Christ.[35]

The passage elaborates on how the "incomparably great power" is demonstrated in the exaltation of Christ. Syntactically, ἥν ἐνήγργησεν ἐν τῷ Χριστῷ (1:20) qualifies ἐνέργεια in the preceding verse to explain how the power was made effective. God demonstrates this might (a) in/by raising Christ from the dead or (b) when he raised Christ from the dead.[36] Both notions may be deduced from 1:20.[37] The efficacy of God's power and what it does for the church provides assurance for Christ followers. Christ is exalted and seated at the position of authority (right hand) with God in the heavenliness.

The resurrection of Christ is a cardinal tenet in Christianity.[38] The early Christians held with certitude that the one who died on the cross also rose from the grave and ascended to the heavens (Acts 1). "They never think of him as one who is dead, or as one who belongs to the past. They speak of him as one who is present with them."[39] Christ's exaltation accorded him a position of favor[40] and power to sit at the right side of God,[41] from where he reigns with God.[42] The "heavenly realms"[43] as a habitat for spiritual beings is where Christ is enthroned; a place where Christ ascended and from where he exercises lordship (1:22). Christ assumes primacy and superiority over the entire angelic

---

35. Lincoln, *Ephesians*, 51. The scope of inquiry will not permit space to explore the conjecture that this prayer contains hymnic fragments. The evidence in support of any quotation or direct parallel with earlier Christian tradition is sparse at best. It is difficult to see how verbatim quotes from hymns or creeds could have been inserted without making an awkward or clumsy reading. Textual echoes from Psalms 8 and 110 are, however, apparent.

36. Lincoln, *Ephesians*, 61; O'Brien, *Ephesians*, 123; F. F. Bruce, *The Epistle to the Ephesians* (Glasgow: Pickering, 1961), 41; C. L. Mitton, *Ephesians* (NCBC; Grand Rapids: Eerdmans, 1973), 69, etc. These commentators and some others translate it as temporal and give no indication as to whether it could be described syntactically as a participle of means or not.

37. D. B. Wallace, *Greek Grammar beyond the Basics: An Exegetical Syntax of the New Testament* (Grand Rapids: Zondervan, 1996), 642. Wallace explains that it carries a temporal force with the intention to connote the *means* as well.

38. Cf. 1 Cor 15:4; 1 Thess 1:10; 1 Pet 1:21.

39. Mitton, *Ephesians*, 69–70.

40. Cf. Ps 80:18; Jer 22:24; victory (Pss 20:6; 44:3; Isa 41:10).

41. Exod 15:6; Ps 89:13; Isa 48:13.

42. H. A. Kent Jr., *Ephesians: The Glory of the Church* (Chicago: Moody, 1971), 30.

43. W. H. Harris III, "The Heavenlies Reconsidered: οὐρανός and ἐπουράνιος in Ephesians," *BSac* 148 (1992): 77. The phrase appears five times in Ephesians (1:3, 20; 2:6; 3:10; 6:12) to carry a local (locative/sphere) sense. See Andrew Lincoln, "A Re-Examination of the 'Heavenlies,'" *NTS* 19 (1972–3): 476. Lincoln explains that, "the phrase is a formula which should be given the same meaning each time it appears in the letter, and the meaning which is most appropriate to all five contexts is a local one."

creation.[44] This cosmic event is intrinsically linked to activities in the material world and affects the conditions of human lives; the victory of Christ goes to benefit the church and insures the spiritual backbone of the community.[45]

Christ is portrayed in superlatives to accentuate his unmatched status both in the material and spiritual dimensions of human existence. God has exalted him far above every spiritual powers that may threaten the readers' place in Christ. The identity of the powers named in this prayer is, however, a debated matter. Carr argues that they comprise angelic host that surround the throne of God. In this view, Christ is elevated to a higher status above all good angels in the heavenly realms. According to Carr, the idea of hostile evil spiritual beings operating in the cosmos against the church was a later development from the second century CE, post-dating Ephesians.[46] Contrary to what previous chapters show about ancient cosmology, Carr indicates that such powers were unknown or nonexistent in the cosmology of the time.[47] But the belief in personal spiritual beings, pagan deities, magic and astrology was widespread in Greek, Roman and Jewish antiquity. The terms Ephesians uses to describe these principalities and powers were similarly employed to characterize such spiritual agents. In Ephesians, good and evil spirits are active in the cosmos (2:1–3; 5:18–21). Increasingly, modern commentators[48] have come to accept the reading of the powers in Ephesians as personal spiritual beings, especially since the 1987 monograph of Clinton E. Arnold.[49]

Ephesians 1 alludes to Psalm 8:6 to express the supremacy of Christ over evil powers. A first century (*ca.*) Jewish text similarly employs terms adduced to here to characterize evil spiritual powers. "And I saw . . . the incorporeal force (δυνάμεις) and the dominions (κυριότητες) and the origin (ἀρχαί) and the authorities (ἐξουσίαι), the cherubim, and seraphim, and the many-eyed thrones (θρόνοι)."[50] The naming of the "powers" is not meant to be an exhaustive list of spiritual forces but a representative list encapsulating the totality of

---

44. Lincoln, "A Re-Examination of the 'Heavenlies,'" 472.

45. The variant in codices Vaticanus (B), ἐν τοῖς ἐπουρανοῖς, shows a manuscript tradition that confirms that the phrase was understood to have local flavor.

46. Carr, *Angels and Principalities*, 93–111.

47. This problematic reading presents a challenge for Carr in his ability or inability to explain the nature of the powers in 6:12. The struggle to do so leads to the conjecture that the explicit reference to evil powers in 6:12 be seen as an interpolation.

48. O'Brien, *Ephesians*, 141–144, Best, *Ephesians*, 172–180, Schnackenburg, *Ephesians*, 77–79, and Lincoln, *Ephesians*, 61–66.

49. Arnold, *Power and Magic*.

50. *Slavonic Apocalypse of Enoch* 20:1.

these powers. Thus, to state that Christ is ὑπεράνω πάσης ἀρχῆς καὶ ἐξουσίας καὶ δυνάμεως καὶ κυριότητος (far above all rule and authority and power and dominion) is not suggesting the ranking order, but an all-inclusive portrait of spiritual forces that have been subjugated to Christ. The adjective "all" qualifies all four nouns to the exclusion of none. These names,[51] which may evoke fear in citizens of Ephesus, have no sway over Christ followers owing to God's work in Christ.[52] They must come to terms with the magnitude of God's power and the triumph of Christ over otherwise dreadful forces in the cosmic realms.

The phrase παντὸς ὀνόματος ὀνομαζομένου (every name that is named) "in heaven or on earth" seems to include every deity or magical name that is not listed. In light of the magical practices of the time, "every name that is named" would resonate with magical names or spells. To talk about a *name* in the Greco-Roman world conjured more than a label or designation. It was a verbal symbol or an essential part of a person's character.[53] A name was vital to the reality to which it was attached (Gen 2:19–20; Mark 5.9).[54] It defined essence and projected identity. "This efficacy of the name was not limited to what we moderns call personal names but included various honorific titles and official appellations that either human or divine bore."[55] Names of gods, demons and heroes were revered. In magic, it is important that one calls on the right name, pronounces it correctly and follows the recipe closely to yield the desired effect. Thus, παντὸς ὀνόματος ὀνομαζομένου denotes the total personality, power and functionality of every name conceivable with authority in the sphere of spiritual powers. Christ has been exalted above them all in perpetuity.

---

51. These terms feature elsewhere in Ephesians 3:10 and 6:12, and in Colossians (1:16; 2:10, 15) suggesting that they were familiar terms.

52. J. P. Lotz, "The *Homonoia* Coins of Asia Minor and Ephesians 1:21," *TynBul* 50, no. 2 (1999): 173–188. Lotz shows from numismatic evidence from the first to fourth century Asia Minor that inhabitants understood the nature of these powers to be closely associated with politics. He points out that the *Concordia* in Rome and *Homonoia* in Greece, for example, became political ideals (p. 177). He argues that the mention of Christ's supremacy over the powers in Ephesians 1:21 and every name that is named resonate with conceptions of inter-city rivalry in Asia Minor and the religious powers. I agree that politics and religion were fused together, but the portrait of these powers in Ephesians (cf. 1:12; 2:2 and 6:10–12) is spiritual and angelic in nature.

53. G. H. P. Thompson, *The Letters of Paul to the Ephesians, Colossians and Philemon – CBC* (Cambridge: CUP, 1967), 42. Also G. von Rad, *Old Testament Theology Vol. 2*, trans. D. M. G. Stalker (New York: Harper & Row, 1965), 81–82. Von Rad discusses the ancient Babylonian and Egyptian understanding of power inherent in a name, to the extent that "an ill-starred name could threaten its bearer's life (cf. Gen 35:18)."

54. Best, *Ephesians*, 173.

55. T. G. Allen, "God the Namer: A Note on Ephesians 1:21b," *NTS* 32 (1986): 471.

The sovereignty of Christ is not confined to one epoch (1:21c). In other words, his supremacy and session at the right hand of God is not a temporary victory. The aeon concepts here are correlative[56] with one aeon continuing to the other.[57] God will not terminate Christ's supremacy at any stage in history. The expression "to put something under one's feet" (1:22) also conjures up imagery from a royal court where defeated foes pay homage to a victorious lord.[58] God has made all principalities and powers subject to Christ. "All" is not limited to the domain of the church but everything that exists in terrestrial and celestial realms (cf. Phil 2:9–11).[59] The enthroned Christ is made head over "everything" for the church (1:22b).

The word "church" features sometimes in the NT to designate a local congregation[60] or a house church,[61] but Ephesians uses it consistently in the broader sense for the community of Christ followers in general. The appearance of the church in 1:22 has been understood to refer to a "heavenly gathering" around Christ in the cosmic realm where believers already participate and enjoy fellowship with him.[62] However, such reading is inspired by the quest for "realized eschatology" and misconstrues the cosmology of Ephesians. The early Christians imagined activities of spiritual beings in human affairs as a reality not removed from the world of their existence. Christ followers are blessed and seated with him in the heavenly realms (1:3; 2:5–6) and assume a position of triumph with him, as a matter of fact. God has thus exalted Christ to the highest honor and place of authority for the benefit of the church. In

---

56. H. Conzelmann, *An Outline of the Theology of the New Testament – Study Edition* (London: SCM, 1969), 316. Conzelmann explains that the two aeons concept is not meant to draw a sharp contrast, but that they should be read with the view that the enthronement of Christ is in a continuum of now and unto the future.

57. *Contra* F. Foulkes, *Ephesians* (Leicester: IVP, 1989), 73.

58. A. G. Patzia, *Ephesians, Colossians, Philemon* (Peabody: Hendrickson, 1984), 171. Patzia suggests that we consider the phrase as an allusion to Psalm 110:1, illustrating Christ's conquest and authority over his enemies. There are two problems with this reading: first, the text presents God as the subject, the one who exalts and gives dominion to Christ. Christ is not doing anything himself to gain this power so we cannot surmise a scenario where he is fighting his enemies; second, πάντα refers to all in the cosmos and not only to the powers aforementioned. If the author had intended to portray such a scenario, he would have done so in 1:21 where he listed the names of the powers.

59. J. D. G. Dunn, *Christology: The Christ and the Spirit Vol. 1* (Grand Rapids: Eerdmans, 1998), 232. Dunn has argued that Christ's exaltation is the fulfillment of God's original purpose of creating humankind. See W. Hendricksen, *Galatians and Ephesians* (Edinburgh: Banner of Truth, 1968), 102.

60. 1 Thess 1:1–2; 2 Thess 1:1, 4; 2:14; Gal 1:2.

61. Rom 16:5; Col 4:15; Phlm 2.

62. O'Brien, *Ephesians*, 146–147.

other words, members have no reason to be afraid of evil powers as long as they maintained their standing as victors in Christ. The resurrection and exaltation of Christ are powerful manifestations of God's power for the benefit of the church (1:19). "The convert would no longer need to live with fear that perhaps one or a number of supernatural 'powers' could be equal or superior to Christ – Christ's power and the authority is exceedingly superior to all categories of 'powers', indeed, 'every name that is named.'"[63] The privileged position with Christ at his exalted position ought to make the readers gratified about God's initiative to adopt, redeem and seal them with the Holy Spirit to ensure their salvation, security and ultimate destiny with him. As human beings, they are privileged beneficiaries of God's initiative to save them from the evil spiritual powers.

## 4.3 Spiritual Death and God's Initiatives for Salvation 2:1–10

The close conceptual link from the end of chapter one and the entirety of chapter two in the epistle would have been more acute if there were no chapter divisions of our texts, as was in the original.[64] Emphasis on the surpassing greatness of God's power that was demonstrated in Christ – to overcome death and restore life – is immediately followed by statements about spiritual death and divine intervention to make believers alive with Christ. The natural death of Christ parallels the spiritual death in trespasses and sins; the resurrection of Christ corresponds with the idea of being raised with Christ; one deals with physical death and resurrection whereas the other addresses spiritual death and salvific status. By implication, the current condition marked by death in sin and trespasses, lust of the flesh or interethnic hostility explains the condition and predicaments with life apart from Christ. It takes divine intervention to deal with the spiritual entanglements, liberate and accord believers a new life in Christ. The pre-conversion past was apart from Christ (2:1–3) but by God's grace the believers are restored, reconciled to God and are able to live peaceably as members of the multi-ethnic household of God (2:4–22). The syntactical function of καὶ (and) at the opening of 2:1 is contrastive, pointing to the life-giving power of God and exalted position of Christ in contrast to the state of their pre-conversion past and current status of unbelievers.

---

63. Arnold, *Power and Magic*, 56.

64. The chapter division of our New Testament was not part of the original Greek text. They were introduced in the twelfth and thirteenth centuries by the Archbishop of Canterbury, Stephen Langton (1150–1228).

The horrific past is sharply contrasted by God's act of salvation in one long sentence (2:1–7), perhaps to emphasize the gracious underpinning and motivation of God's intervention. They were "dead in transgressions and sins." The inclusive tone (2:3) continues the collective framework of the author and his shared identity with the readers. A close reading reveals no attempt to classify or distinguish Jewish and Gentile Christ followers. The entire human race is dead in transgressions and sins (see Rom 3:23). The fitting verdict is stated as being guilty and deserving the judgment of God or divine retribution: *we* "were by nature children of wrath" (ἤμεθα τέκνα φύσει ὀργῆς ὡς καὶ οἱ λοιποί[2:3 ESV]). Moreover, "death in transgressions and sins" has both moral and spiritual connotations.[65] It is reminiscent of the Lukan parable where the lost son was "dead, and is alive again" (Luke 15:24 ESV). It is not figurative[66] but "a factual statement of everybody's spiritual condition outside Christ."[67] Death and sin were connected in Jewish thought, and a person who sinned could be characterized in these terms.[68] The words (transgressions and sins) are hendiadys buttressing the point of alienation from God – no life with God and hence the consequences of life apart from God. To "transgress" is to take a false step, cross a known boundary or deviate from the right path whereas "sin" is a theological term denoting the idea of missing the mark or falling short of a standard.[69] The two feature elsewhere to encapsulate a wide range of ungodly desires and corrupt mindset (thoughts, inclination etc.).[70] They are also used interchangeably in the NT (see Rom 5:12–21) and seem to denote sin in its fullness in this context.

The "then" and "now" schema makes a sharp contrast between the past condition and current status. The believers once walked[71] or conducted

---

65. Rom 16:13; Rom 7:9, 10, 13.

66. *Epictetus, Diss,* I. 3.3; 2.19.27. The Stoics used the word figuratively and regarded things that are not of highest significance to the mind or spirit as being "dead" (*M. Ant.* 2.12.1; 12.33.2). As Lincoln explains, "that which a person had in common with the animal world and which separated him or her from the divine was deemed to be dead." (Lincoln, *Ephesians,* 92).

67. J. W. R. Stott, *God's New Society: The Message of Ephesians* (Leicester: Inter-Varsity Press, 1979), 71. Despite the fact that νεκρός is not typically used for a living being, the author employs it here to portray their spiritual condition.

68. Ezra 3:7; Wis 2:24; Ecclus 25:24; Ezek 18:20; 4 Ezra 3:25f; 8:59; Baruch 54:15, 19. Cf. Pss 13:1–3; 30:3; 31:12; 88:3–6.

69. Stott, *God's New Society,* 71.

70. J. Eadie, *Ephesians* (Grand Rapids: Baker, 1979), 119.

71. J. P. Samply, J. Burgess, G. Krodel, and R. H. Fuller, *Ephesians, Colossians, 2 Thessalonians, The Pastoral Epistles* (Philadelphia: Fortress, 1971), 14–15.

themselves not as they ought (2:2).[72] Their previous way of life was rather subject to a variety of sins and alienation from God: It was life "according to the age of the world" (κατὰ τὸν αἰῶνα τοῦ κόσμου τούτου). The αἰῶν here is taken (by some) to refer to a personal spiritual power paralleling the "ruler of the . . . air" and "spirit" in 2:2. The appearance of the word in magical texts in reference to spiritual beings is the reason some have suggested that a similar usage is in play here. For example, the "master of all" and "the ruler of the universe" is designated as the "Aion of Aions"[73] in the PGM. As one scholar notes, "the devil had many names in contemporary Judaism and early Christianity and the adoption of the name of a pagan god or evil power would not be unexpected, especially since 'this aeon' already possessed an evil connotation."[74] While the magic usage seems to support the argument for a personal spirit being, αἰῶν in 2:2 rather seems to have temporal connotation, there is no NT usage of the term for a personal evil power. The word αἰῶν features also in 2:7 with temporal connotation; it is rather unlikely that its import here is meant to be different from the second feature in the same sentence. I find the reading that befits the context to be the temporal idea.[75] In other words, they conducted themselves as unbelievers according to the social forces of the age due to their spiritual condition (death in sin). "The *age* of this world" is the systems that contradict God's design for humanity and "represents organized evil in the form of peer pressure, ideologies, systems, and structures that provide us with a script of living life totally apart from God and his purposes."[76] The age of this world engenders corrupt behavior and rebellion against God.

The pre-conversion life is further described as one that was lived under the control of an evil spiritual force – τὸν ἄρχοντα τῆς ἐξουσίας τοῦ ἀέρος.[77] The locale from which the spiritual agent exerts control or mastery is "the heavenly realms." Thus, an unseen spiritual agent controls human lives and affairs – prior to salvation in Christ Jesus.[78] Walter Wink dismisses this spiritual concept and argues for a social and existentialist reading of the text to the effect that

---

72. BDAG, 649.

73. PGM IV. 2190.

74. Best, *Ephesians*, 204.

75. Lincoln, *Ephesians*, 95, and O'Brien, *Ephesians*, 158–159.

76. Arnold, *Ephesians*, 143.

77. Cf. John 12:31; 14:30; 16:11; cf. Matt 9:34; 12:24; Mark 3:22; Luke 11:15.

78. O'Brien, *Ephesians*, 159.

Ephesians describes the past here as a world-atmosphere that was subject to the exploitation of destructive social forces.[79]

> It is rather the invisible dominion or realm created by the sum total of choices of evil. It is the spiritual matrix of inauthentic living . . . it is in short, what we mean today by such terms as ideologies, the *Zeitgeist*, customs, public opinion, peer pressure, institutional expectations, mob psychology, jingoistic patriotism, and negative vibes. These constitute "the power of the air," the invincible but palpable environment of opinions, beliefs, propaganda, convictions, prejudices, hatreds, racial and class biases, taboos, and loyalties that condition our perception of the world long before we reach the age of choice, often before we reach the age of speech.[80]

This reading fails to provide adequate explanation to how the readers in Asia Minor would have understood the phrase "according to the ruler of the power of the air." Wink does not examine the phrase in context and fails to comment on the reference to the sphere of operation given as the "air" (ἀήρ).

As in Ephesians 2, "air" (ἀήρ) customarily denotes the realm or operational jurisdiction of evil spiritual forces in the PGM and in Hellenistic Jewish literature.[81] For example, the Testament of Benjamin refers to ἀερίου πνεύματος (3:4). Wink's interest in social justice, noble as it is, overreaches by importing foreign ideas into the text. The notion being conveyed is that of a world and lives that were subject to the control of a spiritual agent. This spirit controlled the lives of Christ followers prior to conversion and currently work in the lives of unbelievers.[82] This is not a strange concept in the milieu. The NT refers to such a spiritual entity elsewhere as the "prince of demons"[83] and "the ruler of the cosmos."[84] To live according to the "ruler of the air" then may be another

---

79. W. Wink, *Naming the Powers: The Language of Power in the New Testament* (Philadelphia: Fortress, 1984), 84.

80. Wink, *Naming the Powers*, 84. Wink points out that they are evil but cannot be described in terms of demons even though Christians wearing the invisible armor of God could be protected from their influence.

81. PGM I. 115–130, 175–184; IV. 2699; *T. Levi* 3:1–3; Philo, *Spec.* I. 66; *Plant.* 14; *Gig.* 6, 7.

82. Lincoln, *Ephesians*, 97.

83. Matt 9:34; 12:24; Mark 3:22; Luke 11:15.

84. John 12:31; 14:30; 16:11.

way of stating that they were exposed to the influence of Satan.[85] "Paul is *not* asserting that all the unredeemed are indwelt personally by Satan through demons. His working in their lives is so strong, however, it is just as if he were inside them, working inside out."[86]

Paul elaborates on the activities of the spirit among unbelievers. Unbelievers are subject to the influence of the spirit that engineers and energizes people to live in disobedience to God.[87] The feature of two opposing spiritual beings here cannot be missed, namely living κατὰ τὸν ἄρχοντα τῆς ἐξουσίας τοῦ ἀέρος as tantamount to living as children of disobedience to God and subject to the wrath of God. "Sons of disobedience" is a Hebraic term for people whose lives are characterized by rebellion against God.[88] Elsewhere, the phrase describes a people of "unbelief" (John 3:36; Acts 14:1–2) or disobedience (see Rom 10:21; 2 Tim 3:2). In Ephesians 2, it denotes disobedience as rebellion against God. Thus, unbelievers are currently exposed to spiritual dominion, the power that energizes and influences them to act in disobedience to God. The author further describes another aspect of the pre-conversion past (2:3), as a people who conducted themselves in "the cravings of our flesh" (ἐν ταῖσ ἐπιθυμίαις τῆς σαρκὸς ἡμῶν). Επιθυμία is a morally neutral word (1 Thess 2:17; Phil 1:23) usually carrying a negative connotation in the NT. It usually appears in association with the flesh to imply life that is governed by uncontrolled or ungodly passions and a corrupt mindset.[89] The link of "flesh" to the "mind" here underscores the fact that these desires emanate from thought processes and appetites of the body. The mind refers to the "reasoning, reflections, conclusions formed by the thinking mind as these direct our volition and the resulting acts."[90] The word is rarely used outside the Pauline corpus (4:18 and Col 1:2).[91] However, as Arnold observes, "the 'flesh' is the inner propensity and inclination to do evil. It is our creatureliness, infected by the implications of

---

85. Cf. Gombis, "Ephesians 2 as a Narrative of Divine Warfare," 410; R. H. Riensche, "Exegesis of Ephesians 2:1–7," *LQ* 2, no. 1 (1950), 72 (70–74); P. D. Simmons, "The Grace of God and the Life of the Church – Ephesians 2," *RevExp* 76 (1976): 476–506.

86. E. Murphy, *Handbook of Spiritual Warfare* (Nashville: Thomas Nelson, 1992), 397.

87. Patzia, *Ephesians*, 179. Cf. Luke 11:14–26; John 13:2; Acts 5:3; 2 Thess 2:9.

88. Cf. Prov 33:5; 2 Sam 7:10; 2 Thess 2:3.

89. T. K. Abbot, *The Epistle to the Ephesians and to the Colossians* (Edinburgh: T&T Clark, 1974), 43.

90. R. C. H. Lenski, *The Interpretation of St. Paul's Letters to the Galatians, Ephesians and Philippians* (Minneapolis: Augsburg, 1937), 411. See Lenski's explanation on how the use of σάρξ and διάνοια in this sentence relate to the idea that they were objects of God's wrath by their very nature.

91. 1 Pet 1:13; 2 Pet 3:1; 1 John 5:20.

the fall of Adam, that propels us to act in ways contrary to what God would have us do."[92] This portrait of life without Christ (2:1–3) provides important insight into the spirit cosmology. Human life in that world is characterized as "death," implying spiritual distancing from God (sin) and in the capacity to be morally upright (trespasses).[93] Human life is subject to spiritual control and stands inept in the ability to control desires of the flesh. Thus, lack of sound moral judgement, moral failings and ungodly desires are the consequence of having no life with the true God. The alienation from God render humans susceptible to the influences of the age in rebellion against God.

The last clause in 2:3 (first half of the sentence) infers from preceding statements to provide the logical verdict on people under such conditions; they were by nature objects of God's of wrath. In other words, they deserved a punitive response in the form of divine vengeance. It is noteworthy that apart from the community being a pre-planned initiative of God, their prior moral, social and spiritual condition were prone to the wrath of God and subject to chastisement. It is nothing short of anachronism to read "by nature" as referring to the "original sin doctrine." It does not refer to judgment on human character but the state of unbelievers[94] in relation to God.[95] This was the condition of all humanity in relation to God outside the community of faith (2:3).

Ephesians 2:1–3 describes the pre-conversion past as a state of spiritual death and one that is controlled by an evil spirit. Believers are saved from this condition and state of affairs: (i) the environment ("the age of this world"), (ii) the control of a personal spiritual power ("the prince of the power of the air") and (iii) the desires of the flesh, which are sinful acts and thought patterns.[96] Human life is under one spiritual power or the other. There is no neutral ground in divine-human relationships. Unbelievers are under "the prince/ruler of the power of the air" whereas believers are saved to maintain a good

---

92. Arnold, *Ephesians*, 143.

93. I do not dispute the possibility of hendiadys but these two words even as hendiadys may still have this interface connotation.

94. Cf. Rom 1:18; 2:5, 8; 3:5; 4:15; 5:9; 9:22; 12:19; 13:4, 5.

95. Best, *Ephesians*, 211, and F. F. Bruce, *The Epistles to the Colossians, to Philemon and to the Ephesians* (Grand Rapids: Eerdmans, 1984), 285. The way Best explains the phrase fits the context where the author's main aim is to make them aware of the state of unbelievers, a condition in which they once were. On the other hand, Bruce suggests that the dative form of φύσις (φύσει) be translated "by birth" to imply that all humanity (both Jews and Gentiles) inherited some sins from Adam that placed them under the condemnation of God. However, unlike Romans 5 where Paul explicitly put the whole of humanity in such state, our pericope seeks to explain the pre-conversion past and the current state of unbelievers in a manner that makes Best's interpretation preferable.

96. O'Brien, *Letter to the Ephesians*, 162.

standing with God. These motifs are not foreign in the ancient world. Pagan gods did punish people when provoked to wrath or called upon to avenge. Israel saw the severity of God's judgment in punitive retaliation against sin; here God makes a dramatic reversal to accentuate his gracious act of salvation. Paul recalls the horrendous past and sharply contrasts it with God's gracious response before completing the long sentence in Greek (2:1–7).

The second half of the sentence makes antithesis with God's initiative, character and intervention to those who were "by nature deserving of wrath." God abounds with mercy and thus showed mercy (Exod 34:6; Ps 103:8; Jonah 4.2); it is out of his reservoir of mercy that he reaches out towards us with great love. The first person "us" is comprehensive to include the Jewish author and his predominant Gentile readership. Ephesians does not make distinction between Jew and Gentile believers but characterizes the urban church as one interethnic community. Moreover, the inclusive phrase καὶ ὄντας ἡμᾶς νεκροὺς τοῖς παραπτώμασιν (2:5) suggests that the author did not exclude himself in the previous condition that prompted God to act. It is God who made *us*, the spiritually dead, alive together with Christ. As if to say we could not have helped ourselves or earned our way, hence the parenthetic interjection "by grace you [plural] have been saved" (2:5). This chapter does not reason vertically to advance notions of ethnic superiority or inferiority and neither does it promote a supersessionist agenda to make Gentiles succeed Jews in God's eschatological plan. Ephesians does construct horizontal framework that eliminates Jew and Gentile demarcations in God's community. The community is one in which ethnic and racial distinctions are retained in the interethnic and interracial household of God. Notions of ethno-racial hierarchy, replacement theology or color blindness are not addressed in this letter. Members of God's community are saved from Jewish and Gentile backgrounds to belong to a community in which previous stereotypes and boundaries of differentiation do not matter anymore. Ethnicity is not erased or marginalized but helps to demonstrate the powerful image of unification of Jews and Gentiles in God's household (2:19), even to principalities and powers (3:9–10).

God has brought to life the spiritually dead and seated them with Christ in the heavenly realms. This shared exaltation and experience in the heavenly realms has often been misunderstood. The idea of "resurrection" and "sitting with Christ in the heavenlies" are traditionally read as the realization of what was otherwise an eschatological experience. First, the heavenly realm is not apart from life on earth but interfaces with human existence. Second, the dead in question are not presumed to be physically deceased, unlike Christ, but the metaphorical "death" is in reference to their spiritual and moral condition (2:1, 5).

To be raised from death in trespasses and sins may not be misconstrued as premature post-mortem experience or bodily resurrection[97] of the dead; the new life with Christ is not suggestive of future eschatology being realized at the present. The purpose clause indicates that God made this happen so that "in the coming ages he might show the incomparable riches of his grace" (2:7). The idea is that God gives out of his abundant stock; that kindness is made manifest from the large reservoir of his grace to accord salvific and productive lives.

A new sentence opens to buttress the point that salvation comes as a result of divine purpose – τῇ χάριτι ἐστε σεσωσμένοι διὰ τῆς πίστεως (2:8). Forensic reading that associates this phrase (2:8) with a courtroom scenario in which guilty sinners are being acquitted lacks evidence and persuasive power on close reading.[98] The emphasis is on how God redeemed a people dead in trespasses/ sins, from living according to the "age of this world," from being subject to "the ruler of the power of the air," and from following the "desires of the flesh and mind" (2:1–2). Salvation is not by merit but by grace. Grace is a favor received, generous outreach or favor to another person (Gal 2:21; 5:4; Rom 6:14).[99] "Grace is that reality in God that moves Him because of His own character to do good to those who are not only undeserving, but who deserve exactly the opposite."[100] It is the charitable quality of God extended to the spiritually dead and morally bankrupt. "'By grace you have been saved' draws the readers' attention to God's sovereign freedom from obligation in saving them."[101] Humans are not architects of the community; it is God's creation borne of his plan. It is God's initiative to redeem humanity from life under the dominion of one spiritual entity to the control and destiny of their divine Creator.

To avoid misconceptions of human involvement and deflate any sense of pride, Paul negates such posture with two clarifying clauses – (a) "this is not from yourselves, it is the gift of God" and (b) it is "not by works, so than no one can boast' (2:8b–9). The word for gift (δῶρον) carries the sense of a

---

97. Bruce, *Colossians, Philemon and Ephesians*, 286–287. Bruce explains the notion of being raised with Christ as the realization of a future event in the present, namely the resurrection of the dead.

98. Bruce, *Colossians, Philemon and Ephesians*, 289.

99. Deut 5:10; Ps 89:28; Isa 54:8–10.

100. T. Pennington, "All the World's a Stage: Understanding the Ultimate Purpose of Our Salvation (Eph 2:7)," *MSJ* 22, no. 1 (2011): 104.

101. Lincoln, *Ephesians*, 104.

present (Matt 2:11) or votive gift.[102] God is the benefactor while humans are beneficiaries of his unmerited favor. Moreover, believers are not the lead actors of their fate or destiny; they are privileged recipients of God's benevolence. The community did not come about as a result of anything they have earned, mobilized or created on their own – not by works. Some have taken "works" to refer to works of the law[103] but the Gentiles would probably hear "human effort" and caution against pride that accompanies a sense of accomplishment.

The identity of the church as God's new community and their purpose of existence is articulated concisely in 2:10. They are God's handiwork ($\pi o i \eta \mu \alpha$). As a word originating from the textile industry, the implied import is that they are God's product (woven fabric). God created them in Christ Jesus for good works – κτισθέντες ἐν Χριστῷ Ἰησοῦ ἐπι ἔργοις ἀγαθοῖς (2:10). They constitute an entity of God's creation designed to meet his cosmic plan, even their good deeds in the community were planned ahead (2:10). The gift of grace evokes gratitude and inherent obligation for commensurate response.[104] Usually, the benefactor does not oblige stated demands from the beneficiary but the programmatic undertaking of a pre-planned agenda of God's unfolding mystery requires articulation of befitting conduct in the new community. Thus, grace must dispel any sense of entitlement and evoke a deep sense of gratitude – exhibited in good conduct that God has already determined as the fitting *modus vivendi*. God chose them before the foundation of the world (1:4); he predestined them according to the purpose of his will (1:5–6); the mystery of his will is being made known also according to his purpose (1:9, 11); and he plans to unite all things in Christ in the fullness of time (1:10). As his creation, he saved them in order that they might conduct themselves according to the new way of life prepared beforehand. God is in charge and nothing about the community came by coincidence. "Salvation is not from works, but it is *for* works, that

---

102. The language resonates with Greek sacrifice to the gods. Usually, this is the word that is used in such context as we find in Matt 15:5; Mark 7:11. Cf. Demosthenes, *De Corona* 18:109; Aristotle *Ath. Pol.* 55.5.

103. Muddiman, *Ephesians*, 111.

104. See J. M. G. Barclay, *Paul and the Gift* (Grand Rapids: Eerdmans, 2015), 11–78. Barclay's survey of the nature of grace/gift in anthropological studies and ancient texts is very instructive in this regard. The polyvalent or multifaceted understanding of grace or gifts in the ancient world becomes evident. It also becomes apparent that grace does come without reciprocal expectations. I think that Barclay has a tendency to overstretch the nature of the inherent obligation to reciprocate to counter Lutheran theology, but the point cannot be overlooked that grace does not mean free for nothing or reception in the spirit of apathy. Grace or gift does not usually come with demands from the benefactor, as such, but culturally imbedded expectation in the way gratitude is expressed – gratitude was one of the highest virtues in antiquity.

is, living is living obediently and productively."[105] Salvation does not come by following a particular four point protocol followed by a sinners' prayer to attain membership in a local church, but a break from sin, deliverance from the control of evil spiritual powers and freedom from ungodly desires of the flesh and mind. "The salvific vision is more than individualized relationship with God but includes real effect on collective social identity and human interaction across ethno-racial lines."[106]

## 4.4 Fellow Members in the Household of God 2:11–22

The artificial paragraph break between 2:1–10 and 2:11–22 in English misconstrues the portrait of the holistic nature of God's salvific plan, as I have argued elsewhere.[107] The readers are called upon (2:11–12) to remember the spiritual and social divide between Jews and Gentiles prior to the enactment of God's plan. Jews had hitherto employed vitriolic labels for Gentiles and characterized them as the "uncircumcised," and excluded "other" from God's covenant community. The Jewish author acknowledges these stereotypes by calling for a reminder that they (the Gentile believers) were (a) separate from Christ, (b) excluded from citizenship in Israel, (c) stood as foreigners to the covenants of promise and (d) a people without God (2:12) as if to say this was the true condition of who they were in their past. As Gentiles, they had no messianic expectation or hope for redemption.[108] Put differently, they had no relationship with the true God to make such expectation possible. The phrase ἄθεοι ἐν τῷ κόσμῳ does not imply that Gentiles did not worship or know of deities; ἄθεοι is not akin to atheism in their polytheistic social context. It rather describes the posture of those who rejected certain gods. It was the designation used for those who neglected to participate in religious rites that

---

105. K. Snodgrass, *Ephesians: The NIV Application Commentary* (Grand Rapids: Zondervan, 1996), 107.

106. D. K. Darko, "What Does It Mean to Be Saved? An African Reading of Ephesians 2," *Pent* 24, no. 1 (2015): 52. The nature of salvation is couched in a collective framework. I have argued in this article that the usual reading of 2:1–10 as a separate pericope from 2:11–22 misconstrues the nature of salvation expressed in the letter.

107. Darko, "What Does It Mean to Be Saved?," 44–56.

108. C. Hodge, *The Epistle to the Ephesians* (Grand Rapids: Eerdmans, 1994), 128. The expression "having no hope" has been understood by others as a hope for resurrection but the most probable explanation, which most commentators affirm, is reference to the messianic hope. It may be noted that a belief in the resurrection of the dead was not widespread in Judaism. In most cases when the prophets talk about the last days (e.g. Joel and Jeremiah) they were looking at the time when the Messiah would rule with justice, and when he would put a new spirit and mind in the people.

were important to the polis.[109] Josephus used ἄθεος in reference to Jews in this regard.[110] The point in Ephesians 2 is that Jews considered Gentiles to have no relationship with the true God in their pre-conversion past. These stereotypical demarcations and interethnic disparity is a Jewish portrait of the state of affairs outside and prior to membership in God's new community, an effect of spiritual and social conditions marked by "death in sin and transgressions" (2:1–3).

Moreover, hopelessness accompanied life without the true God. "They were, in the widest sense of the word, hopeless."[111] The then-now antithesis (2:13), as in 2:4, indicates a radical change of status brought about by the work of God "in Christ." God is still the main architect in the construction of the new community and its identity. God brought those who were once far near through "the blood" of Christ.[112] Christ functions here in a prominent role as the means and mediator of peace; "Christ can be said to be not only a peacemaker or a bringer of peace but peace in person."[113] He overcame hostilities and neutralized social barriers in his flesh, thereby reconciling Jews and Gentiles to God.[114] Ephesians suggests that the cause of social divisions is a lack of relationship with the true God. It gives no prerogatives to Jews and finds remedy to interethnic disparity to reside first in reconciling both Jews and Gentiles to God. Gentiles are not a mere addition to a Jewish community; both are reconciled on equal terms to God.[115] Christ has reconciled, nullified the "dividing wall of hostility"[116] and created one "new humanity" in himself. In Ephesians, reconciliation is not restoration of broken relationship between two ethnic groups, but conciliation of all humanity to God. God's plan of salvation and his cosmic vision have vertical and horizontal relational effects; Christ reconciles people to God and breaks down walls of separation between people groups.

---

109. M. Y. MacDonald, "The Politics of Identity in Ephesians," *JSNT* 26, no. 4 (2004), 430. MacDonald provides elaborate explanation on the etymology of the word.

110. Josephus, *Ag. Ap.* 2.146–149.

111. Hodge, *Ephesians*, 128.

112. It is unclear whether the "blood" was a ransom or atonement for sins in this verse.

113. Hodge, *Ephesians*, 140.

114. L. Mitton, *Ephesians* (Grand Rapids: Eerdmans, 1989), 105.

115. Lincoln, "The Church and Israel in Ephesians 2," 615.

116. The language of "dividing wall" appears only here in the NT. It could be taken as an allusion to the wall separating Jews and Gentile courts in the temple or a reference to the curtain separating the holy place from the holy of holies. It may also resonate with the rabbinic tradition in which the law fences off heathen Gentiles away from the people of God. Another reading that seems plausible in this context is the notion of the dividing wall as enmity between Jews and Gentiles.

The enmity between Jews and Gentiles,[117] owing to the covenant and regulations pertaining to Jewish particularism, has been neutralized in Christ.[118] The "impenetrable fence protecting Israel from the impurity of Gentiles"[119] no longer exists. Christ has abolished the law and its impetus for ethno-racial divisions in no uncertain terms. Therefore, Gentiles are no longer aliens and strangers but fellow citizens with Jews in God's commonwealth.[120] "Divisions and distinctions no longer exist as far as the standing of any before God is concerned."[121] The community is a new creation by the God of creation.[122] Unity in the multi-ethnic church is not a work in progress but comprises the nature of God's household from its inception. This does not suggest erasure of ethnic differences, but that ethnicity does not matter in the community created by God.[123] Jews and Gentiles have equal access in one Spirit; God is the father of all, and they are both members of God's household (2:18–19). Their new identity is couched in kinship parlance to depict God as the father and members as his adopted siblings (1:5) in the multi-ethnic household (2:19).[124]

117. The ascription, "Gentiles in the flesh" denotes ethnic demarcation vis-à-vis other references to "Gentile" in 3:1, 6, 8 and 4:17 as an adaptation of Jewish stereotypes to describe non-Christians (outsiders).

118. B. L. Melbourne, "Ephesians 2:13–16: Are the Barriers Broken Down?," *JRT* 57/58, no. 2 (2001–2005): 115. Melbourne puts it well: "Distinctions such as liberal and conservative, black and white, Caribbean and Latin American, or Asian and Hispanic are realities that are legitimate because of our diversities, but they should be celebrated and not used to erect barriers that Jesus died to destroy."

119. A. T. Lincoln, "The Church and Israel in Ephesians 2," *CBQ* 49 (1987): 611. Also *Letter of Aristeas*, 139, 142.

120. W. O'Neil, "No Longer Strangers (Ephesians 2:19): The Ethics of Migration," *Word & World* 29, no. 3 (2009): 230.

121. F. Foulkes, *The Epistle of Paul to the Ephesians* (Grand Rapids: Eerdmans, 1979), 81. See A. Resner, Jr. "Maintain the Broken Wall: Ephesians 2:14–18," *ResQ* 32, no. 2 (1990) 121–125. Resner focuses on the social implications of the text relative to contemporary Christian communities. Also W. Barclay, *Galatians and Ephesians* (Philadelphia: Westminster, 1976), 117.

122. Fong, "Addressing the Issue of Racial Reconciliation," 572. Nothing in this text indicates what believers ought to do to promote unity. The text describes what God has done by his grace independent of human effort or merit. "Without destroying what they possessed culturally, racially or linguistically, Christ gave every converted Jew and Gentile a new citizenship that enabled them to fellowship equally with one another in the Church while preserving their ethnicity to mingle among those in the world for the purpose of evangelism" (572).

123. Lincoln, *Ephesians*, 144. B. H. Dunning, "Strangers and Aliens No Longer: Negotiating Identity and Difference in Ephesians 2," *HTR* 99, no. 1 (2006): 16.

124. D. K. Darko, "Kinship in Discipleship: The 'Father' Image of God and Disciples as 'Brothers' in Matthew's Sermon on the Mount," in *Exploring Biblical Kinship*, CBQMS 55, eds. J. C. Campbell and P. J. Hartin (Washington, DC: Catholic Biblical Association of America, 2016), 239–255. Here, I demonstrate how the kinship framework of the Sermon on the Mount sheds light on its ethical message. The notions of concord, loyalty and honor associated with Greco-Roman kinship (natural or fictive) form the basis of early Christianity and professional

The temple imagery advances the notion of kinship with physical structure as a house built on the foundation of apostolic teachings and prophetic traditions – a place being built to become a dwelling place of God by the Spirit (2:20–22). The church then is God's own household with diverse people groups, fulfilling his plan to make the gathering of his people a habitat for his own dwelling.

## 4.5 Unfolding Mystery of God, a Witness to Principalities and Powers 3:1–12

The third chapter of the epistle echoes the notion that God (the divine) is the central figure at work in creating this community by reintroducing Paul as a steward of God (οἰκονομία) in the unfolding mystery. The idea of οἰκονομία defuses potential thought of Paul as the architect of the community and clarifies his role as a mere custodian. The Spirit of God revealed the mystery to the apostles and prophets (3:2–5), but the mystery is not mysterious. It is the unveiling of God's plan to unite Jews and Gentiles. As the least significant of all ministers, Paul was tasked by God to make the riches of Christ known to Gentiles. Two long sentences (in Greek) explain the role of the church in God's plan as it relates to its identity as one body. Paul characterizes his ministry in gratitude as a gift of God (3:7) to participate in the unification of Jews and Gentiles "in Christ Jesus through the Gospel" (3:6). The self-portrait of an unworthy steward is meant to accentuate the supremacy of God in the events. It is a privilege for Paul to be accorded grace to preach Christ. Here, Paul abases himself far below the status and dignity of all other believers. "Whereas in 1 Cor 15:9 Paul uses the superlative of himself, ἐλάχιστος, 'least' here in Ephesians a superlative with a comparative ending is employed for greater emphasis, ἐλαχιστότερος, 'very least (3:8 ESV).' Again, whereas in 1 Cor 15:9 Paul compares himself with the other apostles, here the comparison is extended to one with all believers."[125] It is God who gave him this privilege to serve.

First, grace was given for Paul to preach to the Gentiles.[126] The rhetorical import of this statement cannot be understated. Gentiles are significant in God's plan to the extent that God offers Paul the distinct privilege to make

---

societies' use of fictive kinship to promote in-group identity and internal cohesion. This notion of kinship would make members feel obliged to engage in keeping the honor and concord of God's household intact.

125. Lincoln, *Ephesians*, 183.

126. H. A. Kent, Jr. *Ephesians: The Glory of the Church* (Chicago: Moody, 1971), 53. Paul does not imply that he would not preach to Jews but emphasizes his distinctive commission for Gentile evangelization.

his mystery known to them. The measure of what Christ has done is beyond human comprehension; ἀνεξιχνίαστος appears twice in the NT and translates as incomprehensible, unfathomable or unsearchable.[127] It denotes a reservoir so deep that one cannot reach its bottom[128] or a subject whose footprints cannot be tracked.[129] The word "riches" adds to the notion of a reservoir filled with unfathomed treasures. It "does not mean only the ideas contained in the mystery of Christ (v. 6) but also the reality of salvation mediated by the word of proclamation, the love of Christ which exceeds all knowledge and which includes the Gentiles in God's fullness of life (v. 19)."[130] Paul's disposition is that of a privileged custodian, and the content of his preaching is phrased in superlatives as the surpassing riches of God's grace and glory (1:7; 2:7).[131]

The divine agenda being executed is underscored by the fact that Paul's task is to make the plan known to all humanity.[132] "All" refers to both Jews and Gentiles, as also the content of the mystery refers to unification of Jews and Gentiles. It is uncertain as to why Paul uses two different verbs to explain the mechanics by which the mystery is to be made known – to preach and to bring to make plain (3:8–9). Best explains that Gentile Christians needed to be evangelized and brought into the church; Jewish Christians were already in the church but needed enlightenment about God's plan just as much as Gentile Christians; this may be the reason for the change from the idea of evangelization to that of enlightenment.[133]

While the scope of this work does not allow for elaborate discussion on the question of means, it is important to note that any attempt to assign each of these verbs to specific ethnic group has no particular merit and deviates from the main import.[134]

---

127. W. C. Trenchard, *The Student's Complete Guide to the Greek New Testament* (Grand Rapids: Zondervan, 1992), 52.

128. Mitton, *Ephesians*, 124. Mitton further explains that the unfathomed riches are heavenly treasures available to all believers.

129. Foulkes, *Ephesians*, 104.

130. Schnackenburg, *Ephesians*, 137.

131. O'Brien, *Ephesians*, 241.

132. Lincoln, *Ephesians*, 184.

133. Best, *Ephesians – ICC*, 319.

134. Paul defines the pre-Christian status of Jews and Gentiles as being under the control of the ruler of the power of the air. It will therefore be strange for him to make changes of words just to indicate that the Jews did not need enlightenment. Perhaps, Best's conjecture would be more fitting in Romans, but not in Ephesians.

The Jew-Gentile unification in God's salvific plan,[135] defining the mystery, gives no room for Jewish exclusivism; it renders a decisive blow to the principalities and powers as their wishes to promote disparities are being thwarted.[136] The idea that the community is born out of a divine plan is reiterated by the assertion that this mystery was beyond human reach. It was hitherto concealed in God (1:4–5) but is now being made known to the principalities and powers through the church.[137] What was once concealed and inconceivable has now been realized – Jews and Gentiles are members of one shared community; the multi-ethnic church is the embodiment of the mystery signaling what God is able to do in defeat of the powers. Ταῖς ἀρχαῖς καὶ ταῖς ἐξουσίαις (3:10) is a hendiadys for a host of evil spiritual forces in the heavenly realms (2:2; 6:12).[138]

The church is the entity by which the "manifold wisdom of God" is made known to the cosmic powers. Nothing in the passage talks about verbal proclamation of the Gospel as the means by which the mystery is to be made known. In other words, the very existence of the community in unity speaks to the defeat of evil powers. The Greek word for church appears nine times in Ephesians to refer to the universal church in each case (1:22; 3:10, 21; 5:23, 24, 25, 27, 29, 32).[139] The church serves as a medium of revelation to hostile

---

135. C. C. Caragounis, *The Ephesian Mysterion: Meaning and Context* (Lund: Carl Bloms Boktryckeri AB, 1977), 32–34. Upon an extensive investigation of the etymology and meaning of μυστήριον, Caragounis shows that the word originally meant that which is "hard to understand," "incomprehensible" or "mysterious" but later its meaning was narrowed down to a mere "secret." It was employed in Eleusinian Mysteries where secrets are revealed in divine drama to devotees in special circumstances. The meaning, however, changed in the NT times when it was used in philosophy, magic or apocalyptic literature to refer to "a teaching, truth or goal that transcends the human mind and characterized to be incomprehensible" (Caragounis, 34). Its appearances in the NT has parallels with the usage in Daniel (LXX Dan. 2:18, 19, 27–30, 47), DSS (1QS 11.5–8) and Jewish Apocalyptic literature (1 Enoch 52:1–5; 4 Ezra 4:5; 5:31; 7:1; 10:28–30 etc.).

136. Caragounis, *Ephesian Mysterion*, 141.

137. The aorist translates usually as constative, but it could also be taken as ingressive aorist.

138. *Contra* W. Hendriksen, *Galatians and Ephesians* (Edinburgh: Banner of Truth Trust, 1968), 158–159. See Lenski, *Galatians, Ephesians and Philippians*, 483. Among others, Hendriksen and Lenski argue that "principalities and powers" refer to good angels in the heavenly realm. Others have interpreted them to refer to fallen angels (Bruce, *Colossians, Philemon and the Ephesians*, 321). Bruce posits in light of 1 Peter 1:12 that it does not only refer to hostile forces but to all "created intelligence." He does not explain what he meant by created intelligence though. The powers in Ephesians refer to evil spiritual forces. It is rather inconsistent to read their appearance in 3:10 as a reference to good angels. The most fitting and one that is consistent with the usage in Ephesians is the reference to evil spiritual beings.

139. G. E. Ladd, *A Theology of the New Testament* (Grand Rapids: Eerdmans, 1993), 581–582. See more discussion on how the word is used in different places in the NT in Ladd's discussion on the "church."

powers.[140] Nothing is required of the church to make manifest this mystery to the powers.[141] As Caragounis puts it, "the mystery is shaped by God's wisdom, it is a product of it. At the same time God's wisdom is reflected and revealed in the *mysterion*."[142] The unification of Jews and Gentiles heralds to the powers God's power to overcome their efforts to engineer interethic divisions;[143] that they could not hinder the advancement of God's plan to unite the cosmos.[144] God is thus the author and Jesus Christ is the one in/through whom God is enacting this plan. Human agency is absent both in the planning and execution.[145]

In Christ, the church gains access to God (3:12). Two words are used in 3:12 to describe human interaction with God. The first is παρρησία which translates as boldness, openness or frankness in expression,[146] fearless expression in speech. The LXX uses the word to characterize freedom to speak to God (see LXX Job 22:26; 27:9–10). The second is προσαγωγή meaning unrestrained access. It features three times in the NT (Rom 5:2; Eph 2:18 and 3:12) to denote "access" or "right to enter." Both words are linked by a coordinating conjunction to explain the line of communication between Christ followers and God in terms of the free, bold or unrestricted access to speak with God – he is accessible and can be approached fearlessly. This statement is unprecedented given the limitations of access and fear that were associated with the interaction between humans and gods.

## 4.6 Petition for Divine Strength and Insight 3:14–21

Unrestrained access to God does not engender arrogance in respect to how Paul approaches God in prayer (3:14). He bows his knees in submissive posture or in reverence to God (see Isa 45:23; Rom 14:11; Phil 2:10). The prayer reveals Paul's wishes for God's assistance for the community. The term "father" is sometimes used to refer to male deities in Asia Minor, but its usage here recalls

---

140. R. B. Hays, *The Moral Vision of the New Testament: A Contemporary Introduction to New Testament Ethics* (San Francisco: Harper, 1996), 63.

141. *Contra* Wallace, *Greek beyond Basics*, 434.

142. Caragounis, *Ephesian Mysterion*, 108.

143. Lincoln, *Ephesians*, 187.

144. O'Brien, *Ephesians*, 248.

145. J. D. G. Dunn, *The Theology of Paul the Apostle* (Grand Rapids: Eerdmans, 1998), 247. Also D. Wenham, *Paul: Follower of Jesus or Founder of Christianity?* (Grand Rapids: Eerdmans, 1995), 121–122. Paul includes himself in this experience when he refers to Christ Jesus in the first-person plural as Χριστῷ Ἰησοῦ τῷ Κυρίῳ ἡμῶν. Dunn explains that, "at the very least, κυριος acknowledged dominance and right of the superior over the inferior."

146. Philo, *Spec. Leg.*203 and Josephus, *Ant.* 2:4.4; 5:1, 3.

the father who was previously mentioned (1:2), namely God the Father. The petition is made to the sovereign God over all of creation, suggesting that the scope of his authority extends to every cosmic entity. Literally, God is the one "from whom every family in heaven and on earth derives its name." The "namer" has authority and expresses it by providing identity for the named. Πατριά does not carry biological or genealogical connotation, but collective entities, race, clan or angelic hosts in the celestial and terrestrial realms.[147] "Every family in heaven" includes all angelic hosts and spiritual agents. Some argue that the "every" here does not include evil spirits or rebellious angels but there is no reason to exclude angelic hosts from the stated reference to all families in heaven and on earth.[148] In other words, the prayer is offered to the Father (God) who is supreme over all earthly and cosmic entities, nothing exists outside the scope of his sovereignty.

Paul petitions that the readers may be granted strength through the Spirit in their inner being (3:16). First, the subject of the divine passive (κραταιωθῆναι) is God the Father. Second, the request specifically asks God to meet the need by the agency of the Holy Spirit. Third, the locus or object that needs strengthening is the "inner being" (τὸν ἔσω ἄνθρωπον). Κραταιόω denotes strength to prevail amidst challenges or vigor to thrive (1:19; 6:10). It is divine empowerment for the believers to live up to their new identity or to fight against inner struggles that may hinder their progress. The inner being refers to the unseen properties in theological anthropology (spirit or soul/spirit); it is the unseen dimensions of human personhood that may be energized spiritually.

The ἵνα clause in 3:18 may be taken as an expression of purpose, apposition to the previous line or as a secondary petition for spiritual reinforcement. The prayer as a whole is multidimensional in scope: (a) the inner being (soul/spirit), (b) strength in the heart (center of life and seat of reasoning), (c) knowing cognitively and experientially, and (d) love (relationally) as they all relate to the welfare of the community. The petition for "inward strength" may enable members to maintain a suitable disposition for Christ to dwell in their hearts. The Spirit's empowerment and Christ's indwelling are all mediated through faith (3:17). Faith is the means by which Christ gains access to the heart to secure a habitation. Later, faith is noted as the shield in the combat gear against evil spirits (6:16). Paul further prays for God to help the believers to be rooted

---

147. Bruce, *Colossians, Philemon and Ephesians*, 324–325. For Bruce, πατριά which usually translates as "family" must be translated as fatherhood to retain the import of God's sovereignty over all creation.

148. Schnakenburg, *Ephesians*, 147.

and grounded in love. Here, horticultural and architectural metaphors are utilized as vivid ways to express divine enabling to be grounded and in the expression of love in the community.

Furthermore, Paul prays that God may grant them strength to grasp the essence of the four dimensions (3:18). The word for strength is ἐξισχύω and its import is "total strength, competency or full capability" to be able to comprehend. The unnamed object of the four-dimensional imagery (breadth, length, height and depth) is a debated matter. The earlier assumption that "love" in 3:17 and 3:19 offer good grounds to supply it as the object has been debunked. A better case has been made in support of "the wisdom of God"[149] or "the power of God" as the object of the four dimension imagery.[150] For now, I find the argument suggesting that the manner in which these four dimensions feature in magical texts[151] provides us with the closest parallel in denoting the magnitude of divine power[152] to be persuasive. In other words, the author prays that they may comprehend the magnitude of God's power. Another request follows to ask God to grant them the ability to "know" or comprehend the incomprehensible greatness of the love of Christ (3:19). The love of the father is mentioned in 1:4 and 2:4; they are in the One he loves (1:6) and are dearly loved children (5:1). Later, Paul would urge them to emulate the love of Christ (5:2), but here the focus is on coming to terms with what the love of Christ entails. It seems to be an oxymoron to petition God to enable them to know what is incomprehensible or unknowable but the rhetoric seems to point to the idea that "they come to know the inexhaustible nature of the love of Christ"; that they may also be filled with, consumed by or submerged in the fullness[153] of God.

The one long sentence doxology in 3:20–21 follows the focus on God and divine agency permeating these three chapters of Ephesians.[154] Paul concludes the section with a theocentric evocation and wish for God to be honored in the church. The doxology ascribes glory to God in his greatness. It is a power-full

---

149. Schnackenburg, *Ephesians*, 150–152.

150. Arnold, *Ephesians*, 215–217.

151. PGM IV. 964–974, 979–985.

152. Arnold, *Power and Magic*, 91–92.

153. The term πλήρωμα and its cognates are associated with divine activity in Ephesians (1:23; 4:10; 5:18). It is connected to either Jesus Christ, God or the Holy Spirit, the three spiritual agents working on behalf of the readers are the ones with whom "fullness" or "filling" is associated in the letter.

154. The greeting is immediately followed by invocation stating that, "God and father of our Lord Jesus Christ" is the one who blessed them with "every spiritual blessings" (1:3).

doxology partly because it invokes three terms of spiritual power to underscore the magnitude of God's power – δύναμαι, δύναμις, ἐνεργέω (3:20–21). The glory of God must be understood in terms of his "honor" or "splendor" against the background of ancient notions of "honor and shame." God is all powerful and able to do exceedingly above and beyond anything that can be articulated by words or comprehended in thoughts, according to his power at work "in us" – the community as a whole or inner parts of individuals. The locale in which God's glory manifests is the church and in Christ Jesus forever and ever.

## Conclusion

This chapter has shown that a good grasp of the cosmological framework provides clarity, yields new insights and defuses previous notions such as "realized eschatology" in what the author espouses in Ephesians 1–3. It also brings to light the need to deliberately examine religious texts against the backdrop of the religious worldview – to augment historical-grammatical or social history approaches to the text. This discussion also shows that spiritual beings are the main actors in Ephesians 1–3. I proceed to highlight some of the main observations.

a. *God the Father, Christ Jesus and Holy Spirit in Ephesians 1–3*: The God who is to be blessed for providing "every spiritual blessing" at the beginning (1:3) is also the main subject at the end when the author states, "to him who is able to do immeasurably more than all we ask or imagine . . . be glory" (3:20–21). It is evident that humans are not architects of the community nor shapers of its identity. They are privileged beneficiaries in the unfolding plan of the great benefactor, God. The church has its origin in God's plan that predates the creation of the world; he chose them before the foundation of the cosmos (1:4). In other words, their election occurred before the first human being was created. The plan, purpose and prospects of the community are predetermined and engineered by God himself. He chose, redeemed, adopted, purposed, sealed, saved, and made them one etc. They were spiritually dead and incapable of participating in their own salvation. The unification of Jews and Gentiles in Ephesians 1–3 is not what people work to achieve but the composite of the mystery of God with predetermined *modus vivendi* (2:10). Ephesians 1–3 provides no prescription for members, but underscores (a) what God has done that is praiseworthy, (b) understanding of what God aims to do that requires spiritual agency, and (c) God's future plan (inheritance, summation etc.) that ought to inspire hope. Only, much later, in the second half of the letter (4–6) do we read about the moral aspirations and human responsibilities required to keep God's new community on course.

Relationally, God is portrayed as the father who meets all the spiritual needs and ensures the security of believers in a dreadful world. Their enlistment into the community came by means of election, redemption and adoption into the "household of God." Previous allegiance and ascriptions to pagan deities as "father" or "mother" dissipate as believers find their place as children of a powerful father, who is able to do much more than "we" can ask or imagine. However, nothing in the fictive kinship suggests that God paid a ransom to pagan deities to secure rights for their adoption. God's sovereignty, even over principalities and powers, suggests that he is the one to whom every family in heaven and on earth owe their existence. God is consistently portrayed in superlatives in regard to his riches and incomparably great power (1:18, 19), grace (2:7) and love (2:4; 3:19). Additional relational observation is the fact that the section features three paragraphs on prayer. Proportionately and numerically no letter in the Pauline corpus devotes that much space and frequency to prayer than we find in Ephesians (1:3–14; 15–22; 3:14–21). Prayer is an important feature in divine-human communication. Prayer shows a sense of dependency on God, acknowledges God's ability to provide what believers needed to thrive in his church and conveys a deep sense of gratitude for what God has done and continues to do.

Jesus Christ plays a significant role in God's unfolding mystery as he mediates God's work with sinful humanity. He is the one through whom adoption, salvation and reconciliation takes effect. The readers share one parent with Christ in God as their father. The efficacy of God's power on behalf of the church was made manifest in Christ when he raised him from the dead and seated him at his right side in the heavenly realms. Thus, Christ Jesus has dominion over the forces of evil and works on behalf of the church. The believers share an exalted place with Christ above evil spiritual entities, as they sit with him at the right hand of God in the heavenly realms (2:6). However, authority over evil powers does not mean that the powers have diminished in their operations in the world. Believers share in the victory of Christ over these powers, but they are by no means immune to their influence. Human responsibility in dealing with them is a major theme to be explored in the next chapter. Moreover, salvation is mediated through Christ; the one who broke down the wall of hostility in his flesh so that Jews and Gentiles may be reconciled to God and live at peace with one another. He came to preach peace and he is also the embodiment of peace. Through Christ, God makes his unsurpassed riches known. The phrase "in Christ" and its antecedents feature frequently to point to him as the means/instrument or locus of existence.[155] It is remarkable to observe the prominent feature of spiritual beings in these chapters and wonder why so few in scholarship have shown interest to study their import in the letter.

Similarly, the Holy Spirit is God's agent in meeting the needs of the church: "The promised Holy Spirit" authenticates their place with God (seal) and guarantees their inheritance (1:13). Christ mediates reconciliation whereas access to the father is channeled through the Spirit (2:18). More so, God's habitation in the community comes in the presence of the Holy Spirit (2:22). It is through the Spirit that the mystery of Christ is made known to the apostles and prophets (3:5). Paul even prays that God may grant the believers inner strength through the Holy Spirit so that "Christ may dwell in [their] hearts" (3:17). Believers do not only live with the consciousness of divine activities, but they are also strengthened by spiritual agents. It was not unusual in ancient cosmology for devotees of gods like Dionysius to perform rituals in the hope of divine empowerment. Here, God the father, Christ Jesus and the Holy Spirit work in concert to meet their needs – every spiritual aid or blessing is thus within reach.[156]

b. *Principalities and powers*: This subtitle is my designation for all spiritual powers opposed to God. They feature first in the account expressing the greatness of God's power at work when he raised Christ from the dead in triumph over all cosmic powers (1:20–23). It becomes apparent that these powers are opposed to God's plan for humanity. The "ruler of the power of the air," who exercises control over unbelievers, has no power over Christ followers owing to their salvific status (2:2–7). Salvation in Ephesians includes deliverance from sin, the corrupt world and from the control of evil spiritual forces (2:1–10). The unification of Jews and Gentiles serves as a witness to evil spirits about their failure to retain control over Christ followers (3:10). It is noteworthy that unbelievers are not set against believers in Ephesians (2:1–3). The new community provides the best alternative in life. The church is not instructed to see or relate to unbelievers as enemies – their opponents are spiritual forces of evil.

---

155. Fee, *Pauline Christology*, 639–669. It is important that we do not read the lordship of Christ or references to "in him" as some inconsequential theological expressions. The understanding that members ought to submit to Christ as the master/lord and the sense of his spiritual presence to the early readers must not be overlooked in a world of competing spiritual forces at work in human affairs.

156. Fee, *God's Empowering Presence*, 660. In fact, pneumatology in Ephesians is quite similar to what we find elsewhere in the Pauline corpus.

c. *Spiritual enabling for knowledge and inner strength*: Much of the author's wishes in prayer are directed towards cognitive insight or inner strength for the believers. What they need to know (information) is about who they are, their place in God's plan, and the magnitude of God's power at work on their behalf. Potentially, limited understanding of their identity in God and his power could jeopardize the well-being of the community. The content of the prayers also implies that a spiritual being is able to provide humans with wisdom, enlightening and strength to enhance their day-to-day lives. Believers are not admonished to follow a particular set of instructions or engage in certain spiritual disciplines to acquire knowledge or inner strength but to count on God to provide, at least at this stage.

d. *The cosmos and the new community*: All three uses of the word κόσμος appear in the first two chapters of Ephesians (1:4; 2:2, 12). Paul uses the word in an attempt to explain the timing of salvation as that which did not come as an afterthought, but was a pre-existing plan put in place before the foundation of the world. Ephesians also uses κόσμος to characterize the world without Christ. The domain of evil spiritual influence, where pre-conversion life, marked by hopelessness and alienation, was lived (2:2, 12).[157] The community is a new creation[158] comprising Jews and Gentiles; "this is neither *creation ex nihilo* nor *continua creatio* but creation *out of the old existence or the world* – people are saved (2:8–10), chosen (1:4) or called (1:18; 4:1) out of the world."[159] The conduct of members of the church is predetermined by God (2:10). Members are admonished to embrace the fact that unification of Jews and Gentiles is in "the genetic make-up" of the divine mystery. The church comprises a people of God and serves as the microcosm of God's plan for the universe, which will ultimately be consummated in the summation of all things under Christ (1:9–10). The next chapter examines Ephesians 4–6, which directs more attention to human responsibility in God's plan for the cosmos.

---

157. Darko, *No Longer Living as the Gentiles*, 116–119.

158. E. Adams, *Constructing the World: A Study in Paul's Cosmological Language* (SNTW; Edinburgh: T&T Clark, 2000), 77–80. The study of Adams on κτίσις/κτίζω has shed light on how we understand Paul's use of the term relative to his cosmology. Here, new creation is a continuum from the old as we shall see in the ongoing discussion.

159. Darko, *No Longer Living as the Gentiles*, 110.

# 5

# Spiritual Beings in the Moral Discourse of Ephesians 4–6

The previous chapter recounts what God has done through Christ and the Holy Spirit for the believers and their continued need for divine enablement to maintain communal identity, ethos and in-group solidarity. It is noteworthy that the members of the church are not explicitly admonished to do anything on their part but to reflect, embrace, celebrate and be informed of their place in the unfolding mystery of God. The permeating role of spiritual beings in the epistle's worldview portrays a view of the church not just as a social entity in which individuals are able to negotiate their identity and social boundaries along changing trends in their social location. Conversely, who *they are* (their identity) is rooted in divine initiative and agenda for the cosmos. Their mode of conduct is not contingent on some social phenomena, but what God has prepared beforehand as befitting to the identity of the children of God. Moreover, their readiness to be strengthened, informed and empowered by divine enabling is crucial in overcoming the diabolic influence and moral decadence in the world.

This chapter focuses on Ephesians 4–6 in the continuum to probe further into the role of spiritual beings in the identity construct and ethical imperatives being espoused. It observes how the author constructs the group identity and ascribes group dynamics to the work of spiritual agents. The nature of unity, its basis and obligation to maintain internal cohesion are matters of interest. Moreover, we shall observe the roles of God, the Holy Spirit and Jesus Christ as arbiters, empowering agents and models for moral conduct on the one hand, and the role of evil spiritual powers in the efforts to counteract God's plan for the church on the other. Unlike the first three chapters, Ephesians 4–6 makes a direct appeal for responsible human conduct or activity. This chapter will further explore the interlink of divine activity and human responsibility in the letter's spirit cosmology. In other words, to what extent are humans responsible for moral failings if their way of life is predetermined by God (2:10)? I hope that the contrast between the identity of Christ followers and their conduct as members of God's household, and evil spiritual influence in the world without Christ will become apparent.

## 5.1 The Nexus of Theological and Paranetic Discourse 4:1–3

Scholars have taken for granted that Ephesians 4:1 marks a transition from theology or what I would call theological reflection (vv. 1–3) to a paranetic discourse (vv. 4–6) reflecting a consistent pattern in the writings of Paul (Rom 12:1; 1 Thess 4:1; Gal 5:1; Col 3:1).[1] Some have argued that the literary structure, content, genre and even the style evince a two-part discourse that warrants two separate commentaries.[2] Suffice it to indicate that the notion of theology as a distinct category from ethics is anachronistic and informed by post-enlightenment categories of reasoning. The interwoven nature of doctrine and praxis, identity and ethos or *being* and *doing* has eluded many readers. For example, 4:1–16 reiterates divine acts in the constitution of the community and underscores the theological underpinnings for a befitting *modus vivendi*. The theological statements recount shared commonalities and grace-gifts to equip members for service and mutual interdependence. The first paragraph also points to unity in the church as evidence of maturity in the unfolding plan of God (4:1–16).

I devote an entire chapter to Ephesians 4–6, not only because of the literary structure of this section of the epistle, but also due to the way the author transitions from what God has done in the formation of the community and petitions for divine enabling to focus on human responsibilities in the same line of reasoning. Later, we shall observe the theological framework of the household code (5:21–33), suggesting that the alleged dichotomy between theology and ethics in the letter may not be overstated. Ephesians 4:1–16 is a

---

1. Lincoln, *Ephesians*, xxxvi. Lincoln argues that "recognition of the two parts (doctrinal part chs. 1–3 and *paranesis* chs. 4–6) is determinative for discussion of each of the areas of content, structure, genre and style."

2. M. Barth, *Ephesians 4–6* (Garden City: Doubleday, 1974). See also the first commentary on chapters 1–3. There are legitimate reasons for such division, but we may not overemphasize its import since the structural and conceptual interdependence is apparent.

nexus[3] in its portrait of divine activity and human responsibilities. It clarifies that the status of the church as a community of God obliges commensurate conduct from members for its proper function.

The first half (4:1–3) of a long sentence sets the framework of moral discourse.[4] Some have designated 4:1–3 as the "ethical theme"[5] or the summary of the letter.[6] The opening sentence infers from the entire preceding discourse, not only from the immediate paragraph, to call for human responsibility[7] in what has so far been portrayed as the work of God. Invoking his status as the prisoner of the Lord (see 3:1), Paul asserts his earned (implied) authority to call members to conduct[8] themselves in a manner that befits their privileged calling. The self-ascription "As a prisoner for the Lord" stands in parallel with 3:1 where he used a similar expression in the first person.[9] The "chosen" (1:4–5) and a people "called to one hope" in the glorious inheritance (1:18) are now entreated[10] to conduct themselves as worthy members of the household of God (2:19); God is the subject of the divine passive – he is the one who called them. In the honor and shame culture, they must maintain "ascribed honor" accompanying their new status (1 Thess 2:12; Col 1:10); the honor of God is at stake in regard to how they conduct themselves. Customary kinship obligations require that each member exhibits befitting and praiseworthy conduct in a household of some nobility. The two prepositional phrases underline the

---

3. R. P. Martin, *Ephesians, Colossians, and Philemon* (Atlanta: John Knox, 1991), 46–47. Also Kreitzer, *Ephesians*, 118. Kreitzer indicates that there are many similarities between the two parts in content.

4. The first three words in 4:1 (παρακαλῶ οὖν ὑμας) are the same in Rom 12:1.

5. Muddiman, *Ephesians*, 210.

6. Wallace, *Greek Grammar beyond the Basics*, 652. Wallace explains that, "the action is 'walk worthily of the calling . . . '" He posits that the means by which this command is to be carried out is twofold: (1) negatively, by "forbearing one another in love"; and (2) positively, "by striving to maintain [not originate] the unity of the Spirit." He indicates that Ephesians 4:1–3 seems to provide a summary of what the epistle is all about.

7. Foulkes, *Ephesians*, 116. Foulkes points out that human acts being called upon here presume a depth of gratitude for the work of God in Christ.

8. Περιπατέω is consistently used in Ephesians to bear ethical connotation (cf. 2:2, 10; 4:1, 17; 5:2, 8, 15).

9. Paul's reference to himself as a prisoner is not an appeal for sympathy but that his imprisonment is borne out of his efforts to live a life that pleases God. He hopes that this would motivate the audience to consider such pursuit worthwhile. This also negates a claim to superior standing in Christ.

10. The verb also appears in the *T. Naph.* 9:1 where it conveys the sense of begging in earnest: "And when he had charged them with many such words, he *exhorted* (περιπατέω) them that they should remove his bones to Hebron and should bury him with his fathers. And when he had eaten and drunken with a merry heart, he covered his face and died."

requisite comportments to hold the church together. Humility,[11] gentleness[12] and patience are imperative for interpersonal relations in the community. Members are admonished to accommodate each other in love. Love features seventeen times in Ephesians to convey intentionality expressed in self-giving as exemplified in Christ; it is a divine attribute, motivation for conduct and a cardinal virtue (1:5, 15; 2:4; 3:18–19; 4:3, 15–16; 5:25, 28, 33; 6:23–24). Here, believers are admonished to be diligent and proactive in making every effort to *preserve* the unity of the Spirit. Human effort is not what would create unity. Unity forms part of the DNA of the church and only needs to be preserved; the unification of Jews and Gentiles is what the mystery is all about. In other words, divinely originated oneness ought to be preserved as a matter of necessity by privileged beneficiaries. Subsequent admonitions emphasize the need to guard what members already have in Christ.

The Greek term for "unity" (ἑνότης) features only in Ephesians (here and 4:13) to denote oneness that is brought about by divine agency.[13] The readers have received spiritual blessings (1:3), are sealed by the Spirit (1:13–14) and strengthened in the inner being by the Spirit. They also have access to the father by the Spirit (2:17–18). "The unity of the Spirit recalls in a very direct way 2:18, where Paul says that through Christ we both (Jew and Gentile) together in one Spirit have access to God."[14] Oneness in the household of God makes it a conducive place for him to dwell among his people by the Spirit (2:19–22). Moreover, the unveiling of the mystery of God in the unification of Jews and Gentiles is mediated through the Spirit. Jews and Gentiles are in the closest bond of relationship in their current standing with God; they both are συκληρονόμος, σύσσωμος and συμμέτοχος (3:5–6). It is apparent that the

---

11. Grundmann, *TDNT* VIII, 1–26, and H. H. Esser, 'ταπεινός,' *NIDNTT*, 259–264. Ταπεινοφροσύνη was used generally as a derogatory term denoting abasement in the Greco-Roman world, especially in the context of human relations. "When abasement is that of wickedness or immoderation, it can have positive meaning, but it is not in itself a positive good." The word carries this sense in the works of Aristotle and Epictetus 3:24, 56. It, however, features with positive connotation for modest . . . of subjects, soldiers, children or self-abasement to the gods in cultic settings. Esser explains that "in all these uses there remains the memory of the original physical meaning of below, low, in comparison with that which is above or higher . . . In the Greek world, with its anthropocentric view of man, lowliness is looked on as shameful, to be avoided and overcome by act and thought. In the NT, with its theocentric view of man, the words are used to describe those events that bring a man into a right relationship with God and his fellow-man." Its use in the OT and Essene community carries the positive sense of humility (cf. 1QS 4:2).

12. "Gentleness" is a relational virtue that contrasts harsh dealings with fellow humans.

13. The word features in the writings of Ignatius of Antioch quite frequently. Ignatius, *Eph.* 4:2; 5.1; *Phld.* 2:2; 3:2; 5:2; 8:1; 9:1; *Sm.* 12:2; *Pol.* 8:3.

14. Fee, *God's Empowering Presence*, 700–701.

Spirit is paramount to their very existence and interaction in the community of faith. Elsewhere, Paul makes a similar connection to the Spirit and in-group solidarity when he writes about ἡ κοινωνία τοῦ ἁγίου πνεύματος (2 Cor 13:13). The Spirit and peace are linked in Romans 14:7; 15:13 and Galatians 5:22. Ephesians calls on members to keep (τηρέω) the unity of the Spirit (τὴν ἑνότητα τοῦ πνεύματος) in the bond of peace.

The second half of the sentence (4:4–6) provides seven commonalities believers share as the basis for their bond. There is (1) one Spirit at work on their behalf. They are called to (2) one body. They have (3) one Lord, (4) one faith, (5) one baptism, (6) one God and (7) Father of all. "One Spirit" refers to the Holy Spirit; "one Lord" refers to Jesus Christ. The word "lord" refers to Jesus consistently in this letter with exception to the master/lord of slaves in the *Haustafel*. "God and Father" are ascriptions to the Supreme God, Creator and Architect of the unfolding mystery. He is the one also referred to as the Father of the Lord Jesus Christ. It is noteworthy that all these features are in reference to spiritual beings, even faith or baptism as it relates to "one body" to which members are called.

## 5.2 The Gifts of Christ in the Body of Christ 4:7–16

Ephesians 4:7–16 suggests that the exalted Christ aims to "fill the whole universe" (4:10) and establishes his authority over subterranean, terrestrial and celestial powers prior to distributing grace-gifts to members of the church to facilitate unity and maturity in the body. The author alludes to the psalter to portray Christ as the victorious one who possesses the ability to give others authority and action to render services under his lordship/oversight. Three views are proposed to explain the import of the notion that Christ descended to the lower regions prior to his ascension and gift-giving. First, some early church fathers read the passage to denote a descent to the underworld (Hades), thereby suggesting that Christ rose victoriously and was empowered to deputize believers to carry out his mission. A second view reads Christ's descent as a reference to the "incarnation."[15] In this vein, he descended from the heavenly realms to become human, died and ascended prior to dispensing the gifts. A third view places emphasis on the gifts and interprets the descent as an allusion to the coming of the Holy Spirit on the day of Pentecost (Acts 2). The complex structure of 4:8–10 and the lack of a conceptual parallel in

---

15. B. Chapell, *Ephesians: Reformed Expository Commentary* (Philipsburg: P&R Publishing, 2009), 189.

the NT lends its import to speculation. All three views, however, articulate a cosmology in which a spiritual agent intervenes or breaks into the realm of humanity to empower devotees for productive services. Among the three views, however, one seems to follow the ascent-descent movements in the text closely and corresponds with what we know of the cosmology in Asia Minor at the time; this is the view that understands Christ's descent as his going into the underworld to conquer opposing spirits prior to ascending and apportioning grace-gifts.[16] As Arnold rightly explains,

> The "lower parts of the earth" makes the most sense in its first-century religious context if it is interpreted as an expression for the world or Hades. Underworld themes were prominent in Ephesus and western Asia Minor, where a variety of underworld deities were worshiped. Most prominent was the goddess Hekate, the goddess of witchcraft and sorcery.[17]

The forces that control the cosmos and subterranean regions cannot restrain, undermine or sabotage the endeavors of gifted servants of Christ (see 1:20–23 and 2:1–10). To say Christ gave *gifts* recalls the very fact of salvation as a *gift* from God; he "gave the apostles, the prophets, the evangelists, the pastors and teachers" (4:11). Apostles, prophets and evangelists belong to the cultic context as their commission and message has spiritual or divine origins. While shepherding (pastors) and teaching may be conceived as natural abilities that may be perfected by experience, Ephesians characterizes them as being divinely dispensed to meet God's purpose – for service, stability and growth in the body.

The function of the three subsidiary prepositional phrases in 4:12 is a debated matter.[18] The first reading interprets the phrases as providing grounds to differentiate a gifted clergy from the laity whereas a second argues from the structure of the sentence to suggest the idea of "priesthood of all believers." The clergy-laity reading has seen a decline in support. Most scholars read it to be conveying the sense that Christ gave gifts to prepare the saints for the "work of service" and "to build up" the body. Believers are not saved by works (ἔργον

---

16. Lincoln, *Ephesians*, 242, Best, *Ephesians*, 378–382 and Hoehner, *Ephesians*, 524–530. The difficult sentence in 4:8 and further explanation in 4:9–10 are understood to characterize the defeat of the powers prior to the distribution of the gifts so that members may share in the victorious position as they exercise their gifts.

17. Arnold, *Ephesians*, 254.

18. Hoehner, *Ephesians*, 547–550. Hoehner discusses each of the views in great detail.

[2:9]) but for good works (ἔργοις ἀγαθοῖς [2:10]).[19] Here, Christ gives gifts to equip the people described in cultic parlance as "God's holy people" (1:1, 4) for the work of ministry (ἔργον διακονίας). Service (διακονία) is a spiritual gift (Rom 12:7) and it is associated with spiritual gifts elsewhere in Paul (1 Cor 12:5). The gifts may be utilized to equip the saints and edify the body of Christ until they attain "unity in the faith and in the knowledge[20] of the Son of God" (4:13). It is important to note that this is the only reference to Jesus directly as "the Son of God" in the NT. "Unity of faith comes with the realization that we all have one faith in the one person, Jesus Christ."[21] Moreover, it is anticipated that the believers will ultimately measure up to the fullness of Christ[22] – Christ is the yardstick of maturation.

The pericope (4:1–16) concludes with Christ at the center stage in regard to the execution and ultimate effect of responsible conduct and service in the community identified as "the body of Christ" that members might grow in Christ who is the head (4:15). "Christ as head is both the goal and source of our growth."[23] Schnackenburg puts it succinctly, "the explanation begins with Christ the victor over the powers and the giver of gifts to the church (vv. 8–11); his ruling position which supports the total life of the church is now emphasized once more."[24] In the complex imagery of human anatomy, the body grows in Christ and from Christ – the matrix from which all constituent parts develop. This imagery underscores the culturally collectivist framework in the emphasis on mutual interdependence. "Growing into the head likely refers to being conformed to Christ, becoming more like him, and 'growing into' the unity between believers and Christ. Growing *from* him depicts Christ as the source of the body; he is its origin and provides the stimulus for growth."[25]

---

19. "Good works" (2:10) denotes good conduct. The positive use of the word for "work/s" here is divine product/activity, not human ability (2:9).

20. Knowledge is not only acquired in the pursuit of learning but it also a prayer item, suggesting that God is able to provide such insights to believers (cf. 1:17–18).

21. Hoehner, *Ephesians*, 553.

22. Cf. Ephesians 4:10. To "fill all things" is associated with the descent to the lower regions to defeat the powers and later give gifts to members of the community. While the "fullness of Christ" refers to his presence in the body, it may also be understood as the microcosm of the eschatological vision noted in 1:10 where all things will ultimately be summed up in Christ.

23. Hoehner, *Ephesians*, 567–568.

24. Schnackenburg, *Ephesians*, 188.

25. Campbell, *Paul and the Union with Christ*, 281.

## 5.3 Spiritual Beings in the Old vs New Humanity/Outlook

The exalted Christ gave a variety of gifts to empower the community for a common purpose (4:11–16). Having shown that unity is from God who mediates gifts through Christ, Paul proceeds with admonition for responsible conduct. He instructs them to abstain from their previous way of life and be renewed in their minds (mindset) as a necessity for bearing the image of God in righteousness and in holiness. Solidarity also requires a shared commitment to contribute to the needs of the church.

Paul invokes his standing in the Lord to legitimize (ethos) the admonition for members to alter their mindset and desist from the moral indecency associated with Gentile outsiders. I have argued elsewhere in *No Longer Living as the Gentiles* that τὰ ἔθνη here must be read in light of ethnic stereotype in Jewish rhetoric of differentiation – to entreat the Gentile majority[26] to distance themselves from an unfitting past (3:1, 6, 8). In other words, Gentiles in the flesh (2:11, 15) must no longer conduct themselves according to the mindset and moral decadence of their past.[27] Outsiders are portrayed as a people of darkened minds, ignorance and hard-heartedness[28] (4:17–18; Ps 14:1); they are marked by moral bankruptcy (sensuality, greed and all forms of impurity) in stark contrast to how believers have "learned . . . Christ" (4:20). To "learn Christ" is to presume Christ as a moral example or didactic content of virtue (4:20–21). Morality is linked to identity with Christ as a learned experience for Christ followers. Usually, students learn a subject matter such as moral philosophy but the content here is not a subject of inquiry but a personal spiritual agent. It could either connote the embodiment of Christ, Christian tradition or a call to emulate Christ. We can only surmise that the two pedagogical terms, μανθάνω (learn) and διδάσκω (teach), in these two verses point to knowledge acquisition by means of instruction or observation. Thus, the content of learning and the basis for conduct are all Christocentric in this regard.

---

26. *Contra* Strelan, *Paul, Artemis, and the Jews in Ephesus*, 19. Strelan represents the minority view that the audience are made up of predominantly Jewish population.

27. Hoehner, *Ephesians*, 582, and Barth, *Ephesians 4–6*, 499. Some manuscripts read τὰ λοιπὰ ἔθνη clarifying the rhetorical ambiguity. Cf. λοιπὰ ℵ² D¹ K L P Ψ 104, 630. According to Metzger τὰ λοιπὰ is "an interpretative intrusion" to clarify the nuance. See B. M. Metzger, *Textual Commentary on the Greek New Testament* (London: United Bible Society, 1971), 605.

28. Fisher of Lambeth, "Blind or Hard of Heart?" *Theology* 69 (1966): 25–26; B. Lindars, "Blind or Hard of Heart?" *Theology* 69 (1966): 121; Colville of Culross, "Blind or Hard of Heart?" *Theology* 69 (1966): 171; C. H. Dodd, "Blind or Hard of Heart?" *Theology* 69 (1966): 223–224; and J. A. Robinson, "On πώρωσις and πήρωσις," in *St. Paul's Epistle to the Ephesians* (London: James Clarke & Co.), 264–274. Πώρωσις may translate as stubbornness or hardness of heart when used in conjunction with the heart.

Consequently, they must put off their old identity.[29] Human responsibility is required to curtail previous moral choices and state of mind. Paul's use of the clothing metaphor is a vivid way to drive his point home (4:22–24).[30] The past way of life is characterized as τὸν παλαιὸν ἄνθρωπον ("old humanity"). Some find Adamic Christology in the reference to "old humanity," on grounds of conjecture. The ethical tone further casts doubt on the speculative import of Adamic Christology (2 Cor 5:16–17).[31] It is evident that human identity is intertwined with conduct in the call to dislodge the patterns of life associated with the pre-conversion past. The spiritual and material world are not separable both in the identity construction and in the quest to live up to expectation. The contrastive δὲ in 4:23 suggests a radical change from "the old" in the direction of the new. If the main verb ἀνανεόω is taken to be passive (not middle), as I do, then believers are being entreated to avail themselves or be opened to making their darkened minds subject to renewal or transformation by divine agency. "Spirit" in 4:23 (ESV) refers to human spirit but the divine passive suggests the role of the Holy Spirit[32] or God in bringing the change into effect (Titus 3:5; 2 Cor 3:18).

Moreover, the admonition for a changed outlook[33] resumes the clothing metaphor to call on Christ followers to put on the new humanity (τὸν καινὸν ἄνθρωπον). A renewed mind precedes a new outlook (identity) in this regard. The "new humanity" is not *creatio ex nihilo* but creation from the "old" to become anew "like God."[34] God's new creation takes on a new identity and moral image "created in . . . true righteousness and holiness" (4:24). This recalls the idea that the church and its communal identity is a product of God's creation

---

29. E. D. W. Burton, *Syntax of Moods and Tenses in New Testament Greek*, 3rd ed. (Chicago: University of Chicago, 1900), 53. Burton explains that, "there is apparently no instance in the New Testament of the aorist infinitive in indirect discourse representing the aorist indicative of the direct form." Similarly, I take the aorist infinitives to have the force of imperative as we find in other parts of the NT.

30. Euripides, *Iph. Taur.* 602, Libanius, *Ep.* 968; Apuleius, *Metamorphoses* xi.24; *Acts Thom.* 36.66; Ecclus 45:8; *Ebr.* 86; *T. Levi* 8:2; 1 En 62:14–16; 1QS 4.8; Job 29:14; 35:26; Ps 132:9; Isa 59:17; 61:10; Rom 13:12; 1 Pet 2:1; Heb 12:1; Jas 1:21; Eph 6:11.

31. Barth, *Ephesians 4–6*, 544–545.

32. Fee, *God's Empowering Presence*, 709–712. Fee indicates that the probability that the readers would have thought of the subject as the Holy Spirit is high. However, that is not a good reason to read "spirit" as a reference to the Holy Spirit.

33. Καὶ functions as a coordinating conjunction to make a connection between the "renewing of the mind" and to the admonition to "put on the new man."

34. The phrase κατὰ θεὸν κτισθέντα is ambiguous. God may be understood to be both the source and standard simultaneously. The Creator is the source and is also a model for his creation.

in the unfolding plan (2:10, 19). Here, identity and morality come together in the notion of *imago Dei*.[35] This clothing metaphor is widespread in Greek, Roman and Jewish moral discourses. For Plato it is commendable to wear (clothe) "a virtue instead of clothes" in the public sphere.[36] Without making a sharp distinction between moral reasoning and conduct, Philo indicates that "the mind of the wise is clothed with virtues."[37] Righteousness and holiness also feature in Greco-Roman conventions as noble virtues in religious piety[38] or as the embodiment of virtuous living.[39] According to Plato, "righteousness and holiness" are the most respected and honorable qualities.[40] The two virtues were similarly employed in early Christian writings to denote virtuous conduct[41] and here as moral qualities of God himself befitting a people created in his likeness. Human responsibility and divine enabling in the renewing of the mind are necessary for their new moral identity.[42] It is important to note that the contrast of the "old humanity" to the "new humanity" in no way implies dissociation or antagonism towards unbelieving Gentiles. The accent is on the transition of the believers' previous way of life and their new status with God – not comparison to unbelievers or advocacy for radical social distancing.

## 5.4 A *Topos* for the Devil, and Divine Model for Virtue 4:26–27, 31–32

The discussion on anger brings the influence of spiritual activity to bear on the affairs of humankind in vivid terms. The early Christians did not perceive ethics as mere moral codes to observe for public admiration but that which also had a spiritual dimension and consequences. Unchecked conduct is not only detrimental to the orderly function of society, but the ancients reasoned

---

35. R. A. Wild, "Be Imitators of God: Discipleship in the Letter to the Ephesians," in *Discipleship in the New Testament*, ed. F. F. Segovia (Philadelphia: Fortress, 1985), 127–143, and Best, *Ephesians*, 437–439.

36. Plato, *Rep.* 457A.

37. Philo, *Fug.* 110.

38. Plato, *Gorg.* 507; *Rep.* 10.615; *Laws* 2.663; Josephus, *Ant.* 8.245. Cf. Philo, *Virt.* 47.

39. Philo, *Virt.* 50 and see also *Spec.* I. 304; *Fug.* 63.

40. Plato, *Gorgias* 507c. Also Plato, *Laches* 199d and *Protagoras* 349b.

41. Luke 1:75; 2 Thess 2:10; 1 Clem 14:1; 45:3; 2 Clem 6:9; 15:3; Titus 1:8; Rev 16:5.

42. L. G. Perdue, "The Death of the Sage and Moral Exhortation: From Ancient Near Eastern Instructions to Greco-Roman Paranaesis," *Semeia* 50 (1990): 99. Perdue has demonstrated that disciples usually assume or seek to establish new social identity when their teacher is separated from them or dies. It is possible that the communal identity and moral aspirations we find here and other parts of the *paraenesis* are necessitated by the absence of Paul, or perhaps Paul finds the need to write this towards the end of his ministry to preserve his legacy.

that it could also lead to severe spiritual consequences as well. We proceed to discuss how Ephesians addresses anger and falsehood in light of Greco-Roman spirit cosmology.

The instruction on anger management (4:26–27) flows from a discourse on speech-related ethics (see Ps 4:4–5a LXX) to issue double imperatives on anger: ὀργίζεσθε καὶ μὴ ἁμαρτάνετε. The syntax of the two imperatives is complex (4:26) as the rendering of various English translations shows. In other words, should we read ὀργίζεσθε as an imperative of condition,[43] concession[44] or command in relation to the second imperative? Wallace argues that ὀργίζεσθε denotes neither condition nor concession but serves as a direct command;[45] this would imply that anger is a moral necessity.[46] Anger was not condemned entirely in both Greek and Jewish conventions (Deut 24:15, *T. Dan* 6:8); moralists however placed some checks on the limits of its expression or the extent to which one could harbor anger. Aristotle indicates that a "good temper" is rather honorable;[47] "the man who is angry at the right things and with the right people, and, further, as he ought, when he ought and as long as he ought, is praised."[48] However, he condemns destructive expression thereof.[49] He argues that good people must distance themselves from hot-tempered persons. Plutarch similarly endorsed "righteous indignation"[50] as a good check of evil in society; he cautions against bad temper, which often accompanies drunkenness and vulgarity.[51] Demosthenes also makes the distinction between "just anger" (δικάια ὀργή) and a bad expression thereof.[52] Ephesians seems to work within

---

43. Lincoln, *Ephesians*, 301.

44. J. A. Brooks and C. L. Winberry, *Syntax of New Testament Greek* (Lanham: University Press of America, 1979), 129–130. See Patzia, *Ephesians, Colossians*, 252.

45. Wallace, *Greek Grammar beyond the Basics,* 491–492. Wallace provides robust argument against the notion that ὀργίζεσθε must be taken as conditional.

46. Wallace, 492. Wallace fails to provide persuasive reasons to refute the argument for concession. It is important to note that there is no question about the fact that uncontrolled anger is detrimental to God's people, less we employ grammatical ambiguity as the basis to legitimize destructive anger . . . (Prov 15:1, 18; 22:24; 29:8, 11; Eccl 7:9).

47. Plutarch, *Mor.* 456 & 457 and Aristotle, *Nic. Ethics* IV. 5.

48. Aristotle, *Nic. Ethics* IV. 5, 1125b.

49. Aristotle, *Nic. Ethics* IV. 5, 1126a.

50. Plutarch, *Mor.* 463E.

51. Plutarch, *Mor.* 456E. Also Cicero, *Moral Duties,* 38. Cicero advises orators to "assume the appearance of anger" when addressing serious matters but avoid being angry in the act since no good counsel emerges from anger.

52. Demosthenes, *Or.* 16.19.

this tradition or at the very least it does not deviate from the convention in what appears to be a paradox on the morality of how anger may be expressed.

The imperative[53] establishes the instruction in a religious framework; "in your anger *do not sin*." Sin is breach of religious codes often accompanied by spiritual consequences. So far, the onus is on the community members to exercise restraint. Second, Ephesians sets the appropriate time frame for anger. Members must desist from holding on to anger or provocations (παροργισμός) beyond sunset (see Deut 24:15). The sunset phraseology does not denote a literal sunset, but it must be understood as an idiom suggesting that anger must be short-lived. Plutarch uses the same imagery in noting that, "we should next pattern ourselves after the Pythagoreans, who, though related not at all by birth, yet sharing a common discipline, if ever they were led by anger into recrimination, never let the sun go down before they joined right hands, embraced each other, and were reconciled."[54] Thus, members must refrain and not acquiesce in two areas: (a) to not sin due to excessive expression of anger and (b) to exercise discipline in ensuring that anger is not prolonged. Sin could be defined as a breach of divine order that mars the relationship between the sinner and God; it undermines God's social order and injures others. In view of piety, its social import is that sin is an offense to God's plan for humanity. Both God and fellow humans are affected when sin features in moral discourse. To express anger in a destructive way in God's household (the church) is therefore to undermine internal cohesion and God's plan; the boundaries of acceptable norms and sin against God cannot be overlooked.

The negative effect of anger is further framed to have spiritual import. The community (note plural in 4:27) could create τόπος for the devil by entertaining prolonged anger or individuals could be possessed by the devil if they harbored anger. The clause "do not give a place (τόπος) to the devil" is a subsidiary clause to the preceding sentence in 4.26. The negative particle "and do not" presumes human ability (collectively or individually) and responsibility to prevent diabolic influence. The Greek term τόπος may translate as a place, opportunity, geographical position, place in a room or sphere of operation.[55] It is imperative that members do all within their powers to avoid diabolic influence. The second person plural suggests collective responsibility without excluding individual roles in not harboring anger. The dwelling place of God could become a sphere in which the devil inhabits and

---

53. Seneca, *Ira* I. For Seneca, uncontrolled anger is irrational.
54. Plutarch, *Moralia* 488C.
55. Liddell and Scott, *Greek-English Lexicon*, 1806.

operates if anger is prolonged (2:21–22). The devil is not the cause of anger, but human indiscretion (4:3).[56] The notion of anger as a gateway for diabolic influence is known in Second Temple Jewish literature. The *Testament of Dan* (4:7) indicates that, "anger and falsehood together are double-edged evil, and work together to perturb reason. And when the soul is continually perturbed, the Lord withdraws from it and Beliar rules it." The church or its members could voluntarily or inadvertently give access to the devil by failing to defuse grudges and detrimental forms of anger.

It is a consensus view that διάβολος (4:27) refers to a personal evil spirit otherwise known as the devil. In the Pauline corpus διάβολος feature mainly in correspondence associated with Ephesus or its wider vicinity (others Matt 4:1; John 6:70). Apart from here and 6:11, the devil is mentioned only in 1 Timothy 3:6–7 and 2 Timothy 2:26 in the Pauline corpus. In all these instances, διάβολος is a spiritual adversary who works or exploits the failings of Christ followers to advance his agenda. Letting anger go unchecked invites undesirable spiritual consequences in the topos that may be occupied by the Holy Spirit. The negative particle (μηδὲ) leaves no room for ambiguity as it pertains to human responsibility to resist demonic influence. Morality transcends social life in this cosmology; human failings could trigger or attract evil spiritual influence. Paul had indicated earlier that life without Christ is subject to the control of "the ruler of the power of the air" (2:1–3). In Christ, believers have the power to restrain him in obedience to God and with commendable *modus vivendi*.

Uncontrolled anger was similarly condemned in Judaism and Greco-Roman moral philosophy.[57] In Ephesians, anger is not condemned entirely but ought to be expressed with reasonable disposition and within a specific time frame: (a) it should not lead to sin, (b) be prolonged since, (c) that may pave the way for evil spiritual influence. A list of various forms of anger is subsequently provided on a vice list to admonish culprits to seek deliverance as a necessity: πᾶσα πικρία καὶ θυμὸς καὶ ὀργὴ καὶ βλασφημία ἀρθήτω ἀφ᾽ ὑμῶν σὺν πάσῃ κακίᾳ (4:31). The main verb in 4:31 suggests that the onus is on the community or individuals to initiate the process of deliverance. The term αἴρω means to "take away, carry away" or "to lift up and move from one place to another."[58] The passive imperative (ἀρθήτω) suggests that humans under such

---

56. J. W. Shepard, *The Life and Letters of Paul* (Grand Rapids: Eerdmans, 1950), 552.

57. Cf. Ecclus 1:21–22; 27:30; Prov 15:1, 18; 22:24; 29:8, 11; *T. Dan* 3:5–6; 4:7; 5:1. *T. Dan* links anger to falsehood and evil spiritual influence as well.

58. BDAG, 24.

conditions may be limited in their ability to rid themselves of these destructive passions, and stand in need of divine agency to make it happen. They are to avail themselves to be released from "every form" of anger perhaps by God (4:31). The anger requiring God's deliverance has a broad range: one that is rooted in bitterness (πᾶσα πικρία),[59] anger that engenders "a quite definite reaction of the human soul," to one that manifests in violent reaction.[60] The list includes "angry shouting" (κραυγὴ) and blasphemy. Christ followers trapped in these conditions are injurious to concord and need divine intervention to be free.

The second half of the sentence follows with the contrastive δὲ[61] to highlight desirable qualities in their stead. The first on the list is kindness towards one another (γίνεσθε [δὲ] εἰς ἀλλήλους χρηστοί). Χρηστός conveys a sense of honesty, worthiness, and upright personality in relationships. It denotes integrity and humane disposition in regard to human interaction.[62] The second virtue is appropriately translated as tenderheartedness[63] as opposed to a hardened heart (4:18), and the third is forgiveness or the rendering of favor one to another in forgiving wrongdoings.[64] Thus, anger should be replaced with the virtues of kindness, tenderness and forgiveness in the community of faith. The last clause is particularly instructive in how it appeals to a comparable attribute (forgiveness) of God as the motivation or example for good conduct (4:32b). Having made the case that salvation is by grace (2:6–8) and urged readers to put on the moral qualities of God (4:24), Paul emphasizes that the nature of the forgiveness being called for is similar to the one exemplified by God in his act of forgiveness (see Matt 6:12, 14; 18:21–35).[65] In other words, God is both the motivation and model for forgiveness.

---

59. "πικρία," *NIDNTT*, 1.202, and W. C. Trenchard, *Complete Vocabulary Guide to the Greek NT* (Grand Rapids: Zondervan, 1992), 89.

60. Kleinknecht, *Wrath*, 1–2.

61. The contrastive δὲ is the preferred reading though some mss have ουν to denote inference.

62. Philo, *Virtues*, 182. Philo lists it in a catalogue of virtues associated with those who are devout in their relationship to God; it is sincerity that enhances trust in human interaction.

63. *T. Zeb.* 5:1b. According to the *TTP*, even animals need to be treated with tenderness.

64. See Liddell and Scott, *Greek-English Lexicon*, 1978–1979.

65. I do not deem the choice of word here to be coincidence since the author could have used ἀφίεμι instead. Grace is a prominent theme in this letter in undercutting potential pomposity. I opine that χαρίζομαι here is meant to evoke the idea of beneficiaries of God's grace being called upon to extend grace (forgiveness) to one another.

## 5.5 Grieving the Holy Spirit by Moral Indecency 4:28–30

Ephesians 4:28–30 utilizes a virtue-vice antithesis[66] to promote work ethic and appropriate speech in the church. The language shifts from the previous address in the plural to first person singular to indict any propensity to steal;[67] a more desirable path is to work hard to be able to contribute meaningfully to the community. Stealing has far reaching consequences in the way it undermines solidarity. Conversely, members must endeavor to do profitable or honest work.[68] Hard work was a known virtue among Jews,[69] Greeks and Romans. The author proceeds to condemn vulgarity or inappropriate use of words, especially that which is characterized as rotten speech. The only kind of speech admissible must be true,[70] seasoned, and good for edification.

Significant in this inquiry is the consequence accompanying inappropriate speech, namely grieving the Spirit (4:30).[71] Apparently, foul language has the potential to grieve the Spirit. The imperative with the negative particle (μὴ λυπεῖτε) suggests that it lies within the power of community members to abstain from falsehood. Moral failure may lead to grieving the Holy Spirit of God (4:30). Τὸ πνεῦμα τὸ ἅγιον τοῦ θεοῦ is an unusual expression in the NT referring to the Holy Spirit. Fee posits that Ephesians aims to emphasize the role of the Spirit in ethics with "emphatic declaration that the *Holy* Spirit is none other than the Spirit *of God*."[72] The church stands to undermine "unity of the Spirit"(4:3) by grieving the Holy Spirit of God. This same Spirit is the one by whom they are sealed for their ultimate inheritance in God (1:13–14).[73] "The

---

66. Plutarch, *Mor.* 510. Musonius Rufus, 4.20–25. Plutarch argues that the use of contrastive pattern as a device is an effective mode for instruction and argumentation.

67. Stealing is a vice in both Greek and Jewish conventions (cf. Exod 20:15; Deut 5:19; Isa 1:29; Jer 7:9).

68. See Paul's use of the word for manual work (1 Cor 4:12; 2 Tim 2:6; 1 Thess 1:3; 2:9, and 2 Thess 3:8) and religious work (Rom 16:12; 1 Cor 15:10; Gal 4:11; Phil 2:16; 1 Thess 5:12; 1 Tim 4:10; 5:17).

69. Exod 20:9; Ps 104:23; Prov 6:6; 10:4; 28; Ecclus 7:17; Josephus *Ap.* 2:29.

70. Aristotle, *Nic. Eth.* IV. 7 (1127a).

71. J. Rea, *The Holy Spirit in the Bible: All Major Passages about the Spirit* (Lake Mary, FL: Creation House, 1990), 289–290. Rea suggests that the Spirit plays a prominent part in the unity of the church and as such, all vices – not only speech – undermining unity in the church would grieve the Holy Spirit.

72. Fee, *God's Empowering Presence*, 714, and G. D. Fee, *To What End Exegesis: Essays Textual, Exegetical and Theological* (Grand Rapids: Eerdmans, 2001), 266.

73. R. A. Young, *Intermediate New Testament Greek: A Linguistic and Exegetical Approach* (Nashville: Broadman & Holman, 1994), 31–32. Young explains the syntactical function of the genitive and argues that we read it in light of the eschatological promise for Jews. Thus, "the day of redemption" is akin to "the day in which God redeems his people." Cf. 1 Thess 5:2; 2 Thess 2:2; 1 Cor 1:8; 5:5; 2 Cor 1:14.

Spirit is both the sign of ownership and authentication and the empowering presence of God for living to the glory of God until we finally arrive at the promised glory which is our own inheritance (Rom 8:17)."[74] That human conduct could aggrieve a spiritual entity (Holy Spirit, the Spirit of God) or yield spiritual consequence is evident in the NT and in Second Temple Jewish literature.[75] As one such text indicates, "you shall take care and be alert that you do not grieve the spirit of the Lord."[76]

## 5.6 The Children of God in the Kingdom of God 5:1–5

The discourse proceeds with further appeals to members of the church to identify with God and exhibit commensurate virtue, namely love.[77] The admonition for love in 5:1–2 appeals to kinship and the unwritten code of honor and shame that obliges children to emulate the noble qualities of their father. Ephesians insists that they imitate God as his beloved children (5:1–2). The τέκνα ἀγαπητὰ language assumes that they are beneficiaries of God's love, needing to imitate their father (God) by walking in the manner of love he exemplified through the sacrificial work of Christ. "Imitating God" does not presume mystical experience but a natural outflow of virtue anchored in personal relationship with God. As a community created after the likeness of God (4:24), it is natural to be called upon to bear the character of God. The idea of imitating a god is commonplace in Greek, Roman, and Second Temple antiquity. Devotees are similarly entreated by Philo to exhibit the qualities of God, as we find here.[78] Accordingly, "what one of the men of old aptly said is true, that human beings do nothing more akin to God than showing kindness. For what greater good can there be than they should imitate God."[79] For Musonius, humans ought to imitate God because he is their maker and worthy of emulation.

---

74. Fee, *God's Empowering Presence*, 717, 269, and Robinson, *Ephesians*, 114.

75. J. P. Sampley, "Scripture and Tradition in the Community as Seen in Ephesians 4.25ff," *ST* 2 (1972): 105.

76. *T. Isaac* 4.40. See Isaiah 63:10.

77. Ephesians 1:5, 15; 2:4; 3:18–19; 4:3, 15–16; 5:25, 28, 33; 6:23–24. The prominent feature of "love" in the letter in these verses.

78. Philo, *Spec. Leg.* 4.72ff. See Plato, *Theaet.* 176A–B and Pseudo-Isocrates, *To Demonicus* 9–11. For Plato, this can be actualized when the flight of the soul from the corrupt world occurs. He asserts, "a man becomes like God when he becomes just and pure, with understanding" (*Theaet.* 176A–B).

79. Philo, *Spec.* 4.72–73; Philo, *Fug.* 63.

> In general, of all creatures on earth man alone resembles God
> and has the same virtues as He has, since we can imagine nothing
> even in the gods better than prudence, justice, courage, and
> temperance. Therefore, as God, through the possession of these
> virtues, is unconquered by pleasure or greed, is superior to desire,
> envy, and jealousy; is high minded, beneficent, and kindly (for
> such is our conception of God), so also man in the image of Him,
> when living in accord with nature, should be thought of as being
> like Him, and being enviable, he would forthwith be happy, for
> we envy none but the happy.[80]

For Ephesians, the architect of the community and its identity serves as a good model of conduct for its flourishing; after all, they are created to bear the moral image of God (2:10, 15: 4:24) for the praise of his glory (1:6, 12, 18).

The particle ὡς in the phrase ὡς τέκνα ἀγαπητὰ (5:1) may be read as comparative[81] to imply that members imitate God *just as* dearly loved children would or as an adverb qualifying the manner of conduct, *like/as dearly loved children*. The father image of God and quality as a loving father is implied in either case. It is honorable that children maintain the virtuous legacy of great fathers. Pseudo-Isocrates emphasizes that it is a duty: "You must consider that no athlete is so in duty bound to train against his competitors as are you to take thought how you may vie with your father in his ways of life."[82] In the honor and shame culture,[83] it is only fitting that children imitate their father as a moral necessity for the honor of the household (2:19; 6:1).[84] For Philo, children must exercise prudence in "imitating the nature of their father, do all that is right without delay and with all diligence."[85] Ephesians shares this

---

80. Musonius Rufus, XVIII, citing from Lutz, "Musonius Rufus," 109.

81. This would mean that ὡς functions as a comparative adjective.

82. Pseudo-Isocrates, *To Dominicus* 1–15 citing from Malherbe, *Moral Exhortation*, 126.

83. N. Sherman, *Making a Moral Necessity of Virtue: Aristotle and Kant on Virtue* (Cambridge: CUP, 1997), 38–98. Sherman has demonstrated that the use of such expressions and other concepts to evoke emotional response was important in Stoic moral discourse. Moreover, Aristotle employs this device more frequently as he finds the rhetorical strategy useful to evoke his readers' emotions while challenging the mind at the same time to be effective (p. 380). Ephesians follows the convention in this regard.

84. Hierocles, *On Duties*, 4.25.53 = 4.640, 4–644, 15, citing from Malherbe, *Moral Exhortation*, 91–93. Hierocles reckons that it is natural for children to mimic the qualities of their parents and ought to live in a manner that brings honor to them.

85. Philo, *Sacrifices* 68b.

tradition in framing love as a virtue entwined with the identity of believers as children of God.[86]

Another comparison to a spiritual being is made to further explain the nature of love under consideration.[87] Love must be demonstrated like how Christ loved in self-giving and personal sacrifice. Christ serves as a model for love that is pleasing and befitting to their identity.[88] This clause elucidates how Christ exemplified love in his salvific work and serves as a motivation for beneficiaries. Love is the ability to give of oneself for the good of a neighbor[89] in obedience to God, as exemplified in Christ.

The opening of the *paraenesis* places a strong accent on three cardinal virtues that ought to be expressed in love and in preserving unity of the Spirit (4:1–3). Elsewhere, the author prays that love become the matrix from which the church grows (3:17). The love of Christ features similarly in the household code as a model for husbands in conjugal relations (5:25–28). The seventeen appearances of love in Ephesians range from love as divine attribute, basis for conduct or virtue to exhibit – all in the sense of that which is gracious or sacrificial.[90] It should come as no surprise that Paul links this virtue to the readers' identity as children of God and Christ as the model for conduct (5:1–2). Furthermore, he makes a sharp contrast to the sacrificial love of Christ – as a fragrant offering to God – with incompatible vices to their current status (5:3). Sexual immorality,[91] every form of impurity and greed must be unheard

---

86. Cf. Gal 4:5–6; Rom 5:5; 8:15; Phil 2:15.

87. Cf. Eph 1:5, 15; 2:4; 3:18–19; 4:3, 15–16; 5:25, 28, 33; 6:23–24.

88. Lincoln, *Ephesians*, 311.

89. See *T. Gad*, 4.7. Here, love is the law of God for the salvation of humanity, whereas Satan is the author of hatred. His purpose is to thwart the work of God.

90. Ephesians 1:5, 15; 2:4; 3:18–19; 4:3, 15–16; 5:25, 28, 33; 6:23–24.

91. See E. Schweizer, *The Letter to the Colossians*, trans. Andrew Chester (London: SPCK, 1976), 190. Schweizer argues that the word denotes misguided sexual conduct. Also Vögtle, *Lasterkaloge*, 208–209; A. R. Guenther, "The Exception Phrases: Except πορνεία, Including πορνεία or Excluding πορνεία? (Matthew 5:32; 19:9)," 81–96. Ben Witherington, "Mathew 5.32 and 19.9 – Exception or Exceptional Situation?," *NTS* 31 (1985): 571–576; B. Vawter, "The Divorce Clause of Matt 5:32 and 19:9," *CBQ* 16 (1954): 155–167. D. Janzen, "The Meaning of PORNEIA in Matthew 5:32 and 19:9: An Approach from the Study of Ancient Near Eastern Culture," *JSNT* 80 (2000): 66–80. See also D. C. Allison Jr., "Divorce, Celibacy and Joseph (Matthew 1:18–25 and 19:1–12)," *JSNT* 49 (1993): 3–10. Janzen indicates that the term denotes "sex before marriage" in the Matthean context but it usually applies to sexual immorality in general. Allison provides more discussion on how sexual infidelity during bridal betrothal could be damaging. Mary and Joseph of Nazareth are taken as examples when one considers the immediate plans of Joseph to divorce her as a result of her pregnancy.

of in their midst. The argument *ad verecundiam*[92] is effective in the honor and shame culture.[93] Here, the author employs a cultic parlance to refer to them as "God's holy people" to demarcate clear boundaries between them and unfitting sexual practices (see Mark 7:22; 1 Cor 5:10). Πορνεία[94] and its cognate in 5:5 often received more attention in early Christian literature due to the prevalence of sexual laxity in sacred and social settings[95] of Greek antiquity. Sexual immorality,[96] impurity and greed similarly appear in 5:5 where it is

---

92. G. Heyworth and R. Liberman, *Stylebook: The Writing and Revision Stylebook* (New Haven: Cooper Hill, 2000), 225. Literally *argument to shame* – appeal to shame or embarrassment as the basis to distance oneself from unfitting conduct.

93. W. R. Domeris, "Honour and Shame in the New Testament," *Neot* 27, no. 2 (1993): 285, and 283–295. See Cicero, *On Moral Duties*, 2. Cicero aptly articulates the widespread notion of honor and shame, though writing in the Roman context, "in the observance of duty lies all that is honorable, and in neglect of it all that is dishonorable . . . He who severs the highest good from virtue and measures it by interest and not by honor, if he were true to his principles and did not at times yield to his better nature, could not cultivate friendship, justice or liberality."

94. It is condemned in the NT (Matt 5:32; 19:9; Acts 15:20, 29; 21:25; 1 Cor 5:1).

95. See Demosthenes, *Against Neaera*, 123. Here, Apollodoros indicates that "mistresses we keep for the sake of pleasure, concubines for the daily care of our persons, but wives to bear us legitimate children and to be faithful guardians of our households." In *Laws,* VIII, 841, Plato's notion of sexual decency allows for secret affairs as long as the spouse of the subject is kept in the dark. Plato indicates, "(1) Ideally, no one will dare to have relations with any respectable citizen woman except his own wedded wife, or sow illegitimate and bastard seed in courtesans or sterile seed in males in difference of nature. (2) Alternatively, while suppressing sodomy entirely, we might insist that if a man does have intercourse with any woman (hired or procured in some other way) except the wife he wed in holy marriage with the blessing of the gods, he must do so without any other man or woman getting to know about it. If he fails to keep his affair secret, I think we'd be right to exclude him by law from our state honors, on grounds that he's no better than an alien" (trans. Trevor J. Saunders). Musonius Rufus, however, condemns homosexuality, bisexuality and adultery, and argues that all forms of sex outside heterosexual marital relationship is shameful and unacceptable (Musonius Rufus, XII.1–5). Jewish literature similarly condemns sexual immorality in no ambiguous terms (Gen 34:31; 1 Kgs 15:12; 22:47; Amos 7:17 and *T. Levi* 14:5–6; Sir 23:16; cf. Hos 9:1; Jer 3:6; Ezek 23:19; 1 Ch 5:25; Ps 72:27; En 8:2). Philo expresses the norm succinctly in the discourse *On Joseph* where he states, "in other nations the youths are permitted, after they are fourteen years of age, to use concubines and prostitutes, and women who make gain by their persons, without restraint. But among us a harlot is not allowed even to live, but death is appointed as a punishment for anyone who adopts such a way of life. Therefore before our lawful marriage we know nothing of any connection with any other woman, but, without ever having experienced any similar cohabitation, we approach our virgin brides as pure as themselves, proposing as the end of our marriage not pleasure but the offspring of legitimate children" (Philo, *Joseph* IX [43]).

96. R. Kempthorne, "Incest and the Body of Christ: A Study of 1 Cor VI. 12–20," *NTS* 14 (1967/68): 568–574. B. Malina, "Does *PORNEIA* Mean Fornication?" *NovT* 14 (1972): 10–17. J. Jensen, "Does *PORNEIA* Mean Fornication? A Critique of Bruce Malina," *NovT* 20 (1978): 161–184. Jubilees 7:20–21; 20:2–6; 30:7; 33:13–20; 39:6; 41:25. It carries the sense of sexual perversion, including incest, prostitution, harlotry and adultery. Malina alleges that "there is no evidence in traditional or contemporary usage of the word *porneia* that denotes pre-betrothal, premarital, heterosexual intercourse of a non-cultic or non-commercial nature, i.e. what we call 'fornication' today." Further, he argues that its appearance in Jewish literature is in

stated that those who indulge in them shall not inherit the kingdom of Christ and of God. In other words, God's intervention in human history in the advent of Christ is geared towards the construction of a community marked by God's identity and sealed by the Holy Spirit (1:13–14) with moral standards modeled after Christ. Those who refuse to comply with the divinely sanctioned conduct will be barred from the kingdom of God and of Christ.

Christ followers are commanded to desist from certain speech-related vices (5:4), such as foolish talk in general (see 1QS 7:14–18), dirty talk and crude joking. It is important to note that these three vices (αἰσχρότης, μωρολογί,[97] εὐτραπελία[98] – [5.3–4]) are contrasted by one cardinal virtue, namely εὐχαριστία. Εὐχαριστία translates as thanksgiving or gratitude. In the religious circles, it usually denotes an expression of gratitude towards a benevolent deity. The DSS contrasts it with deceit and craftiness (1QS 10:21–23). In Jewish thought, the virtue may be exhibited not only as an attitude but also gratitude expressed in prayers, offerings or in singing praise to God. When it is directed to God it duly summarizes attitudes and words that emerge from sober reflection on what God has done. Philo recalls what Moses said about this important virtue. "And Moses very appropriately says that the fruit of education is not only holy but also praise; for every one of the virtues is a holy thing, but most especially is gratitude (εὐχαριστία) holy . . . Having learnt therefore that there is only one employment possible for us of all the things that seem to contribute to the honor of God, namely the display of gratitude (εὐχαριστία)."[99]

It is not clear if εὐχαριστία in 5:4 has God as the main object or not. The contrast with vices, though, suggests that the virtue is important to cultivate either as a personal quality or an attitude towards God for what he has done (see 1:16). A warning follows (5:6) to recall punitive reaction to acts of disobedience and to "those who are disobedient" (2:2–3), implying that the Holy God detests

---

reference to unlawful sexual practices within the framework of the Torah. Also F. F. Bruce, *I & II Thessalonians* (WBC; Waco: Word Books, 1982), 82. Bruce indicates that "there was no body of public opinion to discourage πορνεία although someone who indulged in it in excess might be satirized on the same level as a notorious glutton or drunkard."

97. Aristotle, *Ethics Eud.* 1234a. It features as a virtue in the works of Aristotle to indicate the middle ground between scandalous ways to insult or injure the reputation of the other and being boorish, but the word is also used as a vice in Aristotle (Aristotle, *Eth. Nic.* 1128 and *Rhetoric* 1389b). Sometimes the word is used to refer to dirty jokes or verbal provocation etc. See P. W. van der Horst, "Is Wittiness UnChristian? A Note on Εὐτραπελία in Ephesians 5:4," in *Miscellenea Neotestamentica Vol. 2*, ed. T. Baarda, A. F. J. Klijn, and W. C. van Unnik (Leiden: Brill, 1978): 163–177. Isocrates, *Areopagiticus* 49. *Antidosis* 296.

98. Plato, *Gorg.* 525a. This is obscenity perpetrated by or associated with vulgar language.

99. Philo, *Plant.* 126 and 131.

misconduct whether it is associated with the pre-conversion past or prevailing among Christ followers. God's children must be obedient, exhibit good conduct or face God's wrath. They are now "light in the Lord" and thus expected to conduct themselves as "children of light"[100] in discerning what is pleasing to the Lord (5:8); they must desist from "fruitless deeds of darkness" (5:11) that are shameful even to name among them.[101] Here, spiritual beings not only shape who the believers are (identity), but also how they conduct themselves (ethics).

## 5.7 The Marks of the Spirit-Filled Community 5:15–21

This pericope makes a sharp contrast between "the foolish" and "the wise" to press for the need for Christ followers to choose wise ways. To be wise here is not to be philosophically enlightened but to exercise wise judgement in the ways of the Lord (5:18–21).[102] The antithesis underscores the necessity for vigilance and sound moral judgment under the lordship of Christ (5:15).[103] In Stoic philosophy, the fool lacks common sense for moral judgment[104] vis-à-vis prudence.[105] "If the essence of virtue be intelligence, then the essence of vice must be ignorance,"[106] they argued. The Hebrew tradition personified "wisdom" as the source, bearer[107] or figure on whom humans depend to acquire the knowledge of God.[108] The wise person makes judicious use of time and

---

100. J. Frey, "Different Patterns of Dualistic Thought in the Qumran Library," in *Legal Texts and Legal Issues: Proceedings of the Second Meeting of the International Organization for Qumran Studies*, eds. Moshe Bernstein et al. (Leiden: Brill, 1997), 283–285.

101. L. J. Kreitzer, "'Crude Language' and 'Shameful Things Done in Secret' (Ephesians 5:4, 12): Allusions to the Cult of Demeter/Cybele in Hierapolis," *JSNT* 71 (1998): 51–77. Kreitzer argues that the language here and 5:4 appealing to shame and vices associated with darkness are all allusions to practices in the cult of Demeter of Hierapolis.

102. Aristotle, *Eth. Eud.* III.7, 1234a. Cicero, *Fin.* III.55. T. Irwin, *Plato's Ethics* (New York: Oxford University, 1995), 347–350. The wise possesses virtue and practical wisdom, but the fool does not. To be wise then is to possess ability to make sound moral judgement in life.

103. Cf. Deut 32:6; Jer 4:22; Prov 1:22; 6:12.

104. M. E. Reesor, "The Stoic Wise Man," in *Proceedings of the Boston Area Colloquium in Ancient Philosophy Vol. V*, eds. J. J. Clearly and D. C. Shartin (Lanham: University Press of America, 1991), 109–110.

105. J. Ferguson, *Moral Values in the Ancient World* (London: Methuen, 1958), 30. See also Plato, *Phaed.* 69a ff. and *Laws* I. 631c. *Prot.* 330a.

106. Ferguson, *Moral Values in the Ancient World*, 30.

107. Prov 1:20–33; 8:1–36; 9:1–6, 10–12.

108. S. W. Crawford, "Lady Wisdom and Dame Folly at Qumran," *Dead Sea Discoveries* 5, no. 3 (1998): 357–359. It is in this light that the Torah is said to be the embodiment of the Wisdom of God.

seizes every opportunity[109] cognizant of the fact that the days are evil.[110] It is imperative then to desist from foolish ways[111] or "moral stupidity"[112] in pursuit of the wishes of the Lord (5:17). This must be a collective endeavor to know the will of the Lord Jesus Christ.

The foolish-wise antithesis pertaining to identity and morality proceeds with subsidiary antithesis to oblige members to desist from liquor-induced vices and endeavor to embrace Spirit-empowered virtues (5:18–21). Drunkenness belongs to darkness and aligns with a foolish[113] way of life whereas prudence is associated with being filled with/by the Spirit (see Prov 23:31). Wine was part of a staple meal in ancient Mediterranean cultures; the text does not aim to condemn alcohol consumption. Christ followers and their unbelieving counterparts would have had wine as part of their regular meal. Rituals and festivities at cultic precincts often included food and wine. Excessive drinking or drunkenness is what is at issue here. For example, excessive drinking[114] was a regular feature at the shrine of Dionysius where devotees considered eating raw meat and drinking (wine) excessively a means to be empowered by the "god of wine."[115] "In order to attain communion with their god the devotees of Dionysius (called Bachantes) drank wine until thoroughly intoxicated . . . thus the influence of their god."[116]

The Hebrews similarly considered abundance of corn or grapes for wine as a blessing from God (Gen 27:28, 37; Joel 2:24 LXX). Wine was used in sacrifices and in other rituals.[117] However, drunkenness was deemed a vice and condemned.[118] Here, Christ followers are being barred from inebriation by alcohol and its moral consequence in the form of sexual laxity or prodigality

---

109. R. M. Pope, "Studies in Pauline Vocabulary – Of Redeeming the Time," *ET* 22 (1910–11): 553. Marcus Aurelius, *Med.* II. XII, XXV.

110. Best, *Ephesians*, 504. Cf. Pelagius; Origen, *Matt. Cat.* 134; GCS 41, 67.1; *Judges Hom* GCS 30, 467.15ff.

111. Josephus, *B. J.* 1.32.3 and 2.14.8.

112. Foulkes, *Ephesians*, 157.

113. Plutarch, *Mor.* 503E, 504B; Philo, *Ebr.* 95, 125–126, *Plant.* 140–147; Prov 23:29–35 LXX; 2 Kgs 11:13.

114. *TDNT* V.162.

115. E. Fergusson, *Early Christianity*, 243, and R. S. Kraemer, "Ecstasy and Possession: The Attraction of Women to the Cult of Dionysius," *HTR* 72/1–2 (1979): 57. See Darko, "The Role of Spiritual Beings in Relation to Ethics," 9–35.

116. B. M. Metzger, *The New Testament: Its Background, Growth, and Content* (Nashville: Abingdon, 1965), 69.

117. Num 6:3; Judg 13:4, 7; Luke 1:15; 7:33.

118. Luke 15:13; 1 Cor 6:10; Gal 5:19–21; 1 Tim 3:3, 8; 5:23; Titus 2:3.

(ἀσωτία). Rogers suggests that we read 5:18a against this backdrop since the rituals of Dionysius were widespread in Asia Minor at the time.[119] Three reasons are offered to this effect: First, that the connection between drunkenness and licentiousness describes the ritual scene at the shrine. Second, the contrast between "drunkenness and debauchery" and "the Spirit and virtue" in one sentence seems to allude to a spiritual context of sort. "If the filling of the Spirit has to do with a supernatural infilling of the Spirit of God, it would only be logical to suppose that the 'drunk with wine' could have a supernatural implication."[120] Third, the mention of "hymns and songs from the Spirit" as a resultant effect from spiritual experience parallels rituals on the shrine of Dionysius where singing and dancing were a regular feature. The idea that spirits were able to influence human conduct to exhibit either virtue or vice was widespread, and we have no reason to doubt that Ephesians 5:18a would have resonated with converts and inhabitants where these religious activities were rampant. We cannot, however, establish with certitude that any particular religious activity serves as the background to this instruction. Gosnell argues that 5:18a may be read rather against the background of a Greco-Roman mealtime, which was often accompanied by drinking and singing in praise to the gods.[121] It was common for members of a polis to gather for symposia, rituals in homes and/or festivities at sacred precincts. It would be problematic to locate a particular background to this phrase. That spiritual powers were capable of enabling humans to flourish was common sense in the milieu.

Paul seems to be more interested in the work of the Spirit to empower members for life in the community (5:18b–21); he simply warns against drunkenness and its accompanying moral failings in order to accentuate the antithetical counterparts in pursuit of the will of the Lord; they must be filled continually with/by the Spirit. The "Spirit" refers to the Holy Spirit,[122] not to the human spirit.[123] The syntax of ἐν is a debated matter – whether it expresses the means by which people are filled or the substance that fills the believers.

---

119. C. L. Rogers, Jr. "The Dionysian Background of Ephesians 5:18," *BSac* 136.543 (1979): 249.

120. Rogers, Jr. "The Dionysian Background of Ephesians 5:18," 256.

121. P. W. Gosnell, "Ephesians 5:18–20 and Mealtime Propriety," *TynBul* 44, no. 2 (1993): 363–371. Also Plutarch, *Mor.* I. 614D615C.

122. Fee, *God's Empowering Presence*, 21, and A. J. Kostenberger, "What Does It Mean to Be Filled with the Holy Spirit? A Biblical Investigation," *JETS* 40, no. 2 (1997): 232–233.

123. See Abbot, *Ephesians*, 161–162; Wescott, *Ephesians*, 81.

The usual translation "Instead, be filled with the Spirit"[124] denotes that the Spirit is the content or substance.[125] Some argue to the contrary that when the preposition ἐν features with πληρόω in the NT it consistently expresses the means by which the filling occurs.[126] "The parallel with οἴνῳ as well as the common grammatical category of *means* suggest that the idea intended is that the believers are to be filled *by means of* the (Holy) Spirit,"[127] argues Wallace. If we accept this reading then the substance is unnamed; we may, however, surmise that God or Christ is in view as we find in other features of πληρόω in Ephesians (1:23; 3:19; 4:10–11).[128] The thrust of the matter is that if the Holy Spirit is content/substance then God/Christ is doing the filling and if it functions as the means (instrumental) then the substance would be God/Christ. Without rehearsing the entire argument, the parallels with wine and context of Ephesians seems to support the notion that the Spirit is the means, mediating the infilling of the fullness of God/Christ.[129] Thus, the readers must be filled by the Spirit to the extent that they come to know God in all his fullness and exhibit qualities that would foster in-group solidarity and better relationship with God.[130]

The five *anarthrous* participles in the subordinate clauses to the imperative, "be filled," indicate the tangible results[131] or effects in the community (5:19–

---

124. See the "New Revised Standard Version," "New International Version," "New King James Version," "New American Standard Bible" and the most recent "Today's New International Version."

125. H. C. G. Moule, *Ephesian Studies* (London: Hodder & Stoughton, 1900), 275–276.

126. Wallace, *Greek Grammar beyond the Basics*, 93, and Fee, *God's Empowering Presence*, 721. They indicate that the verb usually takes the genitive to convey such meaning in the NT (cf. Rom 1:29; 2 Cor 7:4; Luke 2:40).

127. Wallace, *Beyond the Basics*, 375. Also O'Brien, *Ephesians*, 391–392.

128. O'Brien, *Ephesians*, 392, Wallace, *Greek beyond the Basics*, 375 and Lincoln, *Ephesians*, 344.

129. O'Brien, *Ephesians*, 392. Cf. Wallace, *Beyond the Basics*, 375. Wallace gives similar explanation as I have given above and concludes that 5:18b suggests that the "believers are to be filled *by* Christ *by means of* the Spirit *with* content of the fullness of God." Also Lincoln, *Ephesians*, 344. The syntax alone is not sufficient to reach a definite conclusion. For the purposes of our discussion, the Spirit, God and Christ are all spiritual beings working in concert on behalf of the church. In that sense, the import of Spirit empowerment for human conduct does not change much whether the Spirit is taken as *means* or *substance* by which believers are filled.

130. Fee, *God's Empowering Presence*, 722.

131. T. G. Gombis, "Being the Fullness of God in Christ by the Spirit: Ephesians 5:18 in Its Epistolary Setting," *TynBul* 53, no. 2 (2002): 259–271, J. Gnilka, *Der Epheserbrief*, HTKNT 10, no. 2 (Freiburg: Herder, 1971), 270, and H. Schlier, *Der Brief an die Epheser: Ein Kommentar* (Dusseldorf: Patmos, 1971), 246. Gombis advances an earlier interpretation of Gnilka and Schlier that the participial clauses express the means by which people are filled by the Spirit. For Gombis, speaking, singing, making melody, thanksgiving and submission describe "the way in which the

21).[132] First, this will take the form of mutual edification in the way members speak to one another (5:19). The mention of psalms, hymns and songs from the Spirit may not overshadow the import of the verb λαλέω, which means "to speak, talk or intelligible speech" and rarely applied to music.[133] The referent is that of a Spirit-filled community in which members speak to one another by means[134] of psalms,[135] hymns[136] and songs from the Spirit.[137] The second result of being compliant to and availing themselves for the filling with/by the Spirit takes the form of worship; singing and making melody in their hearts to the Lord.[138] The terms ἄδοντες καὶ ψάλλοντες seem to be hendiadys depicting a wide array of singing in worship. The Lord Jesus is the one to whom praise is due, and the kind of worship is that which is marked by sincerity from the heart. The heart is the center of human personality, intellect and will.[139] Worship is "offered from the heart where the Spirit dwells (Rom 5:5; 2 Cor 1:22; 3:3; Gal 4:6); it comes from the deepest level of existence and is not purely emotional (hearty) froth but contains considerable intellectual content; the singing was singing with understanding."[140] The third resultant effect recalls a virtue that previously contrasted speech-related vices, namely thanksgiving (5:20).[141] In a community filled by/with the Spirit, members give thanks always for everything. This sense of gratitude is channeled to God in the name of Jesus Christ (John 14:13–14; Acts 4:9–19; Phil 2:9–10). The fourth and final result is that Spirit-filled members submit[142] to one another out of reverence

---

church carries out its identity as the dwelling place of God in Christ by the Spirit." He further clarifies that, "the five participles do not *lead to* the filling by the Spirit, rather they indicate the *means by which* the command is carried out" (p. 270).

132. Wallace, *Greek Grammar beyond the Basics*, 637–639. These are participles of result.

133. Aristotle, *Eud. Eth.* 801a 29, and Liddell and Scott, *Greek-English Dictionary*, 1026.

134. The prepositional phrase could be taken as instrumental or means.

135. Luke 20:42; 24:44; Acts 1:20; 13:33; 1 Cor 14:26 and Col 3:16.

136. It is anachronistic to surmise that it refers to what we call hymns today. The word simply means songs of praise.

137. Rev 5:9; 14:3; 15:3. It is not unthinkable that spiritual songs may be found in a community filled by the Holy Spirit. Various forms of expressions may be deemed spiritual experience in that regard.

138. Cf. Josephus, *Ant.* 11, 67; 12:349. Cf. 1 Cor 14:15; Pss 7:18; 9:12; 107:4 LXX.

139. Best, *Ephesians*, 165.

140. Best, 513.

141. Rom 1:9; 1 Cor 1:4; Phil 1:4; 4:4; Col 1:3; 1 Thess 1:2; 2 Thess 1:3, 11; Phlm 4; *Did.* 9.2, 3.

142. J. H. Greenlee, *Introduction to New Testament Textual Criticism* (Peabody: Hendrickson, 1995), 64. The verse and paragraph divisions that makes 5:21 a separate sentence are misleading. The paragraph and verses were not introduced until 1551 when Robert Esteinne built on the

for Christ (5:21).[143] They are blessed with spiritual blessings and indeed the Spirit works and mediates the flourishing of the community as a whole. As the diagram shows, the Spirit empowers believers to conduct themselves with moral decency and graceful demeanor.[144]

> And do not be drunk with wine
> which leads to (results in) debauchery
> But be *filled by the Spirit*
> > *speaking* to one another in psalms, hymns and spiritual songs
> > *singing* and *making melody* in your heart to the Lord
> > *giving thanks* always for all things in the name of the Lord Jesus
> Christ to God the father
> > *submitting* to one another in reverence for Christ.

Thus, ethical living is a natural outcome in a community whose members submit to the filling by/with the Spirit (5:18–21). Human responsibility is, however, required for the divine enabling to occur. The Spirit's empowerment should not be equated with ecstatic experiences such as speaking in tongues or prophecy, but an infilling that ultimately engenders suitable demeanor and good conduct. Instead of unwise undertakings fueled by alcohol, members are admonished to be filled by/with the Spirit as the wise alternative to enhance mutual edification, decency and right attitude. It is imperative that they comply with this instruction if they are to benefit from what the Spirit offers to the body of Christ. These admonitions are important as both the individual and collective endeavor to bear witness to outsiders. Consequently, the call "to be filled by/with Spirit" follows with how members of the house churches have to conduct themselves in the households, as Christ followers.

## 5.8 Household Conduct in Christological Framework 5:22 – 6:9

The admonition to the wife draws seamlessly from the Spirit-filled effects in the community[145] in which members submit to one another out of the

---

work of Archbishop Stephen Langton, who had divided the NT into chapters in 1205. The punctuation of NA 28 is misleading in this regard.

143. Cf. E. Käsemann, "Ministry and Community in the New Testament," in *Essays on New Testament Themes*, trans. W. J. Montague, eds. C. F. D. Moule et al. (London: SCM, 1964), 98.

144. Darko, *No Longer Living as the Gentiles*, 65–66. I shed more light on the structure there.

145. In some critical texts Ephesians 5:19–24 forms one sentence.

fear of the Lord (5:21).[146] The *Haustafel* derives from pneumatic activity, framed in Christocentric parlance, and grammatically linked to the preceding foolish-wise antithesis, underscoring how Spirit-filled members may conduct themselves in their households. That spiritual beings – the Holy Spirit and Jesus Christ – feature in such admonition should not come as a surprise in Ephesians. Marriage is the pursuit of the wise who are empowered by the Spirit for good conduct in the locus where Christ reigns as Lord.[147] The call for wives to submit to their husbands[148] emerges as a natural outworking of pneumatic experience – the participle retains its force as an imperative of entreaty requiring wives to act voluntarily (middle voice)[149] "out of reverence for Christ."[150] Customarily, it is right and honorable[151] that the wife submits to her husband, even to his religion. In the wider scope of submission, Plutarch advises that a wife embrace the household gods as her best friends: "Wherefore it is becoming for a wife to worship and to know only the gods that her husband believes in, and to shut the door tight upon all queer rituals and outlandish superstitions."[152] Plutarch also challenges the husband to love his wife, be a good example and keep concord in the household. He forbids her to use magical

---

146. F. Watson, *Agape, Eros, Gender: Towards a Pauline Sexual Ethic* (Cambridge: Cambridge University Press, 2000), 222–223.

147. Darko, *No Longer Living as the Gentiles*, 81–93. O. L. Yarbrough, *Not Like the Gentiles: Marriage Rules in the Letters of Paul* (SBLDS 80; Atlanta: Scholars Press, 1985), 31–63. Will Deming, *Paul on Marriage and Celibacy: The Hellenistic Background of 1 Corinthians 7* (SNTSMS 83; Cambridge: Cambridge University Press, 1995), 50–107. Yarbrough and Deming discuss the Stoic-Cynic debate on the value of marriage. Following their findings, I show how the Stoics make a strong case to consider marriage as the pursuit of wise men. Ephesians follows a similar thought pattern by indicating that marriage belongs to the wise and "wise ways" with the Lord.

148. Osiek, "The Bride of Christ (Ephesians 5:22–33)," 32. Osiek argues that the word for submission "carries the connotation of respectful rather than servile yielding, but very definitely of inferior subject to authoritative superior."

149. R. W. Wall, "Wifely Submission in the Context of Ephesians," *CSR* 17 (1988): 276–284; J. R. Beck, "Is There a Head of the House in the Home? Reflections on Ephesians 5," *JBE* 1 (1989): 61–66; S. H. Gritz, *Paul, Women Teachers, and the Mother Goddess at Ephesus: A Study of 1 Timothy 2:9–15 in Light of Religious and Cultural Milieu of the First Century* (Lanham: University Press of America, 1991), 90–91, and C. S. Keener, *Paul, Women and Wives: Marriage and Women's Ministry in the Letters of Paul* (Peabody: Hendrickson, 1992), 157–183. The filling by the Spirit obliges members to submit to one another. The participle in the "middle" implies no external pressure but voluntary initiative of the wife to submit as a spiritual act that also commands public respect.

150. F. Stagg, "The Domestic Code and Final Appeal: Ephesians 5:21–6:24," *RevExp* 76 (1979): 545. Fear does not imply authoritarianism or a destructive shadow of Christ over the people. It is not submission or acquiescing to intimidation but doing so under love and authority of the Lord.

151. Plutarch, *Mor.* 142E.

152. Plutarch, 140D.

spells as love charms, but endeavor to woo him by good conduct, conversation and companionship.[153] Spiritually, the gods presided over weddings[154] and all affairs of the household.

> The beauty of a household consists in yoking together of a husband and wife who are united to each other by fate, are consecrated to the gods who preside over the weddings, births, and houses, agree with each other and have all things in common, including their bodies, or rather their souls, and who exercise appropriate rule over their household and servants, take care in rearing their children, and pay an attention to the necessities of life which is neither intense nor slack, but moderate and fitting.[155]

Josephus insists that a wife, as the inferior partner, submits to her husband.[156] In the religious worldview, deities had significant influence on the conduct and prosperity of households – be it Greek, Jewish or Roman.

The motivation for bridal submission (5:22) is christologically grounded.[157] Κύριος is a common title for heads of households, spiritual agents or persons of authority. The ascription assigns certain superiority and prerogatives to the object/person referred to as lord.[158] The phrase ὡς τῷ κυρίῳ may be read as urging wives to submit to their husbands "as lords" or referring to the lordship of Jesus Christ as the point of reference. I opine that "as you do to the Lord" seems to be referring to Jesus as the Lord. Thus, Christ is the master of the household of believers, not family gods.

The headship of Christ over the church is appealed to in claiming the analogous position of the husband to Christ and invoking that as the basis for the wives to submit to husbands (5:23–24). The Christ-church analogy suggests that the wife's voluntary submission be seen as a gesture towards a husband who has her highest interest at heart. The husband's obligation to love his wife is similarly framed in Christ-church analogy to imply one that is exemplified in self-giving for her well-being; the husband's primary obligation is to love

---

153. Plutarch, 141B.

154. Plato, *Laws* VIII, 841.

155. Hierocles, *On Duties*. On Marriage (4.22.21-24=4.502, 1-507, 5 Hense; 24:14=4.603, 8-605 Hense) cited by Malherbe, *Moral Exhortation*, 102.

156. Josephus, *Ag. Ap.* 2.201. The religious obligation also provides a strong check on the conduct of the husband who stands under the oversight of God himself.

157. J. P. Sampley, *And the Two Shall Become One Flesh: A Study of Traditions in Ephesians 5:21–33* (Cambridge: CUP, 1971), 121–124.

158. Dunn, *Theology of Paul the Apostle*, 247. See D. Wenham, *Paul: Follower of Jesus or Founder of Christianity?* (Grand Rapids: Eerdmans, 1995), 121–122.

his wife as Christ loves the church (5:25, 28, 33). Customarily, husbands were expected to love their wives and promote concord.[159] To invoke Christ as a model for a husband's conduct is to place a higher demand to the effect that he exercises his roles honorably as a higher obligation. Love for the wife is divinely sanctioned and Christ serves as a model for human conduct. The nature of the love in question is the sacrificial love exemplified in the person and work of Christ. It is not unique for ancient moralists to admonish husbands to love their wives.[160] What is distinct here is the Christocentric framework and its strong religious underpinning. As husbands model their relationship after Christ, so may they be aware of the purpose of Christ's love for the church – to sanctify her, present her to himself in splendor, and to make her spotlessly pure. These virtues required of wives and husbands are necessary to harness marital union that is comparable to the Christ-church relationship, and this is a profound mystery (5:32). Paul appeals to the Hebrew scriptures to validate his case for marital union as divinely sanctioned and modelled after the Christ-church relationship.[161]

The fitting *modus vivendi* in the child-parent relationship shares most of its features with conventional moralists.[162] The religious impetus is overt in Ephesians though. For example, Dionysius indicates that obedience and respect for parents are commendable virtues for children to exhibit.[163] Ephesians calls on children to obey parents "in the Lord" and appeals to the scriptures to

---

159. Osiek, "The Bride of Christ (Ephesians 5:22–33)," 32. Also Grubbs, *Law and Family in Late Antiquity*, 212–213.

160. Plutarch, *Mor.* 143A. It is misleading to claim that ancient moralists did not encourage husbands to love their wives as a way to set Paul apart, suggesting that Paul departs from conventional patriarchal norms to promote love. The evidence rather supports the fact that emphasis on ancient marriages is placed on mutuality and concord. Men were admonished to love their spouses and, in some cases, they were encouraged to do more to maintain the honor in their households. For example, Plutarch indicates that "the marriage of a couple in love with each other is an intimate union; that of those who marry for dowry or children is of persons joined together; and that of those who merely sleep in the same bed is of separate persons who may be regarded as cohabiting, but not really living together" (Plutarch, *Mor.* 143A). See S. Dixon, "Sex and the Married Woman in Ancient Rome," in *Early Christian Families in Context: An Interdisciplinary Dialogue*, eds. D. L. Balch and C. Osiek (Grand Rapids: Eerdmans, 2003), 113. Dixon discusses the pursuit of love and romantic obsessions/infatuation of some men in how they expressed love to their wives in antiquity.

161. Sampley, *And the Two Shall Be One Flesh*, 75–76; P. R. Rodgers, "The Allusions to Genesis 2:23 at Ephesians 5:30," *JTS* 41 (1990): 92–94. Sampley argues that the OT quote forms the basis for the instruction on wife-husband relationship. Cf. Andrew T. Lincoln, "The Use of the OT in Ephesians," *JSNT* 14 (1982): 16–57. Lincoln argues that its import is significant but Sampley's conclusion has no strong basis to it (pp. 35–36).

162. Dionysius of Halicarnassus, *Rom. Ant.* II. 26.

163. Dionysius of Halicarnassus, 26.

buttress the point, indicating that compliance comes with God's promise for longevity and prosperity (Exod 20:12; Deut 5:16). Jewish writers argued that the Torah requires children to obey their parents, and failure to do so could warrant capital punishment.[164] Ephesians does not threaten children but instructs fathers[165] to do their part by providing them with instruction and discipline in the Lord in self-restraint,[166] not provocation.

Greeks and Romans shared the virtue that children obeyed their parents. They also emphasized the idea of spiritual reward or punishment[167] pertaining to the conduct of children. "The gods reward children who honor their parents . . . they punish the children who fail to honor their parents."[168] As one philosopher puts it, "that everyone should obey his mother and father seems a good thing, and I certainly recommend it."[169] It was a legal obligation and morally just that children do so and provide for the needs of their aged parents.[170] Honor to parents was paramount and second only to honor to the gods.[171] Plato explains that the gods would not answer the prayers of children who failed their duty to honor their parents; gods may rather heed the summons of parents to punish children who refuse their duty in this regard.[172] Plato gives a practical example.

> Oedipus, when he was dishonored (so our story runs), invoked upon his children curses which, as all men allege, were granted by Heaven and fulfilled; and we tell how Amyntor in his wrath cursed his son Phoenix, and Theseus cursed Hippolytus, and countless other parents cursed countless other sons, which curses of parents upon sons it is clearly proved that the gods grant; for a parent's

---

164. Josephus, *Ag. Ap.* 2.28 (206) and also Philo, *Dec.* 31 (165–167).

165. It was important that each of the members of the household followed the direction of the male head. He was responsible for provision, protection and guidance in the administration of the household (cf. Prov 4:4; Deut 21:18–21; Sir 3:6; Matt 5:9; Eph 5:1–2; *Gospel of Thomas* 55:1–2; 101:1).

166. Josephus, *Ag. Ap.* 2.26 (204). Josephus indicates that it is the responsibility of parents "to bring those children up in learning and to exercise them in the laws, and make them acquainted with acts of their predecessors." This is not only Jewish value; we find it also in Greco-Roman moral philosophy. Cf. Seneca, *Anger* 2.21.1–6.

167. Plato, *Laws* XI 932B–C. According to Plato children who refused to honor their parents may be whipped, imprisoned or summoned to the courts.

168. P. Balla, *The Child-Parent Relationship in the New Testament and Its Environment* (Peabody: Hendrickson, 2005), 77.

169. Musonius Rufus, "Musonius Rufus – The Roman Socrates," 101.

170. Plato, *Laws* XI 932A.

171. Plato, 917A.

172. Balla, *Child-Parent Relationship*, 25–27.

curse laid upon his children is more potent than any other man's curse against any other, and most justly so. Let no man suppose, then, that when a father or a mother is dishonored by the children, in that case it is natural for God to hearken especially to their prayers, whereas when the parent is honored and is highly pleased and earnestly prays the gods, in consequence, to bless his children – are we not to suppose that they hearken equally to prayers of this kind, and grant them to us? For if not, they could never be just dispensers of blessings; and that, as we assert, would be most unbecoming in gods.[173]

This spirit cosmology helped to place a check on the conduct of children. Children here includes young ones at home and older offspring with living parents. Slavery was common in the Greco-Roman world, even to the extent that the poor could afford to own slaves.[174] Slaves lived with the other members in the household with reasonable conditions and were able to dine together,[175] in some cases.[176] Some performed their duties in the domestic setting whereas others served in the fields. The evidence abounds that slave ownership extended to Jews[177] and members in early Christian churches.[178] Ephesians instructs slaves to obey and honor their masters, not as those performing their duties simply to impress their masters (ὀφθαλμοδουλία) or as people pleasers (ἀνθρωπάρεσκος [6:6]). Conversely, slaves ought to see their roles as slaves of Christ doing "the will of God" from the sincerity of heart. Their labor is service to the Lord, not the earthly masters (6:9). Ephesians thus presents the duty of the slave as

---

173. Plato, *Laws* 931.

174. J. J. Meggit, *Paul, Poverty and Survival* (Edinburgh: T&T Clark, 1998), 129–131. Cf. J. Byron, *Slavery Metaphors in Early Judaism and Pauline Christianity* (WUNT 2.162; Tübingen: Mohr Siebeck, 2003). J. Byron, "Paul and the Background of Slavery: The *Status Quaetionis*, in New Testament Scholarship," *CBR* 3, no. 1 (2004): 133.

175. Koester, *History, Culture and Religion*, 59–62, and A. A. Bell Jr. *A Guide to the New Testament World* (Scottdale: Herald, 1994), 195.

176. A. Wallace-Hadrill, *Houses and Societies in Pompeii and Herculaneum* (Princeton: Princeton University Press, 1994), 103; D. L. Balch, "Rich Pompeiian Houses, Shops for Rent, and the Huge Apartment Building in Herculaneum as Typical Spaces for Pauline Churches," *JSNT* 27, no. 1 (2004): 32–37; and M. MacDonald and H. Moxnes, "Domestic Space and Families in Early Christianity: Editors' Introduction," *JSNT* 27, no. 1 (2004): 5. Also A. Wallace-Hadrill, "*Domus* and *Insulae* in Rome: Families and Housefuls," in *Early Christian Families in Context: An Interdisciplinary Dialogue*, eds. D. L. Balch and C. Osiek (Grand Rapids: Eerdmans, 2003), 3–18.

177. Philo, *Spec. Leg.* 2.123. Exod 20:10; 21:20–21; 23:7–12; Deut 5:14.

178. J. A. Glancy, *Slavery in Early Christianity* (New York: OUP, 2002), 130–152. It was a legitimate practice in the early churches to own slaves but there is nothing to suggest that early Christians were given a religious mandate for savagery or abuse of slaves.

divinely sanctioned and as service to a spiritual being with the ability to reward human conduct, namely God.[179] The import is significant. It is not merely a concept, but is reality rooted in ancient cosmology. The "believing slaves who perform their household duties as slaves of Christ will also be doing the will of God, since that has been expressed supremely in Christ."[180] Doing the will/wishes of God and functioning in the framework of Christ reverberates the notion that members of the church are participants in the cosmic plan of God being rolled out by the agency of Jesus Christ and the Holy Spirit. Doing the will of God is also working within moral boundaries corresponding to their new identity.

Slave masters are admonished to exercise their lordship under the supreme lordship of Christ. As masters (κύριος), they must avoid the use of threats to make slaves do their bidding because both (masters and slaves) are all servants of an impartial lord (κύριος) who would ultimately judge slaves and masters accordingly. The check on morality is the oversight of the "Master . . . in heaven." The spiritual lord[181] of the household is an impartial judge. Spirit cosmology permeates and provides the framework for household ethics in Ephesians. These are not abstract concepts but portraits of realities in their worldview. Each member receives reciprocal admonition[182] with Christocentric basis, motivation, and/or model for conduct. In a nutshell, responsible conduct in the household is the will of God. The quest for concord is evident by the customized obligations of each party and implied notion that they are all members of God's community. In other words, members of the Spirit-filled community ought to conduct themselves in a manner that meets the will of God and harnesses concord.

---

179. G. S. Nathan, *The Family in Late Antiquity: The Rise of Christianity and the Endurance of Tradition* (London: Routledge, 2000), 74–106, 133–158, 169–184 (p. 171).

180. Patzia, *Ephesians*, 279.

181. Cf. T. G. Gombis, "A Radically New Humanity: The Function of the *Haustafel* in Ephesians," *JETS* 48, no. 2 (2005): 317–330. The author rightly indicates the radical change of status and expectations for Christ followers. Yet, one may guard against the tendency to characterize or even exaggerate prescribed conduct for Christ followers as radically distinct in character from the ideals of Greco-Roman society.

182. D. Darko, "The Haustafel in Ephesians versus Contemporary African Family Dynamics," *TJCT* 14, no. 2 (2004): 20. Here, the Christocentric framework is emphasized as I teased out the similarities and differences of marriage in the African context.

## 5.9 Christian Living as Spiritual Warfare 6:10–20

Ephesians 1:20–23 indicates God's great work in Christ that led to the subjugation of all "principalities and powers" under his feet. His triumph does not render the powers inert, impotent or incapable of influencing human affairs. Conversely, the victory has more to do with the status of Christ in relation to the powers and his ability to deal with them on behalf of those who come to believe in him. Salvation changes the status of spiritual lordship and agency at work on behalf of Christ followers; the powers are not rendered powerless but they stand below Christ. As previously noted, moral failings among Christ followers could pave the way for the influence of malevolent forces. This particular pericope of 6:10–20 provides one of the clearest portraits of the letter's spirit cosmology as it pertains to the identity, standing with God and moral aspirations for Christ followers. A misreading of the cosmology would leave many unanswered questions about the nature and import of the spiritual battle that is described. It will become apparent that Paul's call for mortal beings to wrestle with spiritual beings is not outlandish in the world concept of Asia Minor.[183]

Ephesians 6:10–20 serves as the end of the body of the letter, revisiting the dominant cosmological framework and human responsibility for believers to maintain their salvific status in Christ. That God intervened in the condition of humanity under the control of an evil spiritual power (2:2) lies behind the intensity and urgency in the framing of the spiritual battle. Without repeating conditions of the past, this passage encapsulates the nature of the current standing of the readership with God relative to cosmic powers from whose dominion they are saved.[184] The epistolary form and conceptual framework provide appropriate indicators to suggest that it is the *peroratio* of the letter.[185] *Peroratio* is "the final section of a speech that sought to sum up the main themes and to arouse the audience into action."[186] The battle imagery evokes a sense of urgency, not fear, to engender vigilance, discipline and preparedness to mitigate spiritual threats to their standing with God. The passage seeks to promote confidence and security amidst diabolic influence.[187] One may even

---

183. *Contra* Best, *Ephesians*, 385–386. Best argues that the passage does not deal with identity and moral failings but suggests that we read it as a spiritual battle to lead believers to salvation. Parts of the armor are virtues yet Best fails to explain what we should do with the ethical content.

184. O'Brien, *Ephesians*, 457.

185. Lincoln, *Ephesians*, 432.

186. O'Brien, *Ephesians*, 459.

187. Cf. 1 Thess 5:8; 2 Cor 6:7; 10:3–5; Phil 2:25; Phlm 2; Rom 13:12.

posit that it purports to immunize "Christian readers against the influences of their pagan environment and to activate them to a more determined realization of a Christian existence."[188]

Conceptually, 6:10–20 may be divided into three parts namely, (a) the nature of the spiritual battle and identity of opponents (vv. 10–12), (b) combat readiness to engage the opponent (vv. 13–17), and (c) open communication lines (prayer) with God – for Paul and his fellow believers (vv. 18–20). Syntactically, the prepositional phrase in 6:18–20 draws from the preceding discourse to call for vigilance and prayers. Τοῦ λοιποῦ opens the pericope (6:10–20) to denote finality.[189] They are commanded to "be strong in the Lord." The imperative ἐνδυναμοῦσθε is in divine passive calling on members to actively seek or avail themselves to be strengthened in the Lord. In 3:16, God the Father is the one petitioned for such strength. The ability to overcome malevolent forces comes not by physical fitness but by divine enabling. It is a community endeavor, not an individual undertaking (the main verb is plural). This is to say that the first note of caution is to disavow false confidence in human ability, acknowledge the need for divine aid and draw strength from God. The locus of strengthening is "in the Lord" and the means is "in his mighty power." Christ followers are in a battle not to gain or occupy a geographical or spiritual territory but to maintain their standing in the Lord. The reader observes the recurrent reference to power and divine enabling in 6:10; the believers must be strengthened (ἐνδυναμόω) in the Lord, and in his mighty (κράτος) power (ἰσχύς) of his might/strength (ESV). This is not a call to self-actualization but to dependence on divine enablement. The language of the pericope clearly puts accent on transcendent realities and their engagement in human affairs. It is, however, not unusual that such emphasis is put on the need for spiritual help.

Members are commanded to clothe themselves (aorist middle) with the whole armor of God; it is a corporate undertaking and responsibility to make God's armor their own.[190] Elsewhere, they are admonished to enrobe with the moral image of God in holiness and in righteousness (4:24). Here, they need the entirety of God's armor – the emphasis on "completeness" suggests the exclusion of none. Polybius gives a detailed account of what the Roman armor

---

188. Schnackenburg, *Ephesians*, 270.

189. The phrase is sometimes used with a temporal force to mean "from now on" or "in the future" (cf. 1 Cor 7:29; Heb 10:13) but the sense it conveys here is finality, conclusion or summation hence the word "finally" as my preferred translation (cf. Phil 4:8; 2 Cor 13:11; 1 Thess 4:1; 2 Thess 3:1).

190. Mitton, *Ephesians*, 220.

entailed.[191] Paul does not aim to draw parallels with every single armor, since he leaves some out, but the seriousness of cosmic warfare and necessity for adequate preparation. Elsewhere, Paul similarly characterizes Christian living as a warfare (1 Thess 5:8; cf. Isa 11:4–5; 59:17). The word πανοπλία appears only in this passage and in Luke 11:23 to denote a complete armor. The list in 6:10–17 is not exhaustive; it must be taken as representative. The complete armor belongs to God, τὴν πανοπλίαν τοῦ θεοῦ. The children of God must put on the armor of God in the battle to keep good standing as members in the household of God.

The armor of God is necessary to ensure that the adopted children of God (1:5) are able to withstand the stratagems of the devil.[192] "Standing" implies stability and defense of their new identity yet it also denotes vigilance in the face of threat. The salvific status accords privileges and responsibilities pertaining to their standing with God. The tactics of the adversary are characterized as τὰς μεθοδείας τοῦ διαβόλου. The "devil" (6:11) and the "evil one" (6:16) are one and the same spiritual agent, otherwise referred to as the "ruler of the power of the air" (2:2). The devil desires earnestly to keep them away from God. Salvation in Christ has brought about release and redemption from the dominion of evil spirits; the victorious Christ provides a covering from constant onslaught of the powers, which seek to regain control (2:2–3; 4:27). Readers are thus made aware of the stratagems of the devil and their role in curbing devices against the plan of God. Apparently, deployment of the devil's stratagems is fierce and ongoing. Μεθοδεία appears twice in the NT only in Ephesians (see 4:14) to denote trickery, stratagem, scheming or craftiness.[193] Snodgrass explains that it evinces the devil's baits and camouflaged traps for Christ followers.[194]

The ὅτι clause in 6:12 provides further reasons to be enrobed in the armor of God. The first person (plural) suggests that all Christ followers are in view regardless of geographical proximity. Christian living has a spiritual dimension that needs to be guarded. The nature of the struggle characterized by the term πάλη is a hapax legomenon denoting wrestling[195] or physical struggle. Wrestling was a popular body contact sport in Anatolia that featured in the Isthmian and other games of the ancient world. The analogy would reverberate the imagery

---

191. Polybius, *Hist.* 6.23.2–5.

192. The term ἵστημι appears three times in Ephesians (6:11, 13, 14) and only in this passage to buttress the point of the author calling on the readers to solidify their place in the unfolding mystery of God and draw on divine strength to keep their standing.

193. BDAG, 499.

194. Snodgrass, *Ephesians*, 339.

195. Homer, *Ilias* 23.635. Thucydides 1.6.5; Philo, *Leg. All.* 3.68.

of the familiar contact sport as well as the fact that spiritual aid was often sought by athletes to help them to defeat their opponents.[196] As indicated earlier, it was not uncommon for athletes to solicit spiritual support for successful outcomes. Arnold discusses the material evidence from an Ephesian wrestler who utilized the "Ephesians letters" as a talisman to help him succeed in a wrestling match.[197] Apparently, he was successful as long as he wore the talisman and saw demise only when it was detected and taken away from him. Despite the interest in wrestling among elite military officers,[198] Paul makes no connection with wrestling and military preparations but employs the armory as a metaphor to press home the sense of urgency and risk. Moreover, πάλη is an intense sport that aims to sweep an opponent off the feet to the ground. Paul impresses upon his readers that the spiritual battle is a "close-quarter struggling" with a cunning opponent in the spiritual realm[199] whose ultimate aim is to keep them off their feet and rob them of their privilege standing with God. The imagery is that of mortals in an intense fight with an opponent that is not "flesh and blood," but a spiritual agent.[200] This notion permeates the letter both in the way salvation is portrayed (2:1–3) and in the portrait of the spiritual consequence of moral failings. Christ followers must come to terms with the idea that the spiritual adversary lurks in the effort to rob them of their spiritual blessings (1:3).

Paul clarifies the identity of the enemy by stating what they are not (flesh and blood) and their true nature. The struggle is against "rulers" and "authorities." These terms surfaced earlier in 1:21 and 3:10 (see also Col 2:15) to refer to personal evil spiritual powers.[201] However, Carr argues that these terms typically refer to good angels but he concedes that their feature in 6:12 does in fact refer to evil spiritual powers.[202] Not only is there no manuscript evidence to support some of his hypothesis, but there is overwhelming evidence to the contrary.[203] In other words, spiritual beings were believed to exist and operate in human affairs in the cosmology of the time.

The author further characterizes additional opponents, who work in concert with the previously named, as cosmic spiritual powers of the dark

---

196. Arnold, *Power and Magic*, 116–117.

197. Arnold, *Ephesians*, 446–447.

198. Arnold, 445–447.

199. M. E. Gudorf, "The Use of Πάλη in Ephesians 12," *JBL* 117, no. 2 (1998): 334.

200. Cf. Sir. 14:18; 17:31; Matt 16:17; Gal 1:16; 1 Cor 15:50.

201. *Contra* Carr, *Angels and Principalities*.

202. Carr, 110.

203. Arnold, "The 'Exorcism' of Ephesians 6:12 in Recent Research," 71–87.

world – πρὸς τοὺς κοσμοκράτορας τοῦ σκότους τούτου. Darkness is the realm of evil, immorality and depraved minds in Ephesians. It is outside the realm of Christ and the domain of diabolic forces. Κοσμοκράτωρ is *hapax legomenon* in the NT and features elsewhere in another Asia Minor text (*T. Sol.*) referring to cosmic spiritual powers (8:2; 18:2). The word is known in magic recipes and astrology to convey the same meaning.[204] Some deities were believed to operate in darkness (e.g. Artemis, Helios, Serapis). Moreover, the reference to "spiritual forces of evil" may be taken to comprise the summation of all the forces of evil aforementioned and those unnamed,[205] or as a general expression covering the range of spiritual forces that be.[206] Their sphere of operation is darkness – the realm "associated with alienation from God, ignorance, hard-heartedness and debauchery (4:18; 5:8, 11–12)."[207] The gods and goddesses were believed to be spiritual agents capable of influencing human affairs. "The pagan deities are not imaginary or lifeless and therefore harmless, but neither are they omnipotent."[208] For believers, their status and mindset are antithetical to that which is associated with darkness (4:18; 5:6–14). The different names and perhaps functions of these powers do not negate the fact that they work in concert against a common enemy, Christ followers.

Sociopolitical reading of the powers in 6:12 tends to depart from their spiritual identity to suggest that they comprise social structures, kings, institutional powers, laws, traditions and rituals. Proponents see the battle as one that is against "seats of authority, hierarchical systems, ideological justifications, and punitive sanctions which their human incumbents exercise and which transcend these incumbents in both time and power."[209] A leading proponent of this position in the modern era is Walter Wink, who consistently employs the prism of, and passion for, social justice to override obvious cosmological referents in the text.[210] It is, however, a major leap to find sociopolitical systems in the cosmology of 6:12. It is clear that Wink's interest is not to interpret the text in its literary and social context. It is quite anachronistic to employ a post-enlightenment lens as an interpretative tool to

---

204. Arnold, *Power and Magic*, 65–67.

205. Arnold, *Ephesians*, 449.

206. Best, *Ephesians*, 594, and Thielman, *Ephesians*, 421.

207. Thielman, *Ephesians*, 421.

208. Arnold, *Power and Magic*, 67. Cf. PGM, III. 35; IV. 166; IV. 1599, 2198; V. 500; XIII. 619, 637ff and XVIIb. 1ff.

209. Wink, *Naming the Powers*, 85; Wink, *Engaging the Powers*, 42 and 77–78.

210. Wink, *Naming the Powers*.

decipher meaning from a text produced in the first century for first-century readership. The powers are described explicitly as personal spiritual powers that operate in the heavenly realms. They are spiritual in nature; their motivation is evil, and their sphere of operation is cosmic realms – πρὸς τὰ πνευματικὰ τῆσ πονεριάς ἐν τοῖς ἐπουρανίοις (6:12).

Structurally, Ephesians 6:13–17 elaborates on the components of God's armor in analogous terms to the essentials for maintaining identity and moral standing as Christ followers. They must take hold or pick up the full armor of God with a sense of urgency. Paul is concerned that members are able to withstand the stratagems of evil powers in the "day of evil." The day of evil seems to be a dangerous time necessitating total preparedness to mitigate attacks of the enemy. The phrase is sometimes understood in apocalyptic terms to denote a day when evil will intensify – apocalyptic "the day of evil." O'Brien[211] provides a range of interpretations on the import of the term as (a) the age between now and the second coming of Christ, (b) a specific day of tribulation marking the climactic reach of the devil's onslaught, (c) critical times when hostility of evil powers will be intensified, (4) the climactic end of the present evil age, or (5) the day of evil as a specific time of satanic attacks – when believers will come under severe pressure to succumb to the evil powers.

In biblical tradition, "the day of evil" usually refers to the *parousia* or eschatological day of judgment at the end of the present age.[212] One view posits that the armor was needed perhaps to ensure that the readers kept good standing at the moment and even more so in an eschatological day of evil. Such reading implies the *already* but *not yet* eschatological tension in the battle against cosmic powers. Another view suggests that the day of evil is an allusion to Jewish apocalyptic thought, implying *terminus technicus* for the day when evil would be intensified. The problem with the Jewish apocalyptic reading is that Ephesians does not look forward to a future warfare but addresses immediate concerns with future consequences. The battle metaphor aims to challenge the readers to engage their prowess to resist evil's onslaught vigorously then and there; the battle cry demands immediate compliance to withstand the stratagems of the devil lest they become casualties.

Christ followers are further admonished to put on specific units of military attire and arms. First, they must wear the truth as belt – τὴν ὀσφὺν ὑμῶν ἐν

---

211. P. T. O'Brien, "Ephesians 1: An Unusual Introduction to a New Testament Letter," *NTS* 25 (1979): 504–516.

212. Best, *Ephesians*, 596. Cf. Amos 5:18–20; Joel 1:15; 2:32; Zech 14; Dan 12:1; *T. Levi* 5:5; 1 En 55:3; 96:2; *T. Moses* 1:18; *Ap. Abr.* 19:8f; 1 QM 1.10–13; 1 Cor 1:8; 1 Thess 5:2–4.

ἀληθείᾳ (6:14). Literally, they are to have the wrap-around of truth around their waists for easy movement and maneuvering. The belt of the Roman military outfit was a small leather apron tightened or placed under the breastplate for self-protection but also to hold the clothes together for free movement.[213] It is important, however, that we do not let the military imagery overshadow the author's main point. Paul means to say that truth is essential for Christ followers to move freely, fearlessly and steadily. Truth is the antonym to falsehood and dishonesty. "Truth takes up the concern with the ethical quality of truth as the fruit of light in 5:9 and the need for speaking the truth in 4:15 and 5:9."[214] The ancient collective societies regarded honesty as an important virtue in harnessing trust and cohesion (Prov 8:7; 22:21; 26:28). The word features consistently in the LXX to promote solidity and fidelity.[215] The God whose armor is in use is also the "God of truth." God is reliable and follows through with his promises.[216] Girding oneself with truth then is adapting this moral attribute of God in the community of faith. The readiness to exhibit truth corporately would hold the church together against deceitful schemes (4:14). Previously, the church had been commanded to put on the moral identity of God in true righteousness and holiness (4:24). Truth marks the character of those who desist from the works of darkness and walk in the light (5:9). Here, truth is first on the list of virtues required to withstand evil spiritual powers.

The second armor is the "breastplate of righteousness" (τὸν θώρακα τῆς δικαιοσύνης). Θώραξ (breastplate) as an armor is a two-part metal covering to protect the soldier from incoming arrows directed to the chest and against shots to the back in the battlefield. The term "breastplate" features in Isaiah 59:17 as part of God's armor in bringing about justice. The corresponding virtue, righteousness, was a cardinal virtue denoting moral integrity and uprightness.[217] Aristotle explains that righteousness is the sum of all virtues.

> It is complete virtue in its fullest sense, because it is the actual exercise of complete virtue. It is complete because he who possesses it can exercise his virtue not only in himself but towards

---

213. See Best, *Ephesians*, 598.

214. Lincoln, "'Stand, therefore . . . ' Ephesians 6:10–20 as Peroratio," 106.

215. Spicq, *Theological Lexicon of the New Testament Vol. 1*, trans. and ed. James D. Ernest (Peabody: Hendrickson, 1994), 68.

216. Spicq, *TLNT*, 68.

217. See Philo, *Change of Names* 197; *Heir.* 243; *Abraham* 27, 56, 103, 104; *Creation* 80; *Alleg. Interp.* 1:63; 3:77.

his neighbor also; for many men can exercise virtue in their own affairs but not in their relations towards their neighbor.[218]

Lincoln posits that "doing right and practicing justice is equally vital for the Christian soldier in his or her battle against the powers of evil."[219] The lack thereof renders the heart susceptible to spiritual assault. The readers were commanded earlier to disrobe all vices from their past so as to enrobe in the new humanity created after the likeness of God (4:24). So far, the portrait of the units of military attire takes the form of virtue. If we agree with Aristotle that righteousness is the embodiment of all virtues, then Christ followers are in no good standing if they lack it. Moreover, emphases on virtue echoes the notion that human conduct has a spiritual dimension – portrayed here as divine-human warfare.

The author entreats readers to wrap the gospel around their feet (like a shoe) in preparation with the "gospel of peace" (6:15). The exact nature of this footwear is not given though the metaphor seems to allude to *caliga*, the typical sandals for Roman soldiers – a half-boot studded with sharp nails to enhance a firm grip.[220] The main concern though is not the footwear but its spiritual counterpart. The imagery of feet in association with the "gospel of peace" echoes Isaiah 52:7 except that its import in Isaiah is active engagement in proclaiming the gospel of peace whereas in Ephesians it implies readiness to assume defensive posture (see Rom 10:15). The gospel of peace is an essential instrument to enhance mobility, bring peace and enable a soldier to stand firm. The gospel of peace may also be understood to imply a preparation derived from the gospel to take a defensive position[221] or readiness to share the gospel of peace proactively.[222] The stated imperative is to "stand" or "withstand" (6:11, 13–14) the stratagems; this would not necessarily require offensive assault, invasion or seizure of a territory. In any case, the unit would aid believers both to defend themselves or to attack when necessary. Peace is the calm assurance – in the face of spiritual warfare.[223] The language is identical with the portrait

---

218. Aristotle, *Nic. Ethics* 5.1.

219. Lincoln, *Ephesians*, 448.

220. Lincoln, 448.

221. Best, *Ephesians*, 600.

222. O'Brien, *Ephesians*, 477, and P. T. O'Brien, *Gospel and Mission in the Writings of Paul* (Grand Rapids: Baker, 1993), 124.

223. H. C. G. Moule, *Ephesian Studies* (Fort Washington: Christian Literature Crusade, 1937), 328.

of Jesus as the one who came to proclaim peace (εὐηγγελίσατο εἰρήνην [2:17]) to those far and near.

Paul stresses that they take up "the shield of faith" in all circumstances (6:16) and elaborates further on its purpose which is to stop the missiles of the evil one from causing great harm. The "shield" refers to a large Roman shield that covered the entire body in order to neutralize the effects of incoming fiery arrows.[224] Typically, a soldier wore the oblong shield as a unit of his armor, sometimes in a collective positioning as a defensive mechanism of a battalion under attack.[225] Polybius[226] and Josephus[227] emphasize the importance of the shield and its ability to protect against arrows of the enemy. Occasionally, arrows were set alight in combat to maximize damage, set hideouts on fire or inflict more wounds on contact. Apparently, the primary weapon of the Anatolian and Greek Artemis was bow and arrow. It is therefore likely that the accent on the effect of arrows would resonate with the readership as a real threat posed by evil powers in a region with the influence of the Artemis Ephesia.[228]

The shield analogy underscores the import of faith in protecting believers from the stratagems of evil forces. Faith may be conceived of not only as a requisite to become a Christ follower but also as a sustained trust[229] and confidence in God's power at work on their behalf.[230] In a previous section, faith was the means by which members became aware of the manifold power of God (1:19) and gained access to his benefits. Paul commends them for their faith in Christ (1:15), which is also the means by which they obtained salvation, boldness and confidence in their standing with God (2:8; 3:12). The author prays that Christ may dwell in their hearts by means of faith (3:17) in the community marked by shared faith in Christ (4:5, 13). To say faith is the shield in the armor of God is to underline its essence and their potential demise should they stop trusting in God's work in Christ Jesus on their behalf. Faith is a relational term pointing to trust, unwavering commitment or allegiance to a deity (God).[231] The nature of the weapon and identity of the enemy are

---

224. Cf. Gen 15:1; Pss 5:12; 18:2, 30, 35; 28:7.

225. W. Barclay, *Galatians and Ephesians*, 217.

226. Polybius, *Hist.* 6.23.2–5.

227. Josephus, *Jewish Wars*, 3:259.

228. Arnold, *Ephesians*, 458.

229. Cf. Ephesians 1:13, 15; 3:12; 4:13; 6:23.

230. Lincoln, *Ephesians*, 449.

231. See M. Bates, *Salvation by Allegiance Alone: Rethinking Faith, Works, and the Gospel of Jesus the King* (Grand Rapids: Baker Academic, 2017). This important book discusses the need to understand faith in relational terms. Growing up in a collectivist culture in Africa with a

characterized as "flaming arrows" and "the evil one" (6:16). Paul is under no illusion about the real danger posed by the evil one. However, his confidence is articulated to the effect that the fiery arrows could be curtailed by faith in God. A fiery arrow is a dangerous weapon – "it was a dart tipped with tow dipped in a pitch. The pitch-soaked tow was set alight, and the dart was thrown. But the great oblong shield was the very weapon to quench it."[232] The spiritual nature of this battle suggests a deliberate attempt to highlight the need for vigilance in every aspect of Christian living. Faith is a virtue and a gift from God that ought to be active among the saints.

The command to put on "the helmet of salvation" ensures that the mind is protected against diabolic onslaught. The language echoes Isaiah 59:17 (LXX) where God's "helmet of salvation" is the crown of victory in the aftermath of war. However, the helmet in 6:17 is part of God's armor for a spiritual battle. Salvation recalls deliverance from spiritual death – fleshly desires, worldly influence and "the ruler of the power of the air" (2:1–3). The metaphorical helmet guards against cognitive dissonance that pertains to their standing with God. The spiritually charged atmosphere with pagan activities in Asia Minor meant Christ followers could be bombarded by various forms of religious thoughts that could destabilize their salvific standing. The mind is the locus of reason, and thus needed to be guarded against competing religious thoughts. Arnold indicates that to put on salvation "means to realize and appropriate one's new identity in Christ, which gives believers power for deliverance from the supernatural enemies on the basis of their union with the resurrected and exalted Lord."[233] The need for knowledge and understanding regarding their new identity is a recurrent theme in the letter; the mind is the seat of thoughts in Greek thinking and the head houses the mind. Any damage to the head would inevitably affect their cognitive prowess and stability as a whole, whereas unwavering standing in their salvific status would serve as an impenetrable defense. The helmet of salvation thus functions to guard against doubts, distortions and diabolic influence.

The last armor is an offensive weapon that could be utilized defensively as well, namely "the sword of the Spirit, which is the word of God." The sword of the Spirit is that which is made effective by the Holy Spirit. The Greek ῥῆμα is

---

spirit cosmology shared by ancient cultures, I always thought it was a given to conceive of faith/ trust in relational terms until I heard my colleagues explain their previously held propositional prism on what faith entails.

232. Barclays, *Galatians and Ephesians*, 217.

233. Arnold, *Ephesians*, 460.

often used to refer to spoken word or the Hebrew Scriptures.[234] Some read ῥῆμα θεοῦ to be referring to "the faithful speaking forth of the Gospel in the realm of darkness, so that men and women held by Satan might hear this liberating and life-giving word and be freed from his grasp."[235] If we accept this reading then the propagation of the gospel would serve as an offensive assault on the domain of evil powers to release those under their sway. Elsewhere, the spoken word of God is similarly employed as an offensive weapon to overcome the schemes of the evil one.[236] The thrust of this instruction though is to underline the significance of the word of God along with the Spirit in the stand against the schemes of diabolic forces.

The function of 6:18–20 in relation to the armor of God is debated on whether it forms part of the armor or it is a separate pericope in close proximity. Fee suggests that we treat it as part of the overall weapon for the warfare, but not part of the analogy with the armor of God.[237] Some have taken the fact that prayer is left to the end to imply that it is meant to show the effectual impulse or the spirit in which the entire armor may be put into effect.[238] The grammatical structure shows no direct connection, but conceptually it draws from the preceding analogy to appeal for prayer. Prayer is an integral part of the message the author seeks to convey in Ephesians. No other letter in the Pauline corpus devotes that much space to prayer as Ephesians. It is the line of communication with God whose armor is to be worn and on whose side the battle is being fought to keep believers standing. Since the warfare is not geographically bound, members must pray for themselves, for Paul and for other believers to remain faithful to Christ wherever they are. Prayer is in effect the lifeline for staying connected to God in the spiritual battle.

The instruction to take up the "sword of the Spirit" (τὴν μάχαιραν τοῦ πνεύματος [6:17]) is immediately followed by the admonition to pray in the Spirit (ἐν πνεύματι [6:18]). Prayer must be conducted under all circumstances

---

234. The term ῥῆμα features in the NT often to denote a spoken word (cf. John 5:47; 6:63; Acts 10:44; 28:25; Heb 4:12; 1 Pet 1:23–25) whereas λόγος usually refers to the content of a message. The two are sometimes used interchangeably in the NT as well (cf. Acts 16:36–38). While some distinction could be made between ῥῆμα and λόγος in some instances, it is not always the case. For example, there are a few cases in which λόγος was employed to carry the sense of the spoken word (Matt 8:8; 22:46; Luke 7:7; John 2:22; 18:32; 1 Cor 4:19; 1 Thess 1:5). Overemphasis on the import of ῥῆμα could be misleading in this regard.

235. O'Brien, *Ephesians*, 482. I know that this commentary has been deemed problematic in recent years so I use it here with some hesitation.

236. Matt 4:4–10; Luke 4:4–12; Rev 1:16; 2:16; 19:25.

237. Fee, *God's Empowering Presence*, 730.

238. Eadie, *Ephesians*, 471.

ἐν πνεύματι. Every form of prayer and petition must be made to God. This is more than a coping mechanism[239] but an essential part of life in the community where the Spirit of God reigns and fosters togetherness. Prayer in the "Spirit" is prayer that is guided by or made effective by the Holy Spirit. "Proclaiming the word of God is speech directed toward people; prayer is speech directed toward God"[240] and all must be done (ἐν πνεύματι) in the warfare to safeguard a firm standing with God.

The reader is called upon to pray at all times (6:18; see also 1 Esd 8:58; 2 Esd 8:29). Prayer may be made either to express gratitude to God, in worship or in petition. Paul insists on prayer as a spiritual discipline that must not cease; it must comprise every kind of request. Members are further admonished to be vigilant and persevere in prayer for the saints. Nothing in these verses suggests that the primary import of prayer is to deliver people from demonic powers. Believers need prayer to be strengthened in keeping with the unity of the Spirit. It is the means by which they "are to appropriate the divine resources for the battle."[241] In a collective note, Paul asks the churches to pray for him so that he might preach the "mystery of the gospel" fearlessly (see 3:9–10). He needs prayer support to maintain confidence and clarity in his preaching.[242] "The mystery of the gospel Paul preaches is that God has fulfilled the promise made to the Hebrew fathers; and Gentiles are included in that promise."[243]

The mission necessitates prayer. Paul is an ambassador (πρεσβεύω) in chains in need of divine enabling to discharge his duty faithfully. The term ambassador appears only twice in the NT (2 Cor 5:20 and Eph 6:20)[244] to denote

---

239. *Contra* Schnackenburg, *Ephesians*, 281.

240. Fee, *God's Empowering Presence*, 730.

241. Lincoln, "'Stand, therefore . . . ' Ephesians 6:10–20 as Peroratio," 106.

242. G. R. Smillie, "Ephesians 6:19–20 – A Mystery for the Sake of which the Apostle is an Ambassador in Chains," *TJ* 18, no. 2 (1997): 213. Smillie argues that Paul was writing from a prison in Nero's court where he was literally bound in chains; he is here requesting prayer backing to enable him to overcome any intimidation to proclaim the "Mystery of the Gospel" to those in Nero's court.

243. Smillie, "Ephesians 6:19–20," 212.

244. The term originally meant the oldest or eldest, but it later came to be used in connection with functions such as a spokesman, envoy etc. which the wisdom of old age was a necessary requisite (C. Kruse, *2 Corinthians*, Leicester: Inter-Varsity, 1987), 128. In the Hellenistic period, an ambassador was sent by Greek *polis* to another *polis* for negotiations or dialogue with kings. See Ceslas Spicq, *Theological Lexicon of the New Testament Vol. 3*, trans. J. D. Ernest (Peabody: Hendrickson, 1994), 172. In some cases, the envoy carried an authority note to validate his status and job description (Josephus, *Ant.* 12.225, 227; Philo, *Giants* 16). The function included negotiation of treatises of alliance and friendship (1 Macc. 4:11; cf. 8:17; 15:17). It is in this function that a king under attack would send an ambassador to sue for peace (cf. Deut 20:10–12). For instance, "around 200 BCE when the Thracian, commanded by Zoltes, appeared

nobility and humble service. On one hand, it is noble that the ambassador serves on behalf of his country. On the other hand, it is humbling because in Paul's case he is serving a prison term as a price for his ambassadorial duty. As an emissary, he does not do his own bidding, and neither does his message originate from him. He is not the one that matters but Christ; the one who has sent him and whose message he carries (cf. 2 Cor 5:20). Paul is *legatus* of the divine imprisoned for the proclamation of the gospel. He needs God's help as petitioned in prayer to discharge his duties faithfully and effectively.

## Conclusion

The study in this chapter bolsters preceding observations about the dominant role of divine activity in the identity construction and ethical prescriptions of the letter. Corporate solidarity is "unity of the Spirit" yet this unity requires human effort to keep it intact (4:1–3). The author provides a strong basis for oneness that is rooted in shared commonalities and allegiance to God, Jesus Christ and the work of the Holy Spirit. The fusion of divine activity and human responsibility becomes more apparent as leadership and services are framed as gifts from a divine conqueror and benefactor who gave some to be apostles, prophets, evangelists, teachers and pastors to equip members for service (4:9–12). The maturity and stability in/of the church is grounded in and marked by spiritual growth and dependence on Jesus Christ. Without neglecting mortal humans in matters of ethics, it is evinced that spiritual agents are able to influence human conduct for good or ill. Divine activity and human responsibility are thus inseparable in this cosmology.

The literary structure of Ephesians 4–6 is one that accentuates the letter's cosmological framework. The accent on "unity of the Spirit" at its inception is followed by a lengthy theological discourse that establishes the basis of group identity as well as the need for maturation and dependence on Christ (4:1–16). The moral identity of the "new humanity" is purported to bear the image of

---

with an army of consequence in Scythia, marching against the Greek cities that had submitted to Rhemaxos, Agathocles was elected as an ambassador. He crossed the enemy's territory, passing through a good number of tribes, not shrinking from danger, and he persuaded the barbarians not only to do our city no harm but also to track down and return all the livestock that had previously been carried off by the pirates" (Spicq, 74). In the religious circles, ambassador was used figuratively to refer to God's emissaries. Philo, for instance, applies it to angels who deliver God's message to people (*Abr.* 115), and those who are representatives of men before God (*Gig.* 16). He also uses it for Moses as a mediator between God and humankind (*Rer. Div. Her.* 205). Gnosticism, in particular, held the office of an ambassador in high esteem as one who also has a heavenly origin and revelatory task (Bornkamm, *TDNT,* 681).

God in holiness and righteousness (4:24). Inappropriate conduct aggrieves the Holy Spirit and renders members susceptible to demonic influence. Conversely, the wise are filled with the Spirit to exercise sound moral judgment and conduct modelled after Christ (5:18–32). The use of contrastive patterns as a literary device further strengthens the portrait of their alignment with good spiritual agents – be it the old/new, darkness/light or foolish/wise antithesis; they may put on the image of God (4:24), live as light in the Lord Jesus (5:8, 10, 14), and be filled by the Holy Spirit for good life in the community, even in their households (5:18–6:9). The end of the body of the letter and its portrait of Christian identity and conduct as a spiritual battle is of great importance in the structure of the letter (6:10–20). The pericope captures, recaps and accentuates the status of the Ephesians and desired conduct in the cosmological framework of their day. The modern blind spots of radically distancing the transcendent from human affairs and material world obscure what is going on in the letter. Moreover, the epistemology of enlightenment and its antecedents further misconstrue salvation as an individual affair and enrollment in a church body. The Christian's fate is thus left at the whim of human agents who may choose, negotiate and adapt as new trends unfold. Conversely, human beings are not at the helm of affairs in the cosmos. They are rather saved to participate in the execution of God's plan. They were once helpless subjects living according to the age of the world, following the desires of the flesh and controlled by evil spiritual powers (2:1–3). By God's own initiative, he saved, redeemed, adopted and established them as members of his household. Thus, Christ followers need divine enabling in every aspect of their lives to keep their place with God. Their mode of conduct must be governed by God's wishes (2:10) as he enables them in/by the Holy Spirit to model their lives after Christ in advancement of God's plan.

It is noteworthy that nothing in the moral discourse suggests the need for Christ followers to withdraw from their social network in the wider society. Neither do we find any indication of an overt posture to embrace social conventions in an attempt to assimilate into society. Rhetoric of differentiation is aptly employed to highlight their distinctives as God's children and their need to exhibit exemplary lifestyles. Their new identity comes with new praxis that promotes internal cohesion. The boundaries between the in-group and out-group are framed primarily in terms of a cosmic duality pertaining to allegiance to, and influence of, spiritual realities. Ethics is similarly constructed in the same framework in which the devil and his cohorts are associated with vices on one hand while God works in concert with Jesus Christ and the Holy

Spirit to equip believers. Believers are not fighting against unbelievers but against evil spiritual forces seeking to undermine their standing with God.

The discourse climaxes with a portrait of Christian living – identity and ethics – as a spiritual warfare between humans and evil spirits in the cosmic realm. The battle is ongoing and seems to have begun at the point of salvation. The world is divided into two realms: one where believers stand with God through the work of Christ and the Spirit and another where unbelievers live under the control of cosmic evil spiritual forces and impulses of the flesh (2:1–3). This is not a battle of humans against humans (unbelievers) or a combat to reorder social and/or geographical boundaries. It is a warfare between spiritual entities over the fate of Christ followers. Believers are exhorted to maintain strong allegiance to God and fulfil his moral obligations to maintain good standing in their salvific status. According to Ephesians, it is potentially precarious to fall back to the previous way of life hence the call to stand firm with truth, righteousness, the gospel of peace, faith, salvation and the word of God, being always in the spirit of prayer and supplication. Paul does not explicitly indicate the consequences pertaining to one's inability to wear the whole armor of God in the spiritual warfare, but the potential threat to one's ability to stand with God is implied. Thus, the moral discourse of this letter does not reduce ethics to a set of dos and don'ts or a mere list of virtues and vices. Communal identity and moral conduct are intertwined with spirituality – how believers ought to conduct themselves is grounded in who they have become. Their status and conduct are engineered by divine activity. Consequently, divine resources are accorded, made available or suggested to enable them to function well in the community where God dwells (2:19–22). As such, the idea that spiritual forces work for the interest of their devotees is a prominent feature in every chapter of Ephesians.

# 6

# Parallels and Particulars with African Spirit Cosmology

Religious worldview derives from the cultural norms and ideological frameworks of societies. Changes in culture affect expressions of mores, customs and composition of religious texts. Christian origins in the first century have left traces of multicultural exchange, inter-religious encounters and competing theological ideas, even with Jewish sects in matters of piety (Matt 6) and questions about eternal life. Differences in worldview informed by social locations, norms and beliefs are inevitable whenever one religion spreads across geographical borders and time, especially when differing epistemology and cosmology exist in the new contexts. The history of New Testament interpretation reveals the manner in which social location, philosophical trends and cosmological prisms have shaped interpretative approaches.

As a native of Ghana in West Africa with a significant amount of education in Europe, it was apparent to me that the prism with which my European peers and instructors framed thesis statements, probed and reached conclusions often presupposed the eminence of their particular worldview and had philosophical assumptions rooted in the nineteenth century intellectual tradition of Europe vis-à-vis non-Western intellectual traditions. It was intriguing to observe that reading the same first-century Greek text and employing the same historical-grammatical interpretive approach did not mean we saw the same things in the text. In other words, I observed that the knowledge of Greek morphology and syntax was insufficient in understanding a nearly two thousand years old religious text (NT) produced in a different culture and worldview. However, the Western intellectual prowess rather than the irrational approaches[1] of

---

1. K. wa Gatumu, *The Pauline Concept of Supernatural Powers: A Reading for the African Worldview* (Milton Keynes: Paternoster, 2008), 25–59. Wa Gatumu provides a systematic account

non-Western thought becomes the yardstick for deciphering NT texts or determining what qualifies as good scholarship. The idea that political and economic powers have intellectual superiority was an ancient phenomenon that is still alive and well in biblical studies. My previous education in a former British colony prepared me somewhat for the philosophical underpinnings of Western thought, especially its post-enlightenment framework and the fledging post-modernism at the time. However, I soon discovered that I had grossly underestimated the import of these intellectual traditions in prevailing Christian worldview, thought patterns and approach to biblical studies. The portrait of supernatural activity as nonsensical superstitions that prevailed in uncivilized and uneducated parts of the world was commonplace. The approach to religious texts (such as the New Testament) as with any other non-fiction book heightened my curious sensibilities. Their interpretation did not follow the pattern with which Plato, Aristotle, Plutarch and other philosophers were read and neither did the methods used in interpreting them show similarities to how twentieth and twenty-first century non-fiction texts are read, as such. In confusing ways, skeptics of the so-called naive beliefs in supernatural activity and spiritual beings could still express belief in the resurrection of Christ and the Holy Spirit with no apparent contradictions. It is no secret that while the majority of Christians do not live on the continents of Europe and North America, many biblical studies scholars in the global North still disregard the value of non-Western approaches to biblical texts. It is not far-fetched to surmise that a large number of religious studies departments and divinity schools in Europe and North America would today not accept the Jewish native Paul of Tarsus or the Galilean Jesus of Nazareth in their prestigious institutions – their worldview and mode of reasoning, let alone their lives and teachings, would disqualify them.[2]

---

and concrete evidence that indicates how nineteenth century missionaries came to Africa with the notion that Africans are inferior, possess inferior intellect and stand only slightly above apes. This inferior concept provided impetus for the missionaries to dismiss African cultures, worldview and values. Some of the evidence shows how some Bible translators aimed to change the language of some people groups through their works. African beliefs in supernatural powers were thus demonized and dismissed. Lack of respect for Africans allowed for little to no room to make sense of their culture, beliefs and how they relate to Christianity.

2. As a native of Ghana who grew up and worked in the country, I once had an American scholar who insisted that she knew more about women in my particular culture than I do – the only basis being that she had visited the country for two weeks and observed the people closely. Many would think this is laughable, yet we bring such attitudes to biblical interpretation more often than we would like to admit.

This chapter endeavors to show parallels between particulars of spirit cosmology in ancient Asia Minor and those of Africa to concretize scenarios in the reconstruction of ancient worldviews and shed some light on how some parallel worldview with the earliest readers/hearers of Ephesians may inform how we approach the text. Beyond Africa, this spirit cosmology is broadly shared by the majority of Christ followers in the world today. Hopefully, the ancient cosmology and perspectives from Africa will broaden the horizon of the way we ponder ancient or primitive cosmologies. In the case of Ephesians, I hope the import of its spirit cosmology in interpreting the text will become more acute – as a text loaded with lexemes and motifs of spirit cosmology. At the very least, it is anticipated that this chapter will engender a posture of humility in the way we approach texts like Ephesians – intentionally as a cross-cultural endeavor and as a product of, from, and for first-century Christ followers whose cosmology differs significantly from the mainstream of Western academia yet shares commonalities with the African worldview.

## 6.1 Cosmology in African Religious Thought and World Concept

Religion and culture are inseparable in the sub-Saharan African worldview. Western influence in urban development is markedly noticeable from Cairo to Conakry and from Accra to Abuja yet Africans largely retain their indigenous worldview, value systems and religious traditions. The search for meaning in African consciousness is framed and informed by multifaceted ideologies in the form of cosmology, anthropology and mores. The physical, mental and social aspects of human life are perceived to be interfaced and interlinked with the unseen world. The broadly collectivist, polychronic and tribal systems leave people with no particular need for an individual sense of belonging. In much of sub-Saharan Africa, individual identity is connected to that of the community and its ruling deities. A strong sense of spiritual activity in the realms of humanity accounts for a *modus vivendi* that may be characterized as cultures of deep spiritual sensibilities. "What men look for in religious behavior, without exception, are security and satisfaction in their day-to-day world of experience."[3] Africans regard religion as an integral part of culture and human well-being. Anthropologically, the composite of human being in Africa not only comprises material (body) and immaterial (soul/spirit, soul and spirit) elements but it is also believed that a strong connection exists between persons

---

3. M. Assimeng, *Religious and Social Change in West Africa: An Introduction to Sociology of Religion* (Accra: Woeli Publishing, 2010), 65.

and spiritual beings in various forms. Spiritual forces are active in/with human affairs, even in engendering and/or determining people's fate. The creation of the cosmos is God's design, and its governance and sustenance are believed to be under the oversight of God – the Supreme Being. Thus, humans do not control the world or stand at its center to do whatever they want without consequences. At the same time, humans are not preprogrammed robots of God; they have volition to do what they deem fit, with potential spiritual chastisement for wrongdoing and reward for good from divine benefactors.

## 6.2 Supreme God in African Spirit Cosmology

The God concept in African thought does not vary significantly from what we know from the Ancient Near East and Greco-Roman worlds. The notion that the cosmos is the creation of a spirit being is widespread in African spirit cosmology. Since creation theology stands foundational to spirit cosmology among Africans, we proceed to explore the nature of God the Creator in African cosmology. Whether the God these cultures refer to as the Creator can be equated with the biblical God of creation or the one referred to in the monotheistic Abrahamic faiths (Judaism, Christianity, and Islam) as the God of Abraham, Isaac and Jacob is a debated matter. Some Western scholars[4] and missionaries contend that African beliefs, outside Islam and Christianity, subscribe to polytheism and they resist the thought of any African reference to God being associated with the Christian God. Conversely, African scholars have argued against what they deem to be mischaracterization of traditional African beliefs during and after the colonial era. Some argue that African cultures adhere to belief in one Supreme God who works through mediators and subsidiary gods/goddesses, and who may be approached by the agency of other spirit or human agents.[5] African monotheism then may not be misconstrued, in this reasoning.

---

4. See J. Spieth, *The Ewe People: A Study of the Ewe People in German Togo* (Legon: Sub-Saharan Publishers, 2011), 451. Spieth is hesitant but goes on to argue that the Ewe designation of God as *Mawu* does not refer to the Christian God for reasons that Ewes practice syncretism and believe in many gods. Defining the nature of a deity is different from religious traditions that worship many gods, including a particular deity in question. Spieth does not seem interested in discounting the claim that *Mawu* is also the god of creation. However, Bible translators refer to God as *Mawu* in the Ewe Bible with no particular qualification – perhaps as inadvertent reinforcement of tradition.

5. N. K. Dzobo, *Modes of Traditional Moral Education Among Anfoega Ewes* (Cape Coast: Cape Coast University Press, 1971), 4; J. B. Danquah, *The Akan Doctrine of God* (London: Frank Cass, 1968), and K. Gyegye, *African Cultural Values* (Accra: Sankofa, 1996), 4–12.

That God (one Supreme being) is responsible for creation is a widespread belief that preceded Christianity and Islam in Africa. The Supreme God of creation is not confused with (the function of) gods and goddesses.[6] African scholars have argued that in the African worldview God is not distinct from the Judeo-Christian God preached and taught by the missionaries.[7] This is the God who created the world with power and authority and is above all other gods/spiritual beings. Consequently, African scholars of religion argue that Christians and Muslims adopt traditional names, concepts and even appellations to this Supreme Being in translations of their sacred writings and in their religious practices. In Ghana, "the Akan name for the Supreme Being is *Nyame*, the Ewe calls him *Mawu*, which is also the Adangme name while the Ga call him *Nyonmo*. . . . The High God or Supreme Being is generally held to be the Creator of the world and everything in it as well as the source of all powers operating in it."[8] Bible translators make a conceptual transfer and evoke this traditional conception of God in Christian worship. Consistent with Christian theology, sub-Saharan Africans believe that God is omnipotent and omniscient.[9] His omniscience accords him appellations such as "the Wise one" in Zululand, "the Watcher of everything" in Burundi and "the One who knows all and sees all" among the Akan.[10] The Creator is the almighty who governs the universe and all that is within. This God has several anthropomorphic qualities.

> His omnipotent nature implies that He can do whatever He wishes, including assuming any form in any state of existence. He might assume a human or any other form to participate in life's experiences or for any other purpose. He sees all. He knows all, and He rectifies anything that goes wrong in creation when he feels the need to do so. In most cases, however, he does not interfere in the affairs of men. He expects people to behave righteously of their own free will, and He punishes men only when they stray from

---

6. E. K. Larbi, *Pentecostalism: The Eddies of Ghanaian Christianity* (Accra: CPCS, 2001), 2–3.

7. K. Bediako, *Jesus in Africa: The Christian Gospel in African History and Experience* (Carlisle: Paternoster, 2000), 21. The following books provide exhaustive discussion in support of the view. See E. B. Idowu, *Olodumare: God in Yoruba Belief* (London: Longmans, 1962); J. S. Mbiti, *Concepts of God in Africa* (London: SPCK, 1979); and G. M. Setiloane, *The Image of God among the Sotho-Tswana* (Rotterdam: A. A. Balkema, 1976).

8. Nukunya, *Tradition and Change in Ghana*, 56.

9. J. S. Mbiti, *African Religions and Philosophy* (Portsmouth: Heinemann, 1989), 30.

10. Mbiti, *African Religions and Philosophy*, 31.

righteousness and cause disharmony in creation. He may punish unrighteousness Himself or through His agents.[11]

The Supreme God is also called *Odomankoma* (Akan), *Chineke* (Ibo) and *Eleda* (Yoruba) – denoting the God of creation. The gender of God may be neuter, masculine or feminine depending on the people group.

There are various creation mythologies on *how* God created the world – from the imagery of God as a carpenter, a potter and an architect. Each myth has an element of his deliberate and orderly undertaking to bring the cosmos and all that is in it into existence.[12] Aspects of these myths suggest that God once had intimate relationship with human beings but the relationship was marred due to misguided initiatives or acts of human beings. West African traditional religions highlight the reconciling spirit and attributes of God, even when humans strayed. It is noteworthy that animal sacrifice, especially that of unblemished sheep or doves, to the gods and/or ancestors, are an important part of the protocol to bring about reconciliation between two parties, either human and human or human and divine (Eph 2:13–22). God is believed to be just and benevolent. He provides rain for good harvest and children to the barren. Thus, it is not unusual for women blessed with children by God to name their children in acknowledgment of God's benevolence using names such as *Nyamekye* ("gift of God" in Akan), *Mawunyo* ("God is kind" in Ewe), *Mawuli* ("God is alive/exists" in Ewe) or *Oluwasamni* ("God is good to me" in Yoruba).

The significant import of community and family relations in Africa partly accounts for why the role of God, gods/goddesses and ancestors in the community are so pronounced. The Creator and other spiritual entities control atmospheric space and are deeply involved in the terrestrial affairs of the communities. The honorific attributes and appellations are ascribed to the Supreme God relative to his/her function. For example, God is a father who provides, protects, and guides his own. As a mother, she is compassionate, loving, caring and forgiving. Moreover, patron deities of towns or regions as well as gods possess virtuous qualities that adherents may find worthy of emulation (see Eph 5:1–2). People may seek divine enabling to exhibit virtues such as temperance, courage or prudence, which are known to reflect the character of these gods. Kinship lexemes are often employed relative to the gods to engender the shared identity of devotees and enhance solidarity among adherents. The expansive nature of both natural and fictive kinship in African cultures is such

---

11. G. Bannerman-Richter, *The Practice of Witchcraft in Ghana* (Elk Grove: Babari Publishing, 1982), 4.

12. K. A. Opoku, *West African Traditional Religion* (Accra: FEP International, 1978), 21.

that many languages have broader terms for kinsmen and limited vocabulary in distinguishing particularities such as nieces, uncles, cousins, first cousins, second cousins, nephews etc. Common terms for brothers, sisters or uncles strengthen affinity either in fictive kinship relative to a deity or in natural kinship.[13] These kinship lexemes also foster indiscriminate affinity – a sense of closeness, loyalty and community that transcends the Western notion of family or religious community with strong individualistic mindsets. For instance, John Mbiti highlights the father image of God in local worldview when he insisted that the Nuer read the Lord's prayer as, "Our father, it is thy universe, it is thy will, let us be at peace, the souls of thy people be cool; Thou art our father, remove all evil from our path."[14]

In African cosmology God is worshipped in many forms. Some worship him in shrines whereas others call on or petition him/her by means of libation. In some cases, individuals may perform private rituals in gratitude to or as a petition in a private matter. In this cosmology, humankind exists and operates in God's world. God gives life and infuses life in all of his creation. Rivers, earth, trees, mountains and even animals all have a spiritual dimension to their existence or being. Nature can and may even be invited to join in praise to God (see Pss 96:11–12; 97:1–2; 150:6). Thus, the mention of objects like trees, sea or mountains in libation is not senseless homage to inanimate objects, but real petition or invocation to the spirit within or associated with that object.

## 6.3 The Earth, Gods and Goddesses

The Supreme God engages humanity directly or indirectly via rituals, mediums, priests, lesser gods etc. For example, the "Akans believe in lesser spirits, considered to be animate natural objects (roads, rivers, trees). Through them they convey compliments to the Supreme One."[15] In African cosmology, the earth is sacred and in some cases an object of worship. In Akan, *Asase Yaa* (earth spirit [Thursday-born female]) supports life, human dignity and destiny. The Igbos of Nigeria view the earth and water spirits as two prominent female

---

13. This author has been approached more than once to verify if other Africans were making false claims when they referred to other Africans as their brothers or sisters. All-inclusive terms for kinsmen in some African languages do not transfer in English. This conceptual transfer makes it easy for Christ followers to refer to members of their local churches as brothers or sisters with no hesitation.

14. Mbiti, *African Religions and Philosophy*, 64.

15. K. Nkansah-Kyeremateng, *Akan Heritage* (Accra: Sebewie Publishers, 1999), 96.

deities of the land.[16] Some Africans have a custom to give to the earth a drop of water first before they drink or a piece of their food before they eat as an act of worship and gratitude to the divine provider. The earth (with her spirit) provides water and food and thus is deserving of constant tribute in that regard. The earth as a sacred object is treated with respect; as such, there are norms and taboos that regulate propriety thereon. Unwritten codes for privacy and piety are observed in uninhabited space on earth by many cultures; the breach thereof often invites divine retribution. Many communities observe designated days to abstain from tilling the soil, harvesting and other human activities in honor of the earth goddess. Even certain sounds are prohibited by the gods of the land during certain seasons. For example, drumming is prohibited at designated weeks of the year by the Gas in Ghana. Churches and clubs even in the capital city of Accra are prohibited from drumming or increasing decibels of drum bits to a certain level during the period. Engaging in sexual intercourse in uninhabited wild forests defiles the land and rituals and fines are imposed on trespassers to pacify the land or curb the curse of barrenness to the land – implied by the lack of rain and yield in agricultural ventures. In the Igboland of Nigeria, Mother Earth is called Ani. The Akans call her *Asase Yaa* and the Fantes (Ghana) call her *Asase Efua.* For the Igbo,

> Ani is believed to be the fountainhead or source of all increase, not only with regard to crops but also human beings. She is the source of morality as well as the ruler and protector of men. She dwells in the Underworld and is the mistress of countless deities. As Queen of the Underworld, Ani is believed to receive dead bodies into her womb and to rule the ancestors buried in the earth.[17]

Spirits are everywhere at any time and in everything within African communities working for the well-being of the people and regulating human behavior.

Moreover, many tribes have specific times of the year set aside to honor spiritual beings for their contribution to society in the form of town wide festivals,[18] which include the earth spirit, patron gods/goddesses and ancestors.

---

16. S. Jell-Bahlsen, *The Water Goddess in Igbo Cosmology* (Trenton: Africa World Press, 2008), 71–76. According to the Igbos, "the water goddess *Nne Mmiri* is a complementary counterpart to the earth goddess who has her own set of rules, and may also challenge, renew, or modify custom" (p. 72).

17. Opoku, *West African Traditional Religion*, 57.

18. A. Brempong, *Transformations in Traditional Rule in Ghana 1951–1996* (Accra: Sedco, 2001), 85–92. The author provides an exhaustive chart indicating special festivals among various people groups in Ghana, time of the year and the occasion being celebrated.

Like in ancient Ephesus, major festivals include drumming, meals and town-wide processions. In Ghana, the Akans celebrate *Odwira*, the Ga *Homowo*, *Bakatue* or *Aboakyer* is celebrated by the Fante, *Hogbetsotso* among the Ewe, *Kundum* by the Nzema in the southwest and *Gologo* by some tribes in the north.[19] Falola underscores the significance of these festivals in Nigeria: "The most important activities in public life, festivals, celebrations, ritual performance, and various ceremonies connected with rites of passage, all have religious undertones. People are brought together in large gatherings focused by religion, be it the Igbo yam festival or the annual masquerade of the Yoruba."[20] In other words, propensity to the earth spirit, belief in the Supreme God (Creator) and activity of spiritual beings in human affairs are inscribed in African consciousness and celebrated in grand fashion.

The God of creation (usually a father figure) and the earth (mother figure) are cosmic deities who exercise dominion over other spirits (good and bad). The heavens above and earth below are inseparable aspects of one and the same cosmos. The Supreme God rules from the atmospheric realms while Mother Earth is deeply involved in the underworld. "According to various African beliefs, the relationship between this Supreme Being and the other divinities is ordered in such a way that the (minor) gods and goddesses act as intermediaries between human beings and the Supreme Being, God."[21] What happens in the spiritual realm does manifest materially in human affairs. Sub-Saharan Africans puzzle at the dualistic view of heaven and earth as separate entities.

Lesser gods comprise deities whose devotees construct shrines or objects as the point of contact between them and the gods/goddesses. These gods purportedly ensure security from evil omens, harness concord and provide bumper harvests or vocational success. They sanction propriety and chastise misconduct, especially if it undermines social cohesion. Human intermediaries such as priests and priestesses serve to warn trespassers about the punitive reactions of these deities in the event of non-compliance. The "warning must be severe enough to induce the desired changes in human behavior. Once people mend their behavior and harmony is restored, they continue to enjoy the

---

19. T. Ansah, *Kundum: Festival of the Nzemas and Ahantas* (Accra: Onyase Printing Press, 1999), 1–34.

20. T. Falola, *Culture and Customs of Nigeria* (Westport: Greenwood Press, 2001), 34. See also Jacob K. Olupona, *City of 201 Gods: Ile-Ife in Time, Space, and the Imagination* (Berkeley: University of California Press, 2011), 111–250.

21. A. E. Orobator, *Theology Brewed in African Pot* (New York: Orbis Books, 2008), 22.

blessings of the gods."[22] The idea of the "wrath of the gods" is taken seriously. Gods are arbiters and benefactors. "They are strict and impartial in their judgment and are therefore invoked by the weak to intervene on their behalf if their rights are trampled upon."[23] They bless and reward good deeds. They administer justice impartially. They punish by death, diseases and misfortunes on individuals or communities that exploit the innocent, vulnerable and helpless. The gods are "believed to have wide powers; yet each has his or her own area of competence and jurisdiction. Hence, there are gods of war, fertility, epidemics, nation building, agriculture and various other spheres of human endeavor."[24] Africans are usually more fearful of being summoned to the gods for divine retribution than being summoned to courts of law in litigation. The gods are swift in unleashing severe punishment. The notion of spiritual beings as guardians of propriety and social order in collectivist societies partially explains the reduced amount of lawsuit litigations among Africans in Africa. It is not unusual for guilty perpetrators to be killed under a curse pronouncement or suffer misfortune within the set time frame by the administering fetish priest.

There are gods associated with trade and vocation (fishing, farming/harvest etc.) and there are also nature gods such as the goddess of the sea, forest or mountain etc. Patron deities of towns preside over cities and mediate with other spiritual entities for the interest of their devotees – to protect, provide or guide. Other gods/goddesses are believed to cure barrenness, reverse curses, protect citizens and bless devotees. In Ghana, *Kune* is allegedly able to reverse barrenness, prevent miscarriage or help with pregnancy, and cure men who are sexually impotent.[25] Beneficiaries of these services may name their children in honor of the goddess. "Kune" is thus a common name for both males and females in some parts of Ghana.

## 6.4 Human and Spiritual Mediators

In African cosmology, there are different levels and functional intermediaries between the spirit world, especially gods and goddesses, and the human society at large. Two prominent ones are relevant to our discussion, namely (a)

---

22. J. Kuada and Y. Chachah, *Ghana: Understanding the People and their Culture* (Accra: Woeli Publishing, 1999), 38.

23. Kuada and Chachah, *Understanding the People and Their Culture*, 39.

24. Opoku, *West African Traditional Religion*, 55.

25. Assimeng, *Religious and Social Change in West Africa*, 170.

deceased ancestors and (b) priests/priestesses – as they inform the constructs of Christology among African scholars. Ancestors are notable figures who have passed on to the other life (not next life) and continue to pursue the interest of their people in the spiritual realm. Death does not terminate what the noble, respected and responsible citizens have to offer society. They are not dead and gone for good – they are ever-present hence the poor record-keeping of ancestral lineage among some African tribes. This belief is significant in how African Christians conceptualize the role of Christ and the Holy Spirit, as we shall see below. Unlike ancestors, priests and priestesses are human intermediaries that serve religious roles that are analogous to the prophetic ministry and/or priestly functions in ancient Hebrew traditions.

### 6.4.1 Ancestors in African Worldview

Life continues after death in African cultures, but not in the sense of a physical resurrection of the dead. African cultural anthropology regards the non-material aspect of humanity to be as important as the material. Death ends physical existence and visible interaction with the living, but the soul and/or spirit continues to live with the ability to engage with human beings on a regular basis. Africans believe in the existence of ghosts, which must not be confused with ancestors. Ancestors work for the interest of their kinsmen in protecting or preserving family honor – all in the spiritual realm. "The dead do not sever their links with their kinsmen but continue to be members of their individual families, fulfilling their obligations as elders."[26] Deceased members who lived exemplary lives continue to play important roles for their families. They are honored, venerated and called upon in time of need. Occasionally, special rites are performed to honor and seek their assistance.

However, not every deceased person is accorded the status of an ancestor. An ancestor must have left a legacy of dignity and integrity. The manner of death of the person must be a "natural," not an accident or suicide. The person must not be a child. Premature deaths, such as through accidents or the death of a mother during childbirth are disqualifiers. In other words, custom dictates that members detest premature deaths and desist from validating them with ancestral standing. Moreover, "suicide is a disgrace to the person and his/her clan. The corpse is not given a fitting burial and rites are performed to remove whatever curse had forced the person to commit suicide."[27] Those who lived

---

26. Opoku, *West African Traditional Religion*, 37.

27. Kuada and Chachah, *Understanding the People and Their Culture*, 42–43.

irresponsible lives and are known for their nefarious lifestyle are to be forgotten in social memory and cannot be accorded the status of ancestors. Conversely, children are named after the honorable, responsible and successful deceased members; these are ancestors whose contributions are still needed for the betterment of society.

Ancestors are powerful spiritual forces in African cosmology.[28] Apparently, they reside in the underworld under the auspices of the spirit of the earth. They communicate with their kinsmen through dreams, sorcery or soothsaying on a wide range of issues. They intercede and often intercept malevolent attempts to harm their loved ones. Ancestral veneration,[29] as in other parts of the world, includes invoking their names in libations and special rites to plead their cause, all acknowledging their services or giving thanks for their contribution. "The ancestral rites serve as important means of social control. The fact that only people of a certain caliber qualify as ancestors regulates behavior by making individuals and groups not only conform but also to lead such exemplary lives as to enable them to qualify for the honor after their deaths."[30] In some cases, special feasts are dedicated to ancestors who served in leadership roles. The nature of the events range from grand durbars in Ghana to an exclusive rite at the graveside in Sierra Leone.

### 6.4.2. Human Intermediaries: Priests, Priestesses and Herbalists

The main role of priests or priestesses in African cosmology is to serve as mediators between humans and deities or serve as arbiters of the divine in regulating social order. The functions include conveying messages from the gods to the people, performing rituals and administering remedies to those who seek spiritual aid. "Strictly speaking priests are religious servants associated with temples; but in [the] African situation the word is used to cover everyone who performs religious duties in temples, shrines, sacred groves or elsewhere."[31] The phenomenon of priests/priestesses is especially prevalent in West African Traditional Religions than elsewhere on the continent. These

---

28. P. J. Neimark, *The Way of the Orisa: Empowering Your Life through the Ancient African Religion of Ifa* (New York: Harper Collins, 1993), 21–33. The Ifa religious movement places ancestor worship at a prominent place in the beliefs.

29. See E. H. Ofori-Amankwah, *African Culture and Christianity* (Kumasi: KNUST, 2003), 9–17. The entire chapter highlights beliefs in ancestral veneration and offers Christian response but in no substantive manner.

30. Nukunya, *Tradition and Change in Ghana*, 59.

31. Mbiti, *African Religions and Philosophy*, 182.

individuals undergo rigorous training at the shrine to learn the art and craft of priesthood. "The training includes instructions in the laws, taboos, dances, songs, idiosyncrasies of the gods, as well as general priestly duties. In addition, the trainee has to acquire a knowledge of medicine – herbs, roots etc. – and traditional African methods of psychiatry. Every priest is also a herbalist, but a herbalist is not necessarily a priest."[32] Priests are associated with established gods/goddesses and shrines where rituals are performed, and individuals may visit for spiritual assistance. The function of the fetish priest includes blood sacrifice. Certain animals are used for thanksgiving offerings, atonement, breaking curses etc. The deities may range from patron deities of towns, especially in rural areas, to family shrines.

Moreover, the traditional medicine man/witchdoctor who sometimes mediates between the people and spiritual forces may not be a priest/priestess. There are some who are independent or freelance practitioners. The Akan (Ghana) name for them is *dunsinyi* (master of medicine). They employ insights for herbal medicine and spiritual means in administering cures (e.g. Asklepios). Their competences include the "ability to utilize spirit forces for the purpose of saving or destroying physical lives; a knower of medicine must be able to cast spells, neutralize spells, and protect against spells."[33] The *Dunsinyi* play an important role in public health especially where people are not able to access hospitals or orthodox medicine.[34]

### 6.4.3 Beliefs in other Spiritual Forces in Human Affairs

The complex belief systems of the spirit world do not suggest diminished utility of the intellect or complacency in work ethic in African cosmology. Western linear and binary thought patterns often misconstrue spirituality or belief in an active role of spiritual beings for irrational superstitious undertakings or a sluggish lifestyle. Evidently, that is not the case in classical Greek societies, the Greco-Roman world in general or African societies today. However, it is fair to surmise that such beliefs invite unwarranted superstitious activities. Before we consider how the ensuing discussion on spirit cosmology affects the day-to-day life of the African, I will endeavor to provide an overview of beliefs

---

32. Opoku, *West African Traditional Religion*, 74.

33. Bannerman-Richter, *Practice of Witchcraft in Ghana*, 9.

34. I grew up in a small town seventeen miles from the nearest hospital. Most people in my village depended on such people or traditional herbal medicine to meet their primary care needs. In such contexts, the *Dunsinyi* wielded much power and influence.

in witchcraft, sorcery, magic and divinations that parallel what we find in the immediate context of Ephesians in western Asia Minor in the first century.

### 6.4.3.1 Witches and Witchcraft

Belief in witchcraft is commonplace in Africa.[35] Witchcraft is not a mere art or a Halloween-like camouflage but a phenomenon in which humans transform into parahumans to also operate in the unseen world to do good or evil. In African witchcraft, a person may vacate the physical body during sleep hours to engage in nefarious acts with their coven in the spirit world. Witchcraft[36] could be acquired, transferred unknowingly by a relative or knowingly to the recipient. The term for those purportedly born with witchcraft is "witch-incarnate."[37] "Among the many powers of witches is their ability to transform a human being into a sheep or a cow. They seize the ethereal body of the victim, transform it into a desired animal, and then tether it until the day for the feast arrives"[38] – when the person would be killed. "Witches are people, male or female, who are believed to possess inherent supernatural powers which they use to harm others or benefit themselves."[39] Nothing in the way they conduct themselves reveals their status to the ordinary person, not even family members. Witches do not possess any distinguishable features in real life. A spouse or child may not know the identity of a witch in their household. Witches are self-aware about their abilities and recognize their comrades in real life. They are feared for the harm they are able to inflict. For example, "a Ghanaian witch possesses the power to cause sickness, blight her enemies, cause (sexual) impotence and sterility, and death."[40] Witchcraft is often associated with women. In some cases, women who are wrongly accused of being witches

---

35. P. K. Sarpong, *Odd Customs: Stereotypes and Prejudices* (Accra: Sub-Saharan Publishers, 2012), 17–18.

36. See J. Jahn, *Muntu: African Culture and the Western World* (New York: Grove Press, 1961), 29–69. Voodoo is another form of witchcraft. This chapter examines how the Voodoo practice that has its origin in Benin has become popular in Haiti.

37. G. Bannerman-Richter, *Don't Cry, My Baby, Don't Cry: Autobiography of an African Witch* (Elk Grove: Gabari Books, 1984), 21–23. Witch-incarnate is a former witch returning to human existence with their witchcraft as a child.

38. Bannerman-Richter, *Don't Cry, My Baby, Don't Cry*, 23.

39. Nukunya, *Tradition and Change in Ghana*, 59.

40. Bannerman-Richter, *Practice of Witchcraft in Ghana*, 15. This book provides an elaborate discussion on witchcraft in Africa, Ghana in particular, and how some of these activities are brought to the diaspora contexts in Europe and the United States of America.

are ostracized, abandoned and publicly shamed.[41] Elsewhere, traditional beliefs have prompted local members to take the lives of those they considered to be witches responsible for their misfortunes.[42] Death, diseases and accidents have been attributed to witches in Africa. But a former witch confessed that they possess only limited ability to predict what would happen in the future. "Any knowledge a witch has of what will transpire is dictated by the sequence of events prior to that happening. In that respect most witches' ability to know what will happen in the future is not greater than an ordinary person's."[43]

Witchcraft belongs to the realm of *honhom fi* (evil spirits). Unlike the gods that administer justice, witches could inflict harm on the innocent. As such, it is commonplace to seek protection from witchcraft either from a deity, *malam* (Islamic teacher) or a *jujuman* (spiritual man) who may dispense talismans, amulets or other objects for protection. "In many societies, witches are blamed for almost all problems and calamities, from crop failure to mysterious death. Good fortunes and destinies can be altered by witches. Successful marriages can be terminated by them. In periods of economic decline and social unrest, the belief in witchcraft becomes stronger, as individuals and communities seek an external explanation for their misfortune."[44] Individuals may also seek protection against witchcraft from powerful gods. The constant fear of witches in Africa and quest for security from witchcraft cannot be underrated. As one scholar notes, "the forces of evil are always at work against human beings in order to prevent them from enjoying abundant life or fulfilling their *nkrabea* (destiny)."[45] Christian converts expect God to provide such security in Christ Jesus.

### 6.4.3.2 Magic, Sorcery, Soothsaying and Divination

Apart from organized religion, the other aspect of spirit cosmology that dominates human consciousness is the ability to employ magic, soothsaying

---

41. See A. Schauber, "Women and Witchcraft Allegations in Northern Ghana: Human Rights Education Between Conflict and Consensus," in *Ethnicity, Conflicts and Consensus in Ghana*, ed. S. Tonah (Accra: Woeli Press, 2007), 116–148. This essay focuses on Human Rights recounting degrading conditions of women who are charged to be witches and encamped at a village in search of refuge. Society may kill or harm such women since they are deemed dangerous to the well-being of others. Unfortunately, superstitious beliefs in Africa have led to too many such mistreatments of innocent people.

42.  The killing of suspected witches is extra-judicial. Vigilante attacks in some parts of Kenya and Tanzania and eastern Africa are also widely reported in the media these days.

43. Bannerman-Richter, *Don't Cry, My Baby, Don't Cry*, 169.

44. Falola, *Culture and Customs of Nigeria*, 30.

45. Larbi, *Pentecostalism*, 6.

and/or sorcery for benevolent or malevolent ends. Christians and non-Christians explain events, even natural phenomena, to have their origin or causes in magic, witchcraft or some spiritual activity.[46] The online English dictionary at Dictionary.com defines magic first as "the art of producing illusions as entertainment by the use of sleight of hand, deceptive devices." However, what is referred to as magic in this work pertains to spirit cosmology in Africa that departs significantly from this dictionary definition. For Africans, magic has several local names. It is an actual spiritual endeavor and potent force that produces tangible effects. The second definition of magic in Dictionary.com is, "the art of producing a desired effect or result through the use of incantation or various other techniques that presumably assure human control of supernatural agencies or the forces of nature." The ordinary meaning of "magic" in English fails to capture the embodiment of its diabolic and deadly nature in the African worldview.

The "African medicine man" or any ordinary person may acquire the powers to practice magic, sorcery or divination.

> Magicians and sorcerers are consultants whose services are open to utilization by those who need them. These services include: intervention in a promotion exercise; interviews; causing harm to a rival or even having him killed; protection against accidents; protection against conviction in a court case or making it impossible for an opponent or a policeman to appear in court to give evidence; or enabling a lost property to be found.[47]

Magicians and sorcerers are not always affiliated to a particular fetish/shrine; they serve communities with their insights into herbal medicine and spiritual powers. They possess powers to entice partners in conjugal relations or seduce beautiful women or handsome men into sexual acts. "Every village in Africa has a medicine-man within reach, and he is the friend of the community."[48] Among the Ewes in Ghana, Togo and Benin, it is common to deploy *tukpe* (magic) to kill rivals or enemies. The practice may take a form of recitation of a formula or ritual to effect the desired outcome. Such activity, performed miles away against a named person, is able to kill that person within minutes under circumstances that could not be linked to the magician or

---

46. G. K. Nukunya, *Tradition and Change in Ghana: An Introduction to Sociology* (Accra: Ghana Universities Press, 2003), 55.

47. Nukunya, *Tradition and Change in Ghana*, 62.

48. Mbiti, *African Religions and Philosophy*, 162.

conjurer. Magic is used in battles for protection and to defeat enemies. In the words of John Mbiti:

> There is a mystical power which causes people to walk on fire, to lie on thorns or nails, to send curses or harm, including death, from a distance, to change into animals (lycanthropy), to spit on snakes and cause them to split open or die; power to stupefy thieves so that they can be caught red-handed; power to make inanimate objects turn into biologically living creatures; there is power that enable experts to see into secrets, hidden information or the future, or to detect thieves and other culprits. African people know this and they try to apply it in these and many other ways. For that reason, they wear charms, eat 'medicines' or get them rubbed into their bodies; they consult experts, especially the diviners and medicine-men to counteract the evil effects of this power or to obtain powerful "charged" objects containing the same power.[49]

Africans do not treat the existence of evil spirits lightly. It is rare to find Christians or non-Christians who do not know someone that has been impacted directly by malevolent spiritual powers (see appendix 2). The fear of these powers is not merely "perceived" but is real fear rooted in experience. "In the African universe the supernatural can be hyperactive. Against the backdrop of a worldview that takes supernatural evils like the evil eye and witchcraft seriously, it is not uncommon for people to bury all kinds of protective medicines, charms, and amulets on their properties to secure such places against the presence of evil powers."[50] This is partly why it is commonly said, "Do not believe in Jesus unless you are certain of his ability to protect you from evil powers."

Sorcery and divination in this usage include oracular manipulation of objects to discern, choose or understand mysteries with the aid of spirits (comparable with the use of the Urim and Thummim by the high priest in the Old Testament).[51] Diviners unveil mysteries. The objects used in divination or soothsaying include cowry shells, cola nuts, stones or split palm kernels. "The idea behind the operation of every divining system is the supernatural;

---

49. Mbiti, 192–193.

50. J. K. Asamoah-Gyadu, *Contemporary Pentecostal Christianity: Interpretations from African Context* (Oxford: Regnum Africa, 2013), 169.

51. The African practice often looks very much like what we find in ancient Hebrew tradition known as the Urim and Thummim (Exod 28:30; Lev 8:8; Num 27:21; Ezra 2:63; Neh 7:65).

it is the deity or god behind the system that determines how the divination objects will appear to fall."[52] Conflict is usually resolved in the arbitration of the council of elders or people may appeal to a respected person by both parties to mediate. Conflict resolution among the council of elders always opens with a libation to the ancestors and gods of the land. The guilty party may be required to provide animals such as sheep, or birds such as chickens or doves, to atone for their guilt, reconcile with the offended party and pacify spiritual stakeholders of the land. Blood sacrifice is thus a common practice in African cultures and religious practice. Many Africans are at home with the Christian notion of the "shedding blood for the forgiveness of sins." When all such protocols fail, many in rural Africa are likely to consult or appeal to a spiritual agent to address injustice with expediency. Faith in spiritual beings to punish injustice and vindicate the innocent is commonplace. Moreover, magical powers are used in wars and intertribal conflict against opponents. A popular story among the Ewe goes like this:

> In one of the intertribal wars fought many years ago, six juju men were chosen to guard the king's palace. None of them had any weapon but they were armed with charms and amulets. Deep in the night while the soldiers were engaged in a fight several kilometers away, a band of thirty strong men from the enemy camp sneaked into the village to capture the king. On seeing them, three of the juju men dashed forward to meet them with their palms outstretched while chanting *Da male! Da male!* Literally meaning "Shoot, and I'll catch! Shoot, and I'll catch!" The enemies fired their guns and the juju men caught the bullets in their open palms. Terrified the soldiers fled into the bush, some dropping their guns during the flight.[53]

Sorcery and divination also function to reveal sources of evil, ailments or disasters along with prescribed remedies. Practitioners are able to reverse curses, heal diseases and exorcise those possessed by evil powers. Spirits could possess individuals prone to destructive forms of anger, insatiable appetite for sex or aggression. O'Donovan reckons that,

> To be controlled or possessed by a spirit is a common experience in Africa. Most people have witnessed someone under the control of a spirit. When a person is under the control of a spirit, his

---

52. Nukunya, *Tradition and Change in Ghana*, 63.
53. Kuada and Chachah, *Understanding the People and Their Culture*, 45–46.

character and behavior may be dramatically changed. He or she may have unusual physical strength and endurance. The person may speak in a strange language which is not his own language. He or she may speak prophecies or messages from an ancestor or a divinity.[54]

Vices of various forms could be exploited by evil spirits to exercise control over people (see Eph 4:26–27). Epilepsy and mental illnesses are also sometimes associated with the works of evil spirits (see Mark 5:1–17).[55] "During the height of spirit possession, the individual in effect loses his own personality and acts in the context of the 'personality' of the spirit possessing him."[56] It is not always that a spirit possesses an individual for harm. Occasionally, an ancestor may possess a family member as the channel to deliver a message or a god may indwell a person to perform various functions on their behalf. Exorcism is utilized to release victims whose defiant conduct or vices are associated with evil spirits. Tailored rituals may be employed depending on the issue and the powers of the exorcist.

Beyond human activity to employ spiritual powers, there are other spiritual beings in the African world concept. The Akan talks about *Sasabonsam* (evil spirits) or encounters with *Mmoatia* (little people). The Yoruba believe in the existence of *Eshu. Eshu* could bring about severe harm. "Evil tendencies in man are attributed to Eshu and he is generally believed to take great pleasure in causing mischief and confusion among men."[57] *Mmoatia* are spirits that are able to transform into human features to befriend, train or empower human beings to provide healing, counseling and other human services. Unlike the *Sasabonsam*, which are known for malevolent endeavors, *Mmoatia* function for the most part to serve good causes. The experience of a popular healer, soothsayer and counselor in southwestern Ghana called Egya Atta sheds some light on the work of *Mmoatia*. Atta's fame became widespread and important chiefs and leaders consulted him for medical and spiritual remedies in the 1940s and 1950s. "He became a roving physician and settled down in the city of Cape Coast in 1945 at the invitation of a prominent chief. There, he became the chief's court physician and also a traditional doctor to the general

---

54. W. O'Donovan, *Biblical Christianity in African Perspective* (Carlisle: Paternoster, 1995), 142.

55. S. W. Kunhiyop, *African Christian Theology* (Nairobi: Hippobooks, 2012), 57.

56. Mbiti, *African Religions and Philosophy*, 81.

57. Opoku, *West African Traditional Religion*, 70–74.

public."[58] Atta was said to disappear sometimes for days as an infant when he and his twin brother would be laid to sleep. After a town-wide search for three days, the boy would later be found resting calmly by the side of his brother with tangible evidence (spiritual symbols) that he had been well catered to by someone. Frequent disappearance and reappearances for longer durations occurred as the boy grew older. It would later be known that *Mmoatia* had earmarked and befriended the boy from infancy. Apparently, he was trained and empowered by these forces as physician, soothsayer and counselor. Bannerman-Richter explains:

> Egya Atta blended magic and healing. He would initiate treatment by first summoning the soul (okra) of the patient to find out from it the cause of the illness. Many Akan traditional doctors believe that every person's physical condition is closely linked to his spiritual state and that when a person is sick it means that his physical body is out of alignment with his okra (soul). Egya Atta conversed with it to find out from it what was wrong; then he prescribed treatment.[59]

The idea that the spirit of the dead can appear in another form to interact with humans or that spiritual beings engage human beings directly is not unique to Africans, people in the Middle East or Greco-Roman societies shared this belief, which is also prevalent in other parts of the world today.

## 6.5 Spiritual Beings in the African Moral Framework

As in ancient traditions, the broader African spirit cosmology impacts human conduct and social values. The spiritual dimension of ethics does not negate the value of personal responsibility in the African worldview. Human responsibility is rather encouraged by the notion that good conduct attracts divine blessings. The Supreme Being (God) or gods reward responsibility, moral decency and hard work; they do not entertain dishonorable conduct. Moreover, gods possess moral attributes (virtues) that serve as examples for adherents to emulate. God

---

58. G. Bannerman-Richter, *Mmoatia: The Mysterious Little People* (Elk Grove: Gabari Publishing, 1987), 22. The entire book discusses the nature and operations of these spiritual entities. The author provides concrete stories with names and dates to recount alleged experiences with *Mmoatia* in southern Ghana.

59. Bannerman-Richter, *Mmoatia: The Mysterious Little People*, 22. The author proceeds in this chapter to provide accounts of skeptics who visited him and who were confounded by his findings and the ultimate healing he provided.

is good, kind, merciful, and benevolent. "The goodness of God is seen in His averting calamities, supplying rain, providing fertility to people, cattle and fields."[60] God may also express his anger in unleashing misfortunes.[61] "National calamities such as drought, epidemics, locust invasions, wars and floods are beyond human cause or control. They are generally attributed to God's activity, or to a spiritual being."[62]

### 6.5.1 General Framework of Ethics Relative to Spiritual Beings

African morality is not premised on a defined set of laws or written codes (i.e. the Torah) with accompanying consequences for breach thereof. For Africans, the horizontal and vertical dimensions of the cosmos suggest an interlink of the spiritual and physical in the whole creation. Ethics is a human responsibility in conformity to creation and social order. Cultural norms, mores and customs are governed by unwritten codes rooted in relationships, belief systems and precedence of propriety imbedded in the traditions passed on by the forebears. Right or wrong conduct has multilayered foundations in religious beliefs, honor codes, ancestral legacies etc. The idea that spiritual beings have a role to play in social order – to enhance, bless or punish – also affects human sensibility and conscience in private and public conduct. One does not follow a set of ethical principles to attract divine favor but to participate responsibly in good social order with ultimate spiritual ramifications.[63] The people's understanding of society, however, assumes divine presence and agency in matters beyond human ability to control. This notion of how society functions does not mean personal and professional responsibilities are always deferred to spiritual discernment of sorts.

Moral boundaries vary from society to society. What is wrong in peacetime may be virtuous in wartime (i.e. killing) since communal interest almost always trumps personal wishes in the collectivist framework. Moreover, gods and ancestors have stakes in engendering concord in society and, as such, they could inflict punishment on the dishonorable. "The prominent position of the supernatural in the moral order in West African societies is borne out

---

60. Mbiti, *African Religions and Philosophy*, 36.

61. Mbiti, 37.

62. Mbiti, 44.

63. K. Gyekye, *African Cultural Values: An Introduction* (Accra: Sankofa Publishing, 1996), 57. Gyekye further indicates that, "the social values of the African people have a social and humanistic basis, rather than a religious basis and are fashioned according to the people's own understanding of human society, human relations, human goals, and the meaning of human life."

by the fact that breaches of the moral law (in society) are considered to be offences against the gods, the ancestors and God, not so much against the individual."[64] Outstanding contribution to society may thus attract blessings from divine benefactors. It is not unusual for Africans to appeal to "God's will" (Muslim's repeat the Arabic *insha'Allah*) in major or mundane undertakings. Thus, biblical notions of the wrath of God, the will of God or God's blessings do resonate with these cultures. It is partly the responsibility of God or gods to promote harmonious social order; it is in this vein that they protect against, check or indict wrongdoing with retribution. Sin or wrongdoing has social effects, not only personal. Mistreatment of one person affects the entire society and undermines the social order being harnessed by these gods. Individual identity is thus rooted in communal identity. "In African morality, there is an unrelenting preoccupation with human welfare. What is morally good is that which brings about – or is supposed, expected, or known to bring about – human wellbeing. This means, in a society that appreciates and thrives on harmonious social relationships, that which is morally good is what promotes social welfare, solidarity, and harmony in human relationships."[65] Humans work in tandem with spiritual beings to facilitate concord, security and prosperity. Divine activity and human endeavors are inseparable in this moral framework.

In African spirit cosmology, the Supreme God does not cause evil. He is good. He knew that evil would potentially become part of creation. Human volition is, however, responsible for the prevalence of moral evil in the world. Moreover, rogue spiritual beings exist to influence and perpetrate inhumane acts; these powers do not initiate moral evil but enhance existing propensities for evil. In other words, the spiritual powers only empower individuals in their established agenda to do bad or cause harm. For example, people who delight in indiscriminate sexual acts could be possessed by spirits that advance irresistible urges for sex and seduction and it is believed that this is one of the means by which some of the spirits feed. Those who are possessed with spirits of anger, theft or sex may undergo exorcism and be treated at a shrine or by a *jujuman*. This is another way of saying that uncontrollable vices may be cured by deliverance from a pagan god. It is not unusual for Christian leaders to hear about people who dabbled in such activities in their pre-conversion past asking for prayers to break all ties with evil spirits, as they begin afresh with Jesus. Peace and tranquility are sacred; it is God's will that social order prevails.

---

64. K. A. Opoku, *West African Traditional Religion* (Accra: FEP International, 1978), 156.

65. Gyekye, *African Cultural Values*, 57.

The divine quest for social order is the reason sin (breach of divine social order) or wrongdoing has social consequences. Unlike the idea of sin as "breaking God's law," Africans hold that sin violates God's design for human interaction. The Akan believe that sin is an antisocial act with broader social ramifications. It is "basically injury to the interest of another and damage to the collective life of the group."[66]

> In African Religion, wrongdoing relates to the contravention of specific codes of community expectations, including taboos. Individuals and the whole community must observe these forms of behavior to preserve order and assure the continuation of life in its fullness. To threaten in any way to break any of the community codes of behavior, which are in fact moral codes, endangers life, it is bad, wrong or "sinful."[67]

Those who violate social norms may bring disastrous consequences upon themselves or the community as a whole. "The Barundi believe that God gets angry with a person who commits adultery. The Bachwa believe that God punishes people who steal, neglect their ageing parents, murder or commit adultery."[68] God also rewards those who contribute meaningfully to social harmony.

The interplay of spiritual activity and human responsibility along with the interlink of the material and spiritual worlds accounts for why most episodes in life – good or bad – are described by Africans as having a spiritual bearing. Many forms of misfortune are perceived to have a spiritual link. The extremely superstitious find spiritual causality to any misfortune. Social problems and moral failings are attributed to the neglect of, or apathy towards, religious obligations.[69] The use of magic and sorcery to cause harm is considered morally wrong. Society deplores those who use magic to manipulate innocent people against their best judgement. "Those who practice witchcraft, evil magic and sorcery are the very incarnation of moral evil."[70]

---

66. Bediako, *Jesus in Africa*, 26. Also J. Pobee, *Toward an African Theology* (Nashville: Abingdon, 1979), 102.

67. S. W. Kunhiyop, *African Christian Theology* (Nairobi: HippoBooks, 2012), 70. Cf. L. Magasa, *African Religion: The Moral Traditions of Abundant Life* (New York: Orbis, 1998), 166.

68. Mbiti, *African Religions and Philosophy*, 201.

69. J. N. Kudadjie, *Moral Renewal in Ghana: Ideals, Realities and Possibilities* (Accra: Asempa Publishers, 1995), 55, 72–73.

70. Mbiti, *African Religions and Philosophy*, 208.

### *6.5.2 Spiritual Beings/Activity in Marriage and Sexual Relations*

Undoubtedly, the spirit cosmology so far described lends itself to various forms of superstitions and extreme expression thereof. Hence, I now examine the effect of the African spirit cosmology on ethics and social norms in relation to the kinship relations in family and marriage. In the African worldview, the family extends beyond the immediate group consisting of two parents and their children to include the children, grandchildren and great-grandchildren from one's progeny on both the parents' sides of the family. Marriage is a union between two big families, despite the fact that the husband and wife may have their own home and privacy. Families and immediate households venerate their ancestors. There are family gods, especially in rural areas, aiding in protection and prosperity of agrarian enterprises. The ancestors and spiritual agents from either side of the family may be called upon during the customary matrimony to bless the union with peace, offspring and prosperity. A wife is customarily expected to acknowledge the headship and spiritual leadership of the husband in the home. A man's failure to exercise spiritual leadership and provide for the family diminishes his image/honor in the family and society. Usually, African patriarchal roles have more to do with responsibility than male dominance, though abuse of power does occur.

Morality in the marriage or family is linked to the belief systems of the entire family. Spiritual help is solicited in every major undertaking of the family. The gods or spirits are depended upon for provision, good health and security. The powers who are called to ensure a successful marriage during the wedding ceremony are also asked to guard against dissension and facilitate concord in the home. Husbands who suspected their wives for extramarital affairs would use special charms to harm adulterous parties or expose them to public ridicule. For example, the use of the "chastity hex/spell," which is otherwise referred to as *gbolomagba* is common among the Ewe. The spell is sued to keep a cheating wife and her partner together during/after sexual intercourse until their secret act is made public and a *jujuman* (spiritual man) performs certain rituals on the scene while they are naked and still conjoined at their genitals.[71] Apparently, *gbolomagba* "compels a confession to infidelity from an adulterous wife who, subject to her husband's disposition to pity or punish, either has to undergo ritual purification before she is able to re-enter her husband's home or may be ignored by the husband whereupon she goes

---

71. C. Abotsie, *Social Control in Traditional Southern Eweland of Ghana: Relevance for Modern Crime Prevention* (Accra: Ghana Universities Press, 1997), 79–83.

mad."[72] Other tribes check marital infidelity with gonorrhea spells whereby the cheating partner (mostly applicable to the woman) infects her partner with incurable gonorrhea. Moreover, spiritual powers are utilized to expose the potential harm of one partner to the other. In a nutshell, spiritual beings do not only enhance and strengthen conjugal relations, but they also check moral boundaries in the marriage.

Nubility rites (rites of passage that validate eligibility for marriage) are practiced among some West African cultures (e.g. among the Akan, Ewe, Krobo etc.).[73] These rites include pouring libations to all spiritual stakeholders in the cosmic realms. An Akan scholar who is a Catholic bishop recounts what these rites entail,

> The head of her matrilineage takes a bottle of schnapps – in the olden days it used to be palm wine – and pours a libation to thank God (*Onyankopon*), the earth (*Asase Yaa*), the thousand gods of the ancestors (*nananom abosompem*), and the spirits of the dead (*nananom nsamamfoo*) for having looked after one of his children so that she has attained the age of puberty. He then entreats them to stand firmly behind her so that no misfortune may befall her, and the nubility rites being performed in her honor may come to a successful conclusion.[74]

The event includes meals and public presentation of the girl in special traditional costume and bead necklace. The young girl is typically accompanied by her peers as she parades the streets of the town and visits members of the family. Prior to Christian influence, it was deemed a taboo for a girl who had not undergone this rite to marry or bear a child. The pagan/spiritual and social components of this event are inseparable.

Unmarried and married couples are forbidden to engage in sexual intercourse in the bush, where there is no shelter, or in public, because it defiles the land and provokes the wrath of God. Homosexuality and bestiality remain taboo in many parts of the continent. It is considered a violation of norms and an offense to spirits of the land. The debate on homosexuality thus evokes different sentiments with Africans since they consider it not a civil rights issue but a moral issue that violates norms and offends the gods of the

---

72. Abotsie, *Social Control*, 82–83.

73. Abotsie, 25–30. The author further explains the religious import and social significance of this rite in Eweland.

74. P. Sarpong, *Girls' Nubility Rites in Ashanti* (Accra: Ghana Publishing, 1977), 25.

land.[75] The spiritual consequence of sexual misconduct may be severe, and the wrath of the gods is indeed feared.

### 6.5.3 Spiritual Dimension of Professional Ethics and Development

The role of spiritual beings in Africa is not confined to non-professional aspects of life, but plays a role in professional life as well. People of various professions employ spiritual powers to enhance progress or to protect themselves against diabolic attacks. Professional drivers seek spiritual help to protect them against accidents or personal harm in the case of an accident. Politicians consult gods, spiritual men or employ magic to help them defeat their opponents. This practice of calling up spiritual beings for help occurs in private businesses as well as in corporate enterprises. Francis Botchway supplies ample evidence and recounts, in great detail, the use of magic and other spiritual dealings in professional sports in Africa.[76] Sometimes, fear of diabolic attacks engenders unhealthy compromises or affects ethical decisions. Moreover, leadership in African societies has both spiritual and social dimensions. Traditional chiefs and tribal leaders are appointed to discharge their duties with the help of the gods and ancestors.[77] It is not unusual then to hear of leaders in government, corporate and private enterprises soliciting spiritual help for better performance. As one business professor observes, "given the level of superstition in Ghanaian society, wide-spread belief in the supernatural and the sense of insecurity of some chief executives, the juju/spiritual string can be a strong factor."[78] This belief affects performance in corporate leadership, can cause suspicion of work colleagues from tribes known for certain spiritual activities and in office space allocations. It is not unusual for people to link their performance levels and promotion at work to divine intervention.

---

75. This is a sensitive issue as Western countries seek to persuade politicians to enact laws that protect gay rights. African politicians have a lot of persuasion to do with their constituents before they can make laws that can be enforced. This does not necessarily mean most people do not like gays.

76. F. J. Botchway, *Juju, Magic and Witchcraft in African Soccer: Myth or Reality?* (Accra: Presbyterian Press, 2009). The author observes that this is now a spiritual business with sportsmen and women that goes beyond adherents to African Traditional Religions since Christian and Muslim leaders are increasingly occupying the space to meet the needs of soccer players and other athletes.

77. P. K. Dzathor, *The Ewe Nation and Sasabu: A Brief History* (Accra: Berkadams, 1998), 33–64.

78. S. N. Woode, *Values, Standards and Practice in Ghanaian Organizational Life* (Accra: Asempa Publishers, 1997), 24.

The spirit cosmology of Africa and how it permeates every fabric of society, generally parallels the worldview within which the early readers of Ephesians were socially located. Historical and philological inquiry into the religious beliefs and practices of the distant past comes with obvious limitations when the worldview of the investigator is so far removed from the world of the text. Since Africans believe in the active role of spiritual entities in a cosmos where terrestrial and celestial activities are intertwined they do not share in the Western world's dualistic, monochronic and anti-supernatural tendencies. African believers in Christ are therefore converted, like those in Asia Minor, within and from a complex worldview and social framework that believes in the Supreme God, gods/goddesses, ancestors, magic, sorcery and other spiritual realities and their roles in human affairs. These converts do not necessarily dispense with their previous worldview upon conversion but understand their conversion experience from the perspectives within which they are socialized to see the world and reality. Their worldview informs their religious sensibilities, understanding of a text like Ephesians and their ability to make sense of their place in the world.

## 6.6 Christian Conversion, Transformation and Paradigm Shifts

Christian conversion in Africa occurs within the framework of how the people perceive the world, God and how they embrace the gospel to enhance their lives.

### 6.6.1 Holistic Salvation in Christ Jesus

The pre-conversion religious experiences and worldviews of a society shape the paradigms and prisms with which its members embrace the dogma and praxis of new faiths. The effects of antecedent religions and traditions on the reception of Christianity in Africa account for some of the antipathy towards the "missionary gospel" that demonizes the traditions, mores and culture of the people. Largely, post-enlightenment paradigms offer differing views of the world from the African world concept. It is unfortunate to observe the manner in which exaggeration of difference, dualistic cosmology from the West and demonization of African worldviews[79] have obscured, if not blinded, parallel worldviews and proximate norms of Africans and those of the early

---

79. T. Tienou, *The Theological Task of the Church in Africa: Theological Perspectives in Africa* (Achimota: Africa Christian Press, 1990), 19–32.

Christians.[80] Bediako laments the rate at which western theological reasoning has negatively impacted Africans in their readiness to engage biblical studies that are informed by their own cultural perspectives.[81] According to Bediako, Christianity came to invalidate aspects of African traditions and refocus African spirituality, more so on Christ. "Perhaps the Gospel's affirmation of the essential spirituality of the African primal worldview explains why African Theology has so far been predominantly a theology of inculturation."[82] The insistence that cultures that were unaffected by post-eighteenth century reasoning needed to adopt post-enlightenment presuppositions, postures and prisms to be able to decipher the import of first century religious texts has rather curtailed useful insights and checks on anachronisms.

Africans typically do not conceptualize salvation in Christ as the completion of a four-point protocol to gain access to heaven or an esoteric conception of truth to be upheld. Salvation in Christ Jesus ought to align the African belief in a spirit being that is more powerful than the powers that threaten human security and prosperity. Africans need to know the Savior is capable of delivering from spiritual strongholds and protecting believers against demonic forces. The idea that spiritual beings are existentially involved in human affairs further underscores the theological construct of an always present Christ and Holy Spirit, who mitigate intrinsic fears and aid human flourishing. Songs and prayers in Christian churches echo a deep sense of gratitude to the God that meets these needs and continues to work on behalf of his people. Arguably, this partly explains why charismatic activity seems to permeate churches across denominations in the continent. Certainly, the African Pentecostal movement emphasizes these soteriological benefits in the present age than the eschatological rewards in the life to come.[83] "The worldview underpinning the practice of healing and deliverance in African Pentecostalism is based primarily on Jesus's encounters with the powers of affliction and Pauline notions of the wrestle with principalities and powers (Eph 6). The basic theological orientation of the healing and deliverance

---

80. K. Bediako, *Christianity in Africa: The Renewal of a Non-Western Religion* (Edinburgh: University of Edinburgh Press, 1995), 172–186, and D. Tutu, "Whither African Theology," in *Christianity in Independent Africa*, eds. E. Faschole-Luke, R. Gray and A. Hastings (London: Rex Collings, 1978), 336, and K. Bediako, *Jesus in Africa: The Christian in African History and Experience* (Carlisle: Regnum, 2000), 63–75.

81. K. Bediako, "The Roots of African Theology," *IBMR* 13, no. 2 (1989): 58–65.

82. Bediako, *Christianity in Africa*, 177.

83. It is noteworthy that Ephesians seems to emphasize the present privileges and position that believers have with Christ rather than the eschatological perhaps due to prevailing conditions in the church and the wider spiritual climate of the region.

phenomenon is the belief that demons may either possess a person and take his or her executive faculties or simply oppress people through various influence."[84]

Principalities and powers are perceived by Africans to be real spiritual forces that are capable of devastating consequences. In this view of the world, salvation is more than enrollment into a new community but includes deliverance, redemption and reconciliation of human standing with God. "Since 'salvation' in the traditional African world involves a certain view of the realm of spirit-power and its effect upon the physical and spiritual dimensions of human existence, our reflection about Christ must speak to the questions posed by such a worldview."[85] Since evil spirits can operate either through human agency or by direct contact with humans, it is common knowledge that traditional leaders need to and do employ spiritual powers to enhance their ability to discharge their duties. The authority and credibility of these leaders also includes their power to ward off evil omens or malevolent spirits. Thus, Christian leaders find the need and make claims to possess and minister in the power of God – in preaching, exorcism, healing, etc. In this context, it is counterproductive to promote a naturalist view of the world while encouraging people to come to faith in Christ. To many, that is contrary to African realities.

If salvation or becoming a Christian has a spiritual dimension to it then perhaps more clarity is needed in helping converts comprehend the spiritual beings at work on their behalf. The ensuing discussion presents the African worldview that informs response to the gospel for African believers, specifically as it relates to spirit cosmology, theology, Christology,[86] pneumatology, and even demonology in Africa. The focus here is to delineate broad patterns of doctrinal development – convergence and divergence – of indigenous and missionary theologies, to shed light on the intersection of African worldviews and early Christianity, and describe how that may inform the reading of

---

84. J. K. Asamoah-Gyadu, "Born of Water and Spirit: Pentecostal/Charismatic Christianity in Africa," in *African Christianity*, ed. O. U. Kalu (Trenton: African World Press, 2007), 364.

85. Bediako, *Jesus in Africa*, 22.

86. J. M. Vorster, "A Case for a Transforming Christology in South Africa," *JRT* 7 (2013): 310–326. This article provides evidence of how proponents of Reformed, Arminian and Liberation Theologies presented Jesus Christ in the manner that made it possible for believers to oppress people on one hand or to justify violent resistance in the apartheid years in South Africa, on the other. Newspaper articles, sermons and various forms of writings helped to promote Jesus that disregarded human dignity in one way or the other. The author makes an excellent case for a view of the kingdom of God that transcends misguided theologies of (a) the spiritual, (b) historical and political Jesus in South Africa to fuel a sociopolitical agenda of proponents. Our focus here is Christology in the context of spirit cosmology in Africa yet it is noteworthy that theological constructs have the potential to mislead either to social, political or even syncretistic engagements and/or deviations.

Ephesians. The disposition of Christ followers in the continent, owing to their pre-conversion past in African roots, have parallels with the early Christians and enhances our imagination of early Christian reception of Ephesians in its first century context of Asia Minor.

The discussion on the role of God, Jesus Christ, the Holy Spirit, and "principalities and powers" aims to concretize our imagination of the worldview and posture with which Christ followers might conceptualize the cosmology of Ephesians.

### 6.6.2 The Christian God and the Supreme Being

Generally, Africans believe that the God they knew from their traditional belief system (Supreme Being) is the same as the God the Christian missionary taught in their salvific message.[87] God is good. He presides over the world and engages mediators in his interaction with human beings. He is the Creator of the world, all powerful, all present and all knowing. Bible translators concur and employ traditional names, ascriptions and appellations for God in a similar vein. The attributes of the God of the Bible are similar to the pre-Christian conception of God in many ways.[88] African mythologies provide varied explanations to the cause of human separation from God. The African creation myths, which are passed on as oral traditions, usually attribute it to wrongdoing, sin or human acts in disrupting the divine order for society. The need for reconciliation with God to regain his covering and benefit from his ability to ward off evil spiritual powers are thus the impetus for salvation in the African spirit cosmology.[89] Sin is not the breaking of God's law per se since African religions do not appeal to a set of codes. Rather, sin is a violation of God's social order. Sin is antisocial because it violates the norms of human interaction in God's social order.[90] It paves the way for diabolic influence and impairs solidarity in society as a result of the selfish acts of individuals. When the Christian message of salvation is

---

87. Bediako, *Jesus in Africa*, 21.

88. It is misleading for some Western missionaries and others to suggest otherwise. One does not have to create a new God for the Africans. Perhaps, Africans need more clarification about God's nature and his initiative to reconcile sinful humanity to himself in the salvific work of Christ. Historically, this argument came along with demonization of African culture with demeaning posture towards African thought patterns by the colonialist and missionaries who had an imperialist mindset. The missionary portrait of an African's view of God and African articulation of their beliefs is a debate that would not be resolved here. The focus rather is to show what Africans believe and adhere to.

89. Bediako, *Jesus in Africa*, 22.

90. L. Magasa, *African Religion: The Moral Traditions of Abundant Life* (New York: Orbis, 1998), 166, and J. S. Pobee, *Toward an African Theology* (Nashville: Abingdon, 1979), 102.

conveyed with emphasis on sin, the African is convicted of sin in a disposition to repent from sinful and selfish acts both to reconcile to God and to make meaningful contribution to the community. Forgiveness from original sin, important as it is, is deemed incomplete unless true repentance is demonstrated by positive social impact. The notion of conversion as a personal transaction with God or a set of protocols to be fulfilled to get to heaven is found lacking in that regard. In other words, salvation must align the believer to God, ward off the influence of evil forces and unleash the Christ follower to participate in the Christian community.

Christ followers and African theologians in particular do not change their concept of God (Supreme Being) upon conversion to Christianity. Perhaps, the question to ponder is how might Christians imagine the roles of Jesus Christ and the Holy Spirit in this framework? If salvation accords good standing with God, then what role does Jesus Christ and the Holy Spirit play to mitigate the influence of other spiritual forces? Two particular aspects of these questions are worthy of consideration: (a) The conceptual transfer of a believer from traditional belief systems in regard to Christ and the Holy Spirit as spiritual mediators analogous to ancestors or priests in African cosmology, and (b) the role of Jesus Christ and the Holy Spirit in the Christian worldview and praxis – relative to other spiritual forces that are deemed demonic and evil upon conversion.

### 6.6.3 Jesus in African Christian Worldview

The African portrait of Christ ranges from the imagery of a chief/king (*Nana*), spokesman to the traditional chief (*okyeame*),[91] priest or ancestor. Though unstated in articles and books, it seems that the matrix of these theological constructs derives from the idea of the three offices of Christ in Christology (prophet, priest and king). The identity of Christ in African kingly status, mainly in West Africa, is invoked when the subject matter is about his reign as Lord of the kingdom of God. He is conceived as the ultimate chief to whom all humans and spiritual forces in heaven, on earth and in the underworld must bow in submission to his authority. This elevates him above patron deities and atmospheric spirits in various cultures; believers are assured of security in their allegiance and alliance with such a powerful lord/chief (*Nana*). Jesus is occasionally given the ascription *Nana* during praise and worship, and in other forms of prayer. The notion of a spokesman to the chief is limited to his function as a mediator or mouthpiece of the Supreme God. This is an important

---

91. Pobee, *Towards an African Theology*.

role in West African chieftaincy where locals regarded the person occupying this position as the bearer of the chief's message or his emissary.[92]

Two prominent analogies in African Christology are those of Christ as an ancestor and Christ as a (traditional) priest (of a pagan shrine). The "name of Jesus" and the "blood of Jesus" are consequently commonly employed in prayers, songs and sermons as inherently powerful in dealing with evil forces. It is noteworthy that the "ancestor" and "traditional priest" Christology appears mainly in academic discourse. These analogies do not appear in mainstream Christian discussions, sermons or Sunday school classes. However, their value should not be diminished for lack of pragmatic import or usage among the populace. The attempt to make sense of how Africans respond to the Christian faith must invite all ideas to the table for a robust and respectful learning experience. For the purposes of our study, the discussion in regard to Christ as an ancestor and priest would be instructive.

### 6.6.3.1 Jesus Christ as Ancestor

Ancestor worship or veneration is not unique to Africans but is shared by many cultures, both ancient and modern. King has provided a good overview of the conceptions and attitudes towards prominent deceased figures in intertestamental Judaism and other Jewish texts, implying that ancestors occupied a special place in Jewish traditions as well.[93] In Europe, the living honor the dead with flowers, lighting candles and other rituals. King suggests that even the belief in sainthood in some Christian traditions is suggestive of ancestral veneration. However, we discuss Jesus as an ancestor in African Christian worldview not to establish a continuum with ancient or particular religious traditions, but to show how its feature in African spirit cosmology informs conceptions and beliefs in and about Jesus Christ. The incarnation and ascension are alleged to have analogous echoes in Jesus who demonstrated exemplary life on earth and left an unmatched legacy. He is now in the celestial realms serving the interest of his people. The ascension ushers Christ into the spiritual realm to exercise dominion over other spiritual forces for the good of his people, a role similar to that of an ancestor. According to Bediako, Christ has earned the greater right to be conferred with the honor of an ancestor since he accomplished far beyond what any ancestor could have achieved in his

---

92. In my Akan culture (Ghana), the Okyeame carries a special staff bearing the chief's seal in gold to deliver consequential messages on behalf of the chief.

93. F. J. King, "Angels and Ancestors: A Basic Christology," *MS* 11, no. 1 (1994): 10–26. King highlights the notion of the "righteous man" and the patriarchs in the *TTP*, which he does not discuss in great detail, to suggest prevailing thoughts of the deceased within the broader category of what Africans would ascribe to ancestors.

incarnation, resurrection and post-resurrection role as intercessor on behalf of his followers.[94] Christ merits the status also as an exemplar and noble brother.

> Being our True Brother now in the presence of his Father and our Father, he displaces the mediatorial function of our natural "spirit-fathers." . . . He is the Lord over the living and the dead, and over the "living-dead," as ancestors are called. He is supreme over all the gods and authorities in the realm of spirit, summing up in himself all their powers and cancelling any terrorizing influence they might be assumed to have upon us.[95]

Ancestor Christology allows for conceptual transfer to portray Christ in the way believers hitherto counted on their ancestors to preserve family honor, offer security against malevolent forces and promote prosperity in the lineage. To imagine Christ as ancestor does not, however, equate him with other ancestors or diminish his status in relation to the Supreme God – since ancestors are not equal or even close to the level of God in terms power or providence. It only offers a window into the nature, power and relationship that ought to exist between Christ and his followers. As one scholar reckons, "the way is open for appreciating more fully how Jesus Christ is the only real and true Ancestor and Source of life for all mankind, fulfilling and transcending the benefits believed to be bestowed by lineage ancestors."[96]

The concept of Christ as an ancestor has been challenged by some African scholars who find the analogy inadequate and diminishing to the status of Christ. Aye-Addo gives a robust response against the ancestor Christology, contending that ancestors cannot be equated to Christ due to their limitations and lower status in the cosmic arena, even in Akan cosmology. "Akans look for a reality that can overpower the nefarious power and activities of these lesser deities or the spiritual beings . . . . The Akan, therefore, expects Christology in which Jesus Christ will be seen to wield that supernatural power to deal with evil power, magic, sorcery, witchcraft that plagues the society."[97]

---

94. Bediako, *Christ in African Culture*, 38–41.

95. K. Bediako, *Jesus and the Gospel in Africa: History and Experience* (New York: Orbis, 2004), 26–27.

96. Bediako, *Christ in African Culture*, 41–42. Bediako does not argue for syncretism of sorts but for a conceptual transfer to negate and replace loyalty and belief in ancestors with Jesus Christ.

97. C. S. Aye-Addo, *Akan Christology: An Analysis of the Christology of John Samuel Pobee and Kwame Bediako in Conversation with the Theology of Karl Barth* (Eugene: Pickwick, 2013), 165.

Jesus Christ is thus matchless in his power to meet the spiritual needs of his followers (cf. Eph 1:3). However, one does not need to equate him with ancestors simply because he supplies what was hitherto expected of ancestors in the pre-conversion past. Aye-Addo finds it abasing to make such an analogy: "By interpreting Jesus as an ancestor, one reduces him to the level of parent or grandparent, which would leave the Akan with little or no interest in him."[98] The issue here is a cosmology with which conceptions and fears of evil spirits instigate the quest to identify him with spiritual entities that would reduce anxiety and promote stability in the community of faith. In a nutshell, Christ is intimately involved in meeting the needs of Christians – whether his role is imagined as that of an ancestor or a much more powerful spiritual being.

### 6.6.3.2 Christ as Priest

Christ as priest is believed to have a comparable function to that of African priests at fetish shrines who mediate between the gods and human devotees. This is explained in terms of an actual mediator, one who performs sacrifices (as in Hebrews 4–5) and intercedes on behalf of the people. In the case of Christ, the shedding of his own blood evokes significance of blood sacrifice in forgiveness, reconciliation, atonement, even in breaking spiritual bondages.[99] In other words, as a priest Christ atones, breaks bondages and mediates between the people and God.

> This unique achievement of the priestly mediation of Christ renders therefore all other priestly mediators obsolete, so revealing their ineffectiveness. To disregard the surpassing worth of the priestly mediation of Jesus Christ for *all* people everywhere and to choose, instead ethnic priesthoods in the name of cultural heritage, is to fail to recognize the true meaning and end of all priestly mediation, to abdicate from belonging within the one community of humanity and clutch at the shadow and miss the substance.[100]

The view of Christ as priest in African theology could have been enhanced with clear articulation of the parallels that relate to aspects of his humanity and those that apply to his divinity. The fetish priest mediates between the gods

---

98. Aye-Addo, *Akan Christology*, 165.

99. J. D. K. Ekem, *Priesthood in Context: A Study of Priesthood in Some Christian and Primal Communities of Ghana and Its Relevance for Mother-Tongue Biblical Hermeneutics* (Accra: Sonlife, 2009), 177–181. Ekem and other African scholars have drawn from and shown parallels of their ancestor and priestly Christology from African perspectives in the book of Hebrews.

100. K. Bediako, *Jesus in African Culture*, 37–38.

and devotees, but he could not claim the same spiritual status as in the case of the triune God. Moreover, attention to the priest's functions as a mediator, one who performs blood sacrifices, who delivers messages from the gods or ancestors to the people, etc. could be explained as familiar concepts to Africans without clothing Jesus Christ with the unfit garment of a West African fetish priest. Jesus is only a priestly mediator, not *primus inter pares* (first among equals) but one who is incomparable to any other. He is incomparable in his surpassing greatness; he is the one in whom all things on earth and in heaven would be summed up (Eph 1:10).

### 6.6.3.3 The Holy Spirit and "Spirits" of Africa

The "spirit" lexemes and synonymous dictum dominate the African concept of reality and world concept. The spirit cosmology at the backdrop of Christian expressions is that of spiritual influence in every aspect of life. The worldview behind and the language used in Christian texts echo familiar beliefs and situates the work of the Holy Spirit in the realm where other spirits are known to operate. In Africa, the doctrine of Trinity is not a matter of concern and it does not prompt the sense of mystery, paradox and controversy it does in the Euro-American context. God, Jesus Christ and the Holy Spirit do not reside or operate in a realm so removed from the human space in the African worldview. In other words, there is no dualism between the spirit world and the world of human existence. Spiritual forces operate concurrently in the same space and time, often engineering, manipulating or harnessing human activity. African Christians subscribe to a belief in the Holy Spirit as a powerful spiritual agent working in them, with them, through them and on their behalf. They perceive the Spirit in light of their pre-conversion understanding but the Spirit is believed to be surpassing in power above and beyond any other spirit known to Christians.

African Christians, for the most part, follow the precedence of early Christians in perceiving and treating all spiritual beings apart from God, Jesus Christ and the Holy Spirit as evil, demonic or unclean. They project evil status on every other deity, even those believed to be good in traditional religions, and demonize their nature and operations. Western missionaries who believe that some spiritual gifts have ceased in their operation have been quick to demonize African religious practices and reduce them to mere superstition. In so doing, they hinder the prospects of learning and cultivating the ability of African Christians to contextualize their beliefs without compromise.[101] Moreover,

---

101. M. L. Daneel, *Fombidzanu: Ecumenical Movement of Zimbabwean Independent Churches* (Gweru, Zimbabwe: Mambo Press, 1989), 340. Unfamiliar practices to these

a paradox emerges from linguistic limitations as these same missionaries employ local lexemes in the semantic field of African spirit cosmology to translate the name, nature and works of the Holy Spirit in the Bible – words that conjure imageries of spiritual beings known in traditional religions. In trying to find suitable and comparative language to express theological ideas that would be understood and resonate with the Semitic or Greco-Roman background, some translators provide excellent renderings,[102] which in a nutshell contradict the post-enlightenment worldview underpinning their own theological dispositions and positions. Language is part of culture and culture is informed by the worldview of people groups. It is imperative to grasp the framework within which words are appropriated to convey their connotative and denotative meanings – African or Greco-Roman – less we assume the primacy of post-enlightenment prisms without caution. "The difficulty with Western approaches to 'non-Western' religious phenomena – and in this case pneumatological manifestations in Africa – is a dualistic rationalizing that misunderstands a holistic worldview. . . . Theology based on a European model has missed much in biblical pneumatology that speaks directly into the world of Africa – and in fact into the worldview of almost everyone except Western peoples."[103] Christ followers believe that the Holy Spirit is present and active in every aspect of human affairs. The Spirit fills, guides and empowers individuals and communities to excel in their vocations, personal lives and in overcoming opposing spiritual forces intending to sabotage their prosperity.

Theological discourse in regard to the nature of the Holy Spirit ranges from those who portray him as the spirit acting on behalf of the Supreme Being or an ancestor figure mediating on behalf of the people. One scholar in Nigeria posits that we align the work of the Holy Spirit to that of ancestors, who serve as intermediaries between believers and God.[104] "As the ancestor *par excellence,*

---

missionaries and differences in worldview hindered nuanced articulation and deciphering of sound doctrine that addresses the particular questions Africans bring to the church.

102. R. O. Agyarko, "The *Sunsum* of *Onyame*: Akan Perspectives on an Ecological Pneumatology," *JRT* 6 (2012): 254. J. H. O. Kombo, *Theological Models of the Doctrine of the Holy Spirit: The Trinity, Diversity and Theological Hermeneutics* (Carlisle: Langham Global Library, 2016), 112–113. The authors explain the richness and nuanced features that translations provide to enhance meaning. Yet, the different words used and their origins in some cases evoke traditional notions and sentiments of spirits.

103. A. Anderson, "Stretching the Definitions? Pneumatology and 'Syncretism' in African Pentecostalism," *JPT* 10, no. 1 (2001): 102.

104. C. O. Oladipo, *The Development of the Doctrine of the Holy Spirit in the Yoruba (African) Indigenous Christian Movement* (New York: Peter Lang, 1996), 113. A. E. Orobator, *Theology Brewed in an African Pot* (New York: Orbis, 2008), 112–114, 117.

the Holy Spirit is the source of a new life, and the fountainhead of Christian living."[105] The Holy Spirit is, however, deemed more powerful than any ancestor. The portrait of the Spirit as an ancestor in some way negates the belief in the Holy Spirit whose power surpasses all the sorcery, magic or ancestors ever known. Some converts testify to this effect as they compare their previous spiritual encounters to their experience of the Holy Spirit.

The Holy Spirit is widely believed to be instrumental in the conversion experience and in Christian living. The Spirit convicts sinners, seals and guarantees a person's standing with God.[106] Christ followers talk about the "filling" of the spirit, unction to function and the zeal of God to denote the active work of the Holy Spirit, especially in relation to Christian ministry.[107] As one Methodist scholar noted, "my understanding is that the power of God is synonymous with the zeal of God in action, as we see in the work of the Holy Spirit."[108] The notion of "filling/possession of a spirit," anointing of the spirit or divine enabling in the form of gifts or talents is known in African Traditional Religions. A person could be possessed or be overtaken by spirits to the extent of speaking unknown languages or knowledge, in a different voice and manifesting different personalities in unusual ways.

> To be controlled or possessed by a spirit is a common experience in Africa. Most people have witnessed someone under the control of a spirit. When a person is under the control of a spirit, his character and behavior may be dramatically changed. He or she may have unusual physical strength and endurance. The person may speak in a strange language which is not his own language. He or she may speak prophecies or messages from an ancestor or a divinity.[109]

Professionals and leaders at various levels seek Spirit enabling. Leadership in African Indigenous Churches (AIC's) is often confirmed and marked by gifts of prophecy and miracles – claiming to follow the tradition of Elijah and

---

105. Oladipo, *Doctrine of the Holy Spirit*, 107.

106. T. Palmer, *Christian Theology in an African Context* (Bukuru: African Christian Textbooks, 2015), 115, 118.

107. J. K. Asamoah-Gyadu, *Jesus Our Immanuel: An Exercise in Homiletic Theology* (Achimota: African Christian Press, 2012), 70–83.

108. Asamoah-Gyadu, *Jesus Our Immanuel*, 82.

109. W. O'Donovan, *Biblical Christianity in African Perspective* (Carlisle: Paternoster, 1995), 142.

Elisha.[110] More so, anointing "has long been practiced in traditional Africa as part of religious ceremonies confirming someone's spiritual authority, or as a cleansing ritual when commissioning for an assignment, or simply as a medical ritual."[111] Mysteries, revelations and various superstitious phenomena are attributed to the work of the Holy Spirit.

Christians believe that life itself is spiritual warfare that is fought through prayer, fasting and good conduct. It is believed that the Holy Spirit is active in this spiritual warfare as prayers are made to strengthen and provide tactical guidance. Ephesians 6 is a common feature in discussions on spiritual warfare among believers but only a few of them are interested in examining what the entire passage really seeks to convey about the nature of the spiritual warfare.[112] Jesus and the Holy Spirit are called upon interchangeably in the local church context to intervene on a wide range of issues as well.

## 6.7 A Survey of Spirit Cosmology among Christians in Ghana

The study of spirit cosmology in the context of Christ followers in the metropolis of Ephesus (Asia Minor) and African Christians evinces significant commonalities. I conducted a survey in two of the largest metropolitan areas in Ghana (Accra and Kumasi) to aid our understanding and imagining of the framework of the spirit cosmology of the Ephesians. Usually, strong beliefs in spiritual activities are associated with rural customs or mentality that is uninfluenced by "western civilization," which tends to bring about different and more "sophisticated" perspectives of life. In the case of Asia Minor, nothing in our findings suggests departure from broadly held beliefs in spiritual beings anywhere in the Roman empire. Similarly, Accra and Kumasi are two cities with significant western influence and presence, yet the findings therein do not differ from beliefs in less developed parts of the country. The survey was conducted in 2002 but my African students, friends, colleagues and my own observations suggest that there has not been any change to warrant another study since the findings would be the same. The reader should not assume that these beliefs affect intelligence, professional competencies, productivity levels or social interaction with those who do not share this worldview. Some

---

110. A. Anderson, "Stretching the Definitions? Pneumatology and 'Syncretism' in African Pentecostalism," *JPT* 10, no. 1 (2001): 108.

111. Kunhiyop, *African Christian Theology*, 98.

112. O'Donovan, *Biblical Christianity in African Perspectives*, 212–217. Here, the author discusses each of the armors briefly and suggests they be taken seriously along with prayer to combat the influence of spiritual forces.

participants, still echoing these beliefs as part of the reason they worship with African diaspora churches, have since graduated from Russell Group (UK) and Ivy League (USA) universities. It is also the case that the ancient and modern spirit cosmologies under study are shared by the majority of the population elsewhere in Africa, Asia and South America.

Ghana has 27.5 million (2018) people comprising 50.9 percent male and 49.1 percent female. The percentage of Christians has been fairly steady at 71 percent and 17.6 percent identifying as Muslims. The population of Accra is about 3 million compared to 2.5 million in Kumasi, the second largest city. The study targeted the Akans and Ewes ethnic groups. English is the official language in Ghana, but Akan and Ewe are the most dominant language groups in every sector of society – ranging from politics, business/commerce, education, military etc. To understand the way of life of these two ethnic groups is to have a good grasp of life in Ghana. Akan natives are 47.5 percent of the population, though about 70 percent of Ghanaians speak Akan. Ewes are 14 percent but they are geographically widely spread and very influential in the country. Respondents to the survey totaled 320–348 persons as some chose not to answer certain questions (see questionnaire in appendix 1). Fifty-three percent (183) of the respondents self-identified as Akan, and 47 percent (165) as Ewe. There were 59 percent (205) male and 41 percent (143) female respondents. It is noteworthy that 47 percent spent most of their developmental years in Accra, 26 percent in the Volta region, 10 percent in the Ashanti region, and single digits of percentages in Central (4%), Eastern (7%), Western (2%), Upper East (2%), Northern (1%) and Brong Ahafo (1%). Sixty-eight percent of the respondents were 16–30 years old with most attending two of the three most prestigious universities in the country at the time, namely the University of Ghana (Accra) and Kwame Nkrumah University of Science & Technology (Kumasi). The effect of gender, age, denominational affiliation and the region one grew up in were found to have no variant on the outcome from respondents.

The overwhelming majority of respondents said they believed that there is a spiritual dimension to life and that there are spiritual beings involved in human affairs. They emphasized that strong faith was important in mitigating the influence of malevolent forces. Three hundred and two participants (87%) believed that witchcraft in Ghana, as described above, is real with 84 percent indicating that witches are able to cause death, disease and other harm (table 1). Their background, personal experiences and tradition have led them to find a haven in Christianity where they do not need to appeal to gods, "stool spirits" or ancestors to meet their spiritual needs (table 2).

**Table 1**

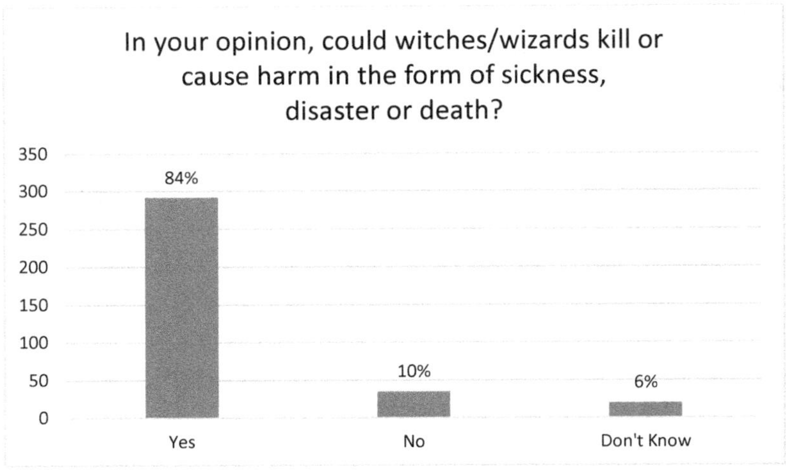


Family gods or stools of chieftaincy are deemed sacred, treated with respect and often named in libation as a contact point between ancestors, gods of the land and adherents.

**Table 2**

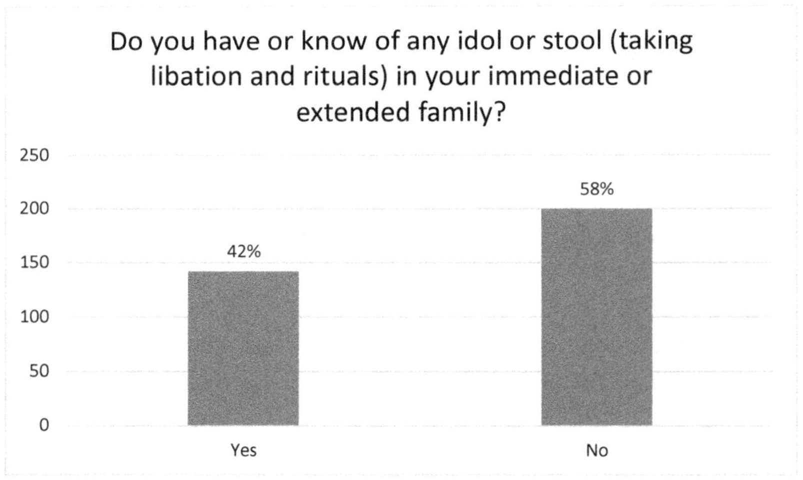


The respondents said that fear and desperation caused nominal Christians to consult witch doctors, Islamic leaders and individuals with magical powers to protect them. Despite religious affiliations as Pentecostals, Charismatics, Independent, Interdenominational and what are called Orthodox churches in Ghana – referring to the Methodist, Presbyterian, and Anglican churches, 64 percent of the participants indicated that they knew Christians who have consulted non-Christian spiritual agents to help improve marriage life, attract a lover or be more attractive to a spouse (tables 3 and 4).

**Table 3**

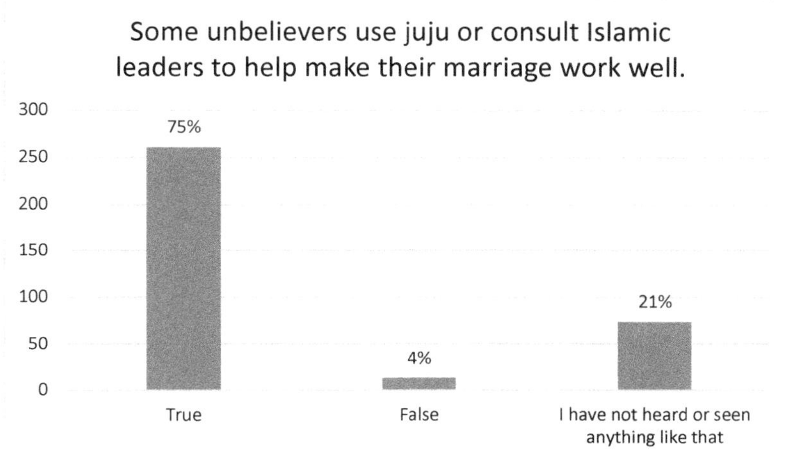


**Table 4**

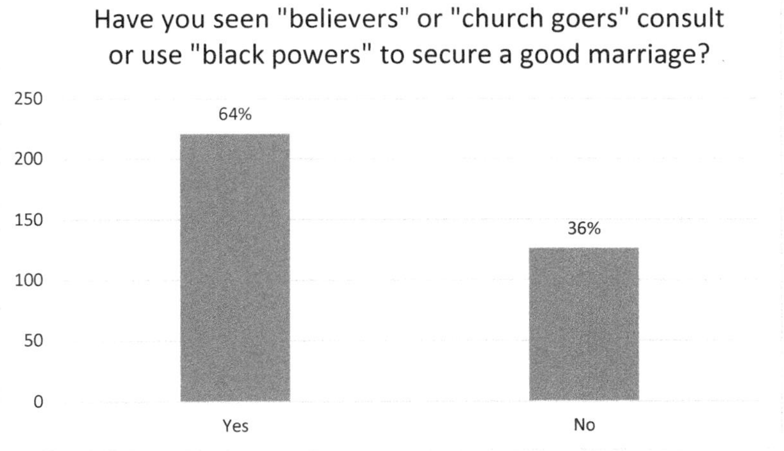


One cannot underestimate how the worldviews of these Christian respondents and what they know to prevail among unbelievers affect how they approach Christianity. They indicated familiarity with the use of juju or sorcery by athletes to enhance performance, for vocational or professional success, promotions, or to cause an enemy to inflict self-harm. Christian leaders are aware that this world concept is the reason conversion to Christianity often requires providing new converts with adequate means of dealing with these realities or compelling evidence of God's power in some shape or form. Christ must be shown to triumph over these spiritual forces. God's ability to provide, protect and promote the welfare of believers is an expectation that comes with conversion (see tables 5, 6 and 7).

**Table 5**

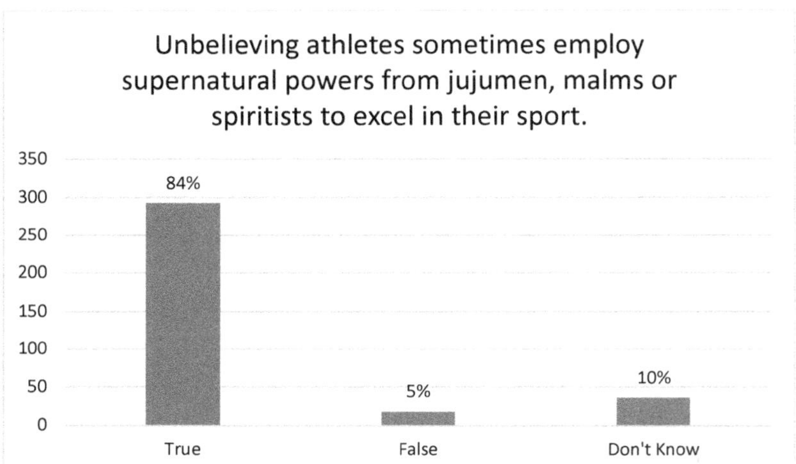


**Table 6**

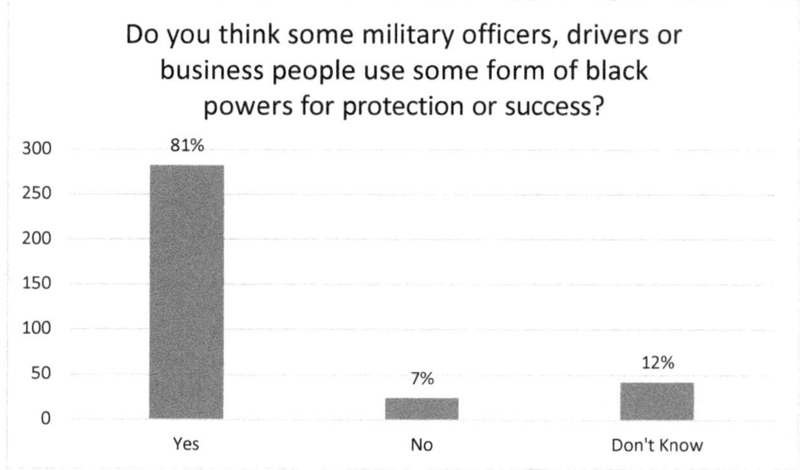

The notion of spiritual blessings among Ghanaian Christians correlates and coincides with people's prevailing interest in the prosperity gospel – where God is expected to deliver spiritual blessings that manifest in the physical realm as material wealth. For the purpose of our subject matter, the findings showed that a significant number of Christians know unbelievers who consult evil powers. It is possible that some believers indulged in such activities prior to conversion to Christianity. To desire spiritual blessings or be blessed with "every spiritual blessing" as in Ephesians 1:3 is not a foreign concept to these Christians.

**Table 7**

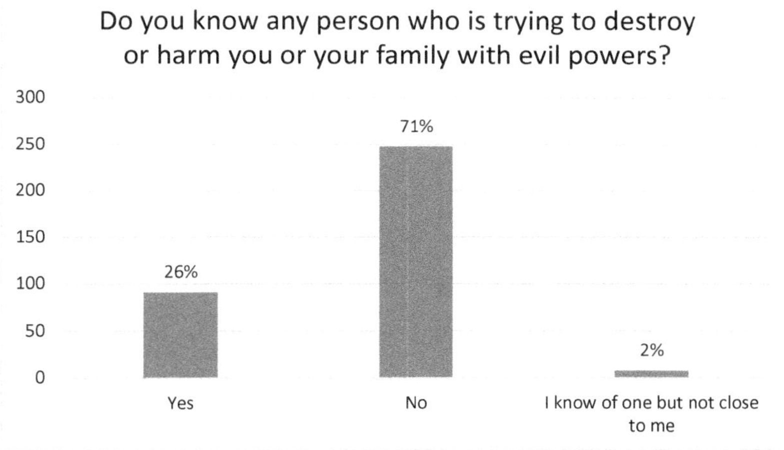


These responses provide insight into how the respondents perceived the spirit world. Forty-five percent said the effects of diabolic forces were personal since their family members had been impacted by such spiritual activity. The mere mention of witchcraft evoked deep and uncomfortable sentiments to some. To them, denying the existence of voodoo or witchcraft was akin to naivete because many could point to tragedies in their family, which they said were caused by witchcraft or a witch doctor. Moreover, unbelievers were purported to use "black magic" to protect their properties from thieves or robbers. Apparently, these powers can punish offenders, influence culprits to embarrass themselves or for malefactors to commit suicide (see tables 8 and 9).

Spiritual activities are prevalent in Africa to the extent that there are lexemes for a variety of spiritual activities in African languages that have no English substitutes. That God must be powerful to meet one's needs is foundational in the decision to accept Jesus as Lord and Savior, among Africans.

**Table 8**

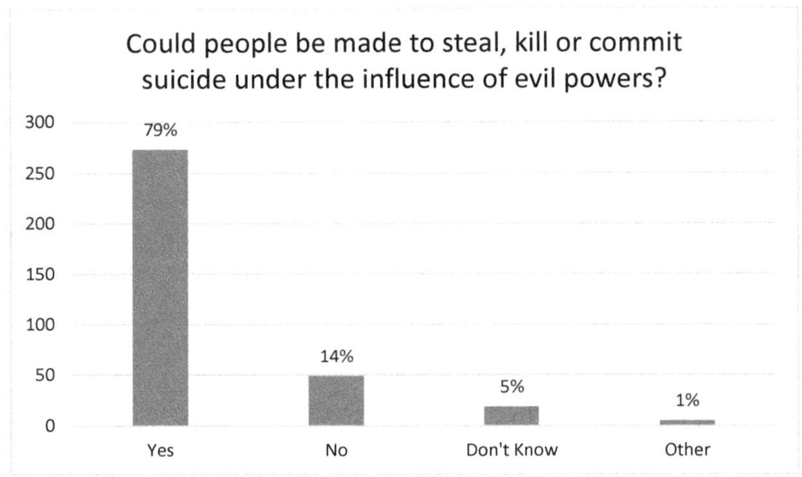



**Table 9**

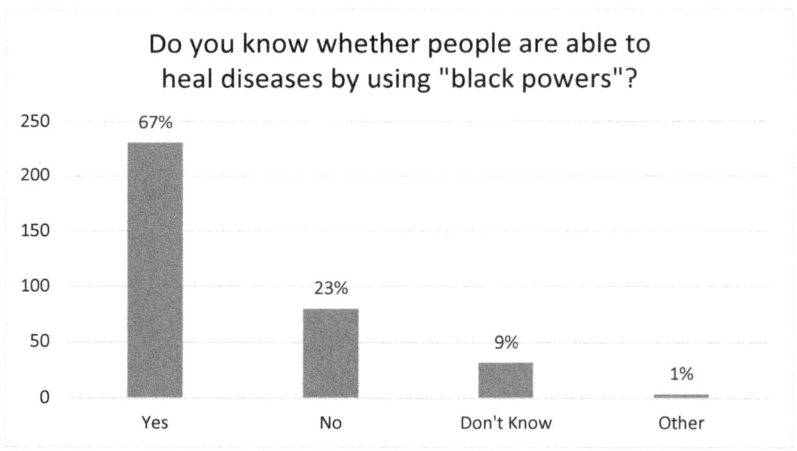



Christians react differently to the existence of dark spiritual powers. There are those who find security in their commitment to Christ and those who find prayers and moral purity as the appropriate means to mitigate the influence of the evil spiritual powers. But there are some Christians who consult witch doctors in times of sickness or difficult conditions. Out of the people surveyed,

74 percent indicated that spiritual protection is "very necessary" (57%) or "necessary" (17%) to them as Christians. Ninety-seven percent indicated that prayer, fasting and moral purity are essential ingredients to be delivered from demonic powers whereas 46 percent said moral behavior/ethics was important in mitigating the influence of demonic powers (see tables 10, 11 and 12).

**Table 10**

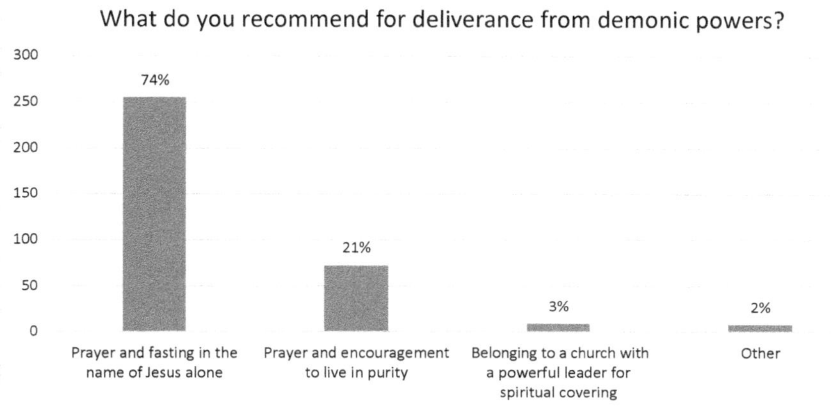


**Table 11**

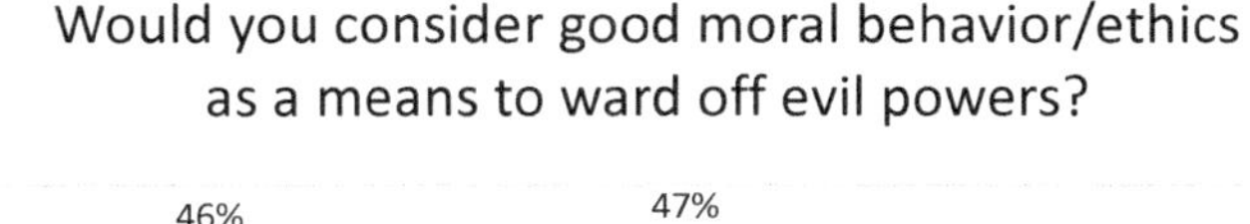

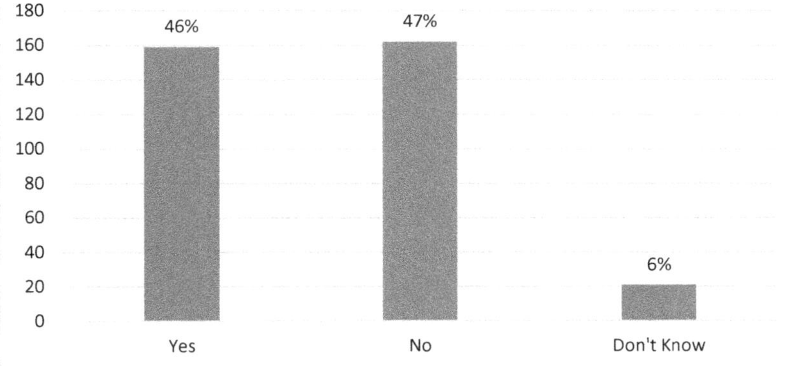

**Table 12**

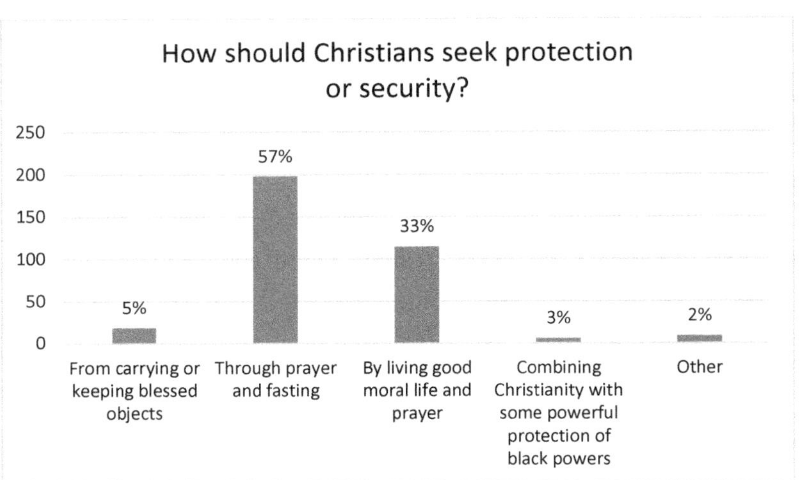


The findings of this survey among the Akans and Ewes further underscore that the spirit cosmology of Christ followers in Ghana, similar to believers in Asia Minor, informs their reception of Christianity, understanding of salvation and the importance of ethics in Christian living. Thus, the converts understand God's salvific work in Christ Jesus in the unfolding mystery, then and now, as one that brings about forgiveness of sins as well as deliverance from cosmic powers to a place of redemption and adoption into the household of God – thereby necessitating the need to stand firm with God and against demonic forces.

## Conclusion

The study of spirit cosmology in Africa reveals parallels with the Greco-Roman world and of first-century Asia Minor conventions in particular. Perhaps, these observations should evoke a new appreciation of the importance of spirit cosmology in a text like Ephesians not in an abstract or in esoteric terms but as one that is dealing with pertinent and prevailing issues in the context of the readership. We are in the field of conjecture in regard to the reception of Ephesians by the earliest recipients. We can only surmise, imagine and assume from similar backgrounds in Africa the import of the framing of Christian identity, new community and spiritual activities for Christ followers in Ephesus as they strived to live out their faith. In this regard, I outline some parallels between the African spirit cosmology and the world of Ephesians as well as some particulars that are distinct to the African context – suggesting the need for some caution in making analogies.

The parallels between the African spirit cosmology and the framework of the Greco-Roman worldview are noteworthy and instructive: (a) They both share in the belief of divine creation of the cosmos. The Creator is identified as the Supreme Being (God) who is known as Theos/Zeus, Nyame, Mawu, Chineku, Eleda, etc. This conception locates human beings, not at the centre of the cosmos, but as stewards and participants in God's creation. For both the ancients and Africans, God is involved in the affairs of humankind, especially by maintaining order in the cosmos. There are subsidiary gods/deities who perform various functions to enhance human flourishing and check human conduct in society. Both worldviews subscribe to the existence of patron deities (gods and goddesses) of fertility, agriculture, mountains, sea and even ancestors. The idea that there are spiritual powers/deities operating in the heavenly realms, on earth and in the underworld is shared as a widespread phenomenon. Other commonalities include: (b) The idea that the Supreme Being and/or other spiritual agents may serve as moral examples for humans; (c) that there are human mediators between spiritual beings and humanity in the form of ancestors and priests. However, Africans elevate the role of ancestors, as noted earlier; (d) both the ancient and modern Africans share the belief in sorcery, magic, divination, soothsaying, etc. They all believe that spiritual powers can enhance human ability to achieve success in business, sports, farming and family life. (e) In light of Ephesians, the ability of witchcraft and other evil spiritual powers to cause harm, sabotage progress, possess individuals and influence people at all levels was shared and continues to be a major issue in African Christianity. Spiritual influence extends to the notion that spiritual beings help humans to develop virtues, exploit moral failings as a gateway for evil ends or influence honorable people to engage in dishonorable conduct. Two additional areas deserving attention are (f) the belief in divine chastisement, vengeance and reward relative to human conduct, and the idea that (g) family gods support, bless and enhance household undertakings and marriage. Gods punish moral failings and bless faithful allegiance.

These parallels underscore the necessity to invite, dialogue and appreciate the perspectives of scholars whose backgrounds are not influenced by the European enlightenment in the study of the New Testament. The limitations of historical critical methods, social history emphasis and post-enlightenment assumptions engender susceptibility to false confidence and blindness to socio-religious issues that may enhance our readings of ancient religious texts. It is apparent to me that the enlightenment has been responsible for certain methodological assumptions and anachronistic presuppositions that need to be revisited in light of what we know about the spirit cosmology of the early Christ followers. They saw the world differently and developed beliefs rooted in that worldview. We may not share in their view of the cosmos, but it is imperative that we interpret their correspondence, customs and ethos in light of that worldview.

Converts to Christianity in Africa clearly embrace their new faith against the backdrop of prevailing and similar spirit cosmologies. They express trust in God, Jesus Christ and the Holy Spirit as spiritual agents responsible for their salvation, deliverance from sin and satanic forces, and as powerful agents to safeguard their security against spiritual onslaughts. Christians frame their identity to comprise a new allegiance and a deep sense of belonging to the community of God. The nature of conversion and its commensurate way of life thus requires radical distancing from previous allegiance to deities, ancestors and practices such as divination, sorcery, soothsaying, etc. All gods, priests, ancestors and pagan festivities are condemned, demonized and regarded as spiritual opposition. Christ followers in Africa like to frame their identity in terms of kinship (God's family), despite tribal stereotypes and intertribal discriminations. Salvation in the African perspective is comprehensive – including forgiveness of sin and admission into God's family, deliverance from the forces of darkness and alignment with God who is able to protect as well as provide for and make his people prosper in their undertakings. Salvation is not limited to admission into the community and/or simply a "visa to heaven." However, many African believers still live in fear of evil spirits here and now – salvation offers a remedy for that as well. The cry for protection, deliverance from enemies and untimely death feature in sermons, songs, prayers and liturgies in African churches.[113] Fear of witchcraft, despite people's faith in God, is dreaded by many African believers. Theological constructs in these settings are thus incursive and oppositional in tone and content – constantly opposing the devil and attributing misfortunes to such spiritual agents. Notions of Christ or the Holy Spirit as ancestor or fetish priest models have their origins and remain products of academic theologizing in African scholarship. Most Christians regard ancestors and fetish priests to be satanic instruments.

---

113. J. A. Adewuya, "Reading Ephesians 6:10–18 in the Light of African Pentecostal Spirituality," in *Global Voices: Reading the Bible in the Majority World*, eds. C. Keener and M. D. Carroll R. (Peabody: Hendrickson, 2013), 83–93. Adewuya provides a very good account of the context in Nigeria and how these beliefs influence worship – in songs, prayers, dispositions etc. His observations from Ephesians 6 underscore the emphases on spirits and spiritual warfare as a major issue in West African Pentecostalism.

There are certain particulars in African spirit cosmology that are not found in the Greco-Roman cosmology or socio-religious framework, at least in the same way. First, there is no phenomena in the Roman world that matches the portrait of witchcraft in West Africa. The idea of evil spirits that are capable of causing severe harm existed in the Greco-Roman world but the African portrait of witchcraft has no close parallel. Second, the post-colonial quest to reimagine Jesus Christ or the Holy Spirit analogously as ancestors and fetish priests is absent in early Christianity, unless we conceive them in light of the offices of Christ as priest, king and prophet. Belief in ancestors and priests existed in the Greco-Roman world but no attempt was made in Ephesians or elsewhere in Paul's writings to construct ancestor Christology or pneumatology for the first-century churches. Perhaps, this lack of precedence should serve as a caution. In the letter of Hebrews, we find priestly and sacrificial analogies from Judaism. This should, however, not be misconstrued since early Christianity was a movement in Judaism (appealing to God and Jewish messianic motifs) until "the parting of the way" sometime in the second century.

Ephesians does not seek to denounce the identity of God (Theos) in non-Jewish thought. The letter assumes the readers have knowledge of God and proceeds to show God's intervention in the unfolding mystery. What we find is that the limitations of Gentile understanding of God are noted and enhanced. For example, the reference to ἄθεος (without God) in Ephesians 2:12 appeals to Jewish stereotypical categories to reorient the Gentile majority about their limited knowledge and experience with the true God. The debate between Western missionaries and Africans on whether native Africans knew or do not know the true God is immaterial since the ultimate aim is to bring people to salvation by grace through faith in Jesus Christ (2:8–10). African Christians may reimagine God afresh in light of their knowledge of his intervention in the cosmos through the work of Christ; the spiritual bondage debarring humans to flourish has been dealt with in Christ. God is now at work through Christ Jesus and in the Holy Spirit to empower and strengthen Christ followers to keep a firm standing with him against principalities and powers. It is likely that fear of evil powers prevailed among Christians in Asia Minor, as we find in Africa today. However, Ephesians does not prescribe a pointed antidote such as "binding and loosing" demonic powers or praying aloud and exorcising as the means to ward off their threats. The high sensitivity to spirits that make Africans find demons behind every object is unwarranted. Christians are saved and must rest in the security accorded in Christ, conduct their lives by the help of the Spirit and strive to keep their stance in God.

# 7

---

# Conclusions

This inquiry has demonstrated the prominent role of spirit cosmology in deciphering the religious identity and moral formation being prescribed for Christ followers in Ephesians. It augments previous studies and highlights what is otherwise relegated to the background – the role of spiritual beings – as a framework that ought to inform the interpreter's task in no small way. The work critiques a one-sided approach to the study of spiritual beings in Ephesians that focuses on the identity and function of "principalities and powers" and argues that such an approach misconstrues the message of the letter. I insist that the nature and function of the powers must be understood in light of their opposing spiritual counterparts (God, Jesus Christ and the Holy Spirit) to fully grasp the message pertaining to the reader's salvific status and conduct in the community. In Ephesians, the referents to the powers make sense only in so far as they are conceived against the backdrop of the work of God through Jesus Christ and the Holy Spirit. This permeating cosmology ought to be engaged closely in any attempt to properly decipher the message being conveyed in Ephesians.

The scope of previous scholarship on this subject has centered around (a) a quest for Jewish apocalyptic origins in explaining the "powers in Paul," (b) Greek and Roman use of similar or related lexemes, (c) twentieth-century attempts to demythologize the powers in advancement of sociopolitical causes, and (d) lexico-grammatical analyses exploring the origins or the broader semantic domain of "principalities and powers" to determine their import in Ephesians. Suffice it to state that those studies have focused on philological analysis. The notion that principalities and powers in Ephesians refer to personal spiritual beings is advanced by underscoring the import of spirit cosmology in the overall framework of the letter. Two things are noteworthy in this regard: First, I argue that a cogent analysis of Ephesians shows a consistent framework of spirit cosmology in the identity construction and communal ethos. It becomes apparent that the worldview with which the broader society and Christ followers made sense of life and livelihood, mores and social order, and even the cosmos as a whole is one that is significantly different from the traditional Western world concept. Evidently, the portrait of spiritual beings in Ephesians is framed in the belief that human responsibility and divine activity in human affairs are inseparable components of life in the cosmos. Second, I contend that a better approach to Ephesians needs intentional and robust engagement with the role of spiritual beings in the framing of the letter, be it the role of evil spirits, God, Jesus Christ or the Holy Spirit. Insufficient attention to spirit cosmology obscures the "spiritual presence" that permeates every page of Ephesians, thereby treating the religious text as if it were philosophical discourse devoid of any spiritual import.

Moreover, religious beliefs of every society tend to be the natural antecedent for its cosmology and vice versa. Social history, literary-grammatical analysis and biblical languages have important place in exegesis, but the issue of genre identification and appropriation in determining a suitable mode of inquiry must not be ignored in the study of sacred texts. Enhanced anachronism that is partly facilitated by post-enlightenment and postmodern epistemology engenders a false sense of confidence that allows a modern interpreter to superimpose their "views" on ancient texts. Profound as our modern questions and interests may be, ethics of interpretation demands of biblical scholars to be mindful of the practice of looking for answers to modern questions in ancient texts. For example, notions of realized eschatology disappear and sociopolitical readings of the powers in Ephesians simply become a false-fit when one pauses to imagine the world in which portraits of spiritual beings in the letter would make sense. Gentile converts and their Jewish counterparts in Asia Minor believed in the reality of personal spiritual beings and their activity in human affairs as the norm. The modern reader may not share this view, but as shown above, the entire discourse is framed with this cosmological understanding.

The socio-religious background studies of Greek, Roman and Jewish societies show broader similarities in their understanding of spiritual powers in the world. As a fledging movement in Second Temple Judaism, the early Christians held monotheistic faith and acknowledged the validity of spiritual powers in pagan societies while asserting the supreme power of their God above all else. Christ followers did not dismiss the potency of demonic powers nor consider opponents to be indulging in mere superstitious beliefs. Conversely, evil spirits are couched as fierce realities and dangerous opponents to contend with in Ephesians 6:10–13. The imagery of the place of human beings in the unfolding mystery is one that may be likened to subjects (children) in a custody battle between two spiritual opponents. Hitherto, they had lost their lives; were living (dead) with God and according to the ruler of the power of the air; they conducted themselves according to the dictates of the world in which they followed the desires of the flesh and the mind (2:2). God took initiative to redeem them out of that condition and adopted them to be participants in his cosmic plan. Life apart from God was life under the control of evil spiritual powers. Ephesians indicates that God exalted Christ above the powers (1:15–23) prior to intervening to save and bring them under his control – ultimately for his glory/honor (1:12, 14, 17). The author is emphatic that their salvific status and life in the community are all aimed for God's δόξα (1:12, 14, 17; 3:13, 16, 21).[1] Central to Christian identity then is the idea of a radical shift from the past with the "ruler of the power of the air" (2:2–3) to becoming members in the household of God (2:19).

The articulation of identity in Christ and what God has done on their behalf (chs. 1–3) sets the stage to state *who they are* as a people "called" to *live* up to their calling and to preserve "the unity of the Spirit" for which they have been called (4:1–3). The basis of who they *have become*, their *conduct* in the new community and *divine enabling* to perform various functions are all framed in theology, Christology and pneumatology (4:4–16). Subsequently, human responsibility is called upon with a reminder of their new status as bearers of the moral image of God in holiness and righteousness (4:23–24), children of God, and those who need to emulate the moral qualities of God/Christ in kinship framework (4:32; 5:1–2, 21–32). Ethics in the community and in domestic settings are supposed to match the honor of being chosen, redeemed and adopted to participate in the plan of God (1:4–14) in concert with Jesus Christ and the Holy Spirit on their behalf. Thus, virtues are not mere civic responsibilities, obligation of a philosophical school, pursuit of happiness or for public notoriety. Virtues are rather prescribed as befitting praxis to their new identity in advancement of solidarity in the household of God. Conversely, vices aggrieve the Holy Spirit and pave way for evil spirits to control transgressors. Ephesians 6:10–20 intensifies the nature of spiritual engagement and calls for human responsibility to maintain unqualified loyalty (to God) and fitting praxis (truth, righteousness, etc.) all in ensuring a firm

---

1. All six mentions of δόξα in Ephesians appear in the first three chapters either in a purpose clause indicating God's ultimate goal or qualifying his status and aims. Christ followers are not the center of attention, but privileged people redeemed by God to participate in a cosmic plan.

standing with God. Consequently, to marginalize this cosmological framework in Ephesians is to miss the import of its message.

The structure and substance of Ephesians speak to the fact that spiritual beings are the main actors of its identity construction and moral framework. The invocation recounting "spiritual blessings" opens the body of the letter (1:3–14), and the author concludes the body with a call to engage in a spiritual warfare (6:10–17). The first three chapters open with "spiritual blessings" and what God has done to choose, adopt, redeem, and seal the status of believers with him (1:3–14); the section also ends with express articulation of God's matchless ability to provide their needs (3:20–21). The second part (chs. 4–6) opens with the exhortation to preserve the "unity of the Spirit" (4:3) and concludes with the portrait of Christian living as a close body contact sport (wrestling) between humans and spiritual agents, thereby necessitating the urgency to enrobe in the full armor of God to secure firm standing with God (6:10–20). Assuredly, members are saved from the world and malevolent forces into a secure place with God under the lordship of Christ and the enabling of the Holy Spirit. Christ, the Holy Spirit and God the Father are all working on behalf of the "saints" to equip them for service, provide spiritual support and harness mutuality. Wisdom, knowledge and virtue may all be obtained by divine enabling to curb spiritual threats to their sense of security. As indicated at the end of chapter four, communal identity is shaped by divine agency to meet God's ultimate goal of "bringing unity to all things in heaven and on earth under Christ" (1:10).

Moreover, the study of spirit cosmology in Africa helps to observe parallels of how unbelievers perceive the world in concrete terms, and what salvation entails spiritually, morally and communally – then and now. It enables us to fathom the extent to which Ephesians encourages Christ followers to mitigate potential fears and the influence of spiritual powers. It becomes evident that portraits of evil spirits would most likely inspire faith in Jesus Christ who has triumphed over them and accorded the church victorious stance with God. The twenty-first century scholar does not have to share this worldview but needs to grasp its import in order to appreciate the message being conveyed in Ephesians. Converts to Christianity in Asia Minor and now in Africa may be rest assured that the all-powerful God is at work on their behalf, his gracious act of salvation through Christ Jesus, and the enabling of the Holy Spirit accord the converts all they need to garner strength to stand firm in their faith. Extremes do exist in societies where this sense of heightened spirituality forms an integral part of the worldview. However, extreme superstitions must not lead scholars to agnosticism in matters of the spirit/spirituality especially if the task is to examine a religious text, like Ephesians, that was authored and received in this framework.

The African analogy further concretizes the reconstruction of spirit cosmology in the Greco-Roman world in a manner that heightens awareness and invites further probing into traditional Western interpretative approaches that focus mainly on grammar, history and thematic studies – with little to no interest in cosmology as a framework (not as a theme).[2] Primitive as it may seem, the early Christians perceived their place in the cosmos in a framework broadly shared by today's Africans. The analogy with African cosmology provides an example of how modern societies unaffected by European enlightenment will be helpful interlocutors in imagining the social and spiritual worlds of the early Christians. While the hub of biblical studies remains in the Euro-American guild with its post-enlightenment prism and posture, I suggest that concerted efforts be made to engage scholars from other cultures in humility for constructive exchange in subjects such as spirit cosmology and kinship in early Christianity. The blind spots of the guild are apparent to scholars from the majority world and churches that are supposed to benefit from our scholarship. I propose that we reconsider and assign a prominent place to the cosmological framework in New Testament interpretation since the Western worldview is so far removed from that of the first century. Evidently, a renewed interest in biblical studies as a cross-cultural endeavor would further increase the value of our discipline in the religion to whom the authors and first readers of our text of inquiry belonged – Christianity.

---

2. I do not suggest that Africans share the experience of first-century Asia Minor in every way. It is, however, imperative the philosophical speculations or abstractions be brought home by showing modern cultures that share similar beliefs.

# Appendix 1

Questionnaire for Akans and Ewes on the role of spiritual beings in human affairs.

Date: March – June 2002. Cities: Accra and Kumasi

1. Which of the following language groups do you belong to?
   a. Akan ( ) b. Ewe ( )

   If you speak both languages, which is your mother tongue? ____________

2. Where did you spend most of your developmental years (10–18 years)?
   a. Greater Accra ( ) b. Ashanti ( ) c. Volta ( ) d. Western ( ) e. Eastern ( )
   f. Upper East or Upper West ( ) g. Northern ( ) h. Brong Ahafo ( )
   i. Central ( ) j. Outside ( )

3. Gender: a. Male ( ) b. Female ( )

4. Which of the following age groups do you belong to?
   a. 10–15 yrs ( ) b. 16–22 years ( ) c. 23–30 yrs ( ) d. 31–39 yrs ( )
   e. 40–49 yrs ( ) d. 50–60 yrs ( ) e. 61 years and above ( )

5. What is your denominational affiliation?
   a. Pentecostal ( ) b. Charismatic ( ) c. Catholic ( ) d. Orthodox ( )
   e. Interdenominational/ independent church ( ) f. Other ________________

6. Do you believe that witchcraft is real in Ghana?
   a. Yes ( ) b. No ( ) c. Don't Know ( )

7. In your opinion, could witches/wizards kill or cause harm in the form of sickness, disaster or death? a. Yes ( ) b. No ( ) c. Don't know ( )

8. Do you have or know of any idol or stool (taking libation and rituals) in your immediate or extended family? a. Yes ( ) b. No ( )
   If yes what is supposed to be the main function of the idol or stool?
   a. Fertility ( )
   b. Protection ( )
   c. Productivity in life, farming and business ( )
   d. Other ________________

9.  Is it possible for someone to use juju or charms to draw a member of the opposite sex to him/herself among unbelievers for sexual activity?
a. Yes ( ) b. No ( ) c. Don't Know ( )

10. It is said that there is a growing number of "believers" or "churchgoers" that consult or use "black powers" to secure a good marriage. Have you heard or seen anything like that? a. Yes ( ) b. No ( )

11. Some unbelievers use juju or consult Islamic leaders to help make their marriage work well.
a. True ( ) b. False ( ) c. I have not heard or seen anything like that ( )

12. Is spiritual protection necessary at all?
a. Very necessary ( ) b. Necessary ( ) c. Not necessary ( )
d. Other_____________________

13. Unbelieving footballers, boxers and other athletes sometimes employ supernatural powers from jujumen, malams or spiritists to excel in their sport. a. True ( ) b. False ( ) c. Don't know ( )

14. Do you think some military officers, drivers or business people use some form of black powers for protection or success?
a. Yes ( ) b. No ( ) c. Don't know ( )

15. Do you think Christians need protection from evil powers?
a. Yes ( ) b. No ( )  c. Don't know ( )

16. How should Christians seek protection or security?
a. From carrying or keeping blessed objects – e.g. cross necklace, special oil, Bible etc. ( )
b. Through prayer and fasting ( )
c. By living a good moral life and prayer ( )
d. Combining Christianity with some powerful protection of black powers ( )
e. Other ______________________________

17. Do you know any person who is trying to destroy or harm you or your family with evil powers? a. Yes ( ) b. No ( ) c. Other ___________

18. Have you had any person in your family or a close relative harmed or affected by some evil spiritual powers?
a. Yes ( ) b. No ( ) c. I know of one but not close to me ( )

19.   What do you recommend for deliverance from demonic powers?
a. Prayer and fasting in the name of Jesus alone ( )
b. Prayer and encouragement to live in purity ( )
c. Belonging to a church with a powerful leader for spiritual covering ( )
d. Other _______________

20.   Would you consider good moral behaviour/ethics as a means to ward off evil powers? a. Yes ( ) b. No ( ) c. Don't know ( )

21.   It is said that people use juju or "black powers" to seek promotion or favour in their work places. Do you believe/know this to be true?
a. Yes ( ) b. No ( ) c. Other _______________

22.   To what extent is it true that some business people consult malams, idols or use juju powers to make their business progress?
a. It is absolutely true ( ) b. I believe it is mere rumor ( )
c. It is generally believed to be true but I do not know it for fact ( )
d. Other _______________

23.   Could people be made to steal, kill or commit suicide under the influence of evil powers? a. Yes ( ) b. No ( ) c. Don't know ( ) d. Other _______________

24.   Do you know whether people are able to heal diseases by using "black powers"? a. Yes ( ) b. No ( ) c. Don't know ( ) d. Other _______________

25.   Is it possible for African traditionalists and jujumen to deliver others being harmed or possessed by evil powers?
a. Yes ( ) b. No ( ) c. Don't know ( ) d. Other _______________

# Appendix 2

This appendix consists of raw data points emerging from the survey in appendix 1 in no particular order. Hopefully, those who endeavor to probe the figures further will find them useful.

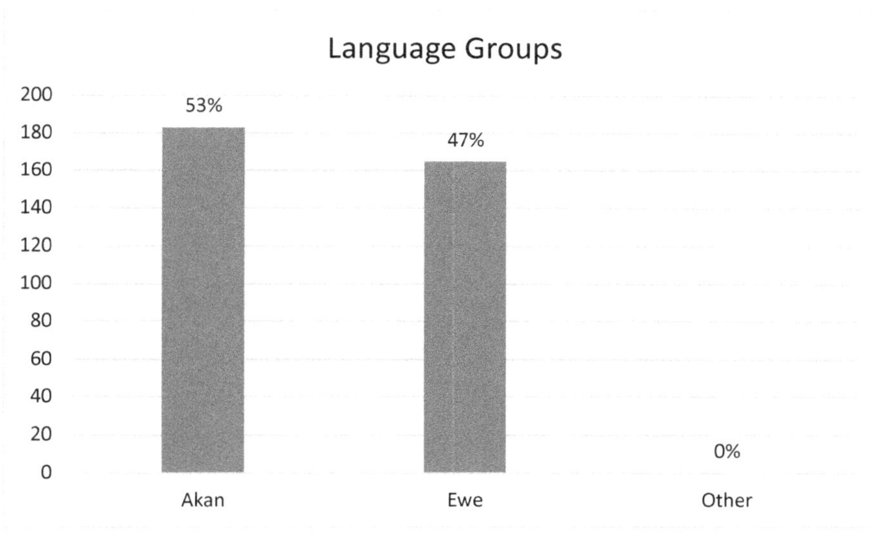



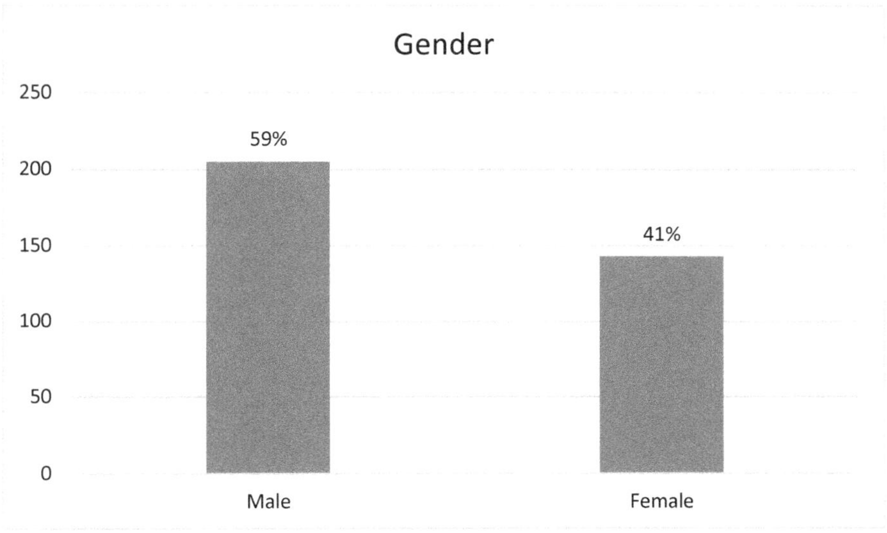

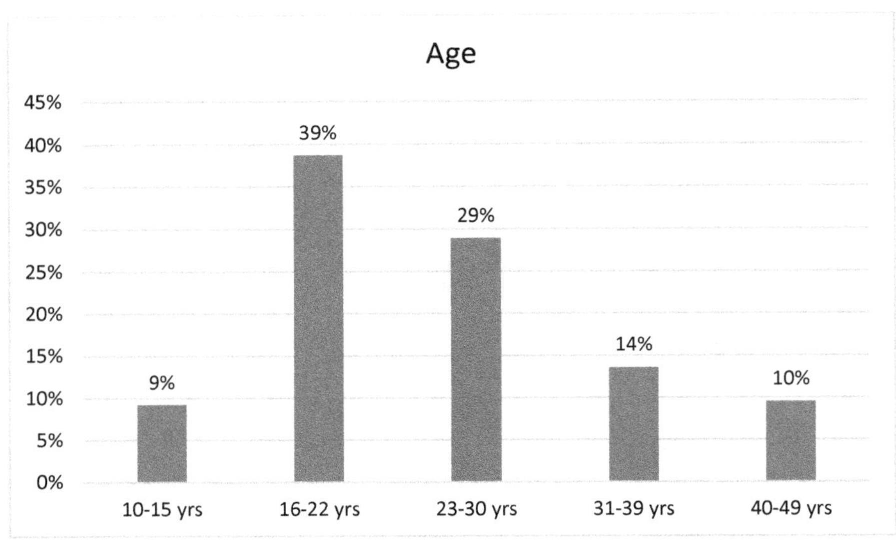
Age
45%
40%
35%
30%
25%
20%
15%
10%
5%
0%
39%
29%
14%
9%
10%
10-15 yrs
16-22 yrs
23-30 yrs
31-39 yrs
40-49 yrs

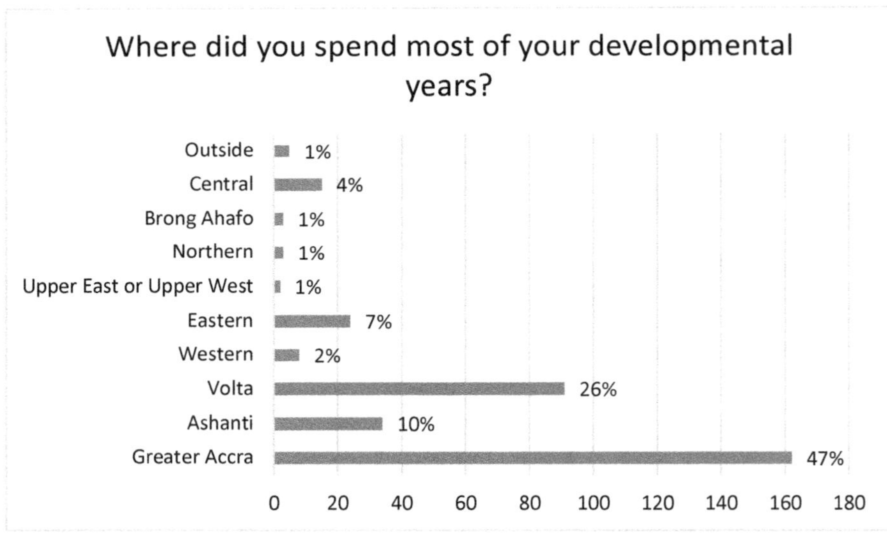
Where did you spend most of your developmental years?
Outside    1%
Central    4%
Brong Ahafo    1%
Northern    1%
Upper East or Upper West    1%
Eastern    7%
Western    2%
Volta    26%
Ashanti    10%
Greater Accra    47%
0    20    40    60    80    100    120    140    160    180

## Denominational Affiliation

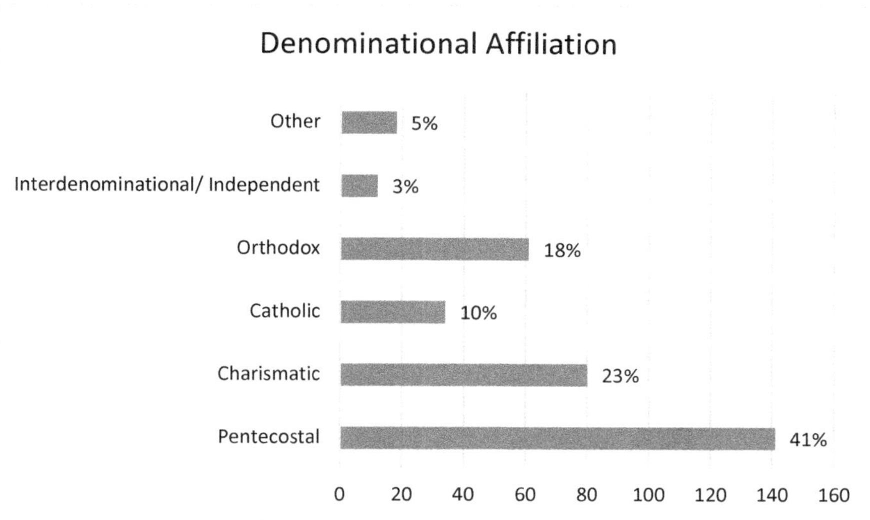


## Do you beleive that witchcraft is real in Ghana?

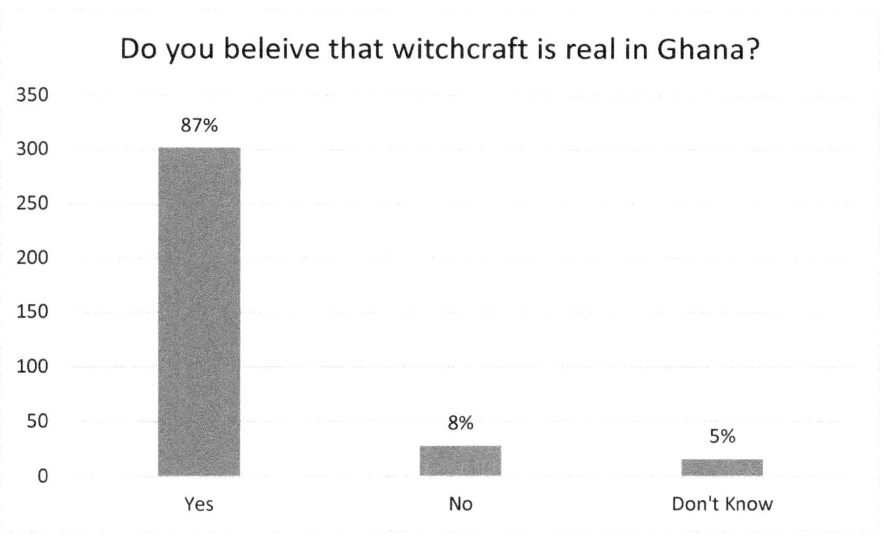

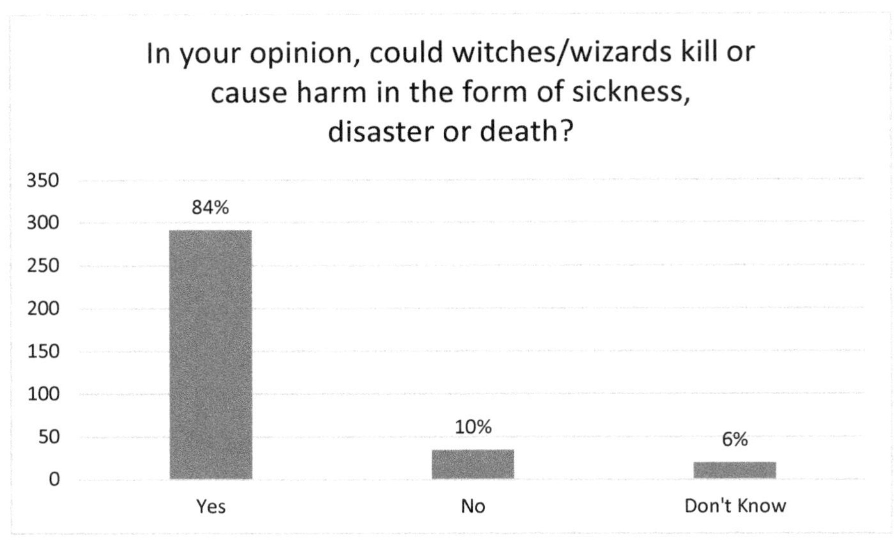

In your opinion, could witches/wizards kill or cause harm in the form of sickness, disaster or death?
350
300
250
200
150
100
50
0
84%
10%
6%
Yes
No
Don't Know


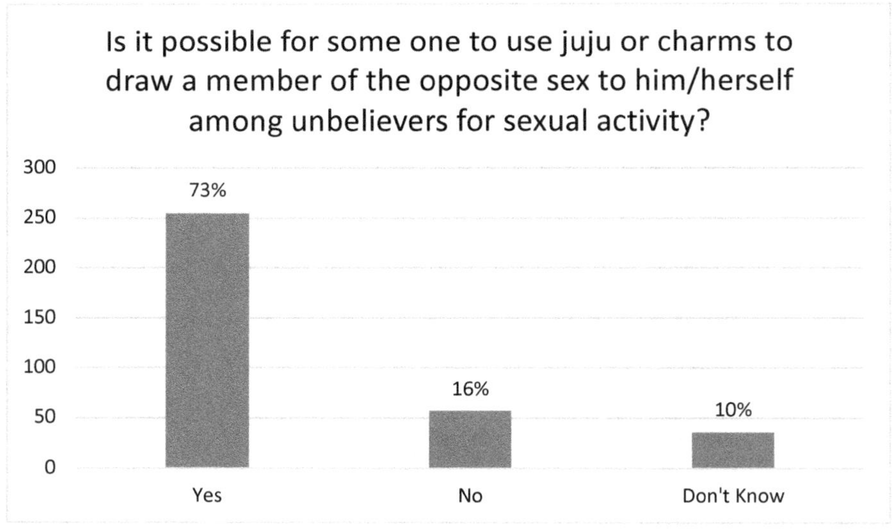

Is it possible for some one to use juju or charms to draw a member of the opposite sex to him/herself among unbelievers for sexual activity?
300
250
200
150
100
50
0
73%
16%
10%
Yes
No
Don't Know

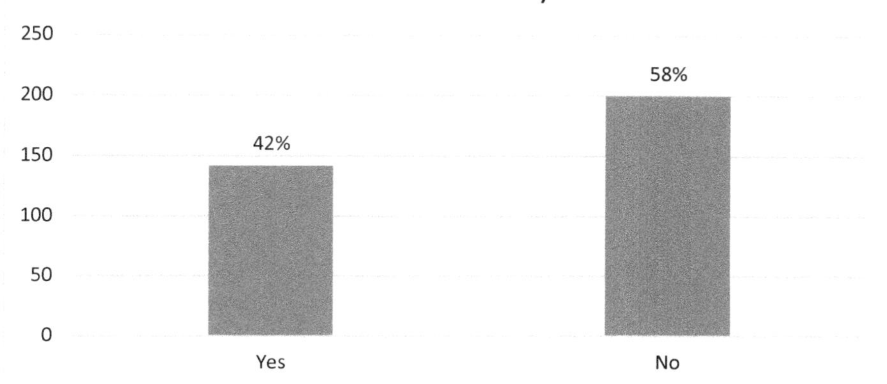
Do you have or know of any idol or stool (taking libation and rituals) in your immediate or extended family?
250
200
150
100
50
0
42%
58%
Yes
No

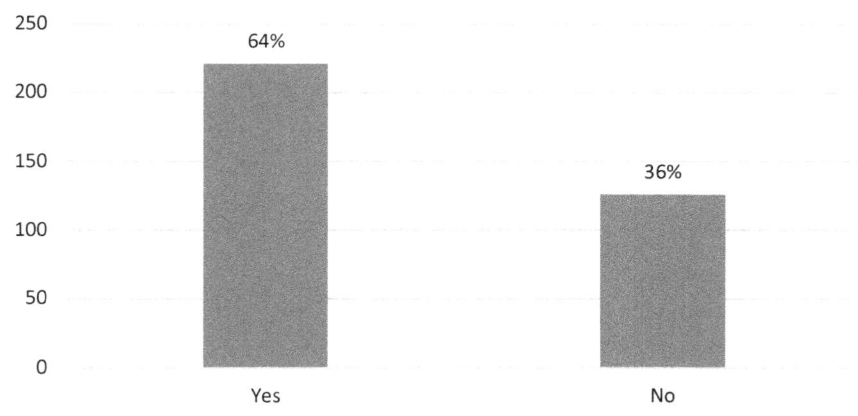
Have you seen "believers" or "church goers" consult or use "black powers" to secure a good marriage?
250
200
150
100
50
0
64%
36%
Yes
No

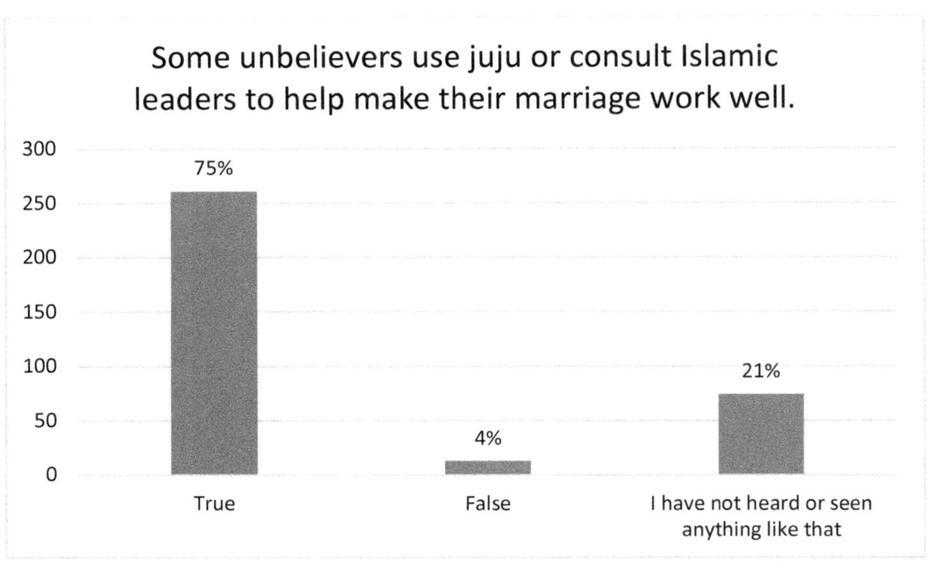

Some unbelievers use juju or consult Islamic leaders to help make their marriage work well.
300
250
200
150
100
50
0
75%
4%
21%
True
False
I have not heard or seen anything like that


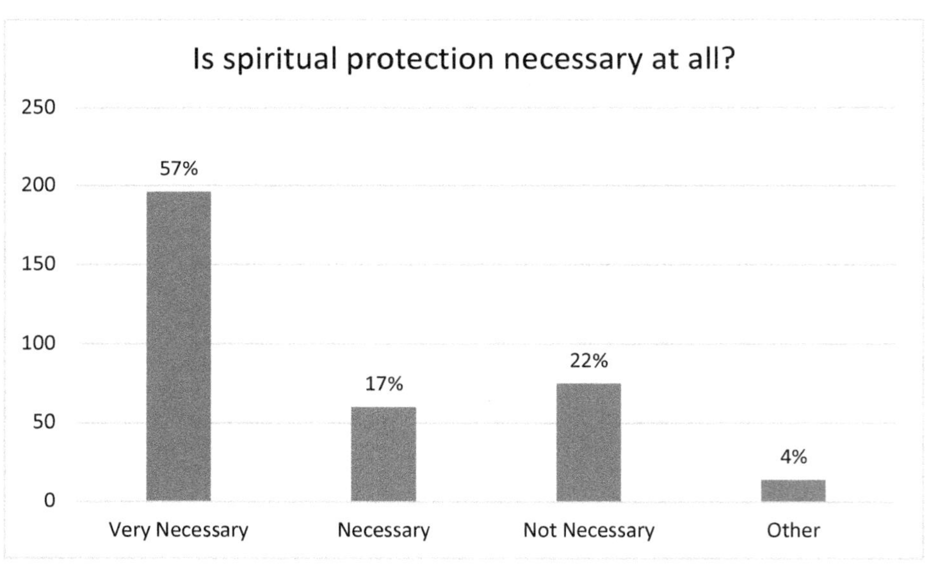

Is spiritual protection necessary at all?
250
200
150
100
50
0
57%
17%
22%
4%
Very Necessary
Necessary
Not Necessary
Other

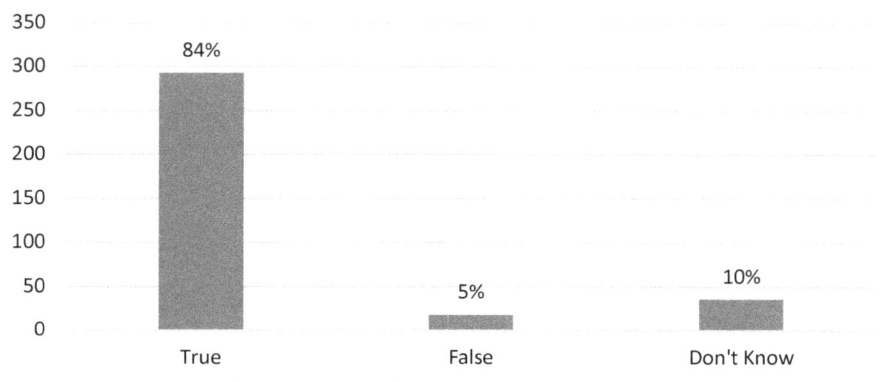
Unbelieving athletes sometimes employ supernatural powers from jujumen, malms or spiritists to excel in their sport.
350
300
250
200
150
100
50
0
84%
5%
10%
True
False
Don't Know

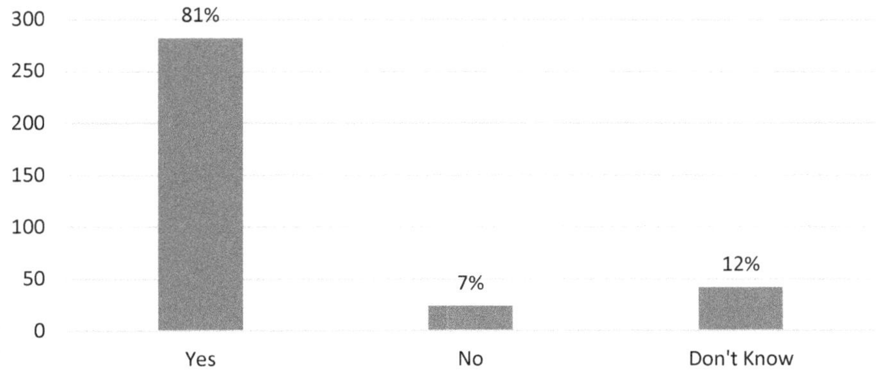
Do you think some military officers, drivers or business people use some form of black powers for protection or success?
300
250
200
150
100
50
0
81%
7%
12%
Yes
No
Don't Know

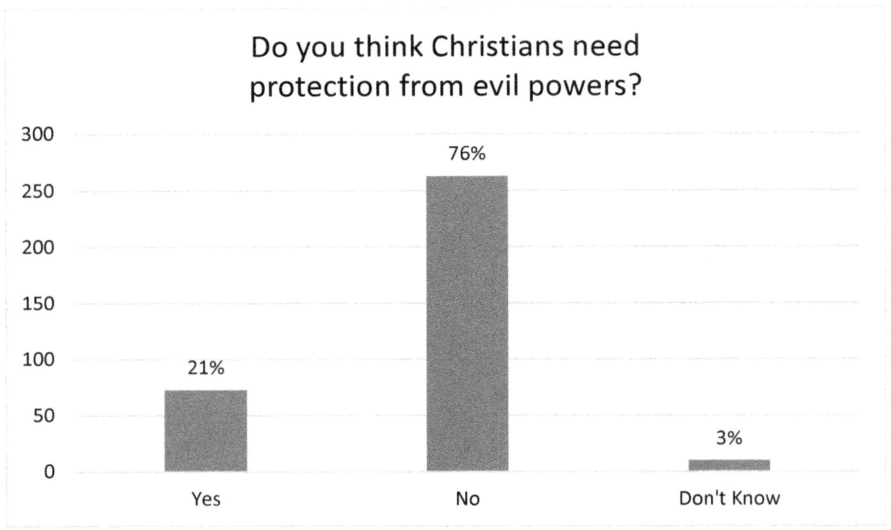

*This question was misunderstood due to poor wording on my part. Some read it to be asking if people who have strong faith in God need further protection. Others thought protection is needed regardless of one's level of faith. Another confusion is in how "protection" was understood – either protection from God or African traditional spiritual leaders. I decided not to include answers to this question in my evaluation and interpretation of data when I discovered the confusion. It is still revealing to observe the thought pattern.*

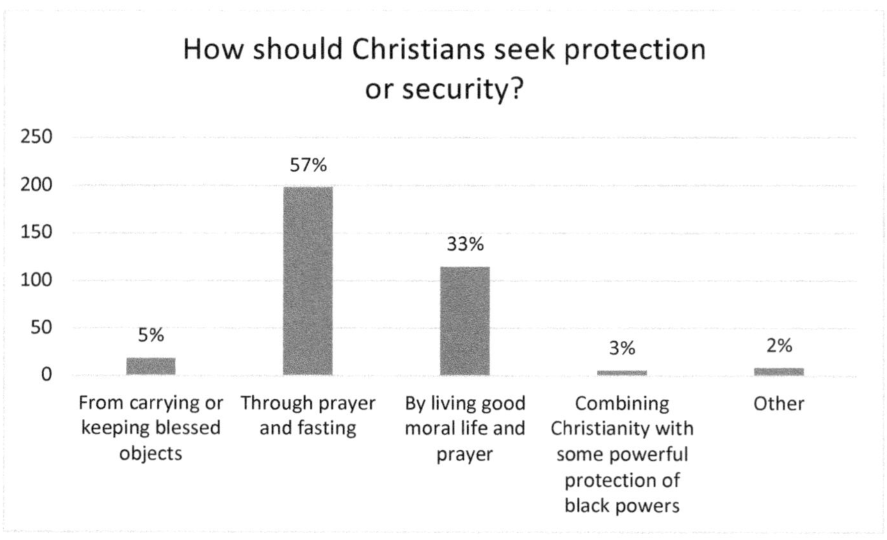

## Do you know any person who is trying to destroy or harm you or your family with evil powers?

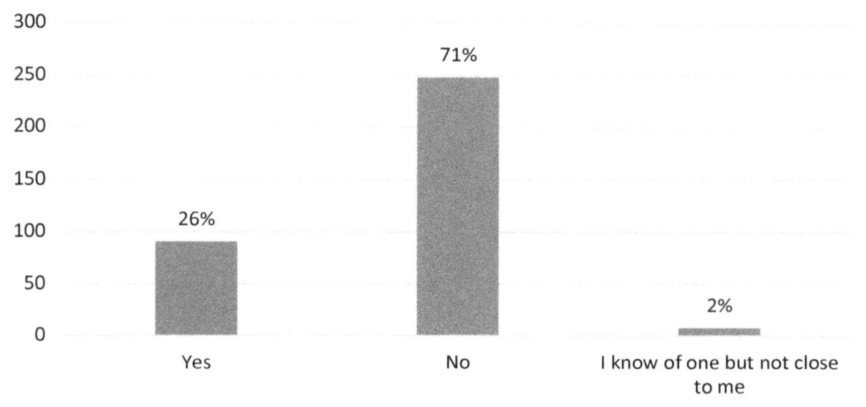



## Have you had any person in your family or a close relative harmed or affected by some evil spiritual powers?

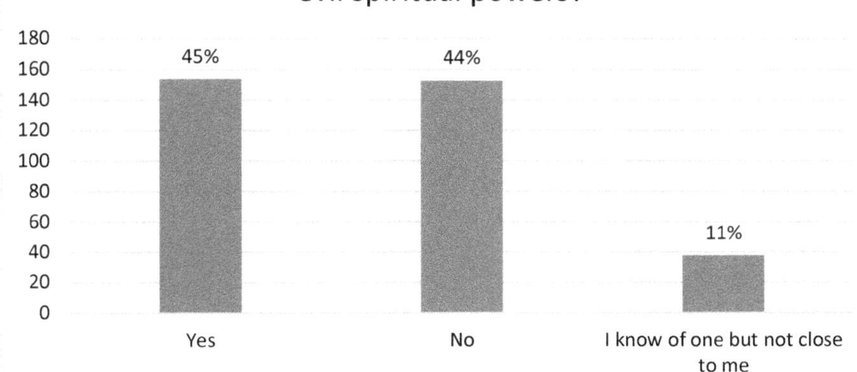

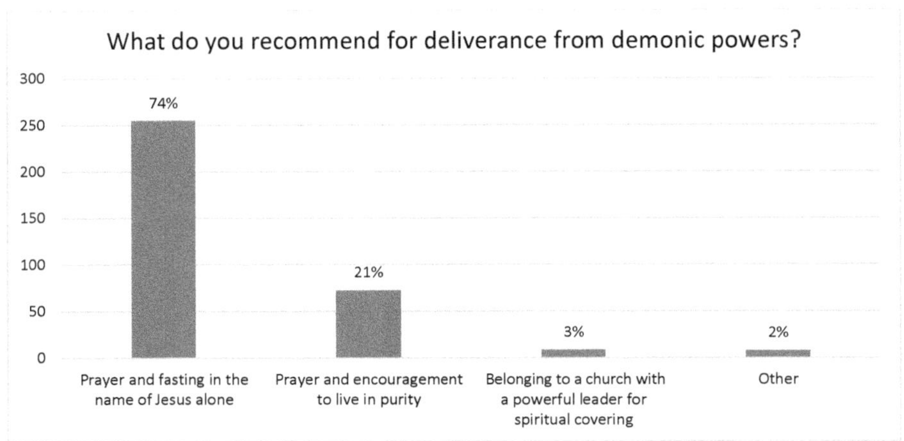

What do you recommend for deliverance from demonic powers?
74%
21%
3%
2%
Prayer and fasting in the name of Jesus alone
Prayer and encouragement to live in purity
Belonging to a church with a powerful leader for spiritual covering
Other

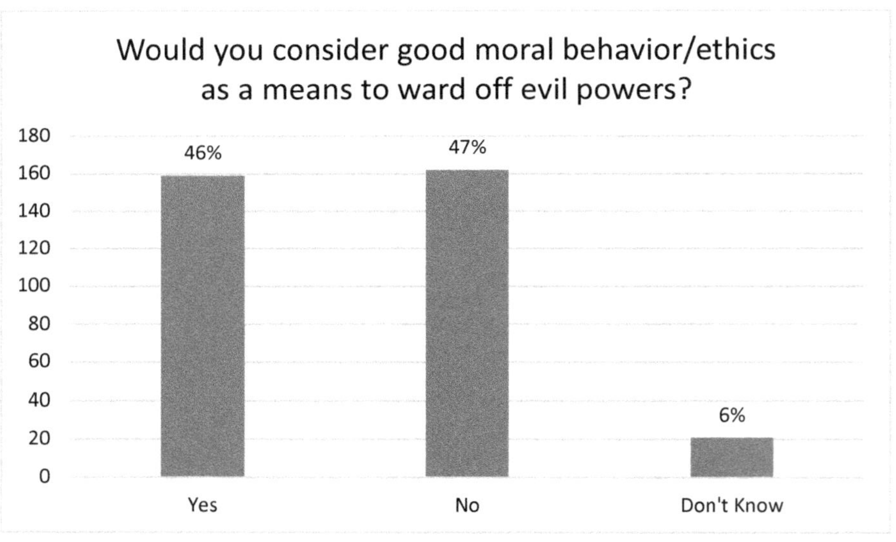

Would you consider good moral behavior/ethics as a means to ward off evil powers?
46%
47%
6%
Yes
No
Don't Know

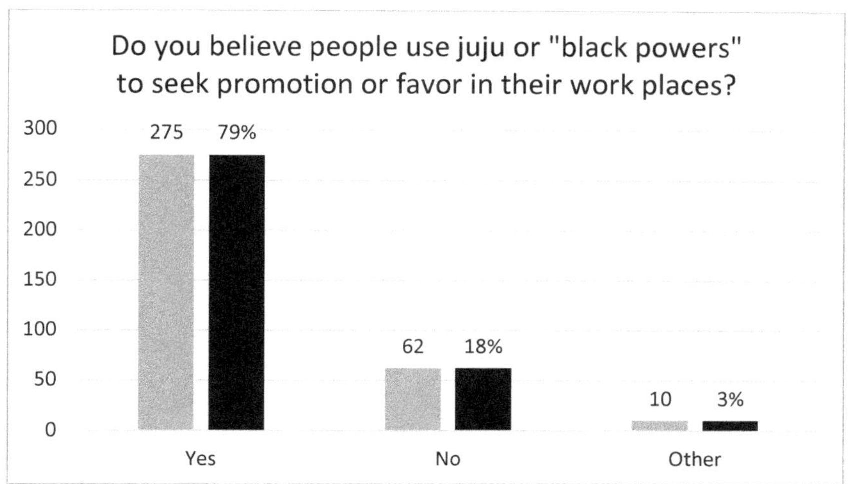

Do you believe people use juju or "black powers" to seek promotion or favor in their work places?
300
250
200
150
100
50
0
275
79%
62
18%
10
3%
Yes
No
Other


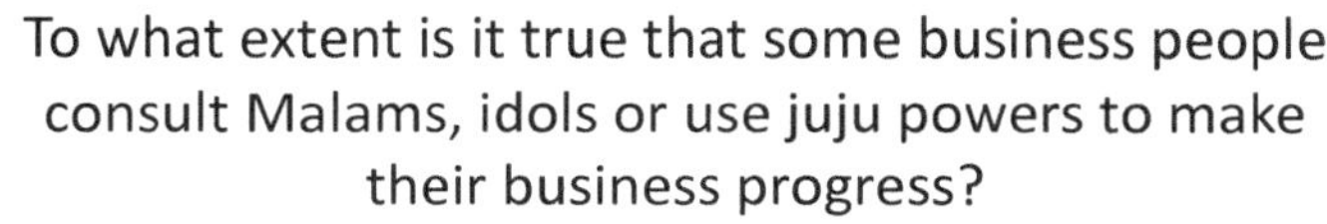

To what extent is it true that some business people consult Malams, idols or use juju powers to make their business progress?


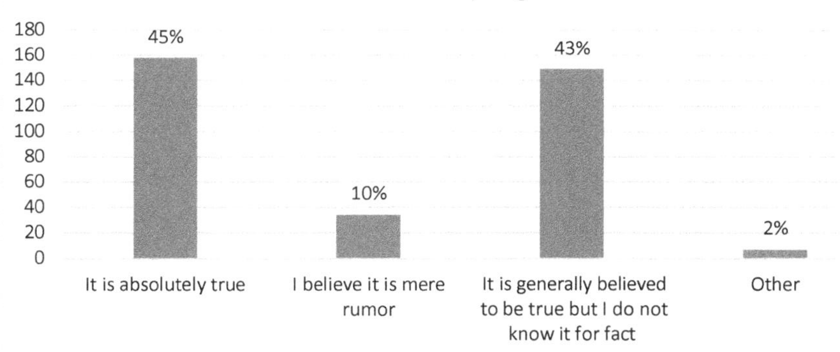

180
160
140
120
100
80
60
40
20
0
45%
10%
43%
2%
It is absolutely true
I believe it is mere rumor
It is generally believed to be true but I do not know it for fact
Other

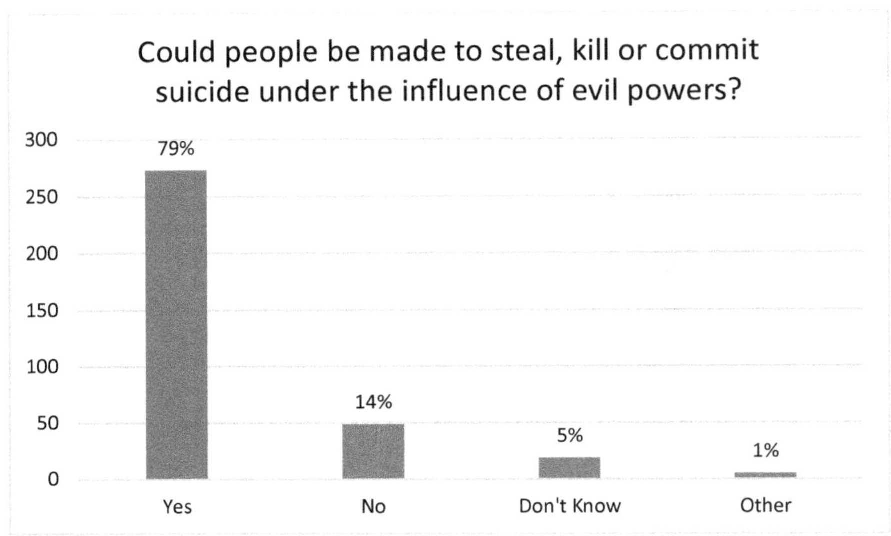


Could people be made to steal, kill or commit suicide under the influence of evil powers?
300
250
200
150
100
50
0
79%
14%
5%
1%
Yes
No
Don't Know
Other


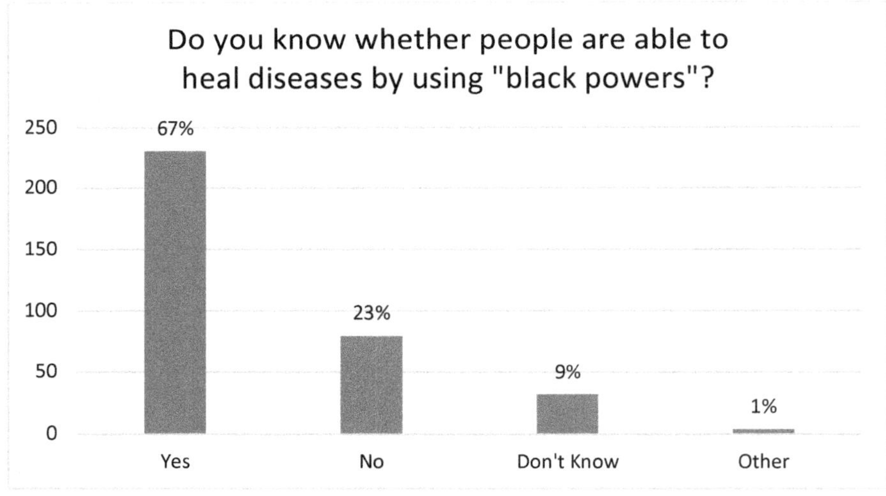


Do you know whether people are able to heal diseases by using "black powers"?
250
200
150
100
50
0
67%
23%
9%
1%
Yes
No
Don't Know
Other

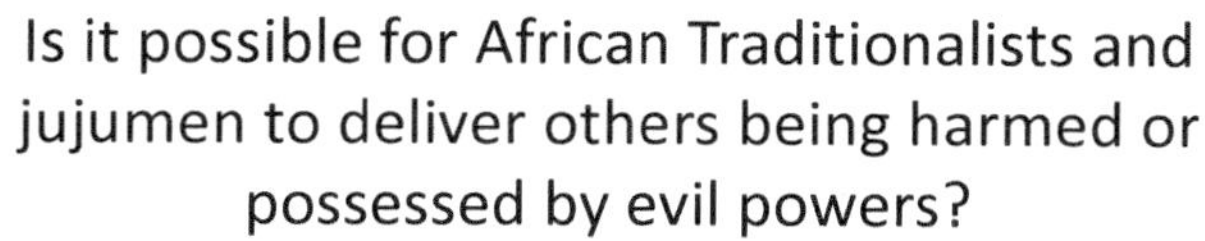

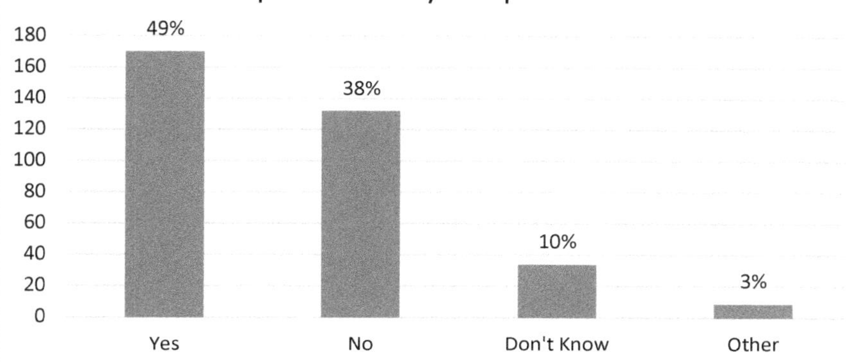
Is it possible for African Traditionalists and jujumen to deliver others being harmed or possessed by evil powers?
49%
38%
10%
3%
180
160
140
120
100
80
60
40
20
0
Yes
No
Don't Know
Other

# Bibliography

## Primary Sources

Apollodoros. *Greek Orators VI: Against Neaira [Demosthenes] 59*. Edited by C. Christopher. Warminster: Aris & Philips, 1992.

Aristotle. *The Art of Rhetoric*. London: Penguin Books, 1991.

———. *The Nichomachean Ethics*. LCL. Translated by H. Rackham. Cambridge: Harvard University Press, 1994.

———. *The Politics*. LCL. Translated by H. Rackham. London: William Heinemann, 1932.

———. *The Works of Aristotle I & II*. Chicago: Encyclopedia Britannica, Inc., 1952.

Aurelius, Marcus. *Meditations*. Edited by Ernest Rhys. London: J. M. Dent & Sons, 1937.

Betz, H. D. *The Greek Magical Papyri in Translation, including Demonic Spells*. 2nd edition. Chicago: University of Chicago Press, 1992.

Charlesworth, J. H. *The Dead Sea Scrolls: Hebrew, Aramaic, and Greek Texts with English Translation: Damascus Document, War Scroll and Related Documents, Vol. 2*. Tübingen: JCB Mohr, 1995.

———. *The Dead Sea Scrolls: Hebrew, Aramaic, and Greek Texts with English Translation: Rule of the Community and Related Documents, Vol. 1*. Tübingen: JCB Mohr, 1994.

———. *The Old Testament Pseudepigrapha Vol. 2: Expansions of the "Old Testament" and Legends, Wisdom and Philosophical Literature, Prayers, Psalms and Odes, Fragments of Lost Judeo-Hellenistic Works*. Garden City: Doubleday, 1985.

———. *The Old Testament Pseudepigrapha Vol. 1: Apocalyptic Literature & Testaments*. Garden City: Doubleday, 1983.

Cicero. *De Finibus Bonorum et Malorum*. LCL. Translated by H. Rackman. London: William Heinemann, 1931.

———. *Orations IX*. LCL. Translated by H. Grose Hodge. Cambridge: Harvard University Press, 1990.

———. *The Basic Works of Cicero*. Edited by Moses Hadas. New York: Random House, 1951.

Danby, H. *The Mishnah: Translated from the Hebrew with Introduction and Brief Explanatory Notes*. Oxford: OUP, 1991.

Demosthenes. *Private Orations Vol. III*. LCL. Translated by A. T. Murray; Cambridge: Harvard University Press, 1939.

Dio Chrysostom. *Dio Chrysostom's Discourses Vol. I–V*. LCL. J. W. Cohoon; London: William Heinemann, 1950.

Dionysius of Halicarnassus. *Roman Antiquities I–XX*. LCL. E. Cary; London: William Heinemann, 1948.

Epictetus. *Epictetus Vol. 2*. LCL. Translated by W. A. Oldfather. London: William Heinemann, 1928.

Herodotus. *Herodotus – Books I–IX*. LCL. A. D. Godley. London: William Heinemann, 1921.

Isocrates. *Isocrates I*. LCL. Translated by George Norlin. London: William Heinemann, 1928.

———. *Isocrates II*. LCL. George Norlin. London: William Heinemann, 1929.

Josephus. *The Works of Josephus*. Translated by W. Whiston. Peabody: Hendrickson, 1987.

Laertus, Diogenes. *Lives of Eminent Philosophers I&II*. LCL. Translated by R. D. Hicks. London: William Heinemann, 1925.

Lutz, C. E. "Musonius Rufus, 'The Roman Socrates.'" Translated by C. E. Lutz. *YCS* 10 (1947): 3–147.

Philo. *The Works of Philo Vol. III, VII–VIII*. LCL. Translated by F. H. Colson and G. H. Whitaker. London: William Heinemann, 1954.

———. *The Works of Philo*. Translated by C. D. Yonge. Peabody: Hendrickson, 1993.

Plato. *Plato: Complete Works*. Edited by J. M. Cooper and D. S. Hutchinson. Indianapolis: Hackett5 Publishing, 1997.

Plutarch. *Moralia II*. LCL. Translated by F. C. Babbit. Cambridge: Harvard University Press, 2002.

———. *Moralia V*. LCL. Translated by F. C. Babbit. Cambridge: Harvard University Press, 1962.

———. *Moralia VI*. LCL. Translated by W. C. Helmbold. Cambridge: Harvard University Press, 1957.

———. *Moralia VII*. LCL. Translated by P. H. De Lay and Benedict Einarson. Cambridge: Harvard University Press, 2000.

Seneca. *Epistulae Morales I&II*. LCL. R. M. Gummere. London: William Heinemann, 1930.

Seneca. *Moral Essays I–III*. LCL. Translated by J. W. Basore. Cambridge: Harvard University Press, 1935.

Xenophon. *Anabasis*. LCL. Translated by C. L. Brownson. London: William Heinemann, 1922.

## Secondary Sources

Aasgaard, R. "Brotherhood in Plutarch and Paul: It's Role and Character." In *Constructing Early Church Families: Family as Social Reality and Metaphor*, edited by Holver Moxons, 166–182. London: Routledge, 1997.

———. "Brothers in Brackets? A Plea for Rethinking the Use of [] in NA/UBS." *JSNT* 26, no. 3 (2004): 301–321.

———. *My Beloved Brothers and Sisters: Christian Siblingship in Paul*. ECC. London: T&T Clark, 2004.

———. "'Role Ethics' in Paul: The Significance of the Sibling Role for Paul's Ethical Thinking." *NTS* 48 (2002): 513–530.

Abbot, T. K. *The Epistles to the Ephesians and to the Colossians*. Edinburgh: T&T Clark, 1897.

Abotsie, C. *Social Control in Traditional Southern Eweland of Ghana: Relevance for Modern Crime Prevention*. Accra: Ghana Universities Press, 1997.

Adams, E. *Constructing the World: A Study in Paul's Cosmological Language*. SNTW. Edinburgh: T&T Clark, 2000.

Adewuya, A. J. "Reading Ephesians 6:10–18 in the Light of African Pentecostal Spirituality." In *Global Voices: Reading the Bible in the Majority World*, edited by C. Keener and M. D. Carroll R., 83–93. Peabody: Hendrickson, 2013.

Agyarko, R. O. "The *Sunsum* of *Onyame*: Akan Perspectives on an Ecological Pneumatology." *JRT* 6 (2012): 251–261.

Algra, K. "The Beginnings of Cosmology." In *Cambridge Companion to Early Greek Philosophy*. A. A. Long. Cambridge: Cambridge University Press, 1999.

Allan, J. A. *The Epistle to the Ephesians: The Body of Christ*. London: SCM Press, 1959.

———. "The 'In Christ' Formula in Ephesians." *NTS* 5 (1958): 54–62.

Allen, T. G. "Exaltation and Solidarity with Christ: Ephesians 1:20 and 2:6." *JSNT* 28 (1986): 103–120.

———. "God the Namer: A Note on Ephesians 1:21b." *NTS* 32 (1986): 470–475.

Allison Jr., D. C. "Divorce, Celibacy and Joseph (Matthew 1:18–25 and 19:1–12)." *JSNT* 49 (1993): 3–10.

Anderson, A. "Stretching the Definitions? Pneumatology and 'Syncretism' in African Pentecostalism." *Journal of Pentecostal Theology* 10, no. 1 (2001): 98–119.

Ansah, T. *Kundum: Festival of the Nzemas and Ahantas*. Accra: Onyase, 1999.

Anthony, M. J., and W. S. Benson. *Exploring the History and Philosophy of Christian Education: Principles for the 21st Century*. Eugene: Wipf & Stock, 2003.

Armstrong, A. H. *An Introduction to Ancient Philosophy*. Boston: Beacon, 1963.

Arnold, C. E. *The Colossian Syncretism: The Interface Between Christianity and Folk Belief in Colossae*. Grand Rapids: Baker Books, 1997.

———. "Ephesus." In *DPL*, edited by G. F. Hawthorne, R. P. Martin and D. G. Reid, 249–253. Leicester: Inter-Varsity Press, 1993.

———. "The 'Exorcism' of Ephesians 6:12 in Recent Research: A Critique of Wesley Carr's View of the Role of Evil Powers in the First Century AD Belief." *JSNT* 30 (1987): 71–87.

———. "Letter to the Ephesians." In *DPL*, edited by G. F. Hawthorne, R. P. Martin, and D. G. Reid, 238–249. Leicester: Inter-Varsity Press, 1993.

———. "Magic." In *DPL*, edited by G. F. Hawthorne, R. P. Martin, and D. G. Reid, 580–583. Leicester: Inter-Varsity Press, 1993.

———. *Power and Magic: The Concept of Power in Ephesians*. Grand Rapids: Baker Books, 1989.

———. *Powers of Darkness: Principalities and Powers in Paul's Letters*. Leicester: Inter-Varsity Press, 1992.

Arzt-Grabner, P. "'Brothers' and 'Sisters' in Documentary Papyri and in Early Christianity." *RivB* 50 (2002): 185–204.

Asamoah-Gyadu, K. J. "Born of Water and Spirit: Pentecostal/Charismatic Christianity in Africa." In *African Christianity*, edited by O. U. Kalu, 339–357. Trenton: African World Press, 2007.

———. *Contemporary Pentecostal Christianity: Interpretations from African Context*. Oxford: Regnum Africa, 2013.

———. *Jesus Our Immanuel: An Exercise in Homiletic Theology*. Achimota: African Christian Press, 2012.

Assimeng, M. *Religious and Social Change in West Africa: An Introduction to Sociology of Religion*. Accra: Woeli Publishing, 2010.

Aune, D. *Greco-Roman Literature and the New Testament: Selected Forms and Genre*. SBLS 21. Atlanta: Scholars Press, 1988.

———. "Magic." In *The International Standard Bible Encyclopedia Vol. 3*. Edited by Geoffrey W. Bromiley. Grand Rapids: Eerdmans, 1990.

———. "Magic in Early Christianity." In *Aufstieg und Niedergang der römischen Welt* II.23.2 (Berlin: Walter de Gruyter, 1980).

———. "The Apocalypse of John and Greco-Roman Revelatory Magic." *NTS* 33 (1987): 481–501.

Aye-Addo, C. S. *Akan Christology: An Analysis of the Christology of John Samuel Pobee and Kwame Bediako in Conversation with the Theology of Karl Barth*. Eugene: Pickwick, 2013.

Baarda, T. et al. *Miscellenea Neotestamentica Vol. 2*. Leiden: Brill, 1978.

———. *Studies in New Testament and Early Christian Literature*. Leiden: Brill, 1972.

Baker, N. L. "Living the Dream: Ethics in Ephesians." *SwJT* 22, no. 1 (1979): 39–55.

Balch, D. L. "Hellenization/Acculturation in 1 Peter." In *Perspectives on First Peter*, edited by Charles H. Talbert, 79–101. Macon: Mercer University Press, 1986.

———. "Household Codes." In *Greco-Roman Literature and the New Testament: Selected Forms and Genre*. SBLS 21. Edited by D. Aune, 25–50. Atlanta: Scholars, 1988.

———. "Rich Pompeiian Houses, Shops for Rent, and the Huge Apartment Building in Herculaneum as Typical Spaces for Pauline Churches." *JSNT* 27, no. 1 (2004): 27–46.

Balch, D. L., and C. Osiek. *Early Christian Families in Context: An Interdisciplinary Dialogue*. Grand Rapids: Eerdmans, 2003.

Balla, P. *The Child-Parent Relationship in the New Testament and Its Environment*. Peabody: Hendrickson, 2005.

Banks, R. *Paul's Idea of Community*. Exeter: Paternoster, 1980.

Bannerman-Richter, G. *Don't Cry, My Baby, Don't Cry: Autobiography of an African Witch*. Elk Grove: Gabari Publishing, 1984.

———. *Mmoatia: The Mysterious Little People*. Elk Grove: Gabari Publishing, 1987.

———. *The Practice of Witchcraft in Ghana*. Elk Grove: Babari Publishing, 1982.

Barclay, J. M. G. *Colossians and Philemon*. NTG. Sheffield: Sheffield Academic, 1997.

———. "The Family as the Bearer of Religion in Judaism and Early Christianity." In *Constructing Early Christian Families: Family as a Social Reality and Metaphor*, edited by H. Moxnes, 66–80. London: Routledge, 1997.

———. *Jews in the Mediterranean Diaspora: From Alexander to Trajan 323 BCE – 117 CE*. Berkeley: University of California Press, 1996.

———. *Paul and the Gift*. Grand Rapids: Eerdmans, 2015.

Barclay, W. *Galatians and Ephesians*. Philadelphia: Westminster, 1976.

———. *The Revelation of John Vol. 1*. Philadelphia: Westminster, 1976.

Barrett, C. K. "New Testament Eschatology." *SJT* 6, no. 4/6 (1953): 136–155.

Barth, M. "Christ and All Things." In *Paul and Paulinism: Essays in Honour of C. K. Barret*. M. D. Hooker and S. G. Wilson, 160–172. London: SPCK, 1982.

———. "Conversion and Conversation: Israel and the Church in Paul's Epistle to the Ephesians." *Int* 17 (1963): 3–24.

———. *Ephesians 1–3*. Garden City: Doubleday, 1974.

———. *Ephesians 4–6*. Garden City: Doubleday, 1974.

———. *The People of God*. JSNTS 5. Sheffield: Sheffield Academic, 1983.

———. "Traditions in Ephesians." *NTS* 30 (1984): 3–25.

Barton, S. C. *Discipleship and Family Ties in Mark and Matthew*. SNTMS 80. Cambridge: Cambridge University Press, 1994.

———. *The Family in Theological Perspective*. Edinburgh: T&T Clark, 1998.

———. "Living as Families in the Light of the New Testament." *Int* 52 (1998): 130–144.

Barton, S. C., and G. H. R. Horsley. "A Hellenistic Cult Group and the New Testament Churches." *JAC* 24 (1981): 7–41.

Bates, M. *Salvation by Allegiance Alone: Rethinking Faith, Works, and the Gospel of Jesus the King*. Grand Rapids: Baker Academic, 2017.

Beasley-Murray, G. R. *Revelation*. Grand Rapids: Eerdmans, 1983.

Beck, J. R. "Is There a Head of the House in the Home? Reflections on Ephesians 5." *JBE* 1 (1989): 61–66.

Bedale, S. "The Meaning of κεφαλη, in the Pauline Epistles." *JTS* 5 (1954): 211–215.

Bediako, K. *Christianity in Africa: The Renewal of a Non-Western Religion*. Edinburgh: University of Edinburgh Press, 1995.

———. *Jesus and the Gospel in Africa: History and Experience*. New York: Orbis, 2004.

———. *Jesus in African Culture: A Ghanaian Perspective*. Accra: Asempa Publishing, 1990.

———. *Jesus in Africa: The Christian Gospel in African History and Experience*. Carlisle: Paternoster, 2000.

———. "The Roots of African Theology." *IBMR* 13, no. 2 (1989): 58–65.

Beker, J. C. *Heirs of Paul: Paul's Legacy in the New Testament and in the Church Today.* Minneapolis: Fortress, 1991.

Bell Jr. A. A. *A Guide to the New Testament World.* Scottdale: Herald Press, 1994.

Benoit, P. "Pauline Angelology and Demonology: Reflexions on the Designations of the Heavenly Powers and On the Origin of Angelic Evil According to Paul." *RSB* 3 (1983): 1–18.

Berger, K. "Hellenistische Gattungen im Neuen Testament." In *ANRW* 2.25.2 (1984): 1340–1341.

Berger, P. L., and T. Luckmann. *The Social Construction of Reality.* Garden City: Doubleday, 1966.

Berkhof, H. *Christ and the Powers.* Translated by H. H. Yoder. Scottdale: Herald Press, 1962.

Bernstein, M. et al. *Legal Texts and Legal Issues: Proceedings of the Second Meeting of the International Organization for Qumran Studies.* Leiden: Brill, 1997.

Best, E. "Dead in Trespasses and Sins (Eph. 2:1)." *JSNT* 13 (1981): 9–25.

———. *Ephesians: A Shorter Commentary.* London: T&T Clark, 2003.

———. *Ephesians.* ICC. Edinburgh: T&T Clark, 1998.

———. "Ephesians: Two Types of Existence." *Int* XLVII, no. 1 (1993): 39–51.

———. *Essays on Ephesians.* Edinburgh: T&T Clark, 1997.

———. *One Body in Christ: A Study in the Relationship of the Church to Christ in the Epistles of the Apostle Paul.* London: SPCK, 1955.

———. "Who Used Whom? The Relationship between Ephesians and Colossians." *NTS* 43 (1997): 72–96.

Best, E., and R. M. Wilson. *Text and Interpretation: Studies in the New Testament Presented to Matthew Black.* Cambridge: Cambridge University Press, 1979.

Betz, H. D. *Galatians.* Philadelphia: Fortress, 1979.

Black, D. A. "The Peculiarities of Ephesians and the Ephesians Address." *GTJ* 2, no. 1 (1981): 59–73.

Blake, E. C., and A. G. Edmonds. *Biblical Sites in Turkey.* Istanbul: Redhouse, 1977.

Block, D. L. *A Theology of Luke and Acts.* Grand Rapids: Zondervan, 2012.

Boon, J. A. *Other Tribes, Other Scribes: Symbolic Anthropology in the Comparative Study of Cultures, Histories, Religions and Texts.* Cambridge: Cambridge University Press, 1982.

Borgen, P. *Early Christianity and Hellenistic Judaism.* Edinburgh: T&T Clark, 1996.

———. "Philo of Alexandria." In *Jewish Writings of the Second Temple Period*, edited by M. E. Stone, 233–282. Philadelphia: Fortress, 1984.

Boring, M. E. "The Language of Universal Salvation in Paul." *JBL* 105, no. 2 (1986): 269–292.

Botchway, F. J. *Juju, Magic and Witchcraft in African Soccer: Myth or Reality?* Accra: Presbyterian Press, 2009.

Botha, P. J. J. "Moral Responsibility and Narrative Rhetoric." *Neot* 28, no. 2 (1994): 495–510.

Brempong, A. *Transformations in Traditional Rule in Ghana 1951–1996*. Accra: Sedco, 2001.

Brinks, C. L. "'Great Is the Artemis of the Ephesians': Acts 19:23–41 in Light of Goddess Worship in Ephesus." *CBQ* 71, no. 4 (2009): 776–794.

Broadie, S. *Ethics with Aristotle*. New York: Oxford University Press, 1991.

Brooks, J. A., and C. L. Winberry. *Syntax of New Testament Greek*. Lanham: University Press of America, 1979.

Brown, C. *New International Dictionary of New Testament Theology* 5.1 on CD-ROM. Zondervan Corporation, 2004.

Brown, P. *The Body and Society: Men, Women and Sexual Renunciation in Early Christianity*. New York: Columbia University Press, 1988.

Bruce, F. F. *I & II Thessalonians*. WBC. Waco: Word Books, 1982.

———. *The Book of the Acts*. Grand Rapids: Eerdmans, 1976.

———. *The Epistle to the Colossians, to Philemon and to the Ephesians*. Grand Rapids: Eerdmans, 1984.

———. *The Epistle to the Ephesians*. Glasgow: Pickering, 1961.

Buell, D. K. "Ethnicity and Religion in Mediterranean Antiquity and Beyond." *RSR* 26, no. 3 (2000): 243–249.

———. "Race and Universalism in Early Christianity." *JECS* 10, no. 4 (2002): 429–468.

———. "Rethinking the Relevance of Race for Early Christian Self-Definition." *HTR* 94, no. 4 (2001): 449–476.

Bultmann, R. *Jesus Christ and Mythology*. New York: Charles Schribner's, 1958.

———. "The Problem of Ethics in Paul (1924)." In *Understanding Paul's Ethics: Twentieth Century Approaches*, edited by Brian Rosner, 195–216. Grand Rapids: Eerdmans, 1995.

Burge G. M. et al. *The New Testament in Antiquity: A Survey of the New Testament within Its Cultural Contexts*. Grand Rapids: Zondervan, 2009.

Burns, E. M., and P. L. Ralph. *World Civilization*. 5th edition, Vol. 1. New York: Norton & Company, 1974.

Burns, R. *The Monuments of Syria. A Guide*. London: Tauris, 1994.

Burton, D. W. *Syntax of Moods and Tenses in New Testament Greek*. 3rd edition Chicago: University of Chicago, 1900.

Butting, K. "Pauline Variations on Genesis 2:24: Speaking of the Body of Christ in the Context of the Discussion of Lifestyles." *JSNT* 79 (2000): 79–90.

Byron, J. "Paul and the Background of Slavery: The *Status Quaetionis* in New Testament Scholarship." *CBR* 3, no. 1 (2004): 116–139.

———. *Slavery Metaphors in Early Judaism and Pauline Christianity*. WUNT 2, no. 162. Tübingen: Mohr Siebeck, 2003.

Caird, G. B. *Paul's Letters from Prison: Ephesians, Philippians, Colossians, Philemon, in the Revised Standard Version*. Oxford: Oxford University Press, 1976.

———. *The Revelation of Saint John*. Peabody: Hendrickson, 1966.

Caragounis, C. C. *The Ephesians Mysterion: Meaning and Context.* Lund: Carl Bloms Boktryckeri, 1977.

Carr, W. *Angels and Principalities: The Background, Meaning and Development of the Pauline Phrase Hai Archai Kai Hai Exousiai.* SNTS 42. Cambridge: Cambridge University Press, 1981.

Carson, D. A. *Exegetical Fallacies.* Grand Rapids: Baker Books, 1984.

Carson, D. A. et al. *An Introduction to the New Testament.* Grand Rapids: Zondervan, 1992.

Chapell, B. *Ephesians: Reformed Expository Commentary.* Philipsburg: P&R Publishing, 2009.

Charles, J. D. *Virtue amidst Vice: The Catalogue of Virtues in 2 Peter 1.* JSNTSup 150. Sheffield: Sheffield Academic, 1997.

Cheon, S. "Three Characters in the Wisdom of Solomon 3–4." *JSP* 12, no. 1 (2001): 105–113.

Cimok, F. *A Guide to the Seven Churches.* Istanbul: A Turizm Yayinlari, 1998.

Clark, S. B. *Man and Woman in Christ: An Examination of the Roles of Men and Women in Light of Scripture and Social Sciences.* Edinburgh: T&T Clark, 1980.

Clarke, A. D. "Equality or Mutuality? Paul's Use of Brother Language." In *The New Testament in Its First Century Setting,* edited by P. J. Williams et al., 151–165. Grand Rapids: Eerdmans, 2004.

Clarke, A. D., and B. W. Winter. *One God, One Lord: Christianity in a World of Religious Pluralism.* 2nd edition. Grand Rapids: Baker, 1992.

Cleary, J. J., and D. C. Shartin. *Proceedings of the Boston Area Colloquium in Ancient Philosophy Vol. V.* Lanham: University Press of America, 1991.

Colville of Culross. "Blind or Hard of Heart?" *Theology* 69 (1966): 168–172.

Conner, R. *Magic in the New Testament: A Survey and Appraisal of the Evidence.* Oxford: Mandrake, 2010.

Conybeare, F. C. "Testament of Solomon." *JQR* 11 (1878): 1–45.

Conzelmann, H. *An Outline of the Theology of the New Testament-Study Edition.* London: SCM, 1969.

Cooper, S. A. *Metaphysics and Morals in Marius Victorinus' Commentary on the Letter to the Ephesians: A Contribution to the History of Neoplatonism and Christianity.* New York: Peter Lang, 1995.

Cotter, W. *Miracles in Greco-Roman Antiquity: A Sourcebook for the Study of New Testament Miracles Series.* New York: Routledge, 1999.

Couch, B. M. "Blessed Be He Who Has Blessed: Ephesians 1:3–14." *IRM* 77 (1988): 213–220.

Coutts, J. "The Relationship of Ephesians and Colossians." *NTS* 4 (1957/58): 201–207.

Crawford, S. W. "Lady Wisdom and Dame Folly at Qumran." *DSD* 5, no. 3 (1998): 357–359.

Cross, F. L. *Studies in Ephesians.* London: A. R. Mowbray & Co., 1956.

Crouch, J. E. *The Origin and Intention of the Colossian Haustafel.* Göttingen: Vandenhoeck und Ruprecht, 1972.

Cullmann, O. *Christ and Time: The Primitive Christian Conception of Time and History.* Vol. 3. Translated by F. V. Filson. London: SCM, 1962.

———. *The Christology of the New Testament.* London: SCM Press, 1959.

Culpepper, H. H. "Ephesians – A Manifesto for the Mission of the Church." *RevExp* 76 (1979): 553–558.

Culpepper, R. A. "Ethical Dualism and Church Discipline: Ephesians 4:25–5:20." *RevExp* (1979): 529–539.

Cumont, F., and L. Canet. "Mithra of Sarapis ΚΟΣΜΟΚΡΑΤΩΡ." In *Comptes rendus des séances de l'Académie des Inscriptions et Belles-Lettres*, 63ᵉ année, N. (1919): 313–328.

Dahl, N. A. "Christ, Creation, and the Church." In *The Background to New Testament and Its Eschatology*, edited by W. D. Davies and D. Daube, 422–443. Cambridge: Cambridge University Press, 1956.

———. "Gentiles, Christians and Israelites in the Epistle to the Ephesians." *HTR* 79, nos. 1–3 (1986): 31–39.

———. *Studies in Ephesians*, WUNT. Edited by D. Hellholm et al. Tübingen: Mohr Siebeck, 2000.

Daneel, M. L. *Fombidzanu: Ecumenical Movement of Zimbabwean Independent Churches.* Gweru, Zimbabwe: Mambo Press, 1989.

D'Angelo, M. R. "Roman Imperial Family Values and the Sexual Politics of 4 Maccabees and the Pastorals." *BibInt* 11, no. 2 (2003): 139–168.

Daniel, R. W. "Notes on the Guilds and Army in Roman Egypt." *BASP* 16 (1979): 37–46.

Danquah, J. B. *The Akan Doctrine of God.* London: Frank Cass, 1968.

Darko, D. K. "Adopted Siblings in the Household of God: Kinship Lexemes in the Social Identity Construction of Ephesians." In *The Handbook to Social Identity and the New Testament*, edited by J. B. Tucker and C. A. Baker, 333–346. London: T&T Clark, 2014.

———. "The Concept of Reconciliation in the Corpus Paulinum: Two Dimensions of Authentic Relationship." *TJCT* 14, no. 1 (2004): 27–36.

———. "The Haustafel in Ephesians versus Contemporary African Family Dynamics." *TJCT* 14, no. 2 (2004): 13–26.

———. "The Issue of Women in Ministry in the Corpus Paulinum with a Particular Reference to the Ghanaian Church and Culture." MA Thesis, OCMS Oxford and University of Leeds (Oxford and Leeds, 2000).

———. "Kinship in Discipleship: The 'Father' Image of God and Disciples as 'Brothers' in Matthew's Sermon on the Mount." In *Exploring Biblical Kinship*, edited by J. C. Campbell and P. J. Hartin, 239–255. CBQMS 55. Washington, DC: Catholic Biblical Association of America, 2016.

———. *No Longer Living as the Gentiles: Differentiation and Shared Ethical Values in Ephesians 4:17–6:9.* LNTS 375. London: T&T Clark, 2008.

———. "The Role of Spiritual Beings in Relation to Ethics According to Ephesians," MTh Thesis, Evangelical Theological Seminary (Osijek, 2001).

———. "The Shadows of the Past: Christian Mission in Sub-Saharan Africa from 1445–1543 and its Implications for Contemporary Missions." *TJCT* 11, nos. 1/2 (2001): 68–82.

———. "Spirit-Cosmology in the Identity and Community of Ephesians." *Pleroma* 15, no. 1 (2013): 59–71.

———. "What Does It Mean to Be Saved? An African Reading of Ephesians 2." *Pent* 24, no. 1 (2015): 44–56.

Dassmann, E., and K. S. Frank. *Pietas: Festschrift für Bernhard Kötting.* Aschendorffsche Verlagsbuchhandlung, 1980.

Dautzenberg, G. *Die Frau im Urchristentum.* Freiburg: Herder, 1983.

Davies, W. D., and D. Daube. *The Background to New Testament and Its Eschatology.* Cambridge: Cambridge University Press, 1956.

Davis, J. J. "Ephesians 4:12 Once More: 'Equipping the Saints for the Work of Ministry.'" *ERT* 24 (2000): 167–176.

Dawes, G. W. *The Body in Question: Metaphor and Meaning in the Interpretation of Ephesians 5:21–33.* Leiden: Brill, 1998.

De Jonge, M. *Jewish Eschatology, Early Christian Christology and the Testaments of the Twelve Patriarchs: Collected Essays of Marinus De Jonge.* Leiden: Brill, 1991.

Deming, W. *Paul on Marriage and Celibacy: The Hellenistic Background of 1 Corinthians 7.* SNTMS 83. Cambridge: Cambridge University Press, 1995.

den Hollander, W. *Josephus, the Emperors and the City of Rome: From Hostage to Historian.* AJEC 86. Leiden: Brill, 2014.

Denton, D. R. "Inheritance in Paul and Ephesians." *EvQ* 54 (1982): 157–162.

Dibelius, M. *An die Kolosser, an die Epheser, an Philemon.* HNT 12; Tübingen: Mohr, 1913.

———. *An die Kolosser, Epheser, an Philemon.* Tübingen: J. C. B. Mohr, 1953.

———. *A Fresh Approach to the Study of New Testament and Early Christian Literature.* Hertford: Nicholson and Watson, 1936.

———. *Die Geisterwelt im Glauben des Paulus.* Göttingen: Vandenhoek & Ruprecht, 1909.

Dickie, M. W. *Magic and Magicians in the Greco-Roman World.* London: Routledge, 2001.

Dillion, J. T. *Musonius Rufus and Education in the Good Life: A Model of Teaching and Living Virtue.* Dallas: University Press of America, 2004.

Dixon, S. "Sex and the Married Woman in Ancient Rome." In *Early Christian Families in Context: An Interdisciplinary Dialogue,* edited by David L. Balch and Carolyn Osiek, 111–129. Grand Rapids: Eerdmans, 2003.

Dodd, C. H. "Blind or Hard of Heart?" *Theology* 69 (1966): 223–224.

———. *The Meaning of Paul for Today.* London: Collin Clear–Type Press, 1973.

———. *The Parables of the Kingdom.* London: Nisbert & Co., 1935.

Domeris, W. R. "Honour and Shame in the New Testament." *Neot* 27, no. 2 (1993): 283–297.

Donelson, L. R. *Colossians, Ephesians, First and Second Timothy and Titus.* Louisville: Westminster John Knox, 1996.

Dudrey, R. "'Submit Yourselves to One Another': A Socio-Historical Look at the Household Code in Ephesians 5:15–6:9." *ResQ* 1 (1999): 27–44.

Duling, D. C. "Solomon, Exorcism, and the Son of David." *HTR* 68, nos. 3/4 (1975): 235–252.

———. "Testament of Solomon: A Translation and Introduction." In *The Old Testament Pseudepigrapha-Apocalyptic Literature & Testaments Vol. 1.* Edited by J. H. Charlesworth. Garden City: Doubleday, 1983.

Duling, D. C., and N. Perrin. *The New Testament: Proclamation and Paranesis, Myth and History.* Fort Worth: Harcourt Brace College, 1994.

Duncan, G. S. "Paul's Ministry in Asia – The Last Phase." *NTS* (1956/57): 211–218.

Dunn, J. D. G. *The Acts of the Apostles.* Valley Forge: Trinity Press International, 1996.

———. *Christology: The Christ and the Spirit Vol 1.* Grand Rapids: Eerdmans, 1998.

———. "The Household Rules in the New Testament." In *The Family in Theological Perspective*, edited by Stephen C. Barton, 43–63. Edinburgh: T&T Clark, 1998.

———. "Once More πιστις Χριστοῦ" *SBLSP* 30 (1991): 730–744.

———. *The Theology of Paul the Apostle.* Grand Rapids: Eerdmans, 1998.

Dunning, B. H. "Strangers and Aliens No Longer: Negotiating Identity and Difference in Ephesians 2." *HTR* 99, no. 1 (2006): 1–16.

Dzathor, P. K. *The Ewe Nation and Sasabu: A Brief History.* Accra: Berkadams, 1998.

Dzobo, N. K. *Modes of Traditional Moral Education among Anfoega Ewes.* Cape Coast: Cape Coast University Press, 1971.

Eadie, J. *The Ephesians.* Grand Rapids: Baker, 1979.

Easton, B. S. "New Testament Ethical Lists." *JBL* 51 (1932): 1–12.

Eckel, P. T. "Ephesians 6.10–20." *Int* XLV (1991): 288–293.

Egger, W. *How to Read the New Testament: An Introduction to Linguistic and Historical Critical Methodology.* Edited by H. Boers. Peabody: Hendrickson, 1996.

Ekem, J. D. K. *Priesthood in Context: A Study of Priesthood in Some Christian and Primal Communities of Ghana and Its Relevance for Mother-Tongue Biblical Hermeneutics.* Accra: Sonlife, 2009.

Elliott, J. H. *Beware the Evil Eye: The Evil Eye in the Bible and the Ancient World – Introduction, Mesopotamia, and Egypt Vol. 1.* Eugene: Cascade, 2015.

———. *Beware the Evil Eye: The Evil Eye in the Bible and the Ancient World Vol. 2 – Greece and Rome.* Eugene: Cascade, 2016.

———. *Beware the Evil Eye: The Evil Eye in the Bible and the Ancient World Vol. 3 – The Bible and Related Sources.* Eugene: Cascade, 2016.

———. *Beware the Evil Eye: The Evil Eye in the Bible and the Ancient World Vol. 4 – Postbiblical Israel and Early Christianity through Late Antiquity.* Eugene: Cascade, 2017.

Engberg-Pedersen, T. "Ephesians 5, 12-14:ἐλέγχειν and Conversion in the New Testament." *ZNW* 80, nos. 1–2 (1989): 89–110.

———. *Paul and the Stoics.* Edinburgh: T&T Clark, 2000.

ErdKamp, P. "Agriculture, Underdevelopment, and the Cost of Rural Labour in the Roman World." *CQ* 49 (1999): 556–572.

Erickson, R. "Ephesians." In *Evangelical Commentary of the Bible.* Grand Rapids: Baker Book House, 1989.

Esler, P. F. *Conflict and Identity in Romans: The Social Setting of Paul's Letter.* Minneapolis: Fortress, 2003.

———. *Galatians.* London: Routledge, 1998.

———. "Keeping It in the Family: Culture, Kinship and Identity in 1 Thessalonians and Galatians." In *Families and Family Relations as Represented in Early Judaisms and Early Christianities: Text and Fictions,* edited by J. W van Henten and A. Brenner, 145–184. Leiden: Deo Publishing, 2000.

Everling, O. *Die paulinische Angelologie und Dämonologie: Ein biblisch-theologischer Versuch.* Göttingen: Vandenhoek & Ruprecht, 1888.

Falola, T. *Culture and Customs of Nigeria.* Westport: Greenwood Press, 2001.

Fee, G. D. *God's Empowering Presence: The Holy Spirit in the Letters of Paul.* Peabody: Hendrickson, 1994.

———. *Pauline Christology: An Exegetical: Theological Study.* Peabody: Hendrickson, 2007.

———. *To What End Exegesis: Essays Textual, Exegetical and Theological.* Grand Rapids: Eerdmans, 2001.

Ferguson, J. *Moral Values in the Ancient World.* London: Methuen & Co., 1958.

Fergusson, E. *Background of Early Christianity.* Second ed. Grand Rapids: Eerdmans, 1993.

Finley, M. I. *Ancient Slavery and Modern Ideology.* New York: Viking, 1980.

Fiorenza, E. S. "Cultic Language in Qumran and in the New Testament." *CBQ* (1979): 159–177.

———. *In Memory of Her: A Feminist Theological Reconstruction of Christian Origins.* London: SCM, 1983.

Fisher of Lambeth. "Blind or Hard of Heart?" *Theology* 69 (1966): 25–26.

Flanagan, J. W., and A. W. Robinson. *No Famine in the Land: Studies in Honour of John L. McKenzie.* Missoula: Scholars Press, 1975.

Foerster, W. *Verbum Dei Manet in Aeternum. Eine Festschrift für Prof. D. Otto Schmitz zu seinem siebzigsten Geburtstag am 16. Juni 1953.* Witten: Luther-Verlag, 1953.

Forbes, C. "Pauline Demonology and/or Cosmology? Principalities, Powers and the Elements of the World in Their Hellenistic Context." *JSNT* 85 (2002): 51–73.

———. "Paul's Principalities and Powers: Demythologizing Apocalyptic? *JSNT* 82 (2001): 61–88.

Foster, P. "The First Contribution to the πίστις Χριστοῦ Debate: A Study of Ephesians 3:12." *JSNT* 85 (2002): 75–95.

Foster, R. L. "Reoriented to the Cosmos: Cosmology & Theology in Ephesians Through Philemon." In *Cosmology and New Testament Theology*, edited by J. T. Pennington and S. M. McDonough, 107–124. London: T&T Clark, 2008.

Foulkes, F. *Ephesians.* Leicester: Inter-Varsity Press, 1989.

———. *Ephesians.* Leicester: Inter-Varsity Press, 1974.

Frey, J. "Different Patterns of Dualistic Thought in the Qumran Library." In *Legal Texts and Legal Issues: Proceedings of the Second Meeting of the International Organization for Qumran Studies*, edited by Moshe Bernstein, et al., 275–335. Leiden: Brill, 1997.

Friendrich, F. "Traditional Ethical Patterns in the Pauline and Post-Pauline Letters and Their Development." In *Text and Interpretation*, edited E. Best and R. McL. Wilson, 195–209. Cambridge: Cambridge University Press, 1979.

Gager Jr., J. G. "Functional Diversity in Paul's Use of End-Time Language." *JBL* 89 (1970): 325–337.

Gardner, J. F., and T. Wiedemann. *The Roman Household: A Sourcebook.* London: Routledge, 1991.

Garland, D. E. "A Life Worthy of the Calling: Unity and Holiness Ephesians 4:1–24." *RevExp* 76 (1976): 517–527.

Garrett, S. R. *The Demise of the Devil: Magic and the Demonic in Luke's Writings.* Minneapolis: Fortress, 1989.

———. "Light on a Dark Subject and Vice Versa: Magic and Magicians in the New Testament." In *Religion, Science, and Magic: In Conflict and in Concert*, edited by J. Neusner et. al., 142–165. New York: Oxford University Press, 1989.

Geller, M. J. et al. *Legal Documents of the Hellenistic World.* London: Warburg Institute/ University of London, 1995.

Geller, M. J., and D. Levene. "Magical Texts from the Genizah (with a New Duplicate)." *JJS* 44, no. 2 (1998): 334–340.

George, M. "Domestic Architecture and Household Relations: Pompeii and Roman Ephesus." *JSNT* 27, no. 1 (2004): 7–25.

Glahn, S. L. "The Identity of Artemis in First Century Ephesus." *BSac* 172 (2015): 316–334.

Glancy, J. A. *Slavery in Early Christianity.* New York: Oxford University Press, 2002.

Gnilka, J. *Der Epheserbrief.* HTKNT 10, no. 2. Freiburg: Herder, 1971.

Gombis, T. G. "Being the Fullness of God in Christ by the Spirit: Ephesians 5:18 in Its Epistolary Setting." *TynBul* 53, no. 2 (2002): 259–271.

———. "Cosmic Lordship and the Divine Gift-Giving: Psalm 68 in Ephesians 4:8." *NovT* 47, no. 4 (2005): 367–380.

———. *The Drama of Ephesians: Participating in the Triumph of God.* Downers Grove: IVP Academic, 2010.

———. "Ephesians 2 as a Narrative of Divine Warfare." *JSNT* 26, no. 4 (2004): 403–418.

———. "Ephesians 3:2–13: Pointless Digression, or Epitome of the Triumph of God in Christ." *WTJ* (2004): 313–323.

————. "A Radically New Humanity: The Function of the *Haustafel* in Ephesians." *JETS* 48, no. 2 (2005): 317–330.

Gordon, M. L. "The Nationality of Slaves under the Early Empire." *JRS* 14 (1924): 93–111.

Gordon, T. D. "'Equipping' Ministry in Ephesians 4?" *JETS* 37 (1994): 69–78.

Gorman, M. J. *Cruciformity: Paul's Narrative Spirituality of the Cross*. Grand Rapids: Eerdmans, 2001.

Gosnell, P. W. "Ephesians 5:18–20 and Mealtime Propriety." *TynBul* 44, no. 2 (1993): 363–371.

Goulder, M. D. "The Visionaries of Laodicea." *JSNT* 43 (1991): 15–39.

Green, J. B. *Conversion in Luke-Acts: Divine Action, Human Cognition, and the People of God*. Grand Rapids: Baker, 2015.

Greenlee, J. H. *Introduction to New Testament Textual Criticism*. Peabody: Hendrickson, 1995.

Greevan and Fichtner. "Πλησίον" *TDNT* 6 (1968): 311–318.

Grenz, S. J. *The Moral Quest: Foundations of Christian Ethics*. Downers Grove: InterVarsity Press, 1997.

Griffiths, J. G. "Xenophon of Ephesus on Isis and Alexandria." In *Hommages a, Maarten J. Vermaseren Vol. 1*. EPRO 68. Leiden: Brill, 1978.

Gritz, S. H. *Paul, Women Teachers, and the Mother Goddess at Ephesus: A Study of 1 Timothy 2.9-15 in Light of Religious and Cultural Milieu of the First Century*. Lanham: University Press of America, 1991.

Grubbs, J. E. *Law and Family in Late Antiquity: The Emperor Constantine's Marriage Legislation*. Oxford: Clarendon, 1995.

Grundmann, W. *Der Begriff der Kraft in der Neutestamentlichen Gedankenwelt*. BWANT 8. Stuttgart: Kohlhammer, 1932.

Gudorf, M. E. "The Use of PALH in Ephesians 6:12." *JBL* 117 (1998): 331–335.

Guenther, A. R. "The Exception Phrases: Except πορνεία, Including πορνεία or Excluding πορνεία? (Matthew 5:32; 19:9)." *TynBul* 53, no. 1 (2002): 81–96.

Gundry, J. M. *Paul and Perseverance: Staying in and Falling Away*. WUNT 2.37. Tübingen: J. C. B. Mohr, 1990.

Gutek, G. L. *Historical and Philosophical Foundations of Education: A Biographical Introduction*. Upper Saddle River: Merrill Prentice-Hall, 2001.

Gyegye, K. *African Cultural Values*. Accra: Sankofa, 1996.

Haase, W. "Commentary on Reesor." In *Proceedings of the Boston Area Colloquium in Ancient Philosophy Vol. V*, edited by J. Cleary and D. C. Shartin, 124–134. Lanham: University Press of America, 1989.

Haenchen, E. *Acts of the Apostles*. Oxford: Basil Blackwell, 1971.

Hall, J. M. *Ethnic Identity in Greek Antiquity*. Cambridge: Cambridge University Press, 1997.

Hamann, H. P. "The Translation of Ephesians 4:12 – A Necessary Revision." *ConJ* 14 (1988): 42–49.

Harris III, W. H. "The Heavenlies Reconsidered: Οὐρανός and Ἐπουράνιος in Ephesians." *BSac* 148 (1992): 72–89.

Harris, W. V. "The Roman Father's Power of Life and Death." In *Studies in Roman Law in Memory of A. A. Schiller*. Leiden: Brill, 1986.

Harrisville, R. A. "The Concept of Newness in the New Testament." *JBL* 74 (1955): 69–79.

Hartman, L. "Some Unorthodox Thoughts on the 'Household-Code Form.'" In *The Social World of Formative Christianity and Judaism*, edited by J. Neusner et. al., 219–232. Philadelphia: Fortress, 1998.

Hauck, F., and S. Schulz. "πόρνη, πορνος, πορνεία" *TDNT* 6 (1968): 579–595.

Hawthorne, G. F. et al. *Dictionary of Paul and His Letters*. Downers Grove: InterVarsity Press, 1993.

Hayman, P. "Was God a Magician? Sefer Yesira and Jewish Magic." *JJS* 40, no. 2 (1989): 225–237.

Hays, R. B. *The Moral Vision of the New Testament: A Contemporary Introduction to New Testament Ethics*. San Francisco: Harper, 1996.

Hendricksen, W. *Galatians and Ephesians*. Edinburgh: Banner of Truth, 1968.

Hengel, M. *Judaism and Hellenism*. Philadelphia: Fortress, 1974.

Heyworth, G., and R. Liberman. *Stylebook: The Writing and Revision Stylebook*. New Haven: Cooper Hill, 2000.

Hitchcock, A. E. N. "Ephesians 1:23." *ExpTim* 22 (1910/11): 91.

Hobbs, R. "The Language of Warfare in the New Testament." In *Modelling Early Christianity: Social-Scientific Studies of the New Testament in Its Context*, edited by P. F. Esler, 259–273. London: Routledge, 1995.

Hodge, C. *The Epistle to the Ephesians*. Grand Rapids: Eerdmans, 1994.

Holladay, J. F. "Ephesians 4.30: Do Not Grieve the Spirit." *RevExp* 94 (1997): 81–87.

Holmberg, B. *Paul and Power: The Structure of Authority in the Primitive Church as Reflected in the Pauline Epistles*. Philadelphia: Fortress, 1980.

Hooker, M. D., and S. G. Wilson. *Paul and Paulinism: Essays in Honour of C. K. Barrett*. London: SPCK, 1982.

Horrell, D. G. "From ἀδελφοί to οι οἶκος θεου – Social Transformation in Pauline Christianity." *JBL* 120, no. 2 (2001): 293–311.

———. *Solidarity and Difference: A Contemporary Reading of Paul's Ethics*. London: T&T Clark, 2005.

———. "Theological Principle or Christological Praxis? Pauline Ethics in 1 Corinthians 8:1–11:1." *JSNT* 67 (1997): 83–114.

Horsley, R. A. *Jesus and Magic: Freeing the Gospel Stories from Modern Misconceptions*. Eugene: Cascade, 2014.

Houlden, J. L. *Paul's Letters from Prison: Philippians, Colossians, Philemon and Ephesians*. Baltimore: Penguin Books, 1970.

Howard, G. "The Head/Body Metaphors of Ephesians." *NTS* 20 (1973/74): 350–356.

Huber, W. "Toward an Ethics of Responsibility." *JR* 73, no. 4 (1993): 573–612.

Hubing, J. *Crucifixion and New Creation: The Strategic Purpose of Galatians 6:11–17.* LNTS 508. London: Bloomsbury, 2015.

Hughes, G. J. *Aristotle on Ethics.* London: Routledge, 2001.

Hui, A. W. D. "The Concept of the Holy Spirit in Ephesians and Its Relation to the Pneumatologies of Luke and Paul." PhD thesis, University of Aberdeen, 1992.

Hultgren, S. J. "2 Cor 6:14–7:1 and Rev 21:3–8: Evidence for the Ephesian Redaction of 2 Corinthians." *NTS* 49 (2003): 39–56.

Hyde, J. A. "Ephesians 4:17–24." *RevExp* 89 (1992): 403–407.

Idowu, E. B. *Olodumare: God in Yoruba Belief.* London: Longmans, 1962.

Irwin, T. *Plato's Ethics.* New York: Oxford University Press, 1995.

Jahn, J. *Muntu: African Culture and the Western World.* New York: Grove Press, 1961.

Janzen, D. "The Meaning of *PORNEIA* in Matthew 5.32 and 19.9: An Approach from the Study of Ancient Near Eastern Culture." *JSNT* 80 (2000): 66–80.

Jell-Bahlsen, S. *The Water Goddess in Igbo Cosmology.* Trenton: Africa World Press, 2008.

Jensen, J. "Does *PORNEIA* Mean Fornication? A Critique of Bruce Malina." *NovT* 20 (1978): 161–184.

Jewett, R. "Tenement Churches and Communal Meals in the Early Church: The Implications of a Form-Critical Analysis of 2 Thessalonians 3:10." *BR* 38 (1993): 23–43.

Johnson, E. E. "Ephesians." In *The Women's Bible Commentary*, edited by C. A. Newsom and S. H. Ringe, 576–580. London: SPCK, 1992.

Johnson, G. "OIKOUMENH and KOSMOS in the New Testament." *NTS* 10 (1963/64): 352–360.

Johnson, L. T. *The Gospel of Luke.* Collegeville: Liturgical, 1991.

Johnson, S. E. "Early Christianity in Asia Minor." *JBL* 77 (1958): 1–19.

Jonge, M. D. *Jewish Eschatology, Early Christian Christology and the Testaments of the Twelve Patriarchs: Collected Essays of Marinus De Jonge.* Leiden: Brill, 1991.

Joubert, S. J. "Managing the Household: Paul as *Paterfamilias* of the Christian Household Group in Corinth." In *Modelling Early Christianity: Social Scientific Studies of the New Testament in Its Context*, edited by P. F. Esler, 213–223. London: Routledge, 1995.

Kasemann, E. "Ephesians and Acts." In *Studies in Luke Acts*, edited by L. E. Keck and J. L. Martyn, 15–32. Philadelphia: Fortress, 1966.

———. *Leib und Leib Christi.* Tubingen: Mohr, 1933.

———. "Ministry and Community in the New Testament." In *Essays on New Testament Themes*, translated by W. J. Montague, edited by C. F. D. Moule et al., 85–88. London: SCM, 1964.

Keck, L. E., and J. L. Martyn. *Studies in Luke Acts.* Philadelphia: Fortress Press, 1966.

Keener, C. S. *Paul, Women and Wives: Marriage and Women's Ministry in the Letters of Paul.* Peabody: Hendrickson, 1992.

Kempthorne, R. "Incest and the Body of Christ: A Study of 1 Cor VI. 12–20." *NTS* 14 (1967/68): 568–574.

Kennedy, G. "'Truth' and 'Rhetoric' in the Pauline Epistles." In *The Bible as Rhetoric: Studies in Biblical Persuasion and Credibility*, edited by M. Warner, 195–202. London: Routledge, 1990.

Kent Jr., H. A. *Ephesians: The Glory of the Church*. Chicago: Moody, 1971.

Kerr, A. J. "Αρραβὼν" *JTS* 39 (1988): 92–97.

Khan, C. H. *Anaximander and the Origins of Greek Cosmology*. New York: Columbia University, 1964.

Kidd, G. "Moral Actions and Rules in Stoic Ethics." In *The Stoics*, edited by J. M. Rist, 247–258. Berkeley: University of California Press, 1978.

King, F. J. "Angels and Ancestors: A Basic Christology." *MS* 11, no. 1 (1994): 10–26.

Kittel, G., and G. Friedrich, eds. *Theological Dictionary of the New Testament*, translated by G. W. Bromiley. 10 Vols. Grand Rapids: Eerdmans, 1964–1976.

Kleinknecht, H. et al. *Wrath: Bible Key Words from Gerhard Kittle's Theologisches Worterbuch zum Neuen Testament*. London: Adam & Charles Black, 1964.

Knibb, M. A. *The Qumran Community*. Cambridge: Cambridge University Press, 1987.

Knibbe, D. "Via Sacra Ephesiaca – New Aspects of the Cult of Artemis Ephesia." In *Ephesos: Metropolis of Asia*. Valley Forge: Trinity Press International, 1995.

Koester, H. "GNWMAI DIAFOROI: The Origin and Nature of Diversification in the History of the Early Church." *HTR* 58 (1965): 279–318.

———. *History, Culture and Religion of Hellenistic Age*. New York: Walter De Gruyter, 1980.

Kombo, J. H. O. *Theological Models of the Doctrine of the Holy Spirit: The Trinity, Diversity and Theological Hermeneutics*. Carlisle: Langham Global Library, 2016.

Konstan, D. "To Hellēnikon Ethnos: Ethnicity and the Construction of Greek Identity." In *Ancient Perceptions of Greek Ethnicity*, edited by I. Malkin, 29–50. Cambridge: Harvard University, 2000.

Köstenberger, A. J. "What Does It Mean to Be Filled with The Holy Spirit? A Biblical Investigation." *JETS* 40, no. 2 (1997): 229–240.

Kraemer, R. S. "Ecstasy and Possession: The Attraction of Women to the Cult of Dionysius." *HTR* 72, nos. 1–2 (1979): 55–88.

———. *Women's Religions in the Greco-Roman World: A Sourcebook*. Oxford: Oxford University Press, 2004.

Kraut, R. *The Cambridge Companion to Plato*. Cambridge: Cambridge University Press, 1992.

Kreitzer, L. J. "Crude Language and Shameful Things Done in Secret (Ephesians 5.4, 12): Allusions to the Cult of Demeter/Cybele in Hierapolis?" *JSNT* 71 (1998): 51–77.

———. *The Epistle to the Ephesians*. Peterborough: Epworth, 1997.

———. *Hierapolis in the Heavens: Studies in the Letter to the Ephesians*. London: T&T Clark, 2007.

———. "The Plutonium of Hierapolis and the Descent of Christ into the 'Lowermost Parts of the Earth' (Ephesians 4:9)." *Bib* 79 (1998): 381–391.

Kroeger, R. C., and C. C. Kroeger. *I Suffer not a Woman: Rethinking 1 Timothy 2:11–15 in Light of Ancient Evidence.* Grand Rapids: Baker, 1997.

Kruse, C. *2 Corinthians.* Leicester, UK: Inter-Varsity Press, 1987.

Kuada, J., and Y. Chachah. *Ghana: Understanding the People and Their Culture.* Accra: Woeli Publishing, 1999.

Kudadjie, J. N. *Moral Renewal in Ghana: Ideals, Realities and Possibilities.* Accra: Asempa Publishers, 1995.

Kuhn, K. G. "Der Epheserbrief im Lichte der Qumrantexte." *NTS* 7 (1960/61): 334–346.

———. "The Epistle to the Ephesians in the Light of the Qumran Texts." In *Paul and Qumran: Studies in New Testament Exegesis,* edited by Jerome Murphy-O'Conner, 115–131. London: Geoffrey Chapman, 1968.

Kunhiyop, S. W. *African Christian Theology.* Nairobi: Hippo Books, 2012.

Ladd, G. E. *A Commentary on the Revelation of John.* Grand Rapids: Eerdmans, 1972.

———. *A Theology of the New Testament.* Grand Rapids: Eerdmans, 1993.

Lamberton, R. *Plutarch.* New Haven: Yale University Press, 2001.

Larbi, E. K. *Pentecostalism: The Eddies of Ghanaian Christianity.* Accra: CPCS, 2001.

Lash, C. J. A. "Where Do Devils Live? A Problem in the Textual Criticism of Ephesians 6:12." *VC* 30 (1976): 161–174.

Laub, F. *Die Begegnung des frühen Christentums mit der antiken Sklaverei.* Stuggart: Verlag Katholisches Bibelwerk, 1982.

Laukamm, S. "Das Sttenbild des Artemidor von Ephesus." *Ang* 3 (1930): 32–71.

Layton, R. A. "Recovering Origen's Pauline Exegesis: Exegesis and Eschatology in the Commentary on Ephesians." *JECS* 8, no. 3 (2000): 373–411.

Lee, J. Y. "Interpreting the Demonic Powers in Pauline Thought." *NovT* 12 (1970): 54–69.

Lemmer, R. "Rhetoric and Metaphor, and the Metaphysical in the Letter to the Ephesians." In *Rhetorical Criticism and the Bible.* JSNTSup 195, edited by S. E. Porter and D. L. Stamps, 459–478. London: Sheffield Academic, 2002.

Lenski, R. C. H. *The Interpretation of St. Paul's Letters to the Galatians, Ephesians and Philippians.* Minneapolis: Augsburg, 1937.

Leonhardt, J. *Jewish Worship in Philo of Alexandria.* TSAJ 84. Tübingen: Mohr Siebeck, 2001.

Leviant, C. *Masterpiece of Hebrew Literature.* Philadelphia: Jewish Publication Society, 2008.

Levine, L. I. *Judaism & Hellenism in Antiquity: Conflict or Confluent?* Seattle: University of Washington Press, 1998.

Liefield, W. L. "Women, Submission and Ministry in Corinthians." In *Women, Authority and the Bible,* edited by A. Mickelsen, 134–153. Downers Grove: InterVarsity Press, 1986.

Lieu, J. M. *Christian Identity in the Jewish and Greco-Roman World.* Oxford: Oxford University Press, 2004.

———. *Neither Jew Nor Greek: Constructing Early Christian Identity*. London: T&T Clark, 2002.

Lillie, W. "The Pauline House-Tables." *ExpTim* (1975): 179–183.

Lincoln, A. T. "The Church and Israel in Ephesians 2." *CBQ* 49 (1987): 605–624.

———. *Ephesians*. WBC 42. Dallas: Word Books, 1990.

———. "The Household Code and Wisdom Mode of Colossians." *JSNT* 74 (1999): 93–112.

———. "A Re-Examination of 'the Heavenlies' in Ephesians." *NTS* 19 (1972/73): 468–483.

———. "'Stand Therefore . . .': Ephesians 6:10–20 as *Preroratio*." *BibInt* 3 (1995): 99–114.

———. "The Use of the OT in Ephesians." *JSNT* 14 (1982): 16–57.

Lincoln, A. T., and A. J. M. Wedderburn. *The Theology of the Later Pauline Letters*. NTT. Cambridge: Cambridge University Press, 1993.

Lindemann, A. *Die Aufhebung der Zeit. Geschichtsverstandnis und Eschatologie im Epheserbrief*. Gutersloh: Mohn, 1975.

Lindesmith, A. R., and A. L. Strauss. *Social Psychology: Third Edition*. New York: Holt, Rinehart & Winston Inc., 1968.

Lintott, A. "The Slave and the Freedman or Woman in the Family." *CQ* 52, no. 2 (2002): 560–565.

Lohmeyer, E. *Die Briefe an die Philipper, and die Kolosser und an Philemon*. Göttingen: Vandenhoeck & Ruprecht, 1930.

Lona, H. E. *Die Eschatologie im Epheser und Kolosserbrief*. Wurzburg: Echter Verlag, 1984.

Long, A. A. *Cambridge Companion to Early Greek Philosophy*. Cambridge: Cambridge University Press, 1999.

Longman III, T., and D. G. Reid. *God as a Warrior*. Carlisle: Paternoster, 1995.

Lotz, J. P. "The *Homonoia* Coins of Asia Minor and Ephesians 1:21." *TynBul* 50, no. 2 (1999): 173–188.

Louw, J. P., and E. A. Nida. *Greek-English Lexicon of the New Testament Based on Semantic Domains*. New York: United Bible Society, 1989.

Luce, J. V. *Introduction to Greek Philosophy*. London: Thames & Hudson, 1992.

Lührmann, D. "Neutestamentliche Haustafeln und amtike Ökonomie." *NTS* 27 (1980): 83–97.

———. "Wo man nicht mehr Sklave oder Freier ist. Überlegungen zur Struktur frühchristlicher Gemeinden." *WD* 13 (1975): 53–83.

MacDonald, M. Y. "Citizens of Heaven and Earth: Asceticism and Social Integration in Colossians and Ephesians." In *Asceticism in the New Testament*, edited by L. E. Vaage and V. L. Wimbush, 269–298. London: Routledge, 1999.

———. *Colossians and Ephesians*. SP. Collegeville: Liturgical Press, 2000.

————. *The Pauline Churches: A Socio-Historical Study of Institutionalization in the Pauline and Deutero-Pauline Writings.* SNTSMS 60. Cambridge: Cambridge University Press, 1988.

————. "The Politics of Identity in Ephesians." *JSNT* 26, no. 4 (2004): 419–444.

MacDonald, M., and H. Moxnes. "Domestic Space and Families in Early Christianity: Editors' Introduction." *JSNT* 27, no. 1 (2004): 3–6.

MacDowell, M. *The Law in Classical Athens.* London: Thames & Hudson, 1978.

MacGregor, G. H. C. "The Concept of the Wrath of God in the New Testament." *NTS* 7 (1961): 101–109.

Magasa, L. *African Religion: The Moral Traditions of Abundant Life.* New York: Orbis, 1998.

Malherbe, A. J. "Antisthenes and Odysseus, and Paul at War." *HTR* 76, no. 2 (1983): 143–173.

————. *Moral Exhortation: Greco-Roman Sourcebook.* Philadelphia: Westminster Press, 1986.

————. *Paul and the Popular Philosophers.* Minneapolis: Fortress, 1989.

Malina, B. "Does *PORNEIA* Mean Fornication?" *NovT* 14 (1972): 10–17.

Malkin, I. *Ancient Perceptions of Greek Ethnicity.* Cambridge, MA: Harvard University Press, 2001.

————. "Introduction." In *Ancient Perceptions of Greek Ethnicity*, edited by Irad Malkin, 1–28. Cambridge MA: Harvard University Press, 2001.

Marshall, I. H. *Acts: Introduction and Commentary.* Leicester: Inter-Varsity Press, 1980.

————. "Mutual Love and Submission in Marriage: Colossians 3:18–19 and Ephesians 5:21–33." In *Discovering Biblical Equality: Complimentarily Without Hierarchy*, edited by R. W. Pierce and R. M. Groothuis, 186–204. Leicester: Inter-Varsity Press, 2004.

————. *The Origins of New Testament Christology.* Downers Grove: InterVarsity Press, 1976.

Martin, D. B. "Slave Families and Slaves in Families." In *Early Christian Families in Context: An Interdisciplinary Dialogue*, edited by D. L. Balch and C. Osiek, 207–230. Grand Rapids: Eerdmans, 2003.

Martin, R. P. *Ephesians, Colossians, and Philemon.* Louisville: John Knox, 1991.

————. "Reconciliation and Unity in Ephesians." *RevExp* 93 (1996): 203–235.

Matera, F. J. *New Testament Christology.* Louisville: Westminster John Knox, 1999.

————. *New Testament Ethics: The Legacies of Jesus and Paul.* Louisville: Westminster John Knox, 1996.

Marxsen, W. *New Testament Foundations for Christian Ethics.* Translated by O. C. Dean. Edinburgh: T&T Clark, 1993.

Mbiti, J. S. *African Religions and Philosophy.* Portsmouth: Heinemann, 1989.

————. *African Religions and Philosophy.* Oxford: Heinemann, 1969.

————. *Concepts of God in Africa.* London: SPCK, 1979.

McCown, C. C. "The Ephesia Grammata in Popular Belief." *Transactions of the American Philological Association* 54 (1923): 120–130.

McGlashan, A. R. "Ephesians 1.23." *ExpTim* 76 (1964/65): 132–133.

McGlone, L. "Genesis 2:18–24; Ephesians 5:21–6:9." *RevExp* 86 (1989): 243–247.

McGuire, M. B. *Religion: The Social Context*, 4th ed. Belmont: Wadsworth Publishing, 1997.

McHugh, J. "A Reconsideration of Ephesians 1:10b in the Light of Irenaeus." In *Paul and Paulinism: Essays in Honour of C. K. Barrett*, edited by M. D. Hooker and S. G. Wilson, 302–309. London: SPCK, 1982.

McKay, K. L. "Aspect in Imperatival Constructions in New Testament Greek." *NovT* 27, no. 3 (1987): 201–226.

McMahan, C. "The Wall Is Gone." *RevExp* 93 (1996): 261–269.

Meeks, W. A. *The First Urban Christians: The Social World of the Apostle Paul.* New Haven: Yale University Press, 1983.

———. *The Moral World of the Early Christians.* Philadelphia: Westminster Press, 1986.

———. *The Origin of Christian Morality: The First Two Centuries.* New Haven: Yale University Press, 1993.

———. "Understanding Early Christian Ethics." *JBL* 105, no. 1 (1986): 3–11.

Meggit, J. J. *Paul, Poverty and Survival.* Edinburgh: T&T Clark, 1998.

Meinardus, O. *St. Paul in Ephesus and the Cities of Galatia and Cyprus.* Athens: Lycabettus, 1979.

Melbourne, B. L. "Ephesians 2:13–16: Are the Barriers Broken Down?" *JRT* 57/58, no. 2 (2001–2005): 107–119.

Merklein, H. *Christus und die Kirche: Die Theologische Grundstruktur des Epheserbriefes nach Eph 2:11–18.* SBS 66. Stuttgart: KBW Verlag, 1973.

Merz, A. "Why Did the Pure Bride of Christ (2 Cor 11:2) Become a Wedded Wife (Eph 5:22–33)? Theses about the Intertextual Transformation of an Ecclesiological Metaphor." *JSNT* 79 (2000): 131–147.

Metzger, B. M. *The New Testament: Its Background, Growth, and Content.* Nashville: Abingdon, 1965.

———. "St. Paul and the Magicians." *PSB* 38 (1944): 27.

———. *Textual Commentary on the Greek New Testament.* London: United Bible Societies, 1975.

Mickelsen, A. *Women, Authority and the Bible.* Downers Grove: InterVarsity Press, 1986.

Mickelsen, B., and A. Mickelsen. "The 'Head' of the Epistles." *CT* 25, no. 4 (1981): 20–24.

———. "What Does Kephale Mean in the New Testament." In *Women, Authority and the Bible*, edited by A. Mickelsen, 97–110. Downers Grove: InterVarsity Press, 1986.

Minear, P. S. "Yes or No: The Demand for Honesty in the Early Church." *NovT* 13 (1971): 1–13.

Mitton, C. L. *Ephesians.* NCBC. Grand Rapids: Eerdmans, 1973.

Mitton, L. *Ephesians*. Grand Rapids: Eerdmans, 1989.

———. *The Epistle to the Ephesians*. Oxford: Clarendon, 1951.

Montague, G. T. *The Holy Spirit: Growth of a Biblical Tradition*. New York: Paulist, 1970.

Morford, M. *The Roman Philosophers: From the Time of Cato the Censor to the Death of Marcus Aurelius*. London: Routledge, 2002.

Moritz, T. *A Profound Mystery: The Use of the Old Testament in Ephesians*. Leiden: Brill, 1996.

———. "The Use of Israel's Scriptures in Ephesians." *TynBul* 46, no. 2 (1995): 393–396.

———. "Summing Up All Things: Religious Pluralism and Universalism in Ephesians." In *One God, One Lord: Christianity in a World of Religious Pluralism*, second edition, edited by A. D. Clarke and B. W. Winter, 88–111. Grand Rapids: Baker, 1992.

Morphew, D. *The Mission of the Kingdom: The Theology of Luke-Acts*. Cape Town: Vineyard International, 2011.

Mott, S. C. "Greek Ethics and Christian Conversion: The Philonic Background of Titus II 10–14 and III 3–7." *NovT* 20 (1978): 22–48.

Motyer, S. "The Relationship between Paul's Gospel of 'All One in Christ' (Galatians 3:28) and the Household Codes." *VE* 19 (1989): 33–48.

Moule, C. F. D. *The Origins of Christology*. Cambridge: Cambridge University Press, 1977.

Moule, H. C. G. *Ephesian Studies*. Fort Washington: Christian Literature Crusade, 1937.

———. *Ephesian Studies*. London: Hodder & Stoughton, 1900.

Mouton, E. *Reading a New Testament Document Ethically*. Atlanta: SBL, 2002.

———. "Reading Ephesians Ethically: Criteria Towards a Renewed Identity Awareness?" *Neot* 28, no. 2 (1994): 359–377.

Moxons, H. *Constructing Early Church Families: Family as Social Reality and Metaphor*. London: Routledge, 1997.

Muddiman, J. *The Letter to the Ephesians*. London: Continuum T&T Clark, 2001.

Müller, K. "Die Haustafel des Kolosserbriefes und das antike Frauenthema. Eine kritische Ruckschau auf alte Ergebnisse." In *Die Frau im Urchristentum*, edited by G. Dautzenberg et al, 263–319. Freiburg: Herder, 1983.

Muller, R. A. *Dictionary of Latin and Greek Theological Terms*. Grand Rapids: Baker Books, 1985.

Munro, W. "Col III.18–IV.1 and Eph V.21–VI.9: Evidence of a Late Literary Strutum?" *NTS* 18 (1972): 434–447.

Murphy, E. *Handbook of Spiritual Warfare*. Nashville: Thomas Nelson, 1992.

Murphy, F. J. *Early Judaism: The Exile to the Time of Jesus*. Peabody: Hendrickson, 2002.

Nash, R. H. *The Gospel and the Greeks: Did the New Testament Borrow Pagan Thoughts?* Philipsburg: P&R Publishing, 2003.

Nathan, G. S. *The Family in Late Antiquity: The Rise of Christianity and the Endurance of Tradition*. London: Routledge, 2000.

Neufeld, T. R .Y. *Ephesians*. Waterloo: Herald, 2002.

Neimark, P. J. *The Way of the Orisa: Empowering Your Life Through the Ancient African Religion of Ifa*. New York: HarperCollins, 1993.

Neusner, J. et al. *The Social World of Formative Christianity and Judaism*. Philadelphia: Fortress, 1998.

Niehoff, M. R. *Philo on Jewish Identity and Culture*. TSAJ 86. Tübingen: Mohr Siebeck, 2001.

Nkansah-Kyeremateng, K. *Akan Heritage*. Accra: Sebewie Publishers, 1999.

Nobbs, A. "'Beloved Brothers' in the New Testament and Early Christian World." In *The New Testament in Its First Century Setting*, edited by P. J. Williams et al., 143–150. Grand Rapids: Eerdmans, 2004.

Nukunya, G. K. *Tradition and Change in Ghana: An Introduction to Sociology*. Accra: Ghana Universities Press, 2003.

O'Brien, P. T. "Ephesians 1: An Unusual Introduction to a New Testament Letter." *NTS* 25 (1979): 504–516.

———. *Gospel and Mission in the Writings of Paul*. Grand Rapids: Baker, 1993.

———. *The Letter to the Ephesians*. PNTC. Grand Rapids: Eerdmans, 1999.

———. "Principalities and Powers: Opponents of the Church." In *Biblical Interpretation and the Church: Text and Context*, edited by D. A. Carson, 110–150. Exeter: Paternoster, 1984.

Odeberg, H. *The View of the Universe in the Epistle to the Ephesians*. Lund: C. W. K. Gleerup, 1934.

O'Donovan, W. *Biblical Christianity in African Perspective*. Carlisle: Paternoster, 1995.

Ofori-Amankwah, E. H. *African Culture and Christianity*. Kumasi: KNUST, 2003.

Oladipo, C. O. *The Development of the Doctrine of the Holy Spirit in the Yoruba (African) Indigenous Christian Movement*. New York: Peter Lang, 1996.

Olupona, J. K. *City of 201 Gods: Ile-Ife in Time, Space, and the Imagination*. Berkeley: University of California Press, 2011.

O'Neil, J. C. "'The Work of Ministry' in Ephesians 4.12 and the New Testament." *ExpTim* 112 (2001): 336–340.

O'Neil, W. "No Longer Strangers (Ephesians 2:19): The Ethics of Migration." *Word & World* 29, no. 3 (2009), 227–233.

Opoku, K. A. *West African Traditional Religion*. Accra: FEP International, 1978.

Orobator, A. E. *Theology Brewed in African Pot*. New York: Orbis Books, 2008.

Osiek, C. "The Bride of Christ (Ephesians 5:22–33): A Problematic Wedding." *BTB* 32, no. 1 (2002): 29–39.

———. "The Family in Early Christianity: 'Family Values' Revisited." *CBQ* 58 (1996): 1–24.

———. "Female Slaves, *Porneia*, and the Limits of Obedience." In *Early Christian Families in Context: An Interdisciplinary Dialogue*, edited by D. L. Balch and C. Osiek, 255–274. Grand Rapids: Eerdmans, 2003.

Osiek, C., and D. L. Balch. *Families in the New Testament World: Households and House Churches*. Louisville: Westminster John Knox, 1997.

Oster, R. "The Ephesian Artemis as an Opponent of Early Christianity." *JAC* 19 (1976): 24–44.

Overfield, P. D. "Pleroma: A Study in Content and Context." *NTS* 25 (1979): 384–396.

Page, S. H. T. "Whose Ministry? A Re-Appraisal of Ephesians 4:12." *NovT* 47, no. 1 (2005): 26–46.

Palmer, T. *Christian Theology in an African Context*. Bukuru: African Christian Textbooks, 2015.

Park, D. M. "The Structure of Authority in Marriage: An Examination of *Hupotasso* and *Kephale* in Ephesians 5:21–33." *EvQ* 59, no. 2 (1987): 117–124.

Parry, R. and Partridge, C. *Universal Salvation?: The Current Debate*. Carlisle: Paternoster, 2003.

Patte, D. "Speech Act Theory and Biblical Exegesis." *Semeia* 41 (1988): 85–102.

Patzia, A. G. *Ephesians, Colossians, Philemon*. Peabody: Hendrickson, 1984.

Pennington, T. "All the World's a Stage: Understanding the Ultimate Purpose of Our Salvation (Eph 2:7)." *MSJ* 22, no. 1 (2011): 99–113.

Perdue, L. G. "The Death of the Sage and Moral Exhortation: From Ancient Near Eastern Instructions to Greco-Roman Paranaesis." *Semeia* 50 (1990): 81–109.

———. "The Social Character of Paraenesis and Paraenetic Literature." *Semeia* 50 (1990): 5–40.

Perkins, P. *Ephesians*. Nashville: Abingdon Press, 1997.

———. "God, Cosmos & Church Universal: The Theology of Ephesians." *SBLSP* (2000): 752–773.

Pierce, R. W., and R. M. Groothuis. *Discovering Biblical Equality: Complimentarily without Hierarchy*. Leicester: Inter-Varsity Press, 2004.

Pobee, J. *Toward an African Theology*. Nashville: Abingdon, 1979.

Pokorný, P. *Der Brief des Paulus an die Epheser*. Leipzig: Evangelische Verlagsanstalt, 1992.

———. *The Genesis of Christology: Foundations for a Theology of the New Testament*. Translated by M. Lefébure. Edinburgh: T&T Clark, 1987.

Pomeroy, S. B. *Families in Classical and Hellenistic Greece: Representations and Realities*. Oxford: Clarendon, 1997.

Pope, R. M. "Of the Heavenly Places." *ExpTim* 33 (1911–1912): 366.

———. "Studies in Pauline Vocabulary – Of Redeeming the Time." *ExpTim* 22 (1910/11): 365–368.

Price, S. *Religions of the Ancient Greeks*. Cambridge: Cambridge University Press, 1999.

Ramsay, W. M. *The Letters to the Seven Churches*. Edited by M. W. Wilson. Peabody: Hendrickson, 1994.

Ratzinger, J. *Jesus of Nazareth: From the Baptism in the Jordan to the Transfiguration*. San Francisco: Ignatius, 2007.

Rawson, B. "The Roman Family in Recent Research." *BibInt* 11, no. 2 (2003): 119–138.

Rawson, B., and P. Weaver. *The Roman Family in Italy: Status, Sentiment, Space*. Oxford: Clarendon, 1999.

Rea, J. *The Holy Spirit in the Bible: All Major Passages about the Spirit.* Lake Mary, FL: Creation House, 1990.

Reardon, B. P. *Collected Ancient Greek Novels.* Berkeley: University of California Press, 1989.

Reesor, M. E. "The Stoic Wise Man." In *Proceedings of the Boston Area Colloquium in Ancient Philosophy Vol. 5,* edited by J. J. Cleary and D. C. Shartin, 107–123. Lanham: University Press of America, 1989.

Reid, D. G. "Vices and Virtues." *DLNTD on CD-ROM,* 2001.

Rengstorf, K.H. "Die neutestamentlichen Mahnungen an die Frau, sich dem Manne unterzuordnen." In *Verbum Dei Manet in Aeternum: Eine Festschrift für Prof. D. Otto Schmitz zu seinem siebzigsten Geburtstag am 16. Juni 1953.* Edited by W. Foerster, 131–145. Witten: Luther-Verlag, 1953.

Resner Jr. A. "Maintain the Broken Wall: Ephesians 2:14–18." *ResQ* 2 (1990): 121–125.

Ridderbos, H. *Paul: An Outline of His Theology.* London: SPCK, 1977.

Riensche, R. H. "Exegesis of Ephesians 2:1–7." *LQ* 2, no. 1 (1950): 70–74.

Rist, J. M. *The Stoics.* Berkeley: University of California Press, 1978.

Roak, C. M. "Interpreting Ephesians 4–6: God's People in Walk Worthy of His Calling." *SwJT* 39, no. 1 (1996): 32–42.

Roberts, M. D. *Ephesians: The Story of God Bible Commentary.* Grand Rapids: Zondervan, 2016.

Robinson, J. A. "On πώρωσις and πήρωσις." In *St. Paul's Epistle to the Ephesians.* London: James Clarke & Co., 1909.

———. *St. Paul's Epistle to the Ephesians.* London: Macmillan, 1903.

Rodger, P. R. "The Allusions to Genesis 2:23 at Ephesians 5:30." *JTS* 41 (1990): 92–94.

Rogers Jr., C. L. "The Dionysian Background of Ephesians 5:18." *BSac* 136, no. 543 (1979): 249–257.

Roitta, R. *Behaving as a Christ-Believer: A Cognitive Perspective on Identity and Behavior Norms in Ephesians.* Linköping: Linköping University, 2009.

Roose, H. "Die Hierarchisierung der Leib-Metaphor im Kolosser- und Epheserbrief als Paulinisierung: Ein Beitrag zur Rezeption Paulinischer Tradition in Pseudo-Paulinischen Briefen." *NovT* 47, no. 2 (2005): 117–141.

Rosner, B. *Understanding Paul's Ethics: Twentieth Century Approaches.* Grand Rapids: Eerdmans, 1995.

Russell, D. A. *Plutarch.* London: Duckworth, 2001.

Sæbø, M. *Hebrew Bible/Old Testament: The History of Interpretation Vol. 1.* Göttingen: Vandenhoeck & Ruprecht, 1996.

Saller, R. "Roman Kinship: Structure and Sentiment." In *The Roman Family in Italy: Status, Sentiment, Space,* edited by B. Rawson and P. Weaver, 7–34. Oxford: Clarendon, 1999.

———. "Women, Slaves, and the Economy of the Roman Household." In *Early Christian Families in Context: An Interdisciplinary Dialogue,* edited by David L. Balch and Carolyn Osiek, 185–204. Grand Rapids: Eerdmans, 2003.

Sampley, J. P. *And the Two Shall Become One Flesh: A Study of Traditions in Ephesians 5:21–33*. Cambridge: CUP, 1971.

———. "Scripture and Tradition in the Community as Seen in Ephesians 4:25ff." *ST* 2 (1972): 101–109.

Sampley, J. P. et al. *Ephesians, Colossians, 2 Thessalonians, the Pastoral Epistles*. Philadelphia: Fortress, 1971.

Samuel, G. *A Short Introduction to Judging and to Legal Reasoning*. Cheltenham: Edward Elgar, 2016.

Sanders, E. P. *Judaism: Practice and Belief 63BCE – 66CE*. London: SCM, 1992.

Sanders, J. T. *Ethics in the New Testament: Change and Development*. London: SCM, 1975.

Sandmel, S. *Philo of Alexandria: An Introduction*. New York: Oxford University Press, 1979.

Santer, M. "The Text of Ephesians 1." *NTS* 15 (1969): 247–248.

Sarpong, P. *Girls' Nubility Rites in Ashanti*. Accra: Ghana Publishing, 1977.

Sarpong, P. K. *Odd Customs: Stereotypes and Prejudices*. Accra: Sub-Saharan Publishers, 2012.

Sasse. "κόσμέω, κοσμος, etc." *TDNT* 30 (1968): 867–898.

Schäfer, P. "Magic and Religion in Ancient Judaism." In *Envisioning Magic: A Princeton Seminar and Symposium*, edited by P. Schäfer and H. G. Kippenberg, 19–43. Leiden: Brill, 1997.

Scharffenorth, G., and K. Thraede. *Freunde 'in Christus warden . . .' Die Beziehung von Mann und Frau als Frage an Theologie und Kirche*. Gelnhausen: Burckhardthaus; Stein/Mfr: Laertare, 1977.

Schauber, A. "Women and Witchcraft Allegations in Northern Ghana: Human Rights Education Between Conflict and Consensus." In *Ethnicity, Conflicts and Consensus in Ghana*, edited by S. Tonah, 116–148. Accra: Woeli Press, 2007.

Schlier, H. *Der Brief an die Epheser: Ein Kommentar*. Dusseldorf: Patmos, 1971.

———. *Principalities and Powers in the New Testament*. London: Burns & Oates, 1961.

Schnackenburg, R. *Ephesians*. Translated by Helen Heron. Edinburgh: T&T Clark, 1991.

Schrage, W. "Zur Ethik der neutestamentliche Haustafeln." *NTS* 21 (1974): 1–22.

Schroeder, D. "Die Haustafeln des Neuen Testaments. Ihre Herkunft und ihr theologischer Sinn." D. Theol. diss. Hamburg Universität, 1959.

Schultz, N. "St. Paul Describes the Spirit as Arrabon. Would St. Luke and St. John have agreed?" *LTJ* 11 (1977): 112–121.

Schweitzer, E. *The Letter to the Colossians*. Translated by Andrew Chester. London: SPCK, 1976.

Scroggs, R. "The Earliest Christian Communities as Sectarian Movements." In *Social-Scientific Approaches to New Testament Interpretation*, edited by D. G. Horrell, 69–92. Edinburgh: T&T Clark, 1999.

Seale, D. "Ephesians 6.12: Struggling Against the Rulers, Against the Authorities." *Evang* 14 (1996): 68–71.

Sedgwick, W. B. "Covetousness and the Sensual Sins in the New Testament." *ExpTim* 36 (1924/25): 478–479.

Segal, F. "Hellenistic Magic: Some Questions of Definition." In *Studies in Gnosticism and Hellenistic Religions*. Leiden: Brill, 1981.

Sellin, G. "Die Paränese des Epheserbriefes." In *Gemeinschaft am Evangelium. Festschrift für Wiard Popkes zum 60*, edited by E. Brandt, P. S. Fiddes, and J. Molthagen, 281–300. Leipzig: EVA, 1996.

Setiloane, G. M. *The Image of God among the Sotho-Tswana*. Rotterdam: A. A. Balkema, 1976.

Shepard, J. W. *The Life and Letters of Paul*. Grand Rapids: Eerdmans, 1950.

Sherman, N. *Aristotle's Ethics: Critical Essays*. Lantham: Rowman & Littlefield, 1999.

———. *Making a Moral Necessity of Virtue: Aristotle and Kant on Virtue*. Cambridge: Cambridge University Press, 1997.

Shkul, M. *Reading Ephesians: Exploring Social Entrepreneurship in the Text*. LNTS 408. London: T&T Clark, 2009.

Simmons, P. D. "The Grace of God and the Life of the Church: Ephesians 2." *RevExp* (1976): 495–506.

Simpson, E. K., and F. F. Bruce. *The Epistles to the Ephesians and the Colossians*. Grand Rapids: Eerdmans, 1975.

Singer, S. *The Authorized Daily Prayer Book of the United Hebrew Congregations of the British Commonwealth of Nations*, 2nd rev. ed. London: Eyre & Spottiswoode, 1962.

Smalley, S. S. "The Eschatology of Ephesians." *EvQ* 28 (1956): 152–157.

Smillie, G. R. "Ephesians 6:19–20 – A Mystery for the Sake of which the Apostle Is an Ambassador in Chains." *TJ* 18, no. 2 (1997): 199–222.

Smith, D. C. "Cultic Language in Ephesians 2:19-22: A Test Case." *ResQ* 31, no. 4 (1989): 207–218.

Smith, G. V. "Paul's Use of Psalm 68.18 in Ephesians 4.8." *JETS* 18 (1975): 181–189.

Smith, J. Z. "The Garments of Shame." *HR* 5 (1965): 217–238.

Smith, M. *Jesus the Magician: Charlatan or Son of God?* San Francisco: Harper & Row, 1978.

Snodgrass, K. *Ephesians: The NIV Application Commentary*. Grand Rapids: Zondervan, 1996.

Spicq, C. *Theological Lexicon of the New Testament*. Translated and edited by J. D. Ernest, 3 Vols. Peabody: Hendrickson, 1994.

Spieth, J. *The Ewe People: A Study of the Ewe People in German Togo*. Legon: Sub-Saharan Publishers, 2011.

Stagg, F. "The Abused Aorist." *JBL* 91 (1972): 222–231.

———. "The Domestic Code and Final Appeal: Ephesians 5:21–6:24." *RevExp* 76 (1979): 541–552.

———. *New Testament Theology*. Nashville: Broadman, 1962.

Standhartinger, A. "The Origin and Intention of the Household Code in the Letter to the Colossians." *JSNT* 79 (2000): 117–130.

Steel, C. *Reading Cicero: Genre and Performance in Late Republican Roman.* London: Duckworth, 2005.

Stephens, W. H. *The New Testament World Pictures.* Nashville: Broadman, 1987.

Stott, J. W. R. *God's New Society: The Message of Ephesians.* Leicester, UK: Inter-Varsity Press, 1979.

Strelan, R. *Paul, Artemis and the Jews in Ephesus.* Berlin: Walter De Gruyter, 1996.

Stronstad, R. *The Charismatic Theology of St. Luke.* Peabody: Hendrickson, 1984.

Suggs, M. J. "The Christian Two Ways Tradition: Its Antiquity, Form, and Function." In *Studies in New Testament and Early Christian Literature*, edited by D. E. Aune, 60–74. Leiden: Brill, 1972.

Swete, H. B. *The Apocalypse of St. John.* New York: Macmillan, 1907.

Tabbernee, W. *Early Christianity in Contexts: An Exploration across Cultures and Continents.* Grand Rapids: Baker, 2014.

Talbert, C. H. *Perspectives on First Peter.* Macon: Mercer University Press, 1986.

Tanzer, S. J. "Ephesians." In *Searching the Scriptures Volume Two: A Feminist Commentary*, edited by E. S. Fiorenza, 325–348. London: SCM Press, 1995.

Taylor, C. C. W. "Politics." *The Cambridge Companion to Aristotle*, edited by J. Barnes. Cambridge: Cambridge University Press, 1995.

Taylor, M. S. *Anti-Judaism and Early Christian Identity: A Critique of the Scholarly Consensus.* Leiden: Brill, 1995.

Taylor Jr., W. F., and J. H. P. Reumann. *Ephesians and Colossians.* Minneapolis: Augsburg, 1985.

Tenney, M. C. *New Testament Times.* London: Inter-Varsity Press, 1965.

Thielman, F. *Ephesians.* Grand Rapids: Baker Academic, 2010.

Thiselton, A. C. *The Holy Spirit: In Biblical Teaching through the Centuries and Today.* Grand Rapids: Eerdmans, 2013.

Thomas, J. "Formgesetze des Begriffs-Katalogs im N.T." *TZ* 24 (1968): 15–28.

Thompson, G. H. P. *The Letters of Paul to the Ephesians, to the Colossians and to Philemon.* Cambridge: Cambridge University Press, 1967.

Thraede, K. "Ärger mit der Freiheit. Die Bedeutung von Frauen in Theorie und Praxis der alten Kirche." In *Freunde 'in Christus warden . . .' Die Beziehung von Mann und Frau als Frage an Theologie und Kirche*, edited by G. Scharffenorth and K. Thraede, 131–182. Gelnhausen: Burckhardthaus; Stein/Mfr.: Laertare, 1977.

———."Zum historischen Hintergrund der Haustafeln des NT." In *Pietas: Festschrift für Bernhard Kötting*, edited by E. Dassmann and K. S. Frank, 359–368. Münster: Aschendorffsche Verlagsbuchhandlung, 1980.

Tienou, T. *The Theological Task of the Church in Africa: Theological Perspectives in Africa.* Achimota: Africa Christian Press, 1990.

Towner, P. H. "Mission Practice and Theology under Construction." In *Witness and Gospel: The Theology of Acts*, edited by I. H. Marshall and D. Peterson, 417–436. Grand Rapids: Eerdmans, 1998.

Trebilco, P. R. *Jewish Communities in Asia Minor.* Cambridge: Cambridge University Press, 1991.

Trenchard, W. C. *The Student's Complete Guide to the Greek New Testament.* Grand Rapids: Zondervan, 1992.

Trümper, M. "Material and Social Environment of Greco-Roman Households in the East: The Case of Hellenistic Delos." In *Early Christian Families in Context: An Interdisciplinary Dialogue*, edited by D. L. Balch and C. Osiek, 19–43. Grand Rapids: Eerdmans, 2003.

Tutu, D. "Whither African Theology." In *Christianity in Independent Africa*, edited by E. Faschole-Luke, R. Gray and A. Hastings, 364–369. London: Rex Collings, 1978.

Umbach, C. "On the Notion of Contrast in Information Structure and Discourse Structure." *JS* 21, no. 2 (2004): 155–175.

Vaage, L. E., and V. L. Wimbush. *Asceticism in the New Testament.* London: Routledge, 1999.

van der Horst, P. W. "Is Wittiness UnChristian? A Note on Eutrapelia in Ephesians 5:4." In *Miscellenea Neotestamentica Vol. 2*, edited by T. Baarda and W. C. van Unnik, 163–177. Leiden: Brill, 1978.

———. "Pseudo-Phocylides: A New Translation and Introduction." In *The Old Testament Pseudepigrapha Vol. 2*, edited by J. H. Charlesworth, 656–573. Garden City: Doubleday, 1985.

———. *The Sentences of Pseudo-Phocylides with Introduction and Commentary.* SVTP 4. Leiden: Brill, 1978.

van Henten, J. W., and A. Brenner. *Families and Family Relations as Represented in Early Judaisms and Early Christianities: Text and Fictions.* Leiden: Deo Publishing, 2000.

van Kooten, G. H. *Cosmic Christology in Paul and the Pauline School: Colossians and Ephesians in the Context of Greco-Roman Cosmology, with a New Synopsis of the Greek Texts.* WUNT 2, no. 171. Tübingen: Mohr Siebeck, 2003.

Vawter, B. "The Divorce Clause of Mt 5:32 and 19:9." *CBQ* 16 (1954): 155–167.

Verhey, A. *The Great Reversal: Ethics and the New Testament.* Grand Rapids: Eerdmans, 1984.

Verner, D. C. *The Household of God: The Social World of the Pastoral Epistles.* SBLDS 71. Chico: Scholars, 1983.

Vogt, P. T. *Interpreting the Pentateuch: An Exegetical Handbook.* Grand Rapids: Kregel, 2009.

Vögtle, A. *Die Tugend- und Lasterkataloge im Neuen Testament.* NTAbh, 16/4-5. Münster: Aschendorff, 1936.

von Rad, G. *Old Testament Theology Vol. 2.* Translated by D. M. G. Stalker. New York: Harper & Row, 1965.

Vorster, J. M. "A Case for a Transforming Christology in South Africa." *JRT* 7 (2013): 310–326.

wa Gatumu, K. *The Pauline Concept of Supernatural Powers: A Reading for the African Worldview.* Milton Keynes: Paternoster, 2008.

Wall, R. W. "Wifely Submission in the Context of Ephesians." *CSR* 17 (1988): 276–284.

Wallace, D. B. *Greek Grammar Beyond the Basics.* Grand Rapids: Zondervan, 1996.

———. "Orgi/zesqe in Ephesians 4:26: Command or Condition?" *CTR* (1989): 353–372.

Wallace-Hadrill, A. "*Domus* and *Insulae* in Rome: Families and Housefuls." In *Early Christian Families in Context: An Interdisciplinary Dialogue*, edited by D. L. Balch and C. Osiek, 3–18. Grand Rapids: Eerdmans, 2003.

———. *Houses and Societies in Pompeii and Herculaneum.* Princeton: Princeton University Press, 1994.

Walters, J. C. "Egyptian Religions in Ephesos." In *Ephesos: Metropolis of Asia.* Valley Forge: Trinity Press International, 1995.

Walvoord, J. F. *The Revelation of Jesus Christ.* Chicago: Moody, 1966.

Warrior, V. M. *Greek Religion: A Sourcebook.* Cambridge: Focus, 2009.

———. *Roman Religion.* New York, NY: Cambridge, 2006.

Watson, F. *Agape, Eros, Gender: Towards a Pauline Sexual Ethics.* Cambridge: Cambridge University Press, 2000.

Weber, M. *Economy and Society.* 3 Vols. New York: Bedminster Press, 1968.

Wedderburn, A. J. M. "Hellenistic Christian Traditions in Romans 6?" *NTS* 29 (1983): 337–355.

Weidinger, K. *Die Haustafeln: Ein Stuck urchristlicher Paraenese.* Leipzig: J. C. Heinrich, 1928.

Weima, J. A. D. *Paul the Ancient Letter Writer: An Introduction to Epistolary Analysis.* Grand Rapids: Baker Academic, 2016.

Wenham, D. *Paul: Follower of Jesus or Founder of Christianity?* Grand Rapids: Eerdmans, 1995.

Wessels, F. "Exegesis and Proclamation: Ephesians 5:21–33 'Wives, be subject to your husbands . . . husbands love your wives . . . .'" *JTSA* 1, no. 67 (1989): 67–76.

Westermann, W. L. *The Slave Systems of Greek and Roman Antiquity.* Philadelphia: American Philosophical Society, 1955.

Whiston, W. "Introduction." In *The Works of Josephus.* Grand Rapids: Hendrickson, 1987.

Whiteley, D. E. H. "Christology." In *Studies in Ephesians*, edited by F. L. Cross, 329–343. London: A. R. Mowbray & Co., 1956.

Wibbing, S. *Die Tugend und Lasterkataloge im Neuen Testament.* BZNW 25. Berlin: Töpelmann, 1959.

Wicker, K. O. "First Century Marriage Ethics: A Comparative Study of the Household Codes and Plutarch's Conjugal Precepts." In *No Famine in the Land: Studies in Honour of John L. McKenzie*, edited by J. W. Flanagan and A. W. Robinson, 141–153. Missoula: Scholars Press, 1975.

Wild, R. A. "Be Imitators of God: Discipleship in the Letter to the Ephesians." In *Discipleship in the New Testament*, edited by F. F. Segovia, 127–143. Philadelphia: Fortress, 1985.

———. "The Warrior and the Prisoner: Some Reflections on Ephesians 6:10–20." *CBQ* 46 (1984): 284–298.

Williams, P. J. et al. *The New Testament in Its First Century Setting*. Grand Rapids: Eerdmans, 2004.

Williamson, P. S. *Ephesians*. Grand Rapids: Baker Academic, 2009.

Williamson, R. *Jews in the Hellenistic World: Philo*. Cambridge: Cambridge University Press, 1989.

Wilson, M. R. *Exploring Our Hebraic Heritage: A Christian Theology of Roots and Renewal*. Grand Rapids: Eerdmans, 2014.

Wink, W. *Naming the Powers: Language of Power in the New Testament*. Philadelphia: Fortress, 1984.

Winter, B. W. *Roman Wives, Roman Widows: The Appearance of New Women and the Pauline Communities*. Grand Rapids: Eerdmans, 2003.

Witherington, B. *The Acts of the Apostles: A Socio-Rhetorical Commentary*. Grand Rapids: Eerdmans, 1998.

———. "Mathew 5:32 and 19:9 – Exception or Exceptional Situation?" *NTS* 31 (1985): 571–576.

Woode, S. N. *Values, Standards and Practice in Ghanaian Organizational Life*. Accra: Asempa Publishers, 1997.

Woodward, K. *Questioning Identity: Gender, Class, Nation*. London: Routledge, 2000.

Wright, N. T. *The New Testament and the People of God*. London: SPCK, 1992.

Yamauchi E. M., and M. R. Wilson. *Dictionary of Daily Life in Biblical & Post Biblical Antiquity Vol. 1*. Peabody: Hendrickson, 2014.

Yarbrough, O. L. *Not Like the Gentiles: Marriage Rules in the Letters of Paul*. SBLDS 80. Atlanta: Scholars, 1985.

Yates, R. "A Re-examination of Ephesians 1." *ExpTim* 83 (1971/72): 146–151.

Yee, T. N. *Jews, Gentiles and Ethnic Reconciliation: Paul's Jewish Identity and Ephesians*. SNTSMS 130; Cambridge: Cambridge University Press, 2005.

Young, R. A. *Intermediate New Testament Greek: A Linguistic and Exegetical Approach*. Nashville: Broadman & Holman, 1994.

Zetterholm, M. *The Formation of Christianity in Antioch: A Social-Scientific Approach to the Separation Between Judaism and Christianity*. London: Routledge, 2003.

# Index of Names

**A**

Abbot, T. K.  97
Abotsie, C.  186
Abraham  60
Adams, E.  114
Adewuya, J. A.  210
Apollonius of Tyana  47
Aristobulus  69
Aristotle  24, 153, 154
Armstrong, A. H.  24
Arnold, C. E.  8, 11, 12, 97, 120
Asamoah-Gyadu, J. K.  179, 191, 199
Assimeng, M.  165, 172
Aune, D. E.  46
Aye-Addo, C. S.  195, 196

**B**

Balla, P.  44
Bannerman-Richter, G.  182
Barclay, J. M. G.  58
Bar-Jesus  76
Bates, M.  155
Beasley-Murray, G. R.  41
Bediako, K.  167, 185, 190, 194
Benoit, P.  8
Berkhof, H.  6, 7
Block, D. L.  72
Borgen, P.  75
Botchway, Francis J.  188
Brempong, A.  170
Brinks, C. L.  33
Bruce, F. F.  75
Bultmann, R.  7
Burton, D. W.  123
Byron, J.  145

**C**

Caird, G. B.  40
Caragounis, C. C.  107
Carr, W.  7, 90, 150
Carson, D. A.  8
Cicero  21, 28, 29, 46
Cimok, F.  75
Clement of Alexandria  40, 48
Colville of Culross  122
Conner, R.  76
Conzelmann, H.  92
Cotter, W.  37
Crawford, S. W.  135
Cullmann, O.  7

**D**

Daneel, M. L.  197
Danquah, J. B.  166
Darko, D. K.  2, 82
De Jonge, M.  63
Deming, W.  141
Dibelius, M.  6
Dickie, M. W.  46
Dillion, J. T.  29
Dio Cassius  46
Dio Chrysostom  27, 30, 43
Dixon, S.  143
Dodd, C. H.  122
Domeris, W. R.  133
Duling, D. C.  37, 60
Dunn, J. D. G.  75
Dzathor, P. K.  188
Dzobo, N. K.  166

**E**

Ekem, J. D. K.  196
Elliott, John H.  51
Epictetus  22
Everling, O.  6

**F**

Falola, T.  171, 177

Fee, G. D.  83, 87
Ferguson, J.  135
Fergusson, E.  39
Fisher of Lambeth  122
Forbes, C.  9
Foulkes, F.  92
Frey, J.  135

**G**
Garrett, S. R.  60
Geller, M. J.  59
Glahn, S. L.  35
Glancy, J. A.  145
Gnilka, J.  138
Gombis, T. G.  10, 138, 146
Gosnell, P. W.  137
Green, J. B.  74
Greenlee, J. H.  139
Grenz, S. J.  27
Griffiths, J. G.  34
Gritz, S. H.  141
Grundmann, W.  6
Gudorf, M. E.  150
Guenther, A. R.  132

**H**
Hayman, P.  59
Hays, R. B.  108
Hengel, M.  51
Hierocles  131
Hubing, J.  14

**I**
Idowu, E. B.  167
Irwin, T.  135

**J**
Jahn, J.  176
Janzen, D.  132
Jell-Bahlsen, S.  170
Jensen, J.  133
Johnson, L. T.  71
Josephus  58, 60, 142, 155
Justin Martyr  77
Kasemann, E.  81

**K**
Kempthorne, R.  133
Kent, H. A.  89, 105
King, F. J.  194
Knibbe, D.  37
Koester, H.  38, 50
Kombo, J. H. O.  198
Kostenberger, A. J.  137
Kraemer, R. S.  33, 39
Kreitzer, L. J.  41, 84
Kruse, C.  158
Kuada, J.  172
Kudadjie, J. N.  185
Kunhiyop, S. W.  181, 185, 200

**L**
Ladd, G. E.  41
Larbi, E. K.  167, 177
Lee, J. Y.  8
Leviant, C.  63
Lincoln, A. T.  15, 16, 154
Livy (Roman historian)  39, 40
Longman, T.  10
Lotz, J. P.  91
Luce, J. V.  22

**M**
MacDonald, M.  85, 103
Magasa, L.  192
Malherbe, A. J.  22
Malina, B.  133
Marshall, I. H.  75
Martin, L. H.  27
Martin, R. P.  117
Matera, R. J.  85
Mbiti, John S.  169, 174, 179, 181, 183
McCown, C. C.  36
Meeks, W. A.  50
Meggit, J. J.  145
Meinardus, O.  48
Melbourne, B. L.  104
Metzger, B. M.  47, 136
Moses  60
Moule, H. C. G.  138, 154
Murphy, E.  97

Murphy, F. J.  70
Musonius Rufus  29, 130

**N**
Nathan, G. S.  146
Neimark, P. J.  174
Niehoff, M. R.  70
Nkansah-Kyeremateng, K.  169
Nukunya, G. K.  167, 174

**O**
O'Brien, P. T.  8, 152
Odeberg, H.  84
O'Donovan, W.  180, 199
Ofori-Amankwah, E. H.  174
Oladipo, C. O.  198
Olupona, J. K.  171
O'Neil, W.  104
Opoku, K. A.  168, 170, 172
Orobator, A. E.  198
Osiek, C.  141
Oster, R.  34

**P**
Palmer, T.  199
Patzia, A. G.  92
Pennington, T.  100
Perdue, L. G.  124
Philo  69, 130, 131, 134
Plato  22, 23, 43, 46, 124, 144
Pliny  47
Plutarch  24, 25, 26, 143
Pobee, J.  192, 193
Polybius  155
Pope, R. M.  84, 136
Price, S.  24

**R**
Ramsay, W. M.  36
Reardon, B. P.  35
Reesor, M. E.  135
Reid, D. G.  10
Reuben  63
Roberts, M. D.  85
Robinson, J. A.  122

Rodger, P. R.  143
Rogers, C. L.  39
Roitta, R.  2

**S**
Sampley, J. P.  130, 142, 143
Sanders, E. P.  58
Sarpong, P. K.  176, 187
Schauber, A.  177
Schlier, H.  6, 81, 138
Schnackenburg, R.  121, 158
Segal, A. F.  46
Seneca  28
Shepard, J. W.  127
Sherman, N.  131
Shkul, M.  2
Simeon  64
Simmons, P. D.  97
Smillie, G. R.  158
Smith, M.  76
Socrates  22, 28
Solomon  60, 62
Spieth, J.  166
Stagg, F.  141
Stephens, W. H.  33
Stott, J. W. R.  94
Strelan, R.  44, 122
Stronstad, R.  71
Suetonius  46

**T**
Tabbernee, W.  77
Tacitus  46
Taylor, W. F.  87
Tenney, M. C.  30
Thiselton, A. C.  69
Thomas Aquinas  4
Thompson, G. H. P.  91
Tiberius  46
Tienou, T.  189
Towner, P. H.  77
Trebilco, P. R.  58, 70
Tutu, D.  190
Vawter, B.  132

**V**

Vogt, P. T.  56
Vorster, J. M.  191

**W**

wa Gatumu, K.  163
Wallace, D. B.  89
Walters, J. C.  31
Warrior, V. M.  31
Watson, F.  141
Weima, J. A. D.  14
Wenham, D.  108, 142
Whiston, W.  58
Wild, R. A.  8, 124
Williamson, P. S.  88
Wilson, M. R.  53
Wink, W.  8, 95
Witherington, B.  47, 132
Woode, S. N.  188

**X**

Xenocrates  24
Xenophon  34

**Y**

Yamauchi, E. M.  68
Yarbrough, O. L.  141
Yee, T. N.  2
Young, R. A.  129

**Z**

Zetterholm, M.  53

# Index of Subjects


**A**

Abrahamic faiths  166
Accra  170, 200, 201
activities
   celestial  189
   terrestrial  189
adulterer  36
African Indigenous Churches (AIC's)
      199
African Pentecostal movement  190
African Traditional Religions  174, 199
Africa, sub-Saharan  165
age of this world  95, 98, 100
agnosticism  21, 216
Aion of Aions  95
Akans, the  169, 195, 196, 201, 208
alienation from God  19, 73, 94, 151
amulets  177, 179, 180
Anatolia  30, 58, 61, 149
Anatolian  75, 155
ancestors  32, 44, 180, 184, 198, 209
   African  173, 174
   deceased  173
   Jewish  194
   prayers to  45
   role of  168
   status  173
   veneration of  186
Ancient Near East  166
angelic creation  90
anger  124–128
   uncontrolled  127
angry shouting  128
antithesis
   foolish-wise  136, 141
   light-darkness  26
   then-now  103
   virtue-vice  129
Aphrodite  43, 49, 59

Apollo  32
apostles  105, 113
   ministry  75
armor of God  148, 149, 152, 157
Artemis  31–36, 49, 52, 61
   mother goddess  43
arts, astrological  50
Asase Efua "Mother Earth" (for the
      Fantes)  170
Asase Yaa "Mother Earth" (for the
      Akans)  170, 187
Asclepius  37, 38, 77
Asia Minor  20, 30, 36, 41, 60, 61, 77,
      78, 120, 137, 189, 200
Asmodeus  62
astrology  12, 21, 24, 41, 46, 50, 51, 58,
      60, 68, 70
atheism  24, 102
athletes  42, 46, 150, 188
Atrahasis  56

**B**

Bacchic rituals  39
Bacchus  39
baptism, of Jesus  72
Beelzebul  76
Beliar  8, 10, 57, 64–67, 127
beliefs
   African  166, 171
   astrological  8
bestiality  187
Bible translators  166, 167, 192
biblical interpretation  4, 20
biblical studies  164
blasphemy  128
blood sacrifice  175
breastplate  68, 153
breastplate of faith  64
bridal submission  142

**C**

*caliga* 154
Catholics 5
celestial 73
Chaldeans 28, 56
charms 42, 48, 179, 186
children of God 83, 115, 132, 149, 215
children's names 168
Chineke (Ibo) 168
Christ followers 192, 193, 198, 199
Christianity 201
Christianity in Africa 189, 210
Christian origins 19, 71, 72, 163
Christ Jesus 112, 208, 211, 216
    as ancestor 194, 195
    as priest 194, 196
Christology 215
    Adamic 123
    African 173, 194
    ancestor 195, 211
    Son of David 60
commonwealth, God's 104
communication 14, 30, 108, 148, 157
    divine-human 112
cosmology 151, 159, 163, 169
    African 166, 169, 172, 174, 193, 217
    ancient 90, 113, 146, 165
    Greco-Roman 211
    spirit 8, 21, 41, 165, 166, 210, 216
cosmos 9, 14, 19, 22–29, 34, 49, 71, 82,
        84–87, 90, 92, 96, 108, 111, 114,
        115, 120, 160, 166, 168, 171, 183,
        189, 209–211, 214, 217
covenant, divine-human 54
craftiness 134, 149
*creatio ex nihilo* 123
creation theology 166
Cybele 41, 253
cymbals 39, 40
Cynics 22


**D**

daemon 26
day of evil 152
death 156, 173, 176, 177, 201

as punishment 172
death, physical 93
deities 30, 36, 83, 165, 171
    cosmic 171
    female 170
    male 108
    pagan 77, 112
    patron 32, 52, 168, 172, 175, 193,
        209
deliverance 67, 74, 127, 156, 184, 191,
        208, 210
demonology 14, 61, 63, 191
devil 12, 19, 56, 57, 66, 126, 149, 210
Dionysius 31, 38, 113, 136, 137
diseases, as punishment 172
disputed letters 6, 9
divination 28, 47, 50, 59, 180, 209, 210
divine activity 13, 16, 72, 115, 159
divisions, ethno-racial 104
dominion 84, 91, 100, 147, 171
dream healing 37
drunkenness 38, 43, 64, 125, 136, 137
*dunsinyi* (master of medicine) 175


**E**

earth spirit 169, 170, 171
Egya Atta 181, 182
Egypt 30, 58, 72
Eleda (Yuroba) 168
Enuma Elish 56
Ephesia Grammata 36, 48, 61, 62
Ephesus 75, 76, 127, 171
Epicureans 22, 26
epilepsy 37, 63
eschatology
    Christian 74
    realized 92, 100, 111, 214
Eshu 181
Essenes 70
eulogy 14, 83, 86
evangelists 120, 159
evil eye 51, 179
evil spirits 2, 8, 57, 64, 71, 77, 161, 211
Ewe 201
exclusion 19, 91, 148

*ex opere operato*  46
exorcism  57, 76, 181, 184, 191

**F**
falsehood  65, 74, 129, 153
family gods  44, 186, 209
family members, deceased  173
fasting  67, 200, 207
Fates  43
father image of God  169
fathers
    apostolic  76
Feralia (festival honoring the dead)  45
festival, yam (Igbo)  171
fire
    molding principle  27
    walking on  179
foolish  134, 135
forgiveness  74, 87, 128, 180
formation  82, 116
foul language  129
framework
    cosmological  13, 43, 72, 111, 147,
        159, 160, 216, 217
    socio-religious  211

**G**
*gbolomagba*  186
Ghana  163, 167, 170, 172, 178, 201
ghosts, African belief in  173
*Giants* (Plato)  69
Global Christianity  20
gods/goddesses  166, 168, 170–172, 175
gonorrhea  187
good spirits  26, 30, 69
gospel of peace  154
grace  85, 87, 93, 99, 101, 112
gratitude  14, 84, 134, 139, 158, 169
greed  29, 65, 67, 131
Greek games
    Isthmian  42
    Nemean  42
    Olympic  42
    Pythian  42
Greek traditions  9

group dynamics  2, 115
group identity  2, 115, 159

**H**
Haustafel  119, 141
healing  191
heavenlies  84, 99
Hekate (goddess)  49, 120
Helios  31, 59, 151
Hellenization  30
herbalist  175
Hercules  37
Hermes  59
Hierapolis  41
hierarchy, ethno-racial  99
Hierocles  44
holiness  122, 123, 153, 215
Holy God  134
Holy Spirit  137, 138, 141, 198, 210, 211
homosexuality  133, 187
*honhom fi* (evil spirits)  177
honor  186, 187, 215
    of the dead  194
honor codes  183
hope  102, 111, 117
hopeless  103
household code  1, 2, 116
household gods  44, 141
household of God  13, 78, 93, 99
human responsibility  16, 114, 117, 127,
    147
humility  165, 217
husband and wife  142, 186
Hygeia  31

**I**
Iao Sabaoth  59
identity
    communal  3, 13, 34, 54, 78, 81, 115,
        123, 161, 184
    social  1, 2, 54, 81
identity construction  82, 159, 214, 216
Igboland  170
image of God  29, 122, 131, 148, 215
*imago Dei*  124

incantations 47
incarnation 73, 119, 185, 194, 195
incubation 38
invocations 59
Ionians 22
Isis 31, 37
Isthmian 149

**J**
Jewish antiquity 81, 90
Jewish particularism 104
Judaism 95, 194, 211
*juju* 180
*jujuman* (spiritual man) 177, 184, 186
just anger 125

**K**
kindness 128, 130
kingdom of God 74, 134, 191, 193
kinship 42, 104, 112, 117, 130
 natural and fictive 168
Krobo 187
Kune 172

**L**
Laodicean Zeus 31
*legatus* 159
lines, ethno-racial 102
Lix Tetrax 61, 62

**M**
magic 68, 70, 75, 91, 95, 195
 definition 178
magical spells 47, 59, 142
*malam* (Islamic teacher) 177
malevolent forces 147, 148, 195, 201,
 216
marriage 25, 26, 31, 43, 45, 143, 186
masquerade, Yuroba 171
Mawu 166
Mawuli 168
Mawunyo 168
medicine, orthodox 37, 38, 175
mental illnesses 181
metaphysics 19

Middle Ages 4
Middle East 51, 182
middle Platonism 9, 24
Miletus 21, 50
miracles 199
missionary gospel 189
Mmoatia (little people) 181
*modus vivendi* 101, 111, 116, 127, 143
monotheism 31
 African 166
moon (Selene) 50
moral failure 64
Mother Earth 171
mountains 27, 209
murderer 36
Muslims 167, 201
mystery cults 78
mythologies 168
 African 192

**N**
name for God
 in Akan 167
 in Burundi 167
 in Zululand 167
neo-Pythagoreanism 24
new humanity 103, 123, 124, 154, 159
Nicolaitans 75
*nkrabea* (destiny) 177
numismatics 14
Nyamekye 168
Nyonmo 167

**O**
occultism 24
Odomankoma (Akan) 168
*oikos* 30, 44
old humanity 123
Oluwasamni 168
Olympus 61, 62
Onoskelis 62
Onyankopon 187
orator 27
orgies 38, 40, 43

**P**

paganism  42, 76
pantheistic  22, 27, 36
Papyri Graecae Magicae  36
*paraenesis*  132
Parentalia (festival honoring the dead)
    45
*parousia*  152
pastors  120, 159
pater familias  44
Pauline corpus  53, 127, 157
Paul's theology  6
peace  154
Pentecost, day of  119
Pergamum  41, 61
Peripatetics  28, 29
*peroratio*  147
Pharisees  54, 59, 70
philosophy, moral  69, 122
physicians  37
piety  126, 163, 170
   religious  124
Platonists  22, 24
Plutarch  24, 25, 26, 126, 141
pneumatology  14, 191, 198, 215
   ancestor  211
polis  24, 31
polytheism  31, 166
power of the air  96, 100
powers  38, 49, 52, 84, 112, 147, 150
   celestial  119
   demonic  79
   evil  58, 93
   healing  37
   spiritual  51
   subterranean  119
   terrestrial  119
practices
   astrological  11
prayer  67, 90, 102, 157, 200, 207
prayer, Daniel's  57
preaching
   of Paul  106, 158
   power of God  191
predestination  86

priesthood  24, 120
   training for  175
   vestments  64
priest(s)/priestess(es)  174, 175
   as intermediaries  171, 173, 174
*primus inter pares*  197
Prince Mastema (evil spirit)  69
principalities  88, 99, 107, 147, 190, 211
principalities and powers  82
prophecy, gift of  199
prophesy  72
   Jewish  74
prosperity  30, 144, 184, 186, 195, 198
   of households  142
Pseudo-Isocrates  131
punishment  22, 144, 183
   capital  144
   from God  64
   of gods  172

**Q**

queen of the cosmos  34

**R**

realm(s)
   celestial  84, 92, 194
   heavenly  14, 99, 107, 112, 119, 152,
      209
   terrestrial  92, 109
recipes  151
Reformation  4
regions, subterranean  120
relationship, divine-human  74, 98
resurrection
   bodily  100
   of Christ  73, 89, 93, 164, 195
   of the dead  70
   physical  173
retribution
   divine  94, 170
   divine, African fear of  172
righteousness  148, 153, 160, 168
rites
   ancestral  174
   nubility  187

of passage  77, 171
religious  102
Roman gods  21
rotten speech  129

**S**
Sabbath  25, 56, 72
Sadducees  54, 59, 70
salvation  73, 93, 95, 99, 103, 112, 120,
    150, 155, 156
Sasabonsam (evil spirits)  181
Satan  6, 8, 11, 79, 157
satanic forces  210
Sceva, sons of  76
scholasticism  4
Second Temple  8, 14, 54, 59, 67, 70,
    127, 130, 214
sectarian  2
Sefer Yesira  59
Sepher Ha-Razim  59
Serapis  31, 49, 151
sexual immorality  132, 133
sexual laxity  133, 136
Shema  54
Shema circumcision  59
shield of faith  155
slaves  44, 119, 145, 146
social anthropology  3, 30
social distancing  124
socio-religious issues  209
Solomon
    association with magic  68
    wisdom of  60
Son of God  19, 72, 121
soothsaying  57, 174, 177, 179, 209, 210
sorcery  45, 50, 57, 76, 174, 178, 185,
    189, 195, 199, 203, 209
sovereignty of Christ  92
spirit cosmology
    African  208, 211
Spirit of God  67, 83, 105, 129, 137, 158
spiritual agents  19, 43, 90, 109, 115,
    142, 151, 160, 209, 210, 216
spiritual powers  47
    evil  6, 7, 15, 90, 93, 153, 160, 192

spiritual warfare  154, 161, 200
spirit world  172, 175, 176, 197, 205
sports  33, 42, 49
steal  129, 185
Stoic philosophy  135
stratagems  14, 149, 152, 155
studies, socio-religious  214
submission  141, 193
    wives  142
submit to one another  139, 140
Suetonius  32
suicide  173
sun (Helios)  50
supernatural powers  24, 48, 176
superstition  24, 26, 188, 197
supremacy of Christ  88, 90
Supreme Being  166, 167, 171, 182, 192,
    198, 209
sword of the Spirit  156, 157
symbols, astrological  52
synagogue  72

**T**
talisman  150
teachers  120, 159
teaching
    apostolic  105
temple prostitution  43
temples  36, 174
    in Ephesus  33
    in Smyrna  41
    pagan  30, 77
tenderness  128
terminus technicus  83, 152
*Testament of Dan* (TTP)  65, 127
*Testament of Solomon*  57, 60, 61
*Testament of the Twelve Patriarchs*
    (TTP)  57, 63
Tiberius, temple of  41
tongues, speaking in  140
transcendent forces  2, 20, 45
transgressions  59, 87, 94, 103
Trinity, doctrine of  197
*tukpe* (magic)  178

**U**
underworld  61, 119, 171, 193, 209
undisputed letters  9
Urim and Thummim  179
veneration, ancestor  174, 194

**V**
*verba*  1
virgins  35, 36, 52, 62
virtue(s)  16, 69, 124, 131, 136, 143,
        153, 161, 168
*voluntas*  1

**W**
warfare, divine-human  154
wine  38, 39, 40, 49, 64, 73
wisdom  11, 40, 60, 88, 135
wise  140, 141
witchcraft  57, 76, 176, 177, 179, 185,
        195, 201, 205, 209
    fear of  210
women  25, 31, 39, 43
world concept  1, 14, 30, 47, 69, 147
    African  181, 189
world, Greco-Roman  91, 145, 166, 175
worldview  197, 200
    African  191, 197
    Greco-Roman  209, 211
    post-enlightenment  198
    sub-Saharan Africa  165
worship  23, 33, 38, 44, 139, 158, 201
    ancestor  194
    Christian  167
    cultic  50
    idol  68
    of earth  169
    places (in Roman world)  28
    places of  77
    synagogue  60
    temple  59
wrestling  150

**Y**
Yahweh  10, 54, 55, 56, 68
Yuroba, the  181

**Z**
Zeus  22, 24, 27, 29, 32, 41, 43, 209
Zeus Soter  41
Zoroaster  26